Mangalwadi's perspective is that of a widely-read Christian from the "Global South." From it he provides a sober, unflattering assessment of our identity crisis, showing how it results from an under-nourished, severely atrophied world-view, increasingly divorced as we are from the biblical foundation that once gave us both coherence and a self transcending sense of purpose.

DAVID LYLE JEFFREY, FRSC, distinguished professor of literature and the humanities (Honors College); distinguished senior fellow and director of Manuscript Research in Scripture and Tradition, Institute for Studies in Religion, Baylor University; guest professor, Peking University, Beijing

Though I do not agree with everything he writes, I think every person who wants to understand the modern world must read this book.

PRABHU GUPTARA, Freeman of the City of London and of the Worshipful Company of Information Technologists and Chartered Fellow of the Chartered Institute of Personnel and Development; Fellow: of the Institute of Directors, of the Royal Commonwealth Society, and of the Royal Society for the Encouragement of the Arts Commerce and Manufactures—Switzerland

A small change in direction could have altered the *Titanic*'s fate. Many are seeing the West headed towards catastrophe, but this highly readable, Eastern overview of our history could reshape our future.

DAVID MCDONALD, HealthTeams International and Mars Hill Foundation, WA

Place this book at the top of your "must read stack" or Kindle queue. You will find yourself cheering as the Bible receives the credit it deserves. Vishal's unique view of Western Civilization through the lens of the East is brilliant!

JAN D. HETTINGA, author and pastor, Seattle, WA

Vishal Mangalwadi stands outside Western civilization today and peers in with eyes enriched by studies in Eastern thought and a perceptiveness unspoiled by Western nihilism. He sees what we apparently no longer see—that Western "exceptionalism" has its taproot in The Bible, and warns us of the coming cultural demise. This book must be read!

JIM MOTTER, president, NORGANIX Biosecurity and director, The Areopagus

Vishal Mangalwadi offers a refreshingly different perspective from what students are taught about what has made America such a source of hope, freedom, and productivity. He explains that America became a shining light because its foundations s read and reread one book. Neglect that book, h

RICHARD

Many modern intellectuals have ridiculed the Bible so loudly and so long that much of the American public is not even aware of its indispensable role in the making of our unique civilization. In *The Book That Made Your World* it is an Indian scholar that turns the tables on Western secularists, shining the light of truth. I believe this compelling and illuminating scholarship will serve as an effective textbook for years to come.

DR. MARK J HARRIS, president, Business for Community Foundation

Read this book for a rich history lesson and a moving reminder of how the Bible has empowered freedom, education, technology, science, and the very soul of Western civilization. Vishal has a unique way of bridging the gap from the East to the West, speaking with prophetic alarm about what civilization will face if it forgets the Bible's positive influence and foundational value.

ROB HOSKINS, CEO, OneHope

Vishal Mangalwadi recounts history in very broad strokes always using his cross-cultural perspectives for highlighting the many benefits of biblical principles in shaping civilization.

GEORGE MARSDEN, author of *Fundamentalism* and *American Culture*

I have been a great admirer of Vishal Mangalwadi, and his latest work only enhances my admiration. His uniquely Indian perspective on the centrality of the Bible for the development of the West and its emphasis on human dignity makes *The Book that Made Your World* essential reading for any thinking Christian. And it serves as a stark warning to the Western world that we forget the Bible and the Christian faith only at great peril to our liberty and even our survival.

CHUCK COLSON, founder of Prison Fellowship and the
Colson Center for Christian Worldview

THE BOOK
THAT
MADE YOUR
WORLD

OTHER BOOKS BY
VISHAL MANGALWADI

The World of Gurus

In Search of Self: Beyond the New Age

Truth and Transformation: A Manifesto for Ailing Nations

Legacy of William Carey: A Model for Transforming Culture

Missionary Conspiracy: Letters to a Postmodern Hindu

India: The Grand Experiment

*Quest for Freedom and Dignity: Caste, Conversion
and Cultural Transformation*

Astrology

THE BOOK THAT MADE YOUR WORLD

HOW THE BIBLE CREATED THE SOUL
OF WESTERN CIVILIZATION

VISHAL MANGALWADI

Thomas Nelson
Since 1798

NASHVILLE   DALLAS   MEXICO CITY   RIO DE JANEIRO

Published in Nashville, Tennessee, by Thomas Nelson. Thomas Nelson is a registered trademark of Thomas Nelson, Inc.

Thomas Nelson, Inc., titles may be purchased in bulk for educational, business, fund-raising, or sales promotional use. For information, please e-mail SpecialMarkets@ThomasNelson.com.

Unless otherwise noted, Scripture quotations are taken from THE ENGLISH STANDARD VERSION. © 2001 by Crossway Bibles, a division of Good News Publishers.

Scripture quotations marked NIV are from HOLY BIBLE: NEW INTERNATIONAL VERSION®. © 1973, 1978, 1984 by International Bible Society. Used by permission of Zondervan Publishing House. All rights reserved.

Scripture quotations marked NKJV are from THE NEW KING JAMES VERSION. © 1982 by Thomas Nelson, Inc. Used by permission. All rights reserved.

Scripture quotations marked KJV are from the KING JAMES VERSION.

ISBN: 978-1-59555-545-8 (TP)

Library of Congress Cataloging-in-Publication Data

Mangalwadi, Vishal.
  The book that made your world : how the Bible created the soul of Western civilization / Vishal Mangalwadi.
    p. cm.
  Includes bibliographical references and index.
  ISBN 978-1-59555-322-5
  1. Bible—Influence—Western civilization. 2. Bible—Influence—Modern civilization. 3. Christianity and culture—India. 4. Christian civilization. I. Title.
  BS538.7.M36 2011
  220.09—dc22   2010051897

Printed in the United States of America

*For the Sincerely Respected Public Intellectual
Member of Parliament and
Former Minister to the Government of India
Honourable Arun Shourie,
whose criticisms of the Bible prompted this inquiry*

CONTENTS

PART VII: GLOBALIZING MODERNITY

FOREWORD

In polite society, the mere mention of the Bible often introduces a certain measure of anxiety. A serious discussion on the Bible can bring outright contempt. Therefore, it is most refreshing to encounter this engaging and informed assessment of the Bible's profound impact on the modern world.

The Book That Made Your World, by Vishal Mangalwadi, brings to mind Alexis de Tocqueville's early-nineteenth-century classic, *Democracy in America*. The invaluable insights of an observant French visitor to America are now a "must read" for virtually every college student in America.

In a somewhat similar vein, Indian scholar, author, and worldwide lecturer Vishal Mangalwadi offers within these pages a fresh and wide-ranging assessment of the Bible's impact on Western culture. *The Book That Made Your World* contains the careful investigation and observations of an "outsider" viewing Western culture from within. What Mangalwadi discovers will surprise many. His book tells the story of the Bible's amazing influence upon the development of modern Western society. It shows why a serious reassessment of the Bible's relevance to contemporary public discourse and education at all levels—public and private, secular and religious—is both urgently needed and much to be desired.

A culture can barely begin, let alone sustain, any serious intergenerational attempt to comprehend, interpret, and respond to the riddles of life and the universe unless it has some reasonably comprehensive worldview. In *The Closing of the American Mind*, Allan Bloom—a Jewish professor—acknowledged that it was the Bible that gave critical impetus to, and sustained, the West's intellectual endeavor of examining all great ideas, be they true or false. Bloom wrote,

> In the United States, practically speaking, the Bible was the only common culture, one that united the simple and the sophisticated, rich and poor, young and old, and—as the very model for a vision of the order of the whole of things, as well as the key to the rest of Western art, the greatest works of which were in one way or another responsive to the Bible—provided access to the seriousness of books. With its gradual and inevitable disappearance, the very idea of such a total book is disappearing. And fathers and mothers have lost the idea that the highest aspiration they might have for their children is for them to be wise—as priests, prophets or philosophers are wise. Specialized competence and success are all that they can imagine. Contrary to what is commonly thought, without the book even the idea of the whole is lost.[1]

Mangalwadi underscores the fact that it was the Western Church that gave birth to the university, in its determined and passionate effort to pursue Truth. Following in the train of the great universities of Bologne, Paris, Oxford, and Cambridge, America's first institution of higher education, Harvard, was founded upon the motto *Veritas*—Truth. Over the course of the last century, however, the motto has been stripped of all meaning. "Leading thinkers" within the academy have succeeded in persuading many that "truth," as such, is largely a function of social convention. The reigning climate of pessimism about our ability to truly know anything significant was most powerfully articulated by the late Richard Rorty, arguably one of the most influential American thinkers of the last forty years.

In What's the Use of Truth?, Rorty contends that there is no privileged position, or any kind of authority, that can provide a rationally justifiable standpoint from which one can know the "real" world. The word *truth*, he insists, has no significant meaning. Traditional distinctions between true and false must be abandoned. In their place, we can only think and speak in terms of webs of language that display greater or lesser degrees of "smoothness" and homogeneity. For Rorty, every assertion of truth is only provisional—at its very core, a form of make-believe—because language itself is merely a product of human society. Our words refer to nothing except insofar as they interpret our experience. Accordingly, Rorty rejected any and all efforts to render reality as meaningful through any means other than that of embracing it as a linguistically constructed, self-referential human social reality.

This very argument, however, also deprived Rorty of any rational basis to support his, or anyone else's, defense of any social structure or view of reality, however compelling or desirable. Indeed, those who embrace such a view consistently cannot even investigate the historical conditions that established the social structures they desire. In *The Future of Religion*, Rorty acknowledged this profound intellectual disability, conceding, "It may be just an historical accident that Christendom was where democracy was reinvented for the use of mass society, or it may be that this could only have happened within a Christian society. *But it is futile to speculate about this*" (emphasis added).[2]

Predictably, Rorty's work, and that of his peers within the academy, has led to a wholesale abandonment of any aspiration to pursue truth, knowledge, and rationality as understood over the long course of Western civilization. The intellectual culture that Rorty represented not only denigrates the classic texts that created the modern world of justice, freedom, and economic opportunity, but also denies any responsibility to introduce students to those foundational ideas that would most certainly contradict the reigning philosophical ideology. In so doing, the long valued "free marketplace of ideas" has been materially and lamentably compromised. For if there is no truth to be discovered—if all truth is merely a function of social constructs—then reason itself has no genuine authority, and in its place, academic fashion and marketing determine what a culture believes. More foreboding still, the risk is real that outright coercion may replace the authority that the modern world once ascribed to Truth. Questions concerning the nature of reality, the meaning of life, of honor, of virtue, of wisdom, and of love are understood to be nothing more than curious relics of old-fashioned thinking.

C. S. Lewis, no stranger to the dictates of academic fashion, credited Owen Barfield, a fellow Inkling, for his deliverance from what Barfield referred to as "chronological snobbery," that is,

> the uncritical acceptance of the intellectual climate common to our own age and the assumption that whatever has gone out of date is on that account discredited. You must find out why it went out of date. Was it ever refuted (and if so, by whom, where, and how conclusively) or did it merely die away as fashions do? If the latter, this tells us nothing about its truth or falsehood. . . . our own age is also "a period" and certainly has, like all periods, its own illusions.[3]

Where does this leave us individually and culturally? If we opt to follow Rorty's lead and the fashion of the day, our only recourse is to join Candide in the cultivation of "our garden." Nothing is "meaningful" except insofar as it satisfies our individual needs and desires. In abandoning Truth, we abandon the only viable means of empowering real community—i.e. through the humble, and yes, "age-old" common pursuit of the Good, the True, and the Beautiful.

Clearly, our "ironic age" desperately needs a more reliable mirror by which to recover and assess our almost forgotten past. We need to re-envision a common and universal hope for human society. We need to learn again from the sources that once so deeply captivated our imaginations, ordered our reason, and informed our wills. It was from and through these very sources that the West realized the transformation of individual lives, families, and whole communities that gave shape to the modern world as we know it. Given the increasing intellectual and spiritual chaos of our time, it strikes me as extremely worthwhile to trace those unique features of the West that helped foster these fertile changes.

Vishal Mangalwadi's immense contribution over the course of the following pages may appear counterintuitive. If so, it is precisely because his arduous research establishes the fact that the Bible and its worldview, contrary to current prevailing opinion, combined to serve as the *single most powerful force in the emergence of Western civilization.*

Where Bloom laments the closing of the American mind, Mangalwadi brings a refreshing optimism. As it happens, he began studying the Bible seriously at an Indian university only after discovering that Western philosophy had lost all hope of finding truth; for all intents and purposes it had become "essentially bankrupt." The Bible aroused his interest in the history of the modern world. His study of world history, in turn, gave birth to a renewed hope that resounds throughout the pages of this rather extraordinary book.

Mangalwadi is an intellectual from the East. He possesses an intimate knowledge of the vast range of Eastern thought and cultures and has also benefited greatly from extensive exposure to the intellectual and spiritual traditions and institutions of the West. This access to the thought of both East and West has afforded him a unique perspective into the mind and heart of Western culture. It enables him to speak to the crisis of our time with incisive clarity and prophetic courage.

These pages introduce us to the poorest of the poor in rural India, as well as to the seminal thinkers of Western civilization. Throughout, Mangalwadi ably demonstrates that the biblical worldview emerges as the critical and unmistakable source of the unique vision of Western thought, values, and institutions. Speaking to the issues raised in the course of Rorty's writings, he documents that the Bible, understood to be the revelation of God to humanity, provided the basis for an admittedly imperfect but nonetheless remarkably humane society. It was, above all, a civilization in which truth was understood to be real, where the collective pursuit of virtue shaped behavior, and the redemptive work of God in the person of Jesus Christ provided a radical and historically verifiable transforming response to the abyss of human selfishness, corruption, and sin.

Weaving careful analysis together with captivating stories, Mangalwadi offers his readers concrete encounters with the full range of human virtue and corruption. He sounds a clarion call to the West not to forget but to remember and return to the unique source of its very life. In the tradition of Ezekiel, this twenty-first-century "watchman on the wall" has spoken. May his words take root and foster a much-needed renewal of the American mind and spirit.

J. STANLEY MATTSON, PH.D.

Founder and President of The C. S. Lewis Foundation, Redlands, California, Stanley Mattson earned his Ph.D. in American Intellectual History from the University of North Carolina–Chapel Hill in 1970. A past member of the faculty of Gordon College,; headmaster of the Master's School of W. Simsbury, Connecticut; and director of corporate and foundation relations for the University of Redlands, Dr. Mattson established the C. S. Lewis Foundation in 1986. He has since served as director of its programs in Oxford and Cambridge, England. The foundation is currently engaged in the founding of C. S. Lewis College as a Christian Great Books College, with a school of the visual and performing arts, just north of the Five College area in western Massachusetts. (For further information, visit the C. S. Lewis Foundation's Web site at www.cslewis.org.)

Prologue

WHY THIS JOURNEY INTO THE SOUL OF THE MODERN WORLD?

In 1994, India's Roman Catholic bishops invited one of our most influential public intellectuals, Dr. Arun Shourie, to tell them how a Hindu looks at Christian missions. Since his illustrious family was a product of missionary education, the bishops may have expected him to commend missions. Shourie, however, condemned missions as a conspiracy of British imperialism.

When Britain colonized India militarily and politically, Shourie argued, missionaries were brought in to colonize the Indian mind. Mission's he said, were the worst form of colonialism, since they harvested our souls; they subverted our culture. From reproaching missions, Shourie went on to attack Jesus and ridicule the Bible as an irrational and immoral book. He then expanded his lecture into two books.[1]

Shourie's books came out when the militant Hindu Bharatiya Janata Party (BJP) was preparing to fight a national election where it emerged as a large enough party in Parliament to form a coalition government. The BJP used Shourie's book to push its platform. It said that the liberal Hindu parties, such as the Indian National Congress, should be voted out because liberal Hinduism had allowed Christians and Muslims to convert our people and subvert Indian culture.

Once the might of a national party got behind Shourie's books, they became national best sellers. His thesis was translated into Indian vernaculars, and excerpts were published as syndicated columns in national and regional newspapers.

I already knew that the Western missionary movement, which the BJP portrayed as the villain of modern India, was, in fact, the single most important force that created contemporary India.* Yet, thanks to Shourie's books, the frontline missionaries, who came from the south to serve North India, began to be accused as dangerous CIA agents. These are some of India's best public servants, sacrificially engaged in uplifting the "untouchable" victims of Hindu philosophy and its oppressive caste system, but they were presumed to have CIA funding to prepare for the Pentagon's neo-colonial designs. The Bible—the book that began and sustained India's education, emancipation, and all-around modernization—was denounced as fit only for fools.

Arun Shourie had gone to India's best Christian college and earned a doctorate from a prestigious American university established by a Protestant denomination to teach the Bible. He had served as an officer of World Bank and headed India's largest newspaper chain. He is a moral crusader whom many of us loved and still do. Why did a learned man like him have such a poor understanding of the Bible and its role in creating the modern West and modern India? Why didn't he understand that the education he received, America's economic system that he studied, the free press that he championed, the political liberties that he cherished, and India's public life that he fought to keep corruption-free had all come from the Bible . . . although much of it had now been secularized and even corrupted?

Dr. Shourie's ignorance was not his fault. The problem was that even his Christian professors in India and in America had little idea of the Bible's importance and how it created the modern world, including its universities, science, economy, and freedoms. Ignorance and unbelief are understandable, but distorting one's own history is costly bias. It undermines the intellectual and moral foundations of the modern world. This reign of ignorant bias in Western universities raises the question: *Must the sun set on the West?*

---

* This includes many British evangelicals who served as civil servants, soldiers, judges, and teachers.

I responded to Dr. Shourie's first book in a series of letters that were published as *Missionary Conspiracy: Letters to a Postmodern Hindu.* I responded to his second book in my preface to Gene Edward Veith's book, *Fascism: Modern and Postmodern.*[2] My Web site www .RevelationMovement.com will soon begin to answer the details of his criticisms of the Bible. *The Book That Made Your World* celebrates the 400th anniversary of the King James Bible, which was the book of the last millennium. This book is also meant to serve those who, like Shourie, seek to build their nations. A little humility will enable anyone to benefit from understanding how the modern world was created.

The sun need not set on the West. Europe and America can be revived again. Light can again shine on nations that have been confused and misled by Western universities and media.

"Myth" has many meanings. Some of them are helpful. However, if *myth* is a view of reality invented exclusively by the human mind, then, by definition, atheism is a myth. During the twentieth century this myth caused havoc in Eastern Europe. Now it has the West by its throat.

A cursory glance may give an impression that this is a book about the Bible. Those who actually read it will know that this is about great literature and great art; great science and liberating technology; genuine heroism and nation building; great virtues and social institutions. If you have a zillion pieces of a puzzle, would you begin assembling them into one picture, without knowing what that picture is supposed to look like? The Bible created the modern world of science and learning because it gave us the Creator's vision of what reality is all about. That is what made the modern West a reading and thinking civilization. Postmodern people see little point in reading books that do not contribute directly to their career or pleasure. This is a logical outcome of atheism, which has now realized that the human mind cannot possibly know what is true and right. This book is being published with a prayer that it will help revive a global interest in the Bible and in all the great books.

VISHAL MANGALWADI
DECEMBER 2010

Part I

THE SOUL OF WESTERN CIVILIZATION

The Bible brought its view of God, the universe, and mankind into all the leading Western languages and thus into the intellectual process of Western man . . . Since the invention of printing, the Bible has become more than the translation of an ancient Oriental literature. It has not seemed a foreign book, and it has been the most available, familiar, and dependable source and arbiter of intellectual, moral, and spiritual ideals in the West.

—H. Grady Davis

Chapter One

THE WEST WITHOUT ITS SOUL

FROM BACH TO COBAIN

For two hundred years we had sawed and sawed and sawed at the branch we were sitting on. And in the end, much more suddenly than anyone had foreseen, our efforts were rewarded, and down we came. But unfortunately there had been a little mistake: The thing at the bottom was not a bed of roses after all; it was a cesspool full of barbed wire . . . It appears that amputation of the soul isn't just a simple surgical job, like having your appendix out. The wound has a tendency to go septic.

—GEORGE ORWELL
Notes on the Way, 1940

On April 8, 1994, an electrician accidentally discovered a dead body in Seattle, Washington. A shotgun had blown the victim's head into unrecognizable bits. The police investigation concluded that the victim of this ghastly tragedy was the rock legend Kurt Cobain (b. 1967) and that he had committed suicide a few days earlier. Cobain's previous attempts at suicide by drug overdose had been unsuccessful. His beautiful wife, singer Courtney Love, is said to have called the police multiple times to have them confiscate his guns before he killed himself or harmed others.

Cobain, the lead singer and gifted guitarist for the rock band Nirvana, captured his generation's loss of anchor, center, or soul so effectively that their album *Nevermind* sold ten million copies, displacing Michael Jackson at the top of the charts.

The phrase "never mind" means "don't bother," "don't concern yourself." Why should you mind, if nothing is true, good, or beautiful in any absolute sense? Should a man be bothered about his adorable daughter's ongoing need for a father? "Never mind" is a logical virtue for a nihilist who thinks that there is nothing out there to give meaning and significance to anything here—be it your daughter, wife, or life. In contrast, the modern West was built by people who dedicated their lives to what they believed was divine, true, and noble.

Nirvana is the Buddhist term for salvation. It means permanent extinction of one's individual existence, the dissolution of our illusory individuality into *Shoonyta* (void, nothingness, or emptiness). It is freedom from our misery-causing illusion that we have a permanent core to our being: a self, soul, spirit, or *Atman*.

Here is a sample lyric expressing Cobain's view of salvation as silence, death, and extinction:

> *Silence, Here I am, Here I am, Silent.*
> *Death Is what I am, Go to hell, Go to jail . . .*
> *Die*[1]

As the news of Cobain's suicide spread, a number of his fans emulated his example. *Rolling Stone* magazine reported that his tragic death was followed by at least sixty-eight copycat suicides.[2]

"Hey, hey, ho, ho, Western Civ has got to go!" The Stanford students of the 1960s who chanted for the demise of the Western civilization were disgusted with hypocrisy and injustices in the West. Yet, their rejection of the soul of their civilization yielded something very different from the utopia they sought. Diana Grains, in *Rolling Stone*, noted that prior to the 1960s, teenage suicide was virtually nonexistent among American youth. By 1980 almost four hundred thousand adolescents were attempting suicide every year. By 1987 suicide had become the second largest killer of teens, after automotive accidents. By the 1990s, suicide had slipped down to number three because young people were killing each other as often as they killed themselves. Grains explained these rising figures among the offspring of the '60s generation:

The 1980s offered young people an experience of unsurpassed social violence and humiliation. Traumatized by absent or abusive parents, educators, police and shrinks, stuck in meaningless jobs without a livable wage, disoriented by disintegrating institutions, many kids felt trapped in a cycle of futility and despair. Adults . . . [messed]-up across the board, abandoning an entire generation by failing to provide for or protect them or prepare them for independent living. Yet when young people began to exhibit symptoms of neglect, reflected in their rates of suicide, homicide, substance abuse, school failure, recklessness and general misery, adults condemned them as apathetic, illiterate, amoral losers.[3]

According to his biographers, Cobain's early years had been happy, full of affection and hope. But by the time he was nine years old Cobain was caught in the crossfire between his divorcing parents. Like far too many marriages in America, his parents' marriage had devolved into an emotional and verbal battlefield. One of Cobain's biographers, commenting on a family portrait when Kurt was six, said, "It's a picture of a family, but not a picture of a marriage."[4] After the divorce, Kurt's mother started dating younger men. His father became overbearing, more afraid of losing his new wife than of losing Kurt. That parental rejection left him displaced, unable to find a stable social center, incapable of maintaining constructive emotional ties either with his peers or with his parents' generation. That instability inflicted a deep wound in Cobain's soul that could not be healed by music, fame, money, sex, drugs, alcohol, therapy, rehabilitation or detox programs. His inner anguish made it easy for him to accept the Buddha's first noble truth that life is suffering.

Psychotherapy failed Cobain. Having questioned the very existence of the *psyche* (roughly, the self or soul), secular psychology is now a discipline in decline. Sigmund Freud and Carl Jung believed in the existence of self,[5] but their followers now recognize that their faith in "self" was a residual effect of the West's Christian past—Jung's father, for example, was a clergyman.

Jung's truly secular followers, such as James Hillman, are recasting the essence of his theory. An increasing number of thinking people are recognizing that theoretically it is impossible to practice psychology without theology. Six centuries before Christ, the Buddha already knew that if God does not exist, then the human self cannot exist either. Therefore, he deconstructed the Hindu idea of the soul. When one starts peeling the onion skin of one's psyche, he discovers that there is no solid core at the center of one's being. Your sense of self is an illusion. Reality is nonself (*anatman*). *You* don't exist. Liberation, the Buddha taught, is realizing the unreality of your existence.

This nihilism is logical if you begin with the assumption that God does not exist. However, it is not easy to live with the consequences of this belief, or rather, this nonbelief in one's own self. To say "*I* believe that '*I*' don't exist" can be devastating for sensitive souls like Cobain. His music—alternately sensitive and brash, exhilarating and depressed, loud and haunted, anarchic and vengeful—reflected the confusion he saw in the postmodern world around him and in his own being. While he was committed to a small set of moral principles (such as environmentalism and fatherhood), he was unable to find a stable worldview in which to center those principles.

He was naturally drawn to the Buddha's doctrine of *impermanence*: there is nothing stable and permanent in the universe. You can't swim in the same river twice because the river changes every moment, as does a human being. You are not the same "thing" that you were a moment ago. Cobain's experience of the impermanence of an emotional, social, spiritual center to his life had tragic consequences. He adopted the philosophical and moral emptiness that other bands lauded as the "Highway to Hell."[6]

MUSIC AFTER GOD'S DEATH

German philosopher Friedrich Nietzsche (AD 1844–1900) realized that having killed God, Europe could not possibly save the civilizational fruits of its faith in God. But not even Nietzsche realized that one philosophical implication of God's demise would be the death of his own self. For fifteen hundred years prior to Nietzsche, the West had followed St. Augustine (AD 354–430) in affirming every human being as a trinity of existence (being), intellect, and will. After denying the existence of the Divine Self, it became impossible to affirm the existence of the human self. Therefore, many intellectuals are reverting to the Buddhist idea that the self is an illusion. As contemporary Jungian psychologist Paul Kuglar explained, in the postmodern philosophy, Nietzsche (the speaking subject) is dead—he never existed, for individuality is only an illusion created by language.[7]

Deconstructionists blame language for creating the illusion of the self, but the Buddha blamed the mind. It cannot be God's image. Therefore, the mind had to be a product of primeval cosmic ignorance, *Avidya*. The Buddha's rejection of the self made sense to the classical skeptics such as Pyrrho of Elea (360–270 BC), who traveled to India with Alexander the Great and interacted with Buddhist philosophers. After returning to Greece, he established a new school of skeptical philosophy to teach that nothing is truly knowable. If so, why should anyone pay philosophers to teach anything? No wonder education, philosophy, and science declined in Greece.

Denying the reality of a spiritual core as the essence of every human being makes it hard to make sense of music, because music, like morality, is a matter of the soul. Those who think that the universe is only material substance and the soul is an illusion find it hard to explain music. They have to assume that music evolved from animals, but none of our alleged evolutionary cousins make music. (Some birds do "sing," but no one has proposed that we, or our music, evolved from them.) Charles Darwin thought that music evolved as an aid to mating. That might be believed if rapists took bands to lure their victims. By evolutionary psychology, rape could be seen as a natural form of mating and morality an arbitrary social control.

Music serves no biological purpose. As Bono, the lead singer for U2 put it, "music is a matter of the spirit." Some contemporary music moves toward God—for example, Gospel Music. Other genres—for example, the Blues—may be running away from God and seeking redemption elsewhere. Nevertheless "both recognize the pivot that God is at the center of the jaunt."[8] Even in the Bible, all prophetic poetry is not singing praises to God. Beginning with Job, biblical poetry includes penetrating questioning of God in the face of suffering and injustice. Music that blames God for evil, affirms God as the only available source of meaning and our right to pass moral judgment.

The Buddhist skepticism that Pyrrho brought to Europe is logical and powerful. The West escaped its paralyzing influence only because thinkers such as St. Augustine succeeded in refuting it. Augustine affirmed the certainty of the human self because the Bible taught that God existed and had created man in his own image. Augustine also affirmed the validity of words. He believed language can communicate truth because communication is intrinsic to the triune God and man is made in the image of a God who communicates. Now, having rejected those biblical foundations, the West has no basis for escaping the Buddha's radical pessimism.

In spite of—or perhaps because of—his inner chaos, Cobain remained so popular that in 2008 the music industry ranked him as the number one "Dead Artist." His albums outsold Elvis Presley's. Years after his death, in 2002 his widow was able to sell the scraps and scribbles in his journals to Riverhead Books for (reportedly) four million dollars. Two decades ago, a publisher anywhere in the world would have rejected his notes as meaningless, misspelled graffiti. At the dawn of the twenty-first century in America, cultural gatekeepers rightly recognize that Cobain represents America's soullessness better than most celebrities. In a sample of relatively meaningful meaninglessness, he wrote:

> I like punk rock. I like girls with weird eyes. I like drugs. (But my Body And mind won't allow me to take them.) I like passion. I like playing my cards wrong. I like vinyl. I like feeling guilty for being a white, American male. I love to sleep. I like to taunt small, barking dogs in parked cars. I like to make people feel happy and superior in their reaction towards my appearance. I like to have strong opinions with nothing to back them up with besides my primal sincerity. I like sincerity. I lack sincerity . . . I like to complain and do nothing to make things better.[9]

I have seen entries similar to Cobain's journals and lyrics in students' private diaries in art exhibitions in American colleges. Prior to Cobain, in the 1960s and '70s, countercultural students at these colleges believed they were on the cusp of inaugurating utopia. By Cobain's time they knew that nihilism leads only to escapism. Steven Blush studied the music of the early 1980s that directly preceded Cobain both chronologically and stylistically. Popularly it is called "hardcore," a genre marked by its brashness and intentional existence outside the mainstream. He concluded:

> Hardcore was more than music—it became a political and social movement as well. The participants constituted a tribe unto themselves. Some of them were alienated or abused, and found escape in the hard-edged music. Some sought a better world or a tearing down of the status quo, and were angry. Most of them simply wanted to raise hell. Stark and uncompromising . . . Lots of [messed]up kids "found themselves" through hardcore . . . the aesthetic was intangible. Most bands couldn't really play that well, and their songs usually lacked craft. They expended little effort achieving prevailing production standards. However, they had IT—an infectious blend of ultra-fast music, thought provoking lyrics, and f[orget]-you attitude.[10]

The postmodern "rebels without a cause" were

Living in a world of my own.[11]

Cobain's music appealed to contemporary America because it was a full-throttled disharmony of rage, anguish, hatred, despair, meaninglessness, and obscenity. His song titles included "I Hate Myself, I Want to Die" and "Rape Me" (later changed to "Waife Me"). Most of what Cobain sang cannot be deciphered, and many of his lyrics that can be deciphered have no apparent meaning. Whether he knew it or not, his lyrics were *Zen koans*, counter-rational sayings such as "what is the sound of one hand clapping?" Such words do not make sense because (in the absence of revelation) reality itself makes no sense. Words are merely *mantras*—sounds without sense—to be chanted or shouted.*

Cobain committed suicide because Nothingness as the ultimate reality does nothing positive. It cannot provide joy to the world, let alone meaning or hope for the mess in one's life. Its only consequence is to inspire people to seek an exit from the world—*Nirvana*. A culture of music does not flourish in the soil of nihilism. Cobain's gift as a musician blossomed because he had inherited a unique tradition of music.

Music seems a natural, perhaps even essential, part of life to the Western mind because it has been an integral part of traditional worship and education. For example, Oxford and Cambridge universities have played pivotal roles in shaping the second millennium. However, a person who has never visited these cities may not know that they are cities of churches and chapels. The chapel is the most important building in traditional colleges and a pipe organ is often the centerpiece of a chapel. That is not the case in every culture.

Turkmenistan is the latest country to put restrictions on music: on state holidays, in broadcasts by television channels, at cultural events organized by the state, in places of mass assembly, and at weddings and celebrations organized by the public.[12] Nations such as Saudi Arabia have had restrictions on music for a long time. In Iran and Afghanistan, women cannot sing on the radio, let alone on television or in person before mixed audiences. In post-Saddam Iraq, radical Muslims have assassinated sellers of music CDs. Mosques do not have keyboards, organs, pianos, orchestras, or worship bands because according to traditional Islam, music is *haraam* or illegitimate.**

These cultures see Western music as inextricably mixed with immoral debauchery. For them, musicians such as Kurt Cobain are undesirable role models. Indeed, on the cover of his album *Nevermind*,

---

* See chapter 6 for a further discussion of how viewing language as mantra affects broader cultural structures.

** The idea that music is "*haraam*" or is illegitimate is based on Qur'an 17.64, 31.6, and 53.59–62. Historically, Islamic theologians working in the tradition of Qur'anic interpretation developed by Ibn Masood, Ibn Abbas, and Jaabir after the death of Prophet Muhammad have interpreted these passages as condemning all music. Other modern interpreters contend that the Qur'an does not ban music.

Cobain brazenly depicted the values he lived by: an infant with a long penis underwater reaching out to a dollar bill on a fishhook. On the back cover, Cobain's mascot, a chipmunk, sits on a vagina. Open debauchery was a part of "pagan" music until the Bible extricated music from it by recentering the locus of the music to God.

> Do not get drunk on wine, which leads to debauchery. Instead, be filled with the Spirit . . . Sing and make music in your heart to the Lord, always giving thanks to God the Father for everything, in the name of our Lord Jesus Christ.[13]

Buddhist monks in Asia developed sophisticated philosophies, psychology, rituals, and psycho-technologies to try to escape life and its sufferings. They perfected techniques such as *Vipasana** to silence not just their tongues but also their thoughts. Buddhism originated in India and prior to its disappearance enjoyed powerful political patronage for centuries. It built such massive monasteries that Buddhist art is a cherished aspect of our national heritage. Yet, Buddhism left no discernible musical tradition or instrument in India. No Buddhist monk started a band such as Nirvana, because in Buddhism salvation is not a heaven filled with music.[14] As a pessimistic philosophy of silence it could not produce music of hope and joy. Buddhism could not celebrate existence because it saw suffering as the essence of life. Some forms of modern Buddhism have embraced music, partially because of the efforts of Western converts, such as Kurt Cobain, who grafted the Western tradition of religious music into the Buddhist faith.

To say that music is a new phenomenon in Buddhist temples is not to suggest that pre-Buddhist Tibet or China had no music.[15] Music is intrinsic to the universe and to human nature even if some worldviews, including Darwinism, do not understand, recognize, or promote it. China's fertility cults and sexual rites involved choirs of boys and girls singing alternately and together to symbolize Yin and Yang dualism as

---

* Yoga attempts to control breathing in its quest to realize *self*. *Vipasana* observes breathing as a means of silencing one's mind to experience that there is no self or soul inside us but only Nothingness, Emptiness, Void, *Shoonyta* or Selflessness.

early as 2000 BC. A thousand years prior to that, the worshippers in Sumero-Mesapotamia used music in their temple rituals.

The musical *ragas* of Hindu magical rituals have survived for thirty-five hundred years. Most of the Vedas are hymns and chants. The Vedic priests understood sound as well as anyone else in the world and developed a highly complex system of chanting, even if Hindu monks and priests did not develop music into the complex medium that Western music became. Thankfully this is changing now. Bollywood has played a great role in inspiring some Hindu ashrams to develop great music. It has also raised the standard of *Qawwali*, which began as a part of Sufi tradition,* but is now loved by Hindus as well as by Muslims—including in Pakistan.

WRITING MUSIC INTO THE WEST'S DNA

St. Augustine, the author of the six-volume *On Music*, was a key figure in inserting music into Western education and worldview. His first five volumes are technical and could have been written by a Greek philosopher. But Augustine was most excited about his sixth book, which gives a biblical philosophy of music. Music is, of course, integral to the Bible, in which the longest book is Psalms. The last psalm, for example, asks creation to praise the Lord with the trumpet, lute, harp, tambourine, strings, pipe, and cymbals.

Why are these physical instruments able to make music? Augustine saw that the scientific basis or essence of music lies in mathematical "numbers" or scores at the core of creation. Since music is mathematical, Augustine argued, it must be rational, eternal, unchangeable, meaningful, and objective—it consists of mathematical harmony. We cannot make a musical sound from just any string. To get a precise note, a string has to have a specific length, thickness, and tension. This implies that the Creator has encoded music into the structure of the universe. This insight was not new. It had been noted by Pythagoras (570–490 BC), whose school Plato attended before starting his Academy.

---

* Sunnis and Shiites consider Sufism a Muslim heresy.

Augustine promoted this "pagan" insight because the Bible presented a view of creation that explained why matter could make music.

Augustine taught that while this musical code is "bodily" (physical), it is made and enjoyed by the soul. For example, the book of Job deals with the problem of inexplicable suffering. In it God himself tells Job of the connection between music and creation: "Where were you when I laid the foundation of the earth? . . . when the morning stars sang together and all the sons of God shouted for joy?"[16]

The Bible taught that a sovereign Creator (rather than a pantheon of deities with conflicting agendas) governs the universe for his glory. He is powerful enough to save men like Job from their troubles. This teaching helped develop the Western belief of a *cosmos*: an orderly universe where every tension and conflict will ultimately be resolved, just as after a period of inexplicable suffering Job was greatly blessed.

This belief in the Creator as a compassionate Savior became an underlying factor of the West's classical music and its tradition of tension and resolution. Up until the end of the nineteenth century, Western musicians shared their civilization's assumption that the universe was cosmos rather than chaos. They composed consonance and concord even when they experienced dissonance and discord. That is not to suggest that classical music did not express the full range of human emotions. It did. A bereaved composer would write a tragic piece; someone abandoned by his love would express his desolation. But such outpourings of a broken heart were understood as snapshots of real life. Given the cultural power of the biblical worldview, no one thought of them as Kurt Cobain did, as evidence of the breakdown of cosmic order or the nonexistence of order in the universe.

In the novel *The Silmarillion*, J. R. R. Tolkien gives us a beautiful, fictional exposition of the Augustinian perspective on the relationship of music, creation, the fall (evil), and redemption. Tolkien's Middle-earth experienced much more suffering than the Buddha's India. Tolkien's "earth" was to be captured, corrupted, and virtually controlled by evil. Suffering was real, brutal, and awful. Yet the Bible taught Tolkien that the Almighty Creator, who was also a compassionate Redeemer, was loving enough and powerful enough to redeem the earth from the greatest possible mess, sin, and suffering. This helped Tolkien to celebrate creation, both in its origin as well as in its ultimate destiny:

> There was Eru, the One, who in Arda is called Iluvatar; and he made first the Ainur, the Holy Ones, that were the offspring of his thought, and they were with him before aught else was made. And he spoke to them, propounding to them themes of music; and they sang before him, and he was glad. But for long while they sang only each alone, or but few together, while the rest hearkened; for each comprehended only part of the mind of Iluvatar from which he came, and in the understanding of their brethren they grew but slowly. Yet ever as they listened they came to deeper understanding, and increased in unison and harmony. . . .
>
> Then Iluvatar said to them: "Of the theme that I have declared to you, I will now that ye make in harmony together a Great Music."
>
> Then the voices of the Ainur, like unto harps and lutes, and pipes and trumpets, and viols and organs, and like unto countless choirs singing with words, began to fashion the theme of a great music; and a sound arose of endless interchanging melodies woven in harmony that passed beyond hearing into the depths and into the heights, and the places of the dwelling of Iluvatar were filled to overflowing, and the music and the echo of the music went out into the Void, and it was not void.[17]

Prior to becoming a follower of Christ, Augustine had been a professor of Greek philosophy. He knew that although music was encoded into the structure of the physical universe, being finite, it could never provide ultimate meaning to life.* Therefore, he reasoned that to be meaningful, music had to be integrated into the ultimate aim of human life, which was to love God and one's neighbors. To love one's neighbor is to "always mind" his welfare.

---

* Augustine's intellectual mentor, Plato, believed that epistemologically no finite particular can make sense without an infinite reference point.

Over the centuries, the influence of Augustine's biblical philoso-phy of music kept growing. Originally, church music was dominated by monophonic plainsong, a single line of melody as in the Gregorian chant. Roman Catholic churches began to develop polyphonic music. This style, which combines several differing voice parts simultaneously, began to flourish at Notre Dame (Paris) by the eleventh century. That development in Christian worship laid the foundation for the entire spectrum of Western classical music, religious and secular.*

In the tenth century AD, Augustine's biblical philosophy of music inspired a group of Benedictine monks to build the world's largest pipe organ in the cathedral of Winchester, England. The organ required seventy men and twenty-six bellows to supply wind to its four hundred pipes. Technologically, the pipe organ was the world's most advanced machine until the invention of the mechanical clock. Europe's organs stood as emblems of the West's unique desire and ability to use the arts, science, and technology for the glory of God as well as for the relief of humanity's suffering and toil.**

Augustine's biblical philosophy of music was an important tribu-tary that contributed to the river of mechanical arts that began to flow out of Christian monasteries and churches. This tradition used tech-nology to worship God and to love one's neighbors.

TAKING MUSIC TO THE MASSES

Martin Luther (AD 1483–1546) took the biblical-Augustinian philoso-phy of music out of the cloister and choir loft to Europe's masses. An Augustinian monk and pioneer of the Protestant Reformation, Luther was and remains a polarizing figure. Some love him; others hate him. Yet many critics agree that Luther may have been the most influential figure of the second millennium.

Luther was a "Protestant" because he saw plenty in his world to protest against. But he did not become a reformer simply because he

---

* Augustine did not have much influence over the Eastern Church and that may be one reason why its music did not develop much beyond the chant.

** See chapter 7 for a discussion of why Western technology became a means of human emancipation.

protested. He changed Europe because he found something worth singing about, something worth living for, and something worth dying for. He found a *covenant* relationship with the Almighty God.* A relationship he could count upon. It was a faith, a worldview upon which his decadent world could be rebuilt. Yet, it was far more than an idea or creed. It was a vibrant relationship with someone who was worth dying for; a love affair worthy of songs.

Luther got excited about the Bible partly because it taught that he could not and *did not need to* do anything to qualify for God's love. Salvation—forgiveness from sin and the restoration of a person's relationship with God—was a free gift of grace to be received by the empty hands of faith. The Bible gave Luther a deep, Abraham-like, inner assurance of God's acceptance. God's friendship gave such a value and meaning to his life that he had something to sing about. Yes, in a world that had rebelled against the Creator, there was suffering. Yet, because God is love, there is hope for pardon, peace, progress, and prosperity. This gospel made the West uniquely optimistic, enabling it to sing, "Joy to the world"—a message opposite to that of Cobain.

Luther helped this biblical worldview to become the soul of Western civilization. His spiritual followers summed up his discovery of the Bible's essence in songs of hope, assurance, and certainty, such as "Amazing Grace," written by reformed slave trader John Newton (1725–1807):

> Amazing grace! How sweet the sound
> That saved a wretch like me!
> I once was lost, but now am found;
> Was blind, but now I see.

Luther became a reformer because he realized that in order to conform to God's Word, all God's children would need to have that Word in their native languages. He translated the Bible into his own

---

* Later some Enlightenment thinkers secularized the biblical idea of divine covenant as "social contract." The idea lies at the root of modern constitutionalism. It enabled the West to become a society built uniquely on trust. See Robert N. Bellah *The Broken Covenant: American Civil Religion in Time of Trial* (New York: Crossroad Books, 1975).

German dialect. His translation went into hundreds of editions and turned his dialect into the "Standard German" for the whole of the German-speaking world. Together with Luther's German hymnal, his Bible forged the soul of the German-speaking nations. Luther's work inspired other reformers, such as William Tyndale, who began translating the Bible into English. That crucial beginning made the Bible the soul also of the English-speaking world.*

Following Jesus and the apostles, the early church sang worship together until Jerome the Great encouraged priests to take over chanted worship in the fifth century. Since then until Luther's time, congregations rarely sang during Christian worship—and then only in Latin, which they did not understand. By and large it was the priest's job to worship and pray. Luther rediscovered the New Testament doctrine of the priesthood of all believers,** which made it necessary for the entire congregation to worship God by singing as well as by prayer and other means. "God," he believed, "has created man for the express purpose of praising and extolling Him."[18] Because of his belief in the priesthood of all believers, Luther wrote hymns in the language of his people—German—and brought music to the lungs and lips of even the poorest peasants in the congregation.

For Luther the reformation of the university was second in importance only to the reformation of the Church, and music had to have a prominent role in education as well:

> I have always loved music; whoso has skill in this art, is of a good temperament, fitted for all things. We must teach music in schools; a schoolmaster ought to have skill in music, or I would not regard him; neither should we ordain young men as preachers, unless they have been well exercised in music.[19]

In putting music at the heart of worship and at the core of his curriculum of education, Luther simply followed the Jewish (biblical)

---

* See chapter 9, "Revolution: What Made Translators World Changers?"
** As we shall see in chapter 15, this profound discovery based on 1 Peter 2:9, Revelation 1:6, etc., became an important source of the West's economic development and political liberty.

tradition of temple musicians and singers who were "prophets" or "sons of prophets." The biblical phrase "sons of prophets" often meant the students of prophets. An early meaning of the phrase "to prophesy" was ecstatic singing accompanied with music.[20] King David—the driving force behind the temple worship in Jerusalem—was Israel's musician, singer, and poet *par excellence*. The Bible calls him a "prophet."[21] The New Testament asked the followers of Christ to seek the gift of prophecy.[22] In the light of the Old Testament, that exhortation had to include learning music, as did the "sons of prophets."

The modern West confirmed Luther's educational philosophy that musical literacy produces people with an intuitive awareness of a logical and orderly universe. It is not a coincidence that universities such as Oxford and Cambridge that have a distinctly Christian heritage still hold music in greater respect than most of the universities founded upon secularism during the twentieth century.

THE FLOWERING OF WESTERN MUSIC

It takes barely five minutes to walk from the Bach house at Eisenach, Germany, to the house where Luther had lived as a student, and it takes less than ten minutes to drive up the hill to the castle of Wartburg where Luther translated the New Testament into German. By the time Johann Sebastian Bach (1685–1750) was born, that area had become a Lutheran province. Philosophically, Johannes Kepler reinforced the biblical-Augustinian-Lutheran view of creation and music by teaching that music mirrors the divinely ordained mathematical harmony of the universe. Bach was a musical genius because he was a mathematical genius who received as a part of his education this (non-polytheistic) biblical outlook of an orderly creation. In that mind-set, aesthetics was inseparable from ultimate harmony. One of his biographers, Wilfrid Mellers said,

> At the school which Bach attended in Ohrdruf the system of education was little changed from the old [Augustinian-Lutheran] prescription. Music was second in importance only to theology,

and was taught by the same master, who believed that music makes the heart ready and receptive to the divine Word and truth, just as Elisius [Elisha] confessed that by harping he found the Holy Spirit.[23]

For Bach, as for Luther, "true music" pursues as its "ultimate end or final goal . . . the honor of God and the recreation of the soul." Bach believed that music was a "harmonious euphony for the glory of God."[24]

Obviously, this is not meant to suggest that Bach's musical talent was nurtured only by theological beliefs. His family was a key factor in developing Bach's talent. In chapter 15 we will see that it was Luther's exposition of the Bible that made his family different from Cobain's family.

In his formative years, Bach drew heavily on his family's musical heritage, which extended back to his great-great-grandfather. The Bach clan had developed into an expansive network of musical apprenticeship and encouragement. This network proved to be pivotal in Bach's development.

Bach and Cobain shared more in common than their talent for music. They both lost their parents when they were nine years old, Cobain's parents to divorce and Bach's to death. A tragic event such as his parents' death could have irreparably upset Bach's emotional balance. But back then the "family" was more than parents and children. Johann moved in with his older brother, who taught him to play the organ and develop his talents as a composer. Following his brother's example, Johann later tutored his own children to become some of the best musicians of their generation. His youngest son became, in his own right, one of the most important influences on Mozart's work.

It is tempting to interpret the order and harmony of Bach's music as a metaphorical reflection of the order of his family. The stability and support of his wider family gave Bach the emotional strength to overcome his heartaches. This strength is reflected not only in his life but also in his work.* Yet, the family alone cannot explain his ability

---

* Chapter 15 will focus on the Western family, for it was one of the most important sources of

to celebrate "The Passion" (suffering) of St. John or St. Matthew. This ability to celebrate suffering came from his faith in the resurrection—God's triumph over suffering and death.

Philosophically speaking, Bach's inner power to cope with his parents' death came from his belief in a sovereign and loving God. His life and his compositions were saturated with *the book* that had given him profound personal and social hope.[25] Life taught him that evil was real and powerful, but the Bible taught him that God was at work redeeming the world, working all things together for good.[26] This biblical faith had been the key to the optimism and music of Western civilization: for Augustine as the Roman Empire was collapsing around him, for Luther as his own life was threatened by a powerful empire and a corrupt religious leadership, and for Tolkien as he lived through the horror of two World Wars.

These people knew evil and suffering, as did the Buddha and Cobain, but the difference was that the Bible gave them a basis for hope in this life as well as in the next. This biblical faith in a Creator who made human beings in his image and loved them enough to come to save them, made it possible for the West to sing, "O come, all ye faithful/ Joyful and triumphant." In contrast, Cobain's career demonstrates that without this faith the West's hope and celebration are turning into a sense of abject despair. If we may borrow the language of musicologists, the West is losing its "tonality"—its "home/key note," its soul, its center, the reference point that allowed the relaxation/resolve of tension.

The Loss of "Tonality" in Western Music

For centuries, Western music was tonal. That is, its hallmark was loyalty to a tonic key/home note. Every single piece gave preference to this one note (the tonic), making it the tonal center to which all other tones were related. The breakup of tonality in Western music is said

the West's greatness and monogamy was a peculiar product of the New Testament. Without the Bible, the West cannot even define family, let alone defend its traditional idea of family against the storms of life.

to have begun with Adolf Hitler's hero, Richard Wagner (1813–1883), who experimented with "atonality" in his opera *Tristan and Isolde*. Claude Debussy (1862–1918), Grand Master of the occult Rosicrucian lodges in France, took that experiment further. The West's descent into the chaos of atonality accelerated in the twentieth century in Vienna, the capital of Europe's cultural decadence.*

Eventually the atonal composers had to create a new organization in their art to replace tonality—an artificial tonality called *serialism*. By dismissing tonality—the center—they lost something they hadn't considered—form. Technically, Cobain retained tonality, but in a philosophical sense the loss of tonality in Western culture culminated in Cobain's music, the icon of America's nihilism and an unfortunate victim of a civilization that is losing its center, its soul. It must be added in his defense that by killing himself, Cobain demonstrated that he lived by what he believed. His sincerity makes him a legitimate icon. Most nihilists do not live in the grip of what they believe to be the central truth about reality. For example, French existentialists Sartre and Camus advocated choice in spite of the nihilism they embraced. In so doing they made a way out of Cobain's problem. For them suicide was not necessary if one could create his own reality by choices.

Cobain remains popular because while many people claim to be nihilists, they don't fully live it out. He did. He lived without creating his own reality through choice (or tonality through serial technique). He lived in the nihilism, in the "atonality," and in that nihilism he died.

In that sense Cobain stands as the direct opposite of the life, thoughts, and work of J. S. Bach. Whereas Bach's music celebrated life's meaning as the soul's eternal rest in the Creator's love, Cobain became a symbol of the loss of a center and meaning in the contemporary West.

While Western music has gone through dozens of phases with thousands of permutations since the time of Luther and Bach, in some ways it was only during the 1980s that a phenomenon like

---

* For example, the second Viennese school of Schoenberg, Webern and Berg.

THE BOOK THAT MADE YOUR WORLD

Kurt Cobain became possible. The rejection of a good, caring, and almighty God and a rejection of the biblical philosophy of sin ensured that there was no way to make sense of suffering—personal, societal, or environmental. Reality became senseless, hopeless, and painful.

THE AMPUTATION OF THE SOUL

Today, many people reject the Bible because they consider it to be irrational and irrelevant. Others believe it to be responsible for racial prejudices, sectarian bigotries, slavery, the oppression of women, the persecution of witches, opposition to science, the destruction of the environment, discrimination against homosexuals, and religious wars. However, this criticism itself reveals the powerful influence the Bible had during the last millennium. During that time, hardly any intellectual position or social practice could become mainstream in Christendom unless it could be defended on biblical grounds, real or mistaken; nor could beliefs and practices be challenged unless their opponents demonstrated that their call for reform was biblical.

Criticisms of the Bible are recognition of its unique cultural power. It has been the West's intellectual and moral compass, the "sacred canopy" (Peter Berger) that gave legitimacy to its values and institutions. The West's rejection of the Bible ushered in what historian Jacques Barzun called its "decadence."[27] It brought an abrupt end to the Modern age* just when Western civilization seemed set to win the world. Now, having amputated the Bible, the Western educational machinery is producing "strays," lost like Cobain. It can make good robots but it cannot even *define* a good man. The postmodern university can teach one how to travel to Mars but not how to live in one's home or nation.[28]

India-born British author George Orwell (1903–50) was a socialist, inclined toward atheism. The horrors of Fascism, Nazism, Communism, and the two World Wars forced him to face the consequences of

---

* By that I mean the period from the sixteenth through the midtwentieth century when the Bible remained the dominant culture-shaping force, even though skeptics, agnostics, and atheists kept condemning the Bible.

the "amputation of the soul." In his "Notes on the Way," Orwell wrote that the writers who sawed off the West's soul included "Gibbon, Voltaire, Rousseau, Shelley, Byron, Dickens, Stendahl, Samuel Butler, Ibsen, Zola, Flaubert, Shaw, Joyce—in one way or another they are all of them destroyers, wreckers, saboteurs." These "Enlightenment" writers led the West into its present darkness.

In his essay Orwell was reflecting on Malcolm Muggeridge's book *The Thirties*, which describes the damage these writers had done to Europe. Muggeridge, then still an atheist, was astute enough to perceive that

> we are living in a nightmare precisely *because* we have tried to set up an earthly paradise. We have believed in "progress." Trusted to human leadership, rendered unto Caesar the things that are God's. . . . There is no wisdom except in the fear of God; but no one fears God; therefore there is no wisdom. Man's history reduces itself to the rise and fall of material civilizations, one Tower of Babel after another . . . downwards into abysses which are horrible to contemplate.[29]

I first discovered the Bible as a student in India. It transformed me as an individual and I soon learned that, contrary to what my university taught, the Bible was the force that had created modern India. Let me, therefore, begin our study of the book that built our world by telling you my own story.

Part II

A PERSONAL PILGRIMAGE

Your word is a lamp to my feet and a light to my path.

—Psalm 119:105 NKJV

Chapter Two

SERVICE

OR A TICKET TO JAIL?

W e tend to assume that our world is normative until we
encounter a society that is fundamentally different. My
culture shock came in January 1976, when my wife and
I left urban India to live in rural, central India. We began our service
to the poor from our little house outside of the village Gatheora in
the Chhatarpur district, then infamous for gangs of armed bandits,
called *dacoits*.* They went around looting, kidnapping for ransom,
and killing, while frequently building temples for their patron deities.
The terrain, terror, and protection offered by other members of their
caste made it easy for them to evade arrest. The most dreaded of these
dacoits, Murat Singh, had led his gang for thirty years. His surrender
to a Gandhian leader,[1] just before we reached Chhatarpur, had cata-
pulted our district onto the national news. But by 1976, his gang had
regrouped around his son, Ram Singh.

Now, in 1978, our neighbors warned us that Ram Singh was
planning to attack us. We noticed some motorcyclists displaying an
unusual interest in our farm. They would stop several times a day
to talk to peasants who worked on farms near ours. Back then it
was deemed dangerous to live on a farm. Farmers lived in compact

---

* A *dacoit* is a member of a class of criminals who engage in organized robbery and murder.

villages, hiding behind mud walls with their kinsmen. This provided some security but entrenched their poverty. A farmer could not grow vegetables and fruit, keep chickens and rabbits, or install an electric pump unless he lived out on the farm to guard them.

For thousands of years the absence of effective law, order, and justice had exacted a debilitating toll from our people. They had been coerced into thinking that it was unwise to be wealthy. Wealth, at least its display, was an invitation to trouble. If a family did manage to save some money for a "rainy day," they neither invested it in comfortable living nor in generating more money. Instead, they dug their cash and jewelry into their floors and walls, burying their wealth.

This timidity and fearfulness is typical of insecure cultures that teach people to hoard their meager capital. Families dare not "squander" it on cultural creativity and personal advancement. Our neighbors lived in the same design of mud huts as their ancestors had two millennia earlier. Our history was frozen. An absence of savings and investment had ensured that no one invented agricultural or domestic appliances. India stagnated while the West advanced. Dreaming, investing, and changing the *status quo* takes courage; but the courage to melt an ice age does not grow in all cultural climates.

CULTURE AND POVERTY

Moribund cultures are fertile fields for fearful, fatalistic worldviews. Only astrologers, fortune-tellers, witch doctors, and sorcerers thrive on such glaciers. Our people's fear warped their folk religion, medicine, witchcraft, child rearing, agriculture, business, travels, and personal habits. They put their "faith" in fate, not in a living God who planned for them a destiny and enabled them to fulfill it. Many of them were devoutly religious. Yet their fear of stars and spirits, rivers and mountains, karma and reincarnation, gods and goddesses, made them vulnerable to exploitation and oppression. Their faith bred terror, not adventure.*

---

* Later we will see how the Bible delivered the West from fatalism and how the West has helped

While the Hindu scriptures can be interpreted to support a case for using arms for righteous ends, we saw no evidence of a religiously motivated defense of the weak. Ram Singh, the new *dacoit* leader of his father's gang, represented a feudal tradition that prevented peasants moving from the village to live on a farm.* Promoting change in such a climate required more than World Bank–approved development projects. It required infusing a new outlook in the people we wanted to serve. But the new faith had to be modeled. We felt that living on a spacious farm would make it possible to install biogas digesters to generate our own cooking gas.[2] Natural gas for rural cooking was unheard-of in 1976. Instead, forests were being depleted by woodcutters and women who spent hours chopping trees. Every day they collected cow dung and made cow-dung cakes for fuel. Our sisters burned this fertilizer, destroying its cooking gas value and harming their lungs.

Electricity had come to our district just before we moved into the village. My brother Vinay had installed an electric pump in our hand-dug well. Other farmers were reluctant to buy water pumps because they feared theft. Electricity was not available for domestic use in villages. Even if it had been, no one had heard of electric kitchen appliances, nor had they the money to buy them. Nor would any have considered them a priority. ("What would women possibly do with the time saved from collecting cow dung or hauling water?")

Our neighbors failed to comprehend our decision to live on an unprotected, isolated farm. What were we up to? How would we ever defend ourselves from the inevitable attacks by robbers? Our neighbors "knew" that the inquisitiveness of the armed motorcyclists was more than natural curiosity. They whispered: "They belong to Ram Singh's gang. He is planning to attack you."

Living on our farm we were very vulnerable. Ruth, Nivedit (our

---

the non-Western world overcome some of the impoverishing effects of traditional worldviews. India and China's new prosperity has prompted some anthropologists to wonder if fatalism necessarily results in poverty.

* In those parts of India where Christianity has had greater influence, e.g., Kerala, people have for ages lived on farms and made much better use of available land.

infant daughter), and Phupha (my elderly uncle) lived in our little house with clumsy wooden doors that could be pushed open. We were only eight kilometers away from the outskirts of Chhatarpur, yet it took thirty minutes to get there on our bicycles. (Bicycles were a recent luxury for a few upper-caste men; most people walked or rode a bullock-cart.) We did not have guns to fight a gang. Our nearest neighbor was more than a kilometer away. No one had a telephone— and there was no 911 to call!

So I prayed. As I read the Bible, I was inspired to confront Ram Singh face-to-face, just as Moses confronted Pharaoh, who had been oppressing the Hebrews. Hearing the voice at the burning bush convinced Moses that God wanted him to speak to Pharaoh, who was enslaving his people.[3] My intellectual quest that had begun at the university had brought me to believe the Bible. My journey into faith taught me to trust God's promise in the Bible that he would be my "shield" and "exceedingly great reward."[4]

Ram Singh was operating out of a suite in the Gupta Lodge near the Chhatarpur bus stand. Until I stepped into his suite, I had assumed that gangsters' dens were fictional inventions of film directors. What I walked into was no movie set. Battle-hardened armed criminals with big twirled-up mustaches guarded the smoke-filled room, littered with liquor bottles. A dozen or so men were drinking and carousing.

"Who are you?" growled one of the bodyguards blocking my entry.

"I am here to talk to Ram Singh," I said, surprised at my resolute declaration.

"About what?" asked the second.

I didn't have to answer. After refilling another drink, Ram Singh introduced himself with astonishing politeness. "I am Ram Singh," he said, addressing me with folded hands (the traditional way to greet people respectfully). "What can I do for you?"

I responded a bit roughly in contrast to his graciousness: "I am Vishal Mangalwadi. I'm told that you are planning to attack me. So I have come here to save you the trouble of finding me."

Silence descended on the room. Ram Singh's politeness turned into embarrassment. Although baffled by my audacity, he tried to remain in command of the situation. He was trying to figure out what I had up my sleeve—was I a decoy for the police? Noticing that I appeared to be unarmed, he motioned to his bodyguards to put down their rifles. Then he protested that the rumors were baseless, spread to malign him: "How could I do such an evil thing? It's MR's gang that is active in your area. They commit the crimes and blame me. Enough is enough. I'm not going to take this nonsense anymore."

Fuming with anger, he turned to two of his followers and abusively ordered them: "Go at once to MR. Tell him to keep his hands off these good people, or this time he will have a real fight on his hands."

Before I could recover from my shock, his men rumbled off on a motorcycle, their rifles slung across their backs. I politely declined his offer of a cigarette and whiskey and bicycled back to our farm.

That encounter ended so well that we did not realize that Ram Singh had turned MR against us both. MR went on to win the next election and become the most powerful politician in our area.

Two years later (1980), I was sitting in an easy chair on the spacious lawns of Chhatarpur's Superintendent of Police. He threatened to murder me if I did not cancel our forthcoming prayer meeting! Wasn't the Superintendent of Police (SP) paid to protect me? Hadn't he taken an oath to defend India's secular, liberal, democratic Constitution, which guaranteed my fundamental rights? Yet here he was, declaring what I only dreamed of hearing from a *dacoit*!

This conflict with our district authorities grew out of our relief work. A week before my conversation with the SP, I lay recuperating from minor surgery in the Mission Hospital, where I had been born thirty years before. Barley was being harvested and the wheat was ripening. Then a hailstorm at harvesttime wrought havoc. It lasted barely two minutes, but hail at harvest is catastrophic for impoverished farmers. Before its din died out people began wailing outside my hospital ward.

None of them were hurt because they had taken shelter in the hospital verandah at the first drops of rain. Finally I could decipher their wails and understand why they were crying. Some cursed the rain god for flattening their crops. Hail shattered their hand-made, partially baked roof tiles. Money scraped together or borrowed for their daughter's dowry now had to go for reroofing and daily bread. Their unpaid debt would skyrocket under ruinous compound interest.*

I heard the peasants curse their fate, their capricious stars, and their cruel gods of rain and hail. I knelt down by my bed and asked God to show us that he, "the Father of mercies and God of all comfort,"[5] was the ruler of this universe, and that it was wrong to resign ourselves to fate. God, as I learned from the Bible, desired all his children to be one family, caring for those outside clan, caste, or culture. Why shouldn't the fortunate share with the unfortunate victims of this natural calamity? Couldn't such tragedies become beautiful occasions of affirming our brotherhood—if indeed we descended from the same original parents?

Early the next morning I received an unexpected visitor—Mr. Chatterjee from the EFICOR relief agency in New Delhi. He had read magazine excerpts of my book *The World of Gurus*.[6] In his relief-and-development circles, people were discussing this "dedicated couple" who had left city life and opportunities in the West to serve the poor in a remote, backward, and dangerous village. Since he was passing through our region to see the temples of Khajuraho,** he decided to visit our work.

Mr. Chatterjee described how the hailstorm struck moments after he got off the bus. He had seen the peasants' reaction. I helped him better appreciate their plight. He offered support for our relief effort if we submitted a project proposal detailing the damage.

A tabloid newspaper turned our relief proposal into front-page news. But even it failed to anticipate the sensation it caused, its story stunned the district. Five days had gone by and everybody knew the storm had flattened crops across more than a hundred villages. Neither district administrators, nor powerful politicians, nor religious leaders

---

* Though India's economy is growing rapidly, that does not translate into relief for peasants. Indebtedness drives farmers to sell their kidneys. Debt drove some 25,000 farmers to suicide from 1997 to 2004.

** These 1,000-year-old temples with explicit erotic sculpture were our district's only claim to fame.

even mentioned *relief*. Yet here we were, a few young social workers, living in mud houses in a "God-forsaken" village* on ten to fifteen dollars a month—with the audacity to promise help to those disaster victims.

I had no idea that simple disaster relief could threaten a calloused and self-serving leadership. I was astonished, therefore, to receive by special courier after-office-hours the District Magistrate's (DM) order banning our relief work! His reason? The newspaper had encouraged the affluent in our district to contribute to our relief effort. That violated state law prohibiting private parties from collecting disaster-relief donations without government permission!

I promised to respect the law and not collect donations. We would only offer relief. The DM insisted that we scrap our project. Why? If you are not collecting, how can you possibly give aid? Your relief project is unauthorized and illegal!

The District Magistrate was an officer of the Indian Administrative Services (IAS),** representing the very best of Indian society. But, like most of the secular, socialist bureaucracy, moral compromises had corrupted him. He was now a puppet of the very gangster-turned-elected politician whom Ram Singh had ordered not to touch us. We decided to obey the biblical injunction to honor and obey civil authorities.[7] I relayed my resolve to obey his order, stop our relief work, and simply pray for relief. The Bible had taught me that God can work things out better than I can.

Help came from an unexpected source—the Gandhi Ashram invited us to hold a nonsectarian, public prayer meeting on their premises. That highly respected institution had negotiated the *dacoits'* surrender before we reached Chhatarpur. I did not realize that their public service had also infuriated the district authorities. They were envious because the Gandhi Ashram's success had exposed their failure to arrest the *dacoits*.

The Gandhi Ashram's leaders felt a kindred spirit with us and

---

* In 1979 we had moved to a new farm, outside of Village Kadari.
** Until the 1980s, the Indian Administrative Services (IAS) drew India's best talent—the best reared, educated, and connected.

respected our work. However, this joint prayer meeting appeared to the authorities as a public rebuff. It legitimized our work. It amplified the potent threat I had become to the established leaders. Therefore, it precipitated the DM's third order: Your prayer meeting is banned! The magistrate judged our prayer was a threat to law and order, "likely to disturb the peace and tranquility of the district."

We met to consider this order. By 1980 our family had grown to a community of about thirty people.[8] Some community members were highly educated; others illiterate. Our community included idealistic young people come to serve others, social dropouts, an ex-prostitute, and some criminals seeking a new life. Everyone agreed that obeying this order was to surrender our God-given freedom, protected by India's Constitution. Our community studied the Bible daily, and the Bible forged a worldview that clashed with the authorities' worldview. We knew our freedoms were from God, not the government's generosity. Government was instituted by God to guard our freedom, not to deprive us of it. Consequently, we could in good conscience disobey the government. The state was not absolute. It did not have the last word. There was a Word above human words.

However, our freedom or right to peaceful assembly was not the issue. Nor was it just relief for disaster victims. The question we faced was, how real was our commitment to the poor and how genuine was our faith in God? The DM asked for no response, so I sent none. Word-of-mouth publicity for the proposed prayer meeting continued, and I retreated to reflect and pray before deciding on my course of action.

The people's enthusiasm for the prayer meeting unnerved the local leadership. They ordered the Superintendent of Police to intimidate me. He called me to his home, sat me down, and assured me that he had read my book reviews and respected me as a public servant. Nevertheless, for two hours he tried to make sure I understood that disobeying him would cost me my life. The SP sensed that I was not taking him seriously. I didn't take his words at face value because I naively trusted India's democracy, judiciary, and free press. How could a police officer murder an innocent social worker and get away with it?

Perhaps the authorities had misread my motives in calling the prayer meeting. To most well-placed Indians, public demonstrations of piety are simply political gimmicks people use to obscure their real motives. But for me, prayer was neither a public gimmick nor a private relaxation exercise. I believed in prayer and expected God to answer because I believed God's invitation in the Bible, "Ask, and it will be given to you"[9] and "You do not have, because you do not ask."[10]

Back at home that night, I talked and prayed with my wife and community. A colleague reminded us that the Bible warns us not to underestimate the spiritual blindness of human rulers. Yet our consensus was that to call off the prayer meeting would be to betray our commitment to serve our people. The Bible authorized us to disobey authorities in order to obey God.[11] Although we couldn't foresee the future, faith required a willingness to accept the consequences of our choices.[12] Faith held that powerful criminal rulers and our powerless communities were not the only players. If there really is a Higher Power, then we must do God's will and trust in him.

The administration must have had spies within our community. At dawn the next day, two truckloads of armed riot police arrived to arrest me. The officer in charge was courteous. He let me eat breakfast with my family and pray with our community before whisking me off to the Bamitha police station. I was arraigned before the Sub-Divisional Magistrate (SDM) in the district headquarters, charged with "threatening" law and order. The SDM said that he would release me on bail if I posted bond not to disturb the district's peace and tranquillity. Signing that bond, I decided, would be slavery. It was better to be imprisoned and retain my freedom to pray. That decision was the ticket to my first trip to jail.

The officials feared that the villagers would throng to see me if they locked me in the local jail. So they incarcerated me in the Tikamgarh jail—a three-hour bus ride away. The authorities were doubly irritated that our prayer meeting was scheduled for Wednesday's market day when thousands of villagers came to the city to buy and sell. Quashing our prayer meeting took a tremendous effort. They turned the entire city into a veritable fortress. Every entry point into the city was barricaded. Potential pray-ers were warned to stay away from the Gandhi Ashram.

Police detained my key supporters for all of Wednesday. Yet, the authorities thought it a tactical necessity to allow a few women, including my wife, Ruth, to reach the premises and pray under the leadership of Dr. D. W. Mategaonker, the highly respected medical superintendent of the Christian hospital. A medical missionary from Maharashtra state, he was known to spend as many as eighteen hours a day serving the sick. He served as the honorary chairman of our governing board. The authorities must have felt that they would appear diabolically oppressive if they also arrested Dr. Mategaonker, the women, and the Gandhi Ashram's leadership who had assembled to pray.

Keeping me in prison soon became an embarrassment for the officials. Once the newspaper discovered that its enthusiasm precipitated my arrest, it decided to make my life in jail front-page news, daily calling on the authorities to come to their senses. A week of such bombardment forced the authorities to unconditionally release me. On my return I undertook a *Padyatra* (footmarch) of thirty some villages, conducting prayer meetings and explaining what had happened. Sitting in peasants' homes and eating their food had a profound effect on me: their plight was no longer a political issue. When the EFICOR relief check finally arrived, we ignored the DM's earlier orders and offered relief to the needy. Having burned their fingers in the earlier confrontation, the district authorities decided not to infuriate the peasants. They looked the other way and bided their time for a more opportune occasion.*

My imprisonment turned into a blessing. The jailor in Tikamgarh had no need to fear a petty politician from another district. Since the local press publicized my story, he granted me the status of a "political prisoner." I had a spacious and airy hall all to myself, together with good food. The jail became an excellent retreat—a time to exercise, pray, and reflect on what nation building meant in

---

* Our community buildings and vehicles were burned down in 1984 during the government-sponsored anti-Sikh riots that followed the assassination of our prime minister, Mrs. Indira Gandhi.

the light of my experience of real (not ideal) India. I revisited my previous questions:

How did modern India get her free press, independent judiciary, and prisons regulated by the rule of law?

What is a just and a free society, and how do we build one?

Why are my people so poor, and how did other nations become so much more prosperous?

How did they free their national institutions from unscrupulous, corrupt, and power-hungry people?

Is it enough to give relief to the destitute and run development projects, or should we find ways to build a better India—a nation where institutions are run in the interest of the people, rather than rulers; where rulers are shepherds, not wolves?

Some of my fellow prisoners told horror stories of being thrown in jail on trumped-up charges of rape and murder for offending some politician or police officer. I wondered if the Superintendent of Police, who held the law and my constitutional rights in contempt, would carry out his threat to kill me.

Was it wise to stand on principles and suffer?

How do I know that these biblical principles are true?

If my beliefs are not true but only my personal preferences, is it prudent to risk my life for them?

Are those friends wrong who prefer to join the corrupt rather than resist evil?

During that imprisonment I began writing *Truth and Social Reform*, which eventually became *Truth and Transformation*.

Chapter Three

QUEST

Can Blind Men Know the Elephant?

My spiritual pilgrimage began in a moral struggle. At a young age I had started stealing and lying. One of my earliest memories is of stealing water chestnuts. I was just over six years old. The chestnuts were meant for the family after lunch but I finished them off before lunch. When confronted I said that the ones I ate were given to me by a friend who got them from a pond.

Why didn't my imagination amuse my father?

He could have said, "Your fertile imagination might do well in Hollywood." But he was rather old-fashioned. He believed that while imagination was good, integrity was more important. So he demanded that I confess the truth.

I insisted that I was telling the truth.

But he was not interested in *my* truth! He wanted *the* Truth.

Exasperated by my insistence that he ought to respect *my* belief, he asked me to take him to my friend.

After we had looked for what seemed like "ages," I suggested that my friend might have gone out of the city to visit some relative.

My father then asked me to take him to the pond from where we got the chestnuts. I made him walk "forever," hoping that he would give up. He kept walking, hoping that I would confess and repent. His anger, frustration, discipline, patience, and love served no purpose. Stealing and lying became habits.

The trivial value of goods I stole or the relative insignificance of lies I told did not concern me. What bothered me was my manifest lack of willpower to control my words and actions. Often in the morning I would decide, "Today I am going to use all my willpower to control myself." But in the evening, when I looked back over my day, I would be ashamed that I had relapsed into the very behavior I loathed and that my efforts at self-reform had failed. I believed my actions were wrong.

Why, then, did I do what I knew was wrong? In the midst of this inner struggle I heard the news that Jesus Christ came to save sinners. That was "good news" to me, as it would be to any alcoholic or adulterer who knew he was wrecking his life and his family. I did need someone to save me, so I asked Jesus to become my Savior. He changed me. I was then able to go to the shops from where I had stolen, offer restitution, and ask for forgiveness. Jesus became the most precious person in my life.

To Think or Not to Think

When I reached university in my late teens, I encountered a number of challenges to my faith. My studies in philosophy, political science, and English literature made it difficult to believe the Bible—the lens through which I had viewed my experience as a youth. One event that caused me to question my belief was a university debate: "This House Believes."*

"Believes" what?

"What" was not the issue. The question was whether we "know" truth or "believe" it. Was the human mind (logic + information obtained through the senses) capable of knowing truth, or did we also need something else—faith, intuition, or mystical experience? Did we need revelation from extraterrestrials, spirits, or God?

---

* This debate happened. However, its content as presented here is "literary," not "literal," truth. I have condensed into one incident ideas that developed over many months. My use of this literary device in other places should be obvious.

One speaker identified himself as a rationalist and atheist. He was so eloquent we were sure he would receive the first prize. The next speaker was dull, but he challenged the rationalists to prove that God does not exist, since they claim to believe only what they can prove. If they couldn't prove it, then they merely *believed* the assertion that God doesn't exist.

True, David Hume had demonstrated that logic cannot prove that God exists—*but can it prove that God does not exist?* If not, how then could a rationalist be an atheist? The rationalist merely believes in logic. He can't prove that the universe is bound by logic. What is our logic? Is it anything more than a product of Western culture? Western philosophy produced rationalism only because the West believed that logos (divine logic) was the power that created and governed the universe. That belief has never been proven. The West believes in reason only by assuming that the human mind is made in the image of a rational God. What if there is no God? What if rationality is not a property of divinity? What if Indian philosophers are right in believing that truth can only be experienced by killing logical thought through meditation.

None of the subsequent speakers answered his challenge satisfactorily. When the motion was put to the vote, the assembly held "This House Believes"—that the university does not know what is true!*

Informal discussions later revealed that not a single professor believed that reason could lead human beings to truth. Our university's existentialists favored a "blind leap of faith." The chief guest, head of the English department, suggested that meditation, not rational quest, might give us a mystical (nonrational) experience of truth. His hope in an intuitive, nonrational, mystical, "right brain" experience was gaining ground worldwide, as I later discovered. It was replacing the West's confidence in the ability of human reason to know truth.

No professor took the trouble to attack my teenage faith. I was driven to doubt by professors appearing more knowledgeable than religious leaders I knew. If learned men were not sure of truth, how could

---

* In chapter 5 we will discuss if common sense is anything more than a cultural belief.

shepherds, fishermen, and tentmakers who wrote the Bible be so certain? Doubting the Bible was not difficult; the harder question was, what do you believe?

I decided to believe what the best philosophers and scientists knew to be true. So, I began reviewing my course in philosophy. Before long

> I knew
> that my professors knew
> that the philosophers knew
> that they did not know
> and that they *could not* know truth.*

No learned person maintained any hope that human logic could discover truth, without divine revelation. The humanist hope that man can discover truth by his reason alone received philosophical support from René Descartes in the mid-1600s. By 1967, when I entered the university world, this confidence in human reason had turned into complete (epistemological) pessimism of the intellectual elite. This doubt over the human ability to know truth was disconcerting.** Just as I became aware of the profound intellectual despair of the postmodern intellectuals, man was within a few months of landing on the moon. What a triumph of the human mind! To realize on this momentous moment that our Age of Reason ended in depressing failure*** was completely confusing. It took four hundred years for Modern**** philosophy to learn what the ancient Greek and Hindu mystics could have told them to begin with: that human reason alone cannot know truth.

The Buddha (563–483 BC) could have saved Modern philosophers

---

* In chapter 6 I discuss how Western civilization first became a thinking civilization and why it is turning to New Age superstitions and mysticism, despising logic (left brain), and exalting feelings or intuition (right brain).
** That implied knowing the truth that it was known that truth is unknown.
*** See chapter 6 on rationality.
**** Throughout this discourse, the word *Modern*, spelled with capital "M," refers to the Modern era (1517–1960s) of intellectual and cultural history, as opposed either to premodern or postmodern.

a lot of trouble. I found that for centuries they had gone around in circles like blind men in a dark room trying to find the door—that wasn't there to begin with. They needlessly made fools of each other and ultimately of their entire clan. Years of thinking, studying, and seeking truth brought the Buddha to realize that the human mind could not discover ultimate truth. Thus, the Buddha described the human intellect as the source of ignorance.* His teaching was known to pre-Christian Greece, yet Western philosophers only rediscovered it at the end of our Modern era. Many now know the "truth" that the human intellect is incapable of knowing truth or putting it in words.

FIVE BLIND MEN AND AN ELEPHANT

According to a Buddhist parable, five blind men tried to understand an elephant. Feeling its feet, one pontificated, "The elephant is like a pillar."

Leaning against the elephant's side, the second scoffed, "That's stupid! The elephant is like a wall."

"Not at all," disputed the third. "The elephant is like a rope!" he exclaimed, grasping its tail.

The fourth, furious, declared: "None of you know the truth! The elephant is like a winnowing fan." He cooled himself with its ear.

The fifth thought the first four were crazy. "The elephant is like a sharp, polished stone," he said, stroking the elephant's tusk.

Our finite minds are like those blind men. During our short lives, we can experience only a small fraction of reality. Can we claim anything to be true beyond our limited experience? Could those five blind men know real truth, even by pooling their information? Or is the only way to know truth through nonrational mystical experience, as my professors were beginning to believe?

---

* It is not always easy to discern what the Buddha himself taught versus what was added by his followers. It is likely that the Buddha did believe that "Ignorance" (*Avidhya*) was the root of creation. For a discussion of *Paticcasamuppada* or the "Chain of Dependent Origination," see chapter 6 on rationality. Assuming that creation, including of the human body, self-consciousness, and rationality, was a product of cosmic "Ignorance," the Buddha sought mystical enlightenment by sidestepping rationality, eliminating self-consciousness, and escaping the body and the world.

What if there was a sixth man who could see? He could say to the first blind man, "Sir, you are holding the elephant's foot, but if you get up and move up four feet, you will feel the wall part, which is the elephant's side."

That would be revelation. Others revealed to me most of what I knew. I couldn't prove that the earth rotated on its axis and revolved around the sun. I believed it because my elders said that the experts said so. That belief helped me understand sunsets and sunrises and why summer changed to winter.

A blind man could test (verify or falsify) many of the sixth person's claims. But when he is told that the tusk is white, he must accept that on faith. Being born blind, he could not comprehend whiteness, let alone verify it. Would this faith be "blind"? Not if he tested the sixth man's other claims about the elephant and found him to be trustworthy. Bigotry is to presume that everyone is blind; that no one knows or can know or communicate the truth, neither an ET (extra-terrestrial intelligent creature) nor a Creator.

WOULD EYES EXIST, IF LIGHT DID NOT?

My professors talked as though while they could speak, their Creator could never speak. They held that while they wrote books, their Creator could never present his point of view. That seemed presumptuous. What if they wrote books because they were made in the image of someone who originated thought and communication?

Some friends maintained that the Bible could not be God's book because it was the product of a particular human culture. Each of the Bible's books bears the imprint of its human authors. Paul's language, vocabulary, and argument are different from John's. This argument seemed convincing until I paused to look at a lotus flower in our garden. It was gorgeous. It clearly depended on chemistry and climate. It *was* chemistry. It was also vulnerable to insects and humans. But could it also be God's handiwork? Each of us wrote what our professors revealed. My notes were different from my friend's notes, just as each lotus was different from the others. Yet what my friends and I wrote were words and thoughts from the same professor. Why couldn't words bearing signatures of several authors be the words of one God?

Though blind men exist, couldn't someone exist who sees? Someone who sees the elephant and communicates with the blind? "Blindness" exists only because sight exists. If no one could see, no one would talk of blindness.

Early Enlightenment philosophers like Descartes made a simple mistake.* They presumed that because we have eyes, we can see for ourselves without nonhuman aid. Our eyes are indeed as wonderful as our intellect. But to see, eyes need light. Why would eyes even exist if light did not? If intellect cannot know truth, perhaps it needs the light of revelation. In fact, intellect can know nothing without revelation.** It seemed to me that the intellect's existence required prior existence of revelation and communication. To a priori rule out revelation was putting confidence in eyes while excluding light.

On the other hand, cynicism seemed indefensible. Human knowledge obviously had some validity. In an age when some sought communication from extraterrestrials, ruling out revelation from God appeared to be arrogant bigotry. I decided to read the world's best-known scriptures to see if the Creator had given revelation.

My professor of Indian philosophy took pains to cultivate in our class a deep respect for the Hindu scriptures. Yet, he never asked us to read the Vedas—the primary and holiest Hindu texts. So I decided to study them. I went to the bookstall of the Gita Press, Gorakhpur—the Bible Society's Hindu counterpart. To my astonishment I was told that I could buy Vedic commentaries, but the Vedas themselves had never been published in Hindi, my mother tongue and India's national language!

"Why?" I asked the bookseller. "Don't priests want us to know God's revelation?"

---

* In many ways Descartes followed Augustine. However, his overconfidence in reason came from Renaissance writers such as Pico della Mirandola. Augustine escaped the trap of the humanist hubris and balanced his belief in intellect with a belief in reasonable faith because skepticism was a part of his intellectual environment.

** Including what theologians call "General Revelation," or "common grace."

The bookseller gently explained that the Vedas could never be translated because they were too sacred and difficult to understand. Besides, understanding was not necessary. They were never written to teach truth. They were mantras to be memorized and correctly chanted with careful pronunciation, enunciation, and intonation. Their magic was in the sound, not in the meaning. To learn the Vedas, I must find a competent guru and spend years at his feet practicing the art of Vedic chanting, while performing prescribed sacrifices.

Disappointed, I queried the Qur'an. *Allahabad*, my city's name, means "the abode of Allah." I again was amazed to learn the Qur'an was published neither in Hindi nor in Urdu—a language I understood because my Muslim friends used it all the time. Since my passion was to know truth, I had little motivation to learn Arabic at that time to study the Qur'an. So I returned to the Bible, which I had already read, to see if it actually was God's revelation.

I was fortunate that my parents, my eldest sister, and several friends encouraged me to read the Bible. Yet deciding to examine the Bible required courage. I had to go against my university's environment.

I found some parts of the Bible to be exciting, others boring, some even repulsive. But I discovered far more than I anticipated.

Chapter Four

SELF

Am I Like Dog or God?

University made it easy to doubt God. My challenge was to discover who I was.

Introduction to Psychology was a required course for those of us studying philosophy at Allahabad University. The department of psychology was the pride of our university. In the late 1960s, the department was dominated by behaviorism, the school of psychology championed by B. F. Skinner. Behaviorism presupposes that there is neither God nor soul. Consequently, human beings are chemicals-turned-animals, qualitatively no different from dogs. Chemistry has no soul or "free will."* It functions as a closed, deterministic system of causes and effects. Behaviorists used Pavlov's dog experiments to explain how human beings are conditioned and could be reconditioned. They reduced human beings to psychochemical machines determined by environment, chemistry, chance, and cultural conditioning. Machines can be damaged, repaired, and reprogrammed, but they are still just machines.

As I started rereading the Bible's first chapter, I found a radically different view of the human self. It says that God created human beings in his image ("man"—both male and female). On one hand

---

* For further discussion of this topic please see chapter 13.

both dogs and I are creatures. We are similar in many ways. For example, we are both mammals. Yet, in fundamental ways we are very different. I cannot know the *essence* of my humanness by studying dogs. If I am made in God's image, would not knowing God be essential to knowing myself? What does this first chapter of Genesis tell me about God and myself?

The Bible opens by declaring: "In the beginning, God created the heavens and the earth." God is the Creator. A dog is only a creature. What am I? If Genesis is right, then I am both a creature (made by God) and a creator (made in the image of the Creator). I am a creative creature.

That was an epiphany for me. Those few short sentences from Genesis matched my experience better than the voluminous words from the department of psychology. The biblical words made sense because they were true to what I knew about myself. Machines produce. Human beings create. What's the difference? We create what we *choose* to create. Freedom, or choice, is the essence of creativity. Determinism explains only a part of me. I eat food when I am driven by the chemistry of hunger pangs. But I can choose to fast. I can choose to fast unto death or choose to break my fast. At the core of my being, I am free.

Ironically, that light of truth dawned on me on a really dark night. I returned home to find that the rest of my family had gone out. Climbing up the stairs with our dog Jackie leading the way, I groped for the light switch and turned it on. But there was no power. I found our hidden key, opened the door, and felt my way to the table where we kept matches and candles, only to find no matchsticks in the matchbox.

My environment "determined" my choice. I sat on the couch, called Jackie to sit by me, and allowed my mind to wander:

What if my family doesn't come back for hours? What if the batteries are dead in the flashlight that my mother carries at night? Well, I guess no homework for me tonight. I'll just go to sleep.

But what if there is no power tomorrow and we still don't have matches? What if matches had never been invented? Well, then, maybe I'd pick up two stones and rub them together to get a spark going. Then we'd have light. But why do we need light? Why doesn't Jackie care whether it is light or dark?

Am I different from dogs? Could it be that I make light—though Jackie doesn't—because I am made in the image of someone who created light?

That last thought was interesting. Jackie accepts what *is*—even darkness. I imagine what *could* be or *ought* to be and try to change what is. That's creativity. I am part of nature, but I am not merely and exclusively a part of nature. By using my imagination, I can transcend nature. I can change nature to become like my imagination. I can invent matches, candles, and electric bulbs. Is that what the Bible implies when it calls God "Creator" and says that I am made in his image?

The creation account in Genesis 1:2–4 continues: "The earth was without form and void, and darkness was over the face of the deep . . . And God said, 'Let there be light,' and there was light. And God saw that the light was good."

Another light turned on inside of me. Perhaps this creative element in the nature of a human was the reason Jesus said: "I am the light of the world. Whoever follows me will not walk in darkness."[1] Jesus' contemporaries had lamps, yet they walked in darkness—moral, religious, social, economic, and political darkness. Jesus called his disciples to be the light in their dark world. How can we change our world if we are merely a part of it? We can invent alloys that are not found in nature and breed flowers and fruits that don't grow in nature. This shows that there is something in us—creative imagination—that transcends nature, culture, and history. We must be free inside to make a difference outside—in nature or in culture.

Determinism (and other forms of reductionism) implies that we don't exist as individual selves but are only products of our chemistry, genes, environment, culture, or language. My professors couched these ideas in scientific/academic terminology. Did that make these ideas any better than traditional fatalism? Fatalism is a worldview with huge social consequences that I could see all around me: poverty, disease, and oppression. Cultures like mine had historically resigned themselves to their "fate." Western civilization, on the other hand, believed that human beings were creative creatures and therefore could change "reality" for the better. This enabled the West to virtually eliminate many of the ills that still plagued my people.

But, I said to myself, *if you were like God, would you wait for your family to return? Wouldn't you just say, "Let there be light," and there would be light?*

Wait a minute! (I was exercising my inner freedom to argue with myself.) *How do we make electricity?*

Don't we read and teach the science and technology of generating and applying electricity before we can make light? Words do come before light. Dogs don't learn to make light because they don't have the gift of language. I use language, but Jackie doesn't. Did we evolve our capacity to use language, or were we made with that capacity because we were created in the image of someone who uses words?

Language does not merely enable us to be creative. Language is itself creative. The best literature is "inspired" language. Inspiration is also key to scientific discoveries, technical breakthroughs, and literary masterpieces. *Inspiration* comes from *"en spiritus"*—in the Spirit. In the dark stillness of that room, I learned what Helen Keller (1880–1964) had learned in a far more dramatic experience: that language makes us humans—persons.

Helen was blind and deaf. Because her condition had developed when she was only nineteen months old, she also became dumb—unable to use oral signifiers (words) for communication. For years, Helen couldn't learn anything because she was locked up within her own world of frustration and anger. In *The Story of My Life* (1902), Helen described her moment of epiphany at age seven:

We walked down the path to the well house, attracted by the fragrance of the honeysuckle with which it was covered. Someone was drawing water and my teacher placed my hand under the spout. As the cool stream gushed over one hand, she spelled into the other the word *water*, first slowly, then rapidly. I stood still, my whole attention fixed upon the motions of her fingers. Suddenly I felt a misty consciousness as if something forgotten—a thrill of returning thought; and somehow the mystery of language was revealed to me. I knew then that "w-a-t-e-r" meant the wonderful cool something that was flowing over my hand. That living word awakened my soul, gave it light, hope, joy, set it free![2]

Her discovery of language enabled Helen to learn to speak by age ten. She learned to write using a Braille typewriter. She became a prolific author, a champion for the blind, and a powerful voice on many social issues.

Helen's excitement about language was opposite of that of Indian mystics. The most enlightened Indian mystics cultivated silence. They saw intellect and language as the source of human ignorance and bondage. Among my friends, Tripathi was the only Hindu who had the courage to agree with the Indian sages. He thought the professors who taught that man was nothing more than an evolved animal were ill informed. Man, Tripathi maintained, was God—the ultimate reality, pure, thoughtless consciousness. It permeates everything. It is everything. It is within us, and we reach it by meditating away all thoughts and words from our minds. Human beings, Tripathi believed, needed to reach a state of consciousness where all dualities, all opposites, merge to become one.

Einstein prevented me from following my psychology professors on the one hand and Tripathi on the other. India's war with China had raised the question whether India should go nuclear. We were proud of the world's reverence for our Gandhian rejection of war, violence, and industrialization. We loved our image of being a nonviolent nation, but would China exploit our lack of nuclear power?

In a sense, the nuclear age began with Einstein's equation $E = mc^2$. Einstein did not arrive at his equation by splitting an atom and measuring the energy it released. He reached this conclusion through his rational imagination and mathematical reasoning. How can a lump of clay (turned fat)—the human mind—know the invisible laws that govern this universe and capture those laws in words, words that can be tested and determined to be true or false? India's nonrational, nonverbal mysticism produced mantras and magic. To develop nuclear power we needed equations and engineering.

Because language is revelatory (as Western science assumes), a team of engineers and scientists can communicate their knowledge to plan a trip to the moon. We use words all the time to reveal truth to each other. We also use words to deceive and manipulate others. But why does language work? If man is merely another animal, like a dog, how can the laws or truths that govern this universe be put into words? Einstein wrote that this problem "leaves us in awe, but which we shall never understand. . . . For the eternal mystery of the world is comprehensibility. . . . The fact that it is comprehensible is a miracle."[3] Yet, he knew some things for sure. He knew the earth was round and that it revolved around the sun. We know enough truth about the solar system to dream of a trip to Mars. Those who maintain that words have nothing to do with truth are clearly wrong. Helen Keller's story gave credence to the biblical idea that our words are revelatory and creative because behind the universe are words—the Creator's words.

Words are tools we use to distinguish solids from liquids, water from milk, and hot milk from cold. If reality were one, as Tripathi believed, we could not know truth without killing language by repeating meaningless mantras or sounds such as *om*. Transcending verbal, intellectual categories would not suffice. Tripathi said that the enlightened sages had to transcend even good and evil. Only then could they merge into the one divine consciousness. Words like morals, he believed, remove us from reality (oneness) into duality or plurality. Our persistence in making value judgments was proof of our metaphysical ignorance.

Tripathi was deeply religious. However, at that time nobody took him seriously. He was virtually alone in his belief, and sometimes not sure if he believed it himself. His belief system gained some respectability in India only in the 1980s—after Western interest in Hindu gurus turned into the New Age movement.

The Bible's beginning gave me a perspective that differed from Tripathi's Hinduism and from academic atheism. God did not merely say, "Let there be light." He judged the light as good. My dog, Jackie, might have a preference between receiving a whole steak or leftover bones. But he did not seem to judge me as good or bad for giving him one or the other. Making value judgments is uniquely human.

My mind went back to the lotus in my garden. *Why was it so beautiful? Plants used fragrant flowers to attract butterflies, but why did they possess beauty? What about those plants that didn't need to attract* insects? *It was not just the flowers that were beautiful. Some trees looked beautiful too! Why were butterflies and trees beautiful?*

If beauty was merely a means of attracting mates, then why do trees and butterflies appear pleasant to us? Their pleasantness seems to harm the flowers and the butterflies: girls pluck flowers and boys chase butterflies (before they start chasing girls!).

Both friends who viewed the universe as a product of blind chance, and Tripathi, who viewed the universe as synonymous with God, rejected the notions of good and bad. For them all value judgments—right and wrong, beautiful and ugly, true and false—were at best subjective and at worst harmful. Boys who claimed that nothing was beautiful or ugly in itself, however, kept looking for beautiful girls—as though beauty was in the girl, not in her eyes. Girls, too, worked hard at looking pretty. Standards of beauty, as of morals, indeed differed from culture to culture and age to age. Did that make all values subjective? Even in the twentieth century, we had entire castes in India whose socially sanctioned profession was to steal. Was stealing then merely cultural preference, or was it bad in itself?

Sitting in that dark room, my mind was illuminated by the little phrase, "And God saw that the light was good." It gave a credible explanation of why we make value judgments:

Moral judgments: This is good; that is evil.
Aesthetic judgments: This is beautiful; that is ugly.
Epistemological judgments: That is true; this is false.

The second chapter of Genesis explains beauty when it says that God planted a garden and made "every tree that is pleasant to the sight."[4] In chapters 3–6, Genesis describes human choices and actions that God said were not good. Could it be that we make value judgments because they are intrinsic to what it means to be a person (like God), as opposed to being mere animals?

My intellectual environment told me that we make a mistake every time we make a value judgment. Those who said we shouldn't judge kept judging those who judged. That showed that making value judgments is an integral, inescapable part of who we are as human beings. It is basic to cultural creativity and to the possibility of reform. We don't fix what is not broken. To change anything, we must first judge what is not good or right or true. The first chapters of the Bible, therefore, seemed to fit reality better than the intellectual options offered by my university or friends. I began to get excited about the Bible because it provided me with explanations. It made greater sense of who I was—a godlike person with a capacity to know, experience, and enjoy goodness, beauty, and truth.

Although I found the early chapters of Genesis exciting, it did not take long to get into the boring and repulsive parts of the Bible. By the time I got to the books of Kings and Chronicles, I had had enough. I was ready to give up. Why was I reading Jewish history? I hardly knew anything of Indian history. Why should I read stories of Jewish kings long dead and gone?

Just as I was contemplating closing this boring book once and for all, something intrigued me. Our folk history told us of great and glorious rulers. This Jewish book, in contrast, told me about the wickedness of Jewish rulers. Why?

The priests must have written the Bible, I thought. It is typical for priests (we call them Brahmins in India) to hate rulers (the Kshatriyas). But no. The Bible said that the priests—in fact, the entire religious establishment of the Jews—became so corrupt that God destroyed his own temple and sent his priests into slavery.

Well then, the Bible must be "subaltern" history, written by ordinary people, oppressed both by priests and kings. But no, this Jewish book seemed more anti-Semitic than almost anything Hitler had penned. These Jewish scriptures (the Old Testament) condemned the Jews* as corrupt, covetous, crooked, stupid, stiff-necked, and rebellious.**

---

* Including the Israelites. Not every descendent of Jacob is a Jew, but in this book I am following the current popular usage.

** Later I realized that the Bible condemned Jews for their immorality, not for being Jews. Not all criticism of a people is racism. Parents who love their children the most, hold them most accountable for their misconducts.

In that case, I thought, the Bible had to be the work of prophets. They love condemning everybody. Another look at those boring books of Kings and Chronicles, however, showed that most of the prophets were false prophets and the good ones lost out. They could not save themselves, let alone accomplish their mission of saving their nation. Their nation disintegrated before their very eyes.

The Bible was a very selective narration and interpretation of Jewish history. It claimed to be God's explanation of why the entire nation was destroyed and when, why, and how it would be rebuilt. Although I studied political science (besides philosophy), none of my professors told us that these "boring" books of the Bible were the very source of modern democracy—including in India. They thought that our democracy had come from Athens. Later in this book, we will examine such secular myths. To continue with my pilgrimage, reading those "boring" books helped me understand one basic difference between literature and revelation.

Literature is something we interpret. Revelation also interprets and evaluates us. It stands above us, judges us, and calls us back to sanity. Repeatedly through Bible history, the Jews degenerated into wickedness. The revelation, however, remained a transcendent standard that promoted self-criticism and reform. It even deconstructed false ideologies that people built around the revelation. That prophetic tradition of self-criticism made the Jews a blessing to the world. Revelation was the source by which humanity could know God's love and judgment simultaneously. This helped me understand why the Bible made it possible for the West to reform itself repeatedly, in spite of many periods of moral and intellectual degeneration. God declared through the prophet Isaiah, "This is the one I esteem: he who is humble and contrite in spirit, and trembles at my word."[5] Only the person humbled by a higher authority could experience true reform.

But why should I, an Indian young man, bother to read the Bible even if it really is God's interpretation of Jewish history?

I had no idea that this simple question was to set the course of my life. At first glance the Bible appeared to be a collection of unrelated books of history, poetry, rituals, philosophy, biography, and prophecy held together only by a binder's stitch and glue. But I only had to read Genesis 11 and 12 to realize that seemingly unrelated and different books of the Bible had a clear plot, a thread that tied together all the books, as well as the Old and the New Testaments. Sin had brought a curse upon all the nations of the earth. God called Abraham to follow him because he wanted to bless all the nations of the earth through Abraham's descendants.[6] It didn't take long to realize that God's desire to bless human beings begins in the very first chapter of Genesis and culminates in the last chapter of the last book with a grand vision of healing for all nations.[7]

The implication was obvious: The Bible was claiming that I should read it because it was written to bless my nation and me. The revelation that God wanted to bless my nation of India amazed me. I realized it was a prediction I could test. It would confirm or deny the Bible's reliability. If the Bible is God's word, then had he kept this word? Had he blessed "all the nations of the earth"? Had my country been blessed by the children of Abraham? If so, that would be a good reason for me, an Indian, to check out this book.

My investigation of whether God had truly blessed India through the Bible yielded incredible discoveries: the university where I was studying, the municipality and democracy I lived in, the High Court behind my house and the legal system it represented, the modern Hindi that I spoke as my mother tongue, the secular newspaper for which I had begun to write, the army cantonment west of the road I lived on, the botanical garden to the east, the public library near our garden, the railway lines that intersected in my city, the medical system I depended on, the Agricultural Institute across town—all of these came to my city because some people took the Bible seriously.

I had always heard that the nineteenth-century "Indian Renaissance" began with Raja Ram Mohan Roy. I was amazed to discover that it actually began with the arrival of the Bible. We were always told that India's freedom was a result of Mahatma Gandhi's struggle; it was a surprise to learn that, in reality, India's freedom was a fruit of the Bible. Before the Bible, our people did not even have the modern notions of nation or freedom. Hindu generals sustained the Mogul rule in India. But that was just the beginning.

The Bible was the very soul of Western civilization.
It was the book of the second millennium after Christ.
It became the force that globalized Western civilization.[8]

Part III

THE SEEDS
OF WESTERN
CIVILIZATION

The Bible was one book that literate Americans in the seventeenth, eighteenth, and nineteenth centuries could be expected to know well. Biblical imagery provided the basic framework for imaginative thought in America up until quite recent times and, unconsciously, its control is still formidable.

—ROBERT N. BELLAH

Chapter Five

HUMANITY

WHAT IS THE WEST'S GREATEST DISCOVERY?

One thousand years ago, the Islamic civilization had surpassed Europe in nearly every respect. Islamic rulers were wealthier, Islamic armies were more powerful, and Islamic intellectuals had advanced further in the arts, scholarship, science, and technology.

But something changed. Now, the people of Spain translate as many books into Spanish *each year* as Arabs have translated into Arabic in the last thousand years. If you take oil out of the equation, then the 5 million people of Finland export more goods and services each year than the 165 million of the Arab world. Oil can be taken out of the equation because the British discovered the oil in the Middle East, American companies began pumping and refining it, the production of oil is sustained by engineers recruited from the Western world, and much of the business depends on the US military keeping tyrants and militants from setting fires to oil wells or disrupting its flow.

What brought about this dramatic rise of the West while the rest of the world stagnated? My secular professors taught that the secret was the West's "discovery" of human dignity during the Renaissance. That is true. But they also taught that the Renaissance humanists discovered this concept in the Greek and Latin classics. That is a myth. Although classical writers held many noble ideals, the inherent value and dignity of each human being was not among them. This unique idea came from the Bible.

SHEELA'S DEATH AND A GLIMPSE INTO MY WORLD

In 1976, Ruth and I left urban India to live with the rural poor outside the village of Gatheora. When we arrived, Ruth decided to visit every family in the village. Every day she would visit a few families to find out how we could serve them. On one such visit, Ruth met Lalta, a ten-year-old girl from a low-caste family. She asked Lalta, "How many brothers and sisters do you have?"

"Four . . . or maybe three," Lalta replied.

"Is it three or four?" Ruth was curious.

"Well, three. The fourth is almost dead."

"May I see him?"

The child was a girl named Sheela. In the middle of a windowless, dingy room, an eighteen-month-old living skeleton was lying on a bare string cot, pus oozing from sores covering her body and head, with flies swarming over her because she could not raise her hand to chase them away. Her thighs were only as thick as an adult's thumb. Sheela was so weak that she could not even cry. She only sighed.

Tears welled up in Ruth's eyes. "What's wrong with her?" she asked the mother.

"Oh, she doesn't eat anything," the mother said with a smirk. "She throws up whatever we give her."

"Why don't you take her to the hospital?"

"How can we afford to see a doctor?"

"Really!" Ruth was astonished by the extent of their poverty. "I will pay for her treatment."

"But where is the time to go to the hospital?" protested the mother.

"What do you mean? Your daughter is dying and you don't have the time to take her to the hospital?"

"I have three other children," said the mother, "and a husband to look after. Besides, I can't find my way around in the hospital."

"Ask your husband to come with you," Ruth suggested.

"He has no time. He has to look after the cattle and the field."

"Tell him I will pay for him to hire someone to look after his field for one day. I will also accompany you. Many hospital staff members are our friends."

The mother found a convenient way to stop being nagged. "I will speak to my husband."

Ruth was delighted. "I will send my husband this evening to talk to your husband. In the morning I will take you to the hospital."

Ruth hurried home to make sure that I would do my part in her mission to save Sheela. When I visited the family that evening, they came out of the house to talk to me. Some neighbors also came out to see what was happening. The couple had decided that they were not going to the hospital.

"Why?" I was surprised.

"We don't have the money."

"But my wife told you that we will pay."

"We don't want to get into debt."

"Well, I'll put it in writing in front of these witnesses," I said, pointing to the neighbors, "that we will never ask for the money to be returned to us. It is a gift."

"We don't have the time."

"But my wife told you that we will pay for you to hire a laborer for the day."

"Why are you bothering us?" They were irritated by my persistence. "She is our daughter."

I couldn't accept that they wanted their daughter to die, because I didn't think that a parent could be so cruel. Yet I couldn't interpret their behavior in any other way. So, I decided to use the pressure of public opinion on them.

"Are you killing this girl?" I asked them bluntly in a slightly raised voice.

"Of course not! But what can we do if she won't eat and will vomit everything we give her?"

"If you can't do anything for her, then why don't you let the doctors do something?"

"Because we can't afford it." They were as stubborn as I.

"Look." I had run out of patience. "If you don't take this girl to the hospital tomorrow, then I am going to the police to report that you are killing her. How can you be so cruel? Why don't you pick up a knife and stab her? Why make her suffer in this way?" Then I turned to the neighbors. "Why don't you say something? Don't you care for this helpless girl?"

I had expected the neighbors to offer moral support. But they looked at me as though I were a fool. Finally, an elderly neighbor helped resolve our dispute. He said to Sheela's parents, "Look! He might actually go to the police. If the police take Sheela to the hospital, then you will have to pay the bill. Therefore it is better for you to go with them."

Dr. Mategaonker admitted Sheela and put her on intravenous medication and feeding. After a week or so, the medical staff was able to start feeding her via a nose tube. After another week, they recommended that we take her to our home and keep feeding her fluids through the same tube until she was healthy enough to eat on her own.

At that time, our family had begun to expand into a community. A few young people lived with us, including Mark, a student from the HNGR (Human Needs and Global Resources) program at Wheaton College in America. They loved caring for Sheela, including hand-washing her dirty, stinky, cloth diapers. Sheela responded to the love and cuddles as much as to the medication and food. She became a delight.

But it didn't last long. One morning her mother came grumbling, "The village folk are saying that you are corrupting our daughter. If she eats in your home, our caste will be polluted and Sheela will become a Christian."

Ruth tried to assure the mother that she was very welcome to take Sheela home with her. We were pleased with what we had been able to do and were glad to hand Sheela back to her parents. Within a few weeks, however, we learned that Sheela was back to her previous condition.

The whole process had to be repeated. Ruth went to persuade the mother. Then I went to persuade and threaten the father. Ruth took Sheela and the mother to the hospital. Sheela was put on an intravenous tube, fed through her nose, and sent to our home. Then her mother came to fight. Ruth assumed that the mother had learned her lesson, so she sent Sheela back to her home again. Before we knew it, Sheela was dead.

Sheela's parents starved her to death because they saw her as a liability. They already had a daughter to babysit their sons and to clean and cook for the family. A second girl was an unnecessary burden. They would have to feed her for ten to twelve years. Then they would need to go into debt to find a dowry to marry her off. Her in-laws might torture her to extract more money from them. In those days, according to our national press, every year in-laws were killing around three hundred young brides in our nation's capital, in efforts to extract more dowry from their parents.* But a dowry is not the end of costs. The daughter would return to her parents' home to deliver her children. Why should they take on this lifelong burden, even if someone was offering free medical care and milk for a few weeks?

Ruth and I could not understand Sheela's parents because our worldview was so different from theirs. They looked at children as assets or liabilities, conveniences or burdens. We looked at them as human beings with intrinsic worth. We believed that God's command, "You shall not murder," gave to every human person a fundamental right to life. We did not expect to gain anything from Sheela. We believed that loving God required loving her.

We intervened because we believed that God's Word commanded us to "speak up for those who cannot speak for themselves, for the rights of all who are destitute. Speak up and judge fairly; defend the rights of the poor and needy."[1]

From the perspective of their own culture, Sheela's parents were not wicked people. They were ordinary human beings, as good or bad as anyone else. They loved their children as much as anyone else did. If they had had an American lawyer, he would have argued that they killed their daughter out of love: it was "mercy" killing—euthanasia—and

---

* See http://www.indianchild.com/dowry_in_india.htm. "According to government figures [nationwide] there were a total of 5,377 dowry deaths in 1993." Such numbers are considered low, as most deaths are recorded as accidents or suicides.

no different than what practically every woman does who aborts her unwanted baby. The parents knew that Sheela's life as an unwanted girl in their caste and culture was going to be especially miserable; her future was doomed to be dark. Therefore, out of their deep compassion for her they shortened her suffering. This, I believe, was indeed the case. The lawyer would have gone on to argue that people in a more privileged position have no right to judge Sheela's parents, who were trapped in a closed circle of poverty.

Sheela's parents believed that, like themselves, Sheela was trapped inescapably in the clutches of poverty. They held to traditional Hindu fatalism. They did not believe they could change history—that they could transcend fate and karma, nature and culture. For them it was too revolutionary to think that as human beings they were history shaping, culture creating creatures and that Sheela's future was *not* fated to be bleak. Thus our conflict was not merely over ethical principles; it was a clash of worldviews.

For a person unfamiliar with the Hindu worldview, it will be hard to understand how parents could kill a child with the implicit consent of a whole village. Perhaps a vision of one of the fathers of modern Hinduism, Ramakrishna Paramhansa, would help. In one of his mystic visions, Ramakrishna saw his Mother-goddess, Kali, arise out of the dark waters of the river. As he watched, she delivered a baby right before his eyes and then proceeded to eat her newborn child. In her hands the child appeared normal flesh and blood, but in her mouth the child seemed to be empty.

The saint interpreted his vision using the same Buddhist concepts that Kurt Cobain lived by, such as, "Life is empty." Although Ramakrishna was a Hindu, he was able to adopt a Buddhist view because the Buddhist teaching of *Anatman* (non-self) has the same practical implication as the Hindu doctrines of reincarnation and *Brahma* (universal self). These doctrines imply that individuality is an illusion and that salvation requires dissolution of an individual's consciousness into a universal consciousness or God.

The Mother-goddess could kill her baby because faith in reincarnation trivializes death as well as life. In the well-known Hindu scriptures, *Bhagavad Gita*, the god Krishna encourages Arjuna to kill his cousins and teachers because reincarnation means that death for a soul is like changing clothes. "As a man leaves an old garment and puts on one that is new, the spirit leaves his mortal body, and then puts on one that is new."[2] The Lord Krishna advised Arjuna not to feel pity for those he was to kill because the soul is never really born and never dies. "Thou dost feel pity where pity has no place. Wise men feel no pity either for what dies or what lives. There never was a time when I and thou were not in existence, and all these princes too, nor will the day come hereafter, when all of us shall cease to be."[3]

Sheela's parents had no hope for her because they did not know that Sheela had another Father in heaven who was not bound by nature, history, culture, or karma. He could change their future as he did for Joseph, who languished in jail for years even though he was not guilty of bad karma.[4]

As I began to see that these differences in worldview were matters of life and death and that fighting poverty required fighting fatalism, I began to speak to our neighbors about our need to know and trust the living God. This connection between the knowledge of God (theology) and the knowledge of man (anthropology) is crucial to understanding the modern West.

HUMANISM

My Indian friends who have been secularized by college education believe, just as I do, that humans can create a different and better future for themselves. They agree that the destiny of a girl like Sheela is not determined by karma. She is not fated to live a life of misery. And my friends don't point to the Bible or to theological creeds to justify this belief. To them, it's common sense.

But such an idea is not common sense in traditional India. Most families that harass, torture, or even kill their daughters-in-law for dowry are well educated. This idea was not common sense in ancient or medieval civilizations. Infanticide was a common practice in ancient Greece and Rome. Notions of human dignity and rights came to India with Christian education. We will look at the consequences of their secularization. For the moment the question is, *how did the West's conception of human beings become so radically different from all the rest? What impact did that have on Western ethics, politics, science, technology, and medicine?*

Europe had become "Christian" long before AD 1500, but that did not make most aspects of its worldview biblical. For example, the biblical view of man was buried under Europe's pre-Christian paganism, the Greco-Roman cosmological worldview, and Islamic fatalism.

Paganism taught the West to fear and worship spirits, demigods, and gods. This folk spirituality continued in medieval Christendom in the form of fear of spirits and prayers to saints and angels. It considered human beings inferior to angels.

While the uneducated masses persisted in pre-Christian paganism, the medieval philosophers, called the scholastics, came under the influence of the ancient Greek cosmological worldview. Most Greeks did not share the contemporary idea that the universe began with a "big bang" recently. They assumed that the cosmos was the ultimate reality. Gods, spirits, angels, ideas, and human beings were all parts of the cosmos. Each had a fixed place in the scheme of things. This meant that even the Supreme God could not change the course of cosmic history. And when man tried to rise beyond the status assigned to him, he committed *hubris*, the sin of arrogance and overweening pride. Neither men, nor gods, nor the Supreme God could change nature or history's downward cycle. Each cycle of cosmic history began as a Golden Age and degenerated into Silver, Bronze, and Iron Ages before being destroyed, only to begin again with another Golden Age.

When Muslims conquered the Byzantine Empire, they acquired Christian monasteries that had preserved Greek learning. These were translated in Arabic and then retranslated into Latin and transmitted into Western Europe. Along with many good things, they also transmitted Islamic fatalism. The cumulative impact of paganism, the cosmological worldview, and fatalism was to make the medieval "Man" a helpless creature who lived in dread of known and unknown forces. Man's "fate" or "fortune" was not in his hands. Some of the forces that ruled his destiny were extremely capricious and completely insensitive. Astrologers and fortune-tellers were of some value, but ultimately they, too, were subject to the same dark forces. Human life, in short, was a tragedy.

One of the most capable of the medieval popes, Innocent III (1160–1216), spelled out this tragic view of life in *The Misery of Man*. He wanted to write its counterpart, *The Dignity of Man*, but never did. A work by that title appeared only in 1486,[5] a century after the pioneers of the intellectual ferment known as the Renaissance discovered in the Bible the idea of humanity's unique dignity and abilities.

My professors believed the secular myth that the notion of human dignity originated in ancient Greece, even though as early as 1885, Henry Thode[6] had already demonstrated that the naturalism of Renaissance art came from the Franciscan tradition, especially from the fourteenth-century thinkers who rejected Platonism and espoused a philosophy called nominalism. Paul Sabatier, who wrote an important biography of St. Francis,[7] supported the same general conclusion. These insights provided a solid interpretational framework for scholars such as Wallace Ferguson[8] and Charles Trinkaus. This century-long research into primary sources culminated in a two-volume work by Trinkaus, *In Our Image and Likeness: Humanity and Divinity in Italian Humanist Thought.*[9] He concluded that although Renaissance humanists read, enjoyed, quoted, and promoted Greek and Roman classics and Islamic scholarship, their peculiar view of human dignity came out of the Bible in deliberate opposition to the Greek, Roman, and Islamic thought.

The Renaissance's new vision of man was inspired by the ancient church fathers, especially St. Augustine and Lactantius, a religious advisor to Constantine I, who wrote excellent Latin even if some aspects of his theology were not well informed. Their view of man, in turn, was derived from the first chapter of the Bible: "Then God said, 'Let us make man in our image, after our likeness.'"[10]

Trinkaus began his study by asserting:

Renaissance humanists evolved and elaborated significant new conceptions of human nature. . . . Beginning with Petrarch, they rarely deviate from a tenure of these visions of man that is difficult to separate from their image of God. Indeed, they find it almost impossible to define man and to discuss him except in terms of his relationship to the nature of the divine and its influence and actions in this world. "Anthropology" and "theology" belong together in Renaissance thought.[11]

The modern West's understanding of man grew out of medieval theology's understanding of God's relationship to the universe, some of which was a deliberate rejection of key Greek ideas. For example, our species has a unique ability: we experience not only the material universe, but also ideas that may or may not correspond to reality. Today many people assume that matter can exist on its own without mind (human or superhuman), but that ideas cannot exist on their own. The Greek philosopher Plato held the opposite belief. He thought that Ideas were the primary reality, and that the material world was a shadow of the Ideas that exist independently. A chair, in other words, was an imperfect shadow of "chairness" that exists in the real realm, the realm of Ideas. Plato's philosophy implied that human beings don't create; we make copies or shadows of reality—Ideas. But what about God: Does he create or does he also copy ideas that already exist in the *true* (Platonic) realm of Ideas?

The medieval nominalists rejected this Greek assumption because the Bible begins with the words, "In the beginning, God created the heavens and the earth."[12] The Greeks had to be wrong, the nominalists reasoned, because God did not copy ideas that already existed. He created out of nothing, *ex nihilo*. The doctrine of creation out of nothing implied that God was not a part of the cosmos—neither of the world of ideas nor of the world of matter. He was free, not bound by any preexisting ideas, order, or logic. The order that we see in the universe is part of his creation.

The next step, exploring human freedom and man's relationship with nature, was the work of Renaissance writers called the humanists. The humanists accepted the nominalists' idea of God's freedom and developed its implications. Since God is free and not bound by the world of preexisting ideas or matter, and since man is made in God's image, man must also be free. That meant man was not created to be a helpless creature trapped in an inescapable cycle of misery.

THE RENAISSANCE DISCOVERY OF MAN

One of the seminal thinkers who formulated the Renaissance conception of human dignity was Coluccio Salutati (1331–1406). His writings wrestle with the ideas of God's providence, man's free will, and man's dignity. He opposed Islamic fatalism on the ground that the God who revealed himself to Moses was free. It was Salutati who reestablished the Augustinian idea of the free will of man—which became a fundamental assumption of Western civilization through thinkers such as Martin Luther and Jonathan Edwards. Following him, Lorenzo Valla (1406–57) became the third key Renaissance figure to discuss the issue of human dignity. Like Petrarch and Salutati, Valla was also a devout Christian, an evangelical Catholic who derived his vision of man from his vision of God.

The Oration on the Dignity of Man was the work of their successor, Pico Della Mirandola (1463–94), who articulated Valla's idea more energetically. Sometimes Mirandola's enthusiasm concerning the dignity of man made him forget that man had misused his mind and his will in rebelling against his Creator. Therefore human intellect was fallen as much as human will. Nevertheless, Mirandola followed St. Augustine in arguing that the dignity of man consisted in the fact that man was not created as a fixed part of the structure of the universe. After the universe had been completed, God gave man the role of viewing it and admiring its maker, with the duty to reaffirm the Creator by imitating his attributes, such as love, rationality, and justice.

Another of Pico's well-known works is *Heptaplus*, a commentary on the first chapter of Genesis. In this he described God's six days of labor and seventh day of rest. This work is the clinching evidence that the Renaissance view of man came from an exegesis of Genesis 1:26. It was the Bible that enabled Pico to reject pagan and Islamic astrology. He wrote, "The stars cannot rule us by their material parts which are as vile as ours, so that we should beware of worshipping the work of the artificer as more perfect than its author."[13] Pico's readers were fascinated with astrology, but he urged them to worship God: "Therefore, let us fear, love and venerate Him in whom, as Paul said, are all created things both visible and invisible, who is the beginning in whom God made heaven and earth, that is Christ . . . Therefore let us form not stellar images in metals but the image of the Word of God in our souls."[14]

THE INCARNATION: THE BASIS OF HUMAN DIGNITY

Islamic intellectuals were as competent as Europeans. They had the Greek classics and even the Jewish (Old Testament) idea of creation. Some Muslim scholars also questioned astrology. Why didn't Muslim scholars make the notion of human dignity an aspect of Islamic culture?

The answer is that the Renaissance writers did not derive their high view of man from only one verse of the Bible that describes the creation of man. They found human dignity affirmed most supremely in the Bible's teaching on the incarnation of Christ. The New Testament taught that God saw the misery of man and came as a man, Jesus Christ, to make human beings sons and daughters of God. But Islam denied God the right to become a man. According to Islam, for God to become a creature as lowly as man would violate his dignity.

By asking rhetorically, "Can God also become a dog?" Muslim apologists reduced man to the level of beasts. They followed the Greeks in putting limits on what God could or could not do. In contrast, the nominalists believed that God was free—he was not limited by our presuppositions or by logical conclusions derived from our assumptions. If God was not bound by human logic, then in order to know truth we had to go beyond logic to *observe* what God had actually done. What if he did love human beings enough to come to this earth to save them and make them his beloved children? Such an act would imply that human beings were unique in the created order.

Far from violating God's dignity, the incarnation was to be the ultimate proof of *man's* dignity: of the possibility of man's salvation, of a man or a woman becoming a friend and child of God. The incarnation would make human beings of greater worth than the angels. Indeed, the Bible portrayed angels as "ministering spirits": "In speaking of the angels . . . 'He makes his angels winds, his servants flames of fire' . . . Are not all angels ministering spirits sent to serve those who will inherit salvation?"[15]

Its failure to appreciate the value and dignity of human beings prevented Islamic civilization from developing the full potential of its people. It trapped the masses without the fundamental rights and liberties that made it possible for the West to overtake Islamic civilization.

The poet Petrarch used the incarnation as a central argument in developing Renaissance humanism. He rested his case on the Bible and focused his criticism on Aristotle and Aristotle's popular Islamic advocate Averröes or Ibn-Rushd (1126–98). Trinkaus wrote that according to Petrarch, "Man's natural knowledge of himself leads only to a knowledge of his misery and hence to despair, since man is even farther from God than earth is from heaven. How then is the gap between man and God bridged? Only by Incarnation which is key to Petrarch's religious thought and of humanist religious thought in general."[16]

Except for Seneca (4 BC–AD 65), all the ancient Greek and Roman writers insisted on the absolute separation of divinity, leaving man in his misery, without remedy. Seneca alone believed that "God will come to men; no mind is good without God." While Petrarch insisted on the infinite distance between man and God, he rejoiced that the distance had been bridged by the mystery of divine grace. His grace brought God close to man. It enabled him to lift man above his misery.

God's descent means man's ascent. Misery, helplessness, despondency, and eternal self-conflict are normal for men. They can be resolved because the transcendent can also be immanent—"Emmanuel," that is, God with us. One who will wipe away every tear and remove the curse of sin, including death. Trinkaus concluded that the incarnation of Christ "is one of the theological foundations of the humanists' much-repeated theme of the dignity and excellence of man."[17] It reversed the traditional emphasis on human lowliness. Petrarch put it this way:

> Surely our God has come to us so that we might go to Him, and that same God of ours interacted with humanity when He lived among us, "showing himself like a man in appearance." . . . What an indescribable sacrament! To what higher end was humanity able to be raised than that a human being, consisting of a rational soul and human flesh, a human being, exposed to mortal accidents, dangers, and needs, in brief, a true and perfect man, inexplicably assumed into one person with the Word, the Son of God, consubstantial with the Father and co-eternal with Him. To what higher end was humanity able to be raised than that this perfect man would join two natures in Himself by a wondrous union of totally disparate elements?[18]

Of course, the Renaissance writers quoted classical writers (more Romans than Greeks) to garnish their treatises on man. But they could not and did not derive their high view of man from the Greco-Roman worldview. It was the Bible's vision of what man was created to be, and saved to become, that became the commonsense view in the West.

It was this biblical view that inspired Ruth to try to save Sheela. Our neighbors did not understand her compassionate impulse because three thousand years of Hinduism, twenty-six hundred years of Buddhism, a thousand years of Islam, and a century of secularism had collectively failed to give them a convincing basis for recognizing and affirming the unique value of a human being.

THE SECULAR MYTH

My professors were confused about the philosophical foundations of human dignity because the myth has impressive pedigree. Romantic poet Percy Bysshe Shelley (1792–1822) was an early creator of the myth. In his poem "Prometheus Unbound" he steals a concept that came out of biblical theology and plants it in a Greek legend. In the original legend Prometheus is bound up because he steals fire from the temple of Zeus and gives it to the hopelessly backward humans. Shelley retained many elements of the Greek myth but gave it a secular flavor. His Prometheus symbolizes man. The supreme god, called by Zeus's Roman name Jupiter, is a phantom tyrant, a creation of the human mind and will. This phantom God abuses the power that Prometheus has given him and begins to oppress man. God becomes the source of evil. In most Greek versions of the myth, Prometheus is released by appeasing Zeus. But Shelley's Prometheus is not so pliable. He does not curry Jupiter's favor. Prometheus ("man") is liberated by rebelling against Jupiter and taking his powers back from his imaginary god.

Shelley's effort to liberate man from God attracted many because so much of the Church was, as we have noted, corrupt and oppressive. Sophisticated mythmakers like Marx, Nietzsche, and Freud garnished his idea. They ignored the facts of intellectual history outlined above, looked at the failures of the church, and assumed that God was the source of human enslavement. They popularized the myth that freedom meant delivering ourselves from a God who exists only in human imagination. Marxist and Nietzschean fascist myths, however, turned out to be far more destructive than the myth that ruled Sheela's culture. These myths caused the murder of more than one hundred million people during the twentieth century.[19] Freud's myth, as we shall see later in this book, is now taking its toll on the West.

It is true that man has invented many gods. But Moses did not invent God for psychological comfort. He was grazing sheep when he saw the burning bush. He didn't believe the voice that was sending him to Egypt, where Freud's ancestors were crying out to God because of their slave masters.[20] Moses and the Hebrews were very reluctant believers. They were forced to believe because God revealed himself in their history. Freud's myth is not about God's death. It is about man's death. If there is no God, then man cannot be a spiritual entity. He cannot be a soul, an imaginative, creative self that transcends nature and acts upon nature as a first cause.

During the twentieth century American culture was still shaped by the Bible. Therefore, it escaped the consequences of this dehumanizing secular myth. But as we noted in the first chapter, the postmodern West has moved close to the Buddha's denial of the soul's existence. Its practical consequences were expressed by a young grunge rocker: "I belong to the Blank Generation. I have no beliefs. I belong to no community, tradition, or anything like that. I'm lost in this vast vast world. I belong nowhere. I have absolutely no identity."[21]

Kurt Cobain was a logical product of this nihilism. If man is not made in God's image, a person cannot be anything special: humanism is arrogance: animalism is a truer philosophy. As Ingrid Newkirk, cofounder of the People for the Ethical Treatment of Animals, put it, "A rat is a pig is a dog is a boy."[22] In other words, Sheela's parents were right: a baby is not innately better and should have no higher privileges than an unwanted dog, pig, or rat.

The Marxists who ruled the Soviet Union were ahead of the philosophical curve. They considered individuality to be a bourgeois concept, a manifestation of the middle-class desire for independence, private property, and a free economy. Therefore, like Islam and Hinduism, they set out to liquidate all expressions of individual identity in favor of a collective, communal consciousness. Post-Marxists like Roland Barthes, Michel Foucault, and Jacques Derrida go further. They hold that our lives are culturally determined: our language shapes our thoughts, and individuality or subject-hood is an illusion. Even if "singularity" is undeniable, individuality is an artificial construct "constituted by a web of forces of which consciousness is the effect rather than the point of origin."[23]

The postmodern deconstruction of individuality implies that Shakespeare was not a creative genius with a unified personality. His works were an expression not of his creativity, but of his culture. Some postmodernists, who think that individuality has to be an illusion, seek to annihilate their sense of individuality through drugs, Tantric sex, yoga, and meditation. Like Hindu gurus, some of them try to merge their individual consciousness into a universal, impersonal nothingness.

The Copenhagen Zoo vividly expressed the secular view of humanity when it exhibited a caged pair of *Homo sapiens* in 1996.[24] Zookeeper information official Peter Vestergaard explained that the exhibit sought to force visitors to confront their origins and accept that "we are all primates." The visitors saw the other hairy primates staring at the ceiling, swinging from bars, and picking lice from each others' pelts. However, the caged *Homo sapiens* (Henrik Lehmann and Malene Botoft) worked on a motorcycle, checked their e-mail, sent and received faxes, read books, and adjusted their air conditioner.

The zoo had a problem. Existing laws, shaped by the "outdated" biblical worldview, demanded that it recognize the fundamental rights of *Homo sapiens*, including their right to freedom. It had to give them the freedom to leave their cage to satisfy "urges" for a night at the opera or a candlelight dinner. The zoo also had to pay them to stay in a cage. These humans refused to heed the call of nature in public and objected to displaying "intimate behavior," claiming "that's not interesting." After a few weeks, both *Homo sapiens* departed the monkey house. The experiment violated their dignity as human beings.

Rebellious Compassion

What Ruth did for Sheela was not unique. Traveling through Africa and Asia, and especially seeing the work of Mother Teresa, the late British journalist Malcolm Muggeridge noted that faith in Christ's incarnation had inspired many Christians to give up their comforts and risk their lives to serve the poorest of the poor. Even though Muggeridge was an atheist at the time, he observed that atheistic humanism had not inspired anyone to devote his or her life to serve the dying destitute of Calcutta.

The West became a humane civilization because it was founded on the precepts of a teacher who insisted that man was valuable. Jesus challenged the inhumanity of his intellectual and religious culture when he declared that the Sabbath was made for man, not man for the Sabbath. The West became humane because the original humanists believed that Christ's incarnation and death defined what a human being is. But now, having rejected its soul, the West has no option but to see human individuality and dignity as illusions, much as Sheela's parents did.

Equally important is the fact that in rejecting its soul, the West is also rejecting the source of its uniquely rational culture. Let us examine that next.

Chapter Six

RATIONALITY

What Made the West a Thinking Civilization?

"I nspired? The Bible is not even intelligent," wrote the militant atheist writer and publisher E. Haldeman-Julius (1889–1951). The Bible, he asserted, was illogical and irrational, "full of absurdities and contradictions."[1]

Historians, on the other hand, tell a different story. In *The Oxford History of Medieval Europe*, editor George Holmes wrote: "The forms of thought and action which we take for granted in modern Europe and America, which we have exported to other substantial portions of the globe, and from which indeed, we cannot escape, were implanted in the mentalities of our ancestors in the struggles of the medieval centuries" (when the Bible was shaping the thought processes of Christendom).[2] Likewise Edward Grant pointed out in *God and Reason in the Middle Ages* that during the latter Middle Ages (AD 1050–1500), the Bible created a peculiar religious person, called the *schoolman* or *scholastic*. He used logic as his primary tool to study divinity. No earlier culture had created such a rational man with the intellectual "capacity for establishing the foundations of the nation-state, parliaments, democracy, commerce, banking, higher education and various literary forms, such as novels and history."[3]

The scientific, technological, military, and economic success of the West came from the fact that it became a thinking civilization.

THE BOOK THAT MADE YOUR WORLD

Was its rationality a coincidence of history? Or did the Bible promote rationality because it informed the West that the ultimate reality behind the universe was the rational Word (*logos*)* of a personal God? It was not, as Indian sages thought, primeval silence, senseless sound (mantra), energy, or impersonal consciousness.

Many in the West followed atheists like Haldeman-Julius in rejecting belief in a rational Creator. It did not occur to them that rejecting the Bible's God might undermine the West's confidence in reason; that it might force their universities to conclude that rationality could not be intrinsic to the universe; that atheism would make reason a chance product of blind chemistry; that logic would become an accidental and dispensable product of Western culture, losing its authority to subject all viewpoints and all cultures to its rules.

Some people think that an accident of history, the printing press, made the West rational. It's true that the easy availability of books helped to disseminate the ideas generated during the Renaissance, Reformation, and Enlightenment. But if printing was the secret, then Asia should have led European thought by centuries. The Chinese had invented the printing press hundreds of years earlier. By AD 972, they had printed 130,000 pages of the sacred Buddhist writings, the *Tripitaka*. Korean printers invented movable metal fonts at least two centuries before the German Gutenberg reinvented them in AD 1450. Why didn't printing reform China or Korea?

SALVATION BY ROTATION

Printing and books didn't reform my continent because our religious philosophies undermined reason. By AD 823, Chinese monasteries had so many books that they invented rotating bookcases. By 836, at least one monastery at Suchow in eastern China had even made a brake to

---

* Greeks used the term *logos* to refer to the spoken word as well as to the unspoken word, still in the mind—reason. They also used the term to mean "the rational principle that governs all things." Some Jews, like Philo of Alexandria, used the term to refer to God. In the New Testament, the apostle John used *logos* to refer to the second person of the Triune God, prior to his incarnation as Jesus. John's use of *logos* became the key to the West becoming a thinking civilization. The term is discussed later in this chapter.

stop the rotation. In the middle of the twelfth century, when some European monasteries and cathedral schools were beginning to blossom into universities, a Buddhist monk named Yeh Meng-te (d. 1148) traveled through the temples and monasteries in eastern China and reported that "in six or seven out of ten temples, one can hear the sound of the wheels of the revolving cases turning day and night."[4]

Were the monks turning the bookcases in order to find and read books? That would have indicated that these temples were centers of tremendous research. But Professor Lynn White Jr., one of the world's greatest authorities on medieval religiosity and the rise of technology, explained that the sound of the rotating bookcases was "not a result of scholarly activity." The monks were meditating on the sound of endlessly rotating cases filled with sacred books. They were not interested in wisdom contained in those books. They sought "salvation by rotation of sacred writings"[5] because they did not believe in words. Their goal was to reach silence through sound-without-sense (*mantra*).

While some Christians do use the names of Jesus or Mary as mantras, according to the Bible, prayer is a rational conversation with God. Talking to God is possible only if the Creator is a person. Because the Buddha denied the existence of God, his followers developed spiritual rituals that involved mindless, mechanical "prayer": mechanically rotating cylinders packed with written prayers and prayers written on flags to flutter in the wind.

A MECHANICAL PATH TO SALVATION

This mechanized piety is now appealing to the postmodern West. Transcendental Meditation (TM), a pseudoscientific religious movement, is a good illustration. I became interested in TM because the Maharishi Mahesh Yogi, a graduate of my alma mater, Allahabad University, had started it. In 1974, the president of the Indian branch of the movement initiated me into the "mechanical path to salvation"[6] in the Maharishi's living room in Rishikesh. He gave me a mantra, the name of a minor Hindu demigod, and asked me to recite this sound silently for twenty minutes, twice a day. When I reached the advanced stages of spiritual development, he told me, I would need to fast and recite the mantra for several hours at a time.

I asked what my mantra meant. He told me not to bother with the meaning. The point was not to know truth, he said, but to empty my mind of all rational thought—to "transcend" thinking. To think is to remain in ignorance, in bondage to rational thought. Meditation is a means of escaping thinking by focusing attention on a "sacred" (meaningless) sound like *om*. Thinking must be stopped and the mind must be silenced because the root of existence is not *logos*, the rational word, but *Avidhya*, ignorance. This belief is best summed up in the Buddhist doctrine of creation summarized in *Paticcasamuppada* or the "Chain of Dependent Origination":

> Out of Ignorance arises Imagination, thence Self-consciousness, thence Name and Form (*i.e.*, corporal [bodily] existence), thence the Six Senses [the sixth being Thought], thence Contact, thence Feeling (or Emotion), thence Craving, thence Attachment, thence Becoming, thence Rebirth, and thence all the manifold ills that flesh is heir to.[7]

The Hindu gurus who taught me were brilliant, but none of them had built a university in sacred places such as Rishikesh and Haridwar.* Swami Dayananda of Haridwar explained the reason: "We use logic to destroy logic." Why? Because "creation," including rationality, is a product of cosmic illusion—*maya*.

My Indian professors were well aware that our philosophical tradition did not cultivate the intellect. But they thought that the West's interest in cultivating rationality came from ancient Greece.

Six hundred years before Christ, beginning with philosophers like Thales and Anaximander, the Greeks indeed cultivated the life of the mind. That tradition continued as long as they respected logic. But it began to die out after they denied the existence of transcendent *logos* and yielded to Gnostic efforts to transcend rationality.

---

* The Maharishi International "University" was founded in the West and started functioning in India some years later.

Professor Raoul Mortley examined the rise and fall of *logos* in ancient Greece. In his study *From Word To Silence,*[8] he pointed out that the idea of *logos,* or the rational word, as the controlling feature of the universe originated in Greece with the pre-Socratic thinkers. It ended with the closing of the Athenian Academy in AD 529.

The Greeks had become suspicious of logic centuries before the Academy closed, however. Their great rhetoricians, the Sophists, used logic for political manipulation. Rhetoric was important in Greek city-states because democracy depends on persuasion. Parties opposing each other use logic. This made Greeks think that logic was for manipulation, not for knowing truth. If seemingly logical arguments could be advanced to support mutually exclusive conclusions, why should anyone trust logic? How could we know that logic is intrinsic to reality? That suspicion enabled Greek skeptics to flourish and demolish the idea of *logos.*[9]

The skeptics were not mystics. But they created an intellectual "climate in which rationalism . . . [was] seen as suspect, becoming the object of doubt and dissatisfaction, thus allowing the claim that real knowledge is to be had independently of the procedures of reason."[10] So mysticism followed on the heels of skepticism.

As Greek philosophy became increasingly skeptical of the human ability to know truth, polytheistic cults began to infuse people's lives with myths, superstitions, and rituals in an attempt to provide some sort of overarching framework and meaning for their lives. Without a rational God who communicates truth, the Greeks had to give up their concept of *logos* and their faith in reason.

While Greek skeptics attacked *logos,* Philo of Alexandria (25 BC–AD 50), a Jew, saved it from going into oblivion. The Jews are "the people of the book," and his culture predisposed Philo to defend the use and function of language, though he also attacked the way Sophists misused language. Mortley points out that for Philo,

> the making of the world may seem incomprehensible, but its principles are nevertheless written somewhere: language is not about to be lightly abandoned, since the word/reason principle stands at the very source of the created world.[11]

The Hebrew Scriptures taught Philo that *logos,* or wisdom, was a part of the being and nature of God.* Therefore, he struggled to save the concept of *logos.* In order to save it he *hypostatized* it. To hypostatize is to think of a concept or abstraction as having real, objective existence.

For the apostle John, *logos* was not an abstract concept. John touched the Word in flesh and blood. John lived with Jesus for three years and witnessed incredible happenings. He saw Jesus' word bring dead men back to life. He was in a drowning boat when Jesus' word stilled a storm. He was nervous when Jesus asked them to feed five thousand men with five loaves and two fish. But afterward he helped collect twelve baskets full of leftover bread. John heard Jesus repeatedly predict his own death and resurrection, but he neither understood nor believed Jesus. But then he saw Jesus die on the cross. Meeting the risen Christ convinced him, like other eyewitnesses, that the Creator had indeed come to save the repentant sinners.

What was John to make of Jesus' declaration, "I am the . . . truth"?[12] How was he to interpret Jesus' testimony before the judge who crucified him? Jesus said to Pilate, "For this purpose I was born and for this purpose I have come into the world—to bear witness to the truth."[13] John's experiences with Jesus drove him to a conclusion that was opposite of the Buddha's. Ultimate reality was not silence but word—*logos.* John began his Gospel with his conclusion: "In the beginning was the Word [*logos*], and the Word was with God, and the Word was God . . . And the Word became flesh and dwelt among us, and we have seen his glory, glory as of the only Son from the Father, full of grace and truth."[14]

If God is Truth, if he can speak to us in rationally understandable words, then human rationality is really significant. The way to know the truth is to cultivate our minds and meditate on God's Word. *These theological assumptions constituted the DNA of what we call Western civilization.*

Raoul Mortley wrote,

---

* The Creation account in Genesis 1, for example, portrays God as thinking, speaking, creating, naming, and judging. It repeatedly says, "And God said, 'Let there be . . .'"

With John's treatment there is an attempt to make *logos* enter time and space: the hypostatized *logos* is now attached to an historical figure, and the Johannine identification of *logos* with Jesus constitutes one of the foundations of Patristic philosophy [of the early church fathers].[15]

John's assertion that in Christ's incarnation the eternal Word had entered time and history made the modern West very different from my culture. Indian philosophy, like Greek Platonism and Gnosticism, is suspicious of time. This is because our incarnations are mythical, not historical.* In fact, Indian thinkers went beyond viewing time as cyclical to declare it as *maya* (illusion). By contrast, the Jews believed that time is real. They had seen God act in history. One day they were slaves in Egypt; the next day they were free, on the other side of the Red Sea, no longer trapped by Pharaoh's army. They therefore had a linear view of history—very different from all other cultures. For Jews, history moves forward.

John's experience reinforced this view of history. The "good news" was that the eternal Word, *logos*, had entered human history. This made the reality of time "a hallmark of Christian orthodoxy."[16] Ultimately it saved the West from Gnosticism.

THE LIGHT OF LOGIC IN THE DARK AGES

St. Augustine (AD 354–430) and Boethius (ca. AD 480–524) were the two church fathers who played the most important roles in preserving logic and laying the intellectual foundations of medieval and modern Western civilization. Augustine exercised a formidable influence throughout the Middle Ages, the Renaissance, and the Reformation. Boethius's role was significant in the early Middle Ages and until the mid-twelfth century.

---

* Westernized Hindus recognize the value of time. Therefore, some are trying to find historical truth behind religious myths. This will definitely help our understanding of Indian history and prehistory. Honest history will help change the nonhistorical nature of our civilization. However, academic myth making in the name of political correctness, however, will further damage us.

Skeptics, mystics, and nihilists questioned whether the human self existed, whether our minds meant anything, or whether our wills were really free. Augustine saved the intellect from the skeptics' attack because he understood the biblical revelation to imply that our minds were God's most precious gift to us. They enabled us to be God's own image, to know him, and to love him. Augustine wrote,

> Far be it from us to suppose that God abhors in us that [the intellect] by virtue of which He has made us superior to other animals. Far be it, I say, that we should believe in such a way as to exclude the necessity either of accepting or requiring reason; since we could not even believe unless we possessed rational souls.[17]

In his authoritative study, *God and Reason in the Middle Ages*, historian Edward Grant stated, "The role that these two scholars assigned to reason and rationality significantly influenced the way reason was viewed and used in the Middle Ages."[18] Grant documented how the biblical worldview, not the secular state, made the West a thinking civilization:

> It is an irony of medieval history that reason and rationality had, for better or worse, virtually everything to do with religion, theology, and the Church, and relatively little to do with the state. This was true in the early Middle Ages prior to the emergence of universities around 1200, but became even more pronounced after their formation.[19]

The church sustained the idea of the *logos* because the Bible's framework provided a rationale for believing in reason. The *logos* had entered history and become flesh. Since rationality was a part of the nature of God that had been given to us, philosophy or rational understanding and systematization of revealed truth (which then included science) was not something to be feared or shunned.

While the Asian monks were altering their rational consciousness through meditation, drugs, and physical and sexual exercises, Augustine's works set the rigorous tone of philosophical studies that has characterized the last fifteen hundred years of religious education in Christendom.

> So impressed was [Augustine] with the "valid rules of logic" that he could not believe they were formulated by human beings. "They are," he boldly proclaimed, "inscribed in the permanent and divinely instituted rationality of the universe."[20]

Boethius built on Augustine's worldview, which was robust enough to integrate Greek insights into biblical revelation. He translated philosophical, medical, and scientific texts from Greek into Latin and also wrote philosophical and theological treatises. He inspired medieval scholars to continue developing their philosophical tradition until the "dawn" of the early Renaissance and Reformation. Grant wrote,

> Boethius guaranteed that logic, the most visible symbol of reason and rationality, remained alive at the lowest ebb of European civilization, between the fifth and tenth centuries. When, in the course of the eleventh century, the new Europe was emerging and European scholars, for reasons we may never confidently know, were aroused to an interest in logic and reason, the legacy of Boethius' "old logic" was on hand to make the revival possible, and was perhaps even instrumental in generating it.[21]

What saved rationality after the Greeks gave it up? It was the Bible's teaching that eternal life was to *know* God and Jesus Christ.[22] That Jesus was someone in whom were hidden the treasures of wisdom and knowledge. An entire section of the Bible is called Wisdom Literature* and teaches that wisdom and understanding are far more important than rubies and diamonds. John of Damascus (ca. AD 676–749) was one church father who taught that to be spiritual was to cultivate the life of the mind. The last of the Greek church fathers, he continued the tradition of Boethius and Augustine.

---

* Books of Job, Psalms, Proverbs, Ecclesiastes, and the Song of Solomon.

John's work *The Fount of Knowledge* reinforced the belief that orthodox, biblical Christianity was a religion of rationality. In the Philosophical Chapters of this work, the very titles of the sixty-eight chapters reveal a heavy emphasis on logic. Much of that emphasis is derived from pre-Christian writers. This is significant because by his time, the Greeks had rejected rationality completely in favor of mysticism. John of Damascus was able to pay tribute to reason and rationality because of his faith in the Bible. This is how he opened his first treatise: "Nothing is more estimable than knowledge, for knowledge is the light of the rational soul. The opposite, which is ignorance, is darkness. Just as the absence of light is darkness, so is the absence of knowledge a darkness of reason. Now, ignorance is proper to irrational beings, while knowledge is proper to those who are rational."[23]

Mass Awakening of the European Mind

The middle of the second millennium witnessed many attempts to bring moral and social reform to Europe. But such attempts were motivated by one of two opposite attitudes. One was intolerance and persecution, the attempt to suppress dissent and bring about conformity by force. This was manifested, for example, in the Spanish Inquisition and the expulsion of Jews and Muslims. The other was the open, questioning attitude of reformers like Wycliffe, Tyndale, Luther, and Calvin, who sought to make the Bible available to people so they could discover the truth for themselves. Macro-historian and economist David Landes explained the Bible's role:

> Dissent and heresy were an old story, but in 1517, when Martin Luther nailed his "Ninety-five Theses" to the church door in Wittenberg, he struck the first blow for secession. Christendom was headed for breakup. In the decades that followed, Protestants in several countries (the English Lollards had preceded them) translated the Bible into the vernacular. People read and started thinking for themselves.[24]

Why did unleashing the Bible into vernacular languages result in a mass awakening of the European mind? Until the sixteenth century, the Germans, Swiss, and English were just as superstitious as the Spanish. And unfortunately the church was often a major source of this irrationality. A bishop would place a "tooth of the baby Jesus" or a "piece of the cross of Christ" in a glass case in a cathedral, and devout Christians would go on pilgrimages to see the relic. They would make a donation in the hope of receiving remission for some of their sins. The donation might shorten their time in purgatory by, say, 336 years, 26 days, and 6 hours. Superstitions like these were the first to disappear as people began to read the Bible.

Once English bishops realized that it had become impossible to prevent people from buying and reading the Bible, King Henry VIII allowed the English Bible to be placed in every parish. The times were turbulent, as the Reformation was raging in continental Europe. Influenced by William Tyndale's book *The Obedience of a Christian Man* (1528), Henry thought that reading the Bible would make Englishmen docile and obedient. He was furious when just the opposite happened.

Almost every alehouse and tavern turned into a debating society.[25] People started questioning and judging every tradition of the church and every decision of the king. People could question religious and political authorities because they now had in their hands the very Word of God. The Word of God was an authority higher than the authority of the church and the state combined. Upset that the Bible had created such intellectual ferment, Henry tried to put the genie back into the bottle. He drafted a second edict withdrawing his permission to read the English Bible. But it was too late; the masses had been aroused. The second edict was never issued, although Henry's document still exists in his own handwriting.

Alehouses became debating clubs as people interpreted and applied the Bible differently to the intellectual and social issues of the day. Some were content to let the church settle their disputes. Others realized that the only way to determine which interpretation was correct was to read the Bible with valid rules of interpretation. This was a bottom-up intellectual revolution. It infused the minds of all literate

Englishmen—not just those in the universities—with a new logical bent. It took no time for that revolution to spread into other aspects of people's lives. Until that time, England was only a middling power. But once the English people began using logic to interpret the Bible, they acquired a skill that propelled their nation to the forefront of world politics, economics, and thought.

Some people think that chance happenings of history, such as guns, germs, and steel, were the keys to the West's ability to colonize the world.[26] Their materialistic perspective overlooks the fact that Catholic nations like Portugal, Spain, and France were the leading naval powers during the sixteenth century. What enabled much smaller Protestant nations such as England and Holland to beat their Catholic rivals?

Cedric B. Cowing, professor emeritus of history in Hawaii, studied the impact of the eighteenth-century biblical "Revival" in England and the "Great Awakening" or "New Light" in America. He concluded that the primary factor that propelled the English-speaking nations ahead of their Catholic rivals was the peculiar relationship between biblical spirituality and intellectual awakening.

The fact that God had communicated his Word motivated people to learn reading and writing. The Bible was already a library—a collection of sixty-six books. On top of that, John Wesley urged his converts to study fifty selected titles. In America the awakening had begun under Jonathan Edwards, America's first philosopher. The attempt to master his books, the recommended books, and the Bible motivated believers to develop a number of learning skills. Cowing said that as a result of these spiritual revivals,

> in Britain, many of the converts of Whitefield and Wesley were
> motivated to learn to read [the Bible] and write, but in the northern
> colonies [e.g., North America] where people were already liter-
> ate—except the Indians and Negroes—the energies and discipline
> released by the New Light were the inspiration needed to master
> abstract religious material. In comprehending theological as well as
> devotional printed matter, the emotions [stirred up by Revivalists]

aided the development of cognitive skills. The novices in focusing on the stages of conversion were studying a process analogous to the still mysterious secular sequence of gathering data, altering hypotheses, and somehow relying upon intuition to synthesize the conclusions. This type of thinking would have a more general utility later. The Great Awakening induced a grass roots intellectualism that ultimately spread in every direction, from belief in God's sovereignty all the way to agnosticism.[27]

These spiritual revivals led to the mass awakening of reason. People were seeking and receiving the promised "Spirit of wisdom and understanding, the Spirit of counsel and might, the Spirit of knowledge and the fear of the Lord"[28]—which is "the beginning of knowledge."[29] By producing an unprecedented hunger for the knowledge of truth, biblical revivals lifted Protestant countries out of the poverty that was chronic worldwide.

In his inquiry into the wealth of the nations, the Scottish economist Adam Smith noted that hard work alone does not result in prosperity. Primitive tribes that hunt and gather the whole day, seven days a week, work hard. The difference between poverty and prosperity is determined by how much "skill, dexterity, and judgment" (in short, thought) is put into work. Letting one's mind direct one's muscles involves many things. Technology is one of them.

The rational use and organization of time, labor, available resources, and capital is equally important. Rational relationships among all the participants in an economic system and the rational sharing of resources, costs, and profits make vital differences in the economic life of a people. These economic relationships are expressed in rational principles, laws, contracts, taxes, and legal and financial institutions. Some of the principles and laws of a rational society are written down. Others are moral virtues taken for granted because they are a part of the culture and its religious ethos. It was the Bible that shaped the ethos of the countries that became Protestant and served as the engine for global development.

All human beings have the same basic intelligence, but not all religious cultures produce economically rational citizens. Scholars in many non-Protestant nations have recognized this fact. Take, for example, Argentina. Until the nineteenth century, all of Argentinean manufacturing—spinning, weaving, potting, soap making, cooking oil production, candle making—was domestic industry, carried out by women. "In a *macho* society with values inherited from Spain, adulthood brought males 'complete independence and idleness.'"[30] Some farsighted citizens realized that the economic transformation of their society required that they recruit new immigrants, especially from Protestant Europe, whom the Argentineans saw "as better educated, harder working, politically mature."[31] This recruiting, however, was unacceptable to the Roman Catholic leadership. That opposition led Argentine political philosopher, patriot, and diplomat Juan Bautista Alberdi (1810–84) to urge his country to respect what the Bible had done in Protestant countries:

> Spanish America, limited to Catholicism to the exclusion of any other religion, resembles a solitary and silent convent of nuns. . . . To exclude different religions in South America is to exclude the English, the Germans, the Swiss, the North Americans, which is to say the very people this continent most needs. To bring them without their religion is to bring them without the agent that makes them what they are.[32]

ARE WE WITNESSING *THE CLOSING* OF *THE AMERICAN MIND*?

Professor Allan Bloom's thesis (1987) regarding the closing of the American mind to things such as truth, things that really matter, is important. He laments the West's loss of confidence and in its own intellectual heritage of Great Books. This confidence was born during the Middle Ages. Following Augustine and John of Damascus, Christians studied the Bible and other great books because they believed that the Creator himself had communicated his thoughts in a book and fashioned the human mind in his own image. God gave the gift of reason to all human beings so that we might love him, know all truth, and understand and manage his creation. Devout Christians cultivated their minds by copying, preserving, and studying great books because they believed that to be God-like meant to develop the intellect, to grow in our knowledge of all truth—whichever individual or culture discovers it first. That is what made the West a thinking civilization. Amputation of its soul cannot but lead to the closing of the American mind.

While Allan Bloom lamented the icons of mindless music, such as Mick Jagger, the most unabashed promoter of anti-intellectualism came to America from India—Osho Rajneesh. He was one of the first public intellectuals to take postmodern thought from the ivory tower to the middle class. He promoted Cobain's nihilism and the Buddhist idea that words had nothing to do with truth; that the ultimate reality was Silence, *Shoonyta*, Void, or Nothingness.

Prior to becoming a guru and coming to America, Rajneesh taught philosophy in the Indian university at Sagar, in the state of Madhya Pradesh. He realized that rationalism paraded in secular universities was an emperor without clothes. His intellectual "honesty" appealed to the university graduates described by Allan Bloom. Rajneesh's writings were peppered with phrases such as, "Intellect is the chief villain" and "Do not use your mind." The meditations he taught were techniques of "killing the mind." He insisted, "Religion is a process to go beyond thinking, to achieve a point in your mind where there is no thinking at all."[33] A famous sign in his ashram read: "Please keep your shoes and your mind outside the temple." Rajneesh has been forgotten, but his ideas are winning the West. To date, Dan Brown's novel *The Da Vinci Code* is the most influential exposition of Rajneesh's teaching that the knowledge of truth comes, not via words and mind, but through sex ritualized with Gnostic mumbo-jumbo.

But the decline of the West and its confidence in reason is a subject for another book. At the start of this chapter, I alluded to Edward Grant's assertion that biblical rationality was the key to the development of the West's freedom and prosperity. Allow me to illustrate the point by focusing on one of its fruits—technology.

Chapter Seven

TECHNOLOGY

WHY DID MONKS DEVELOP IT?

In the summer of 2000, I was invited to the University of the Nations in Jinja, Uganda, to teach a course on the Foundations for Community Development. Unfamiliar with the area, I assumed that I was going to see a desert. But even before the plane landed in the city of Entebbe, I was pleasantly surprised to see lush greenery.

En route to the university campus, I observed hundreds of women and children hauling water on their heads. The sight reminded me of home, although in rural India it is women and girls, not boys, who carry water. Indian cities have water pipes coming into homes, but many of them do not actually bring water. Rapid, unplanned urbanization, coupled with corruption, has made it difficult for cities to keep up with the growing demand for water. It is common to see people lined up at community taps waiting to fill their vessels with water and carry them to their homes.*

My first morning in Jinja, I learned that I was staying on the shores of Lake Victoria, at the source of the legendary White Nile River. I had no idea that Lake Victoria was the world's second largest freshwater lake. Nor had I imagined the Nile to be so gigantic at its origin. It exits

---

* Carrying water is not the only unnecessary and inefficient use of manpower. Laborers carrying bricks and mortar on their heads to build someone's bungalow are a common sight, while heavy machinery may be employed a few blocks away to build a skyscraper!

Lake Victoria with such force that the British built a hydroelectric dam at Jinja, which generates so much electricity that some of it is sold to Kenya.

The abundance of water and electricity made me wonder why women were carrying water on their heads, morning and evening, 365 days a year. Were they unaware of pumping technology? That couldn't be the case, because across the fields from my residence was an industrial complex owned by Indians. I could hear the pump that supplied water to their two thousand homes directly from Lake Victoria.

By the fourth day it became difficult for me to respect a practice that forced women to engage in this drudgery while many men sat and played cards. Using their muscles to bring water was not merely a waste of billions of hours of labor; it also meant that families did not bathe enough, flush enough, or wash enough. Drinking from insufficiently washed glasses, and eating inadequately washed food from unacceptably washed dishes with improperly washed hands or cutlery are sure ways to get infected with easily avoidable diseases. It means wasting further time and resources to cure illnesses. It condemns a whole people to work at a fraction of their energy. It produces stunted women and children who have less time than others to play, learn, and be creative. It epitomizes the oppressive headship of husbands and the callous rule of a community.

That experience raised the questions: Why don't American women haul water on their heads? Why did Western people begin using their minds to do what most cultures used their muscles to do?

Technology is "magic of the mind." When you use the mind—that is, technology—water brings itself to you—water produces electricity and electricity pumps water right into your home. By using their minds instead of their muscles, a handful of people can supply more water to a million homes than can a million people hauling it on their heads.

Neither Africa nor India lacks ingenious minds. The Egyptians living along the Nile built the pyramids while barbarians inhabited Western Europe. The problem was that the engineers who made pyramids to honor the bones of kings and queens did not bother making wheelbarrows for their slaves. Some husbands who care for their wives do, in fact, make wheelbarrows in Uganda. It takes only a few sticks and a wheel.

My experience in Jinja refuted the proverb that "necessity is the mother of invention." Every family needs water. What if a wife cannot bring enough water? In that case most cultures took simpler routes than inventing technology. Men forced their children to work, took additional wives, or bought slaves. The Hindus persuaded a caste that God created them to be water haulers and their "salvation" lay in fulfilling their *dharma*—doing their caste duty generation after generation.

It is fashionable to reject technology. Mahatma Gandhi opposed it, and the city of Jinja has erected a huge statue to honor him. The problem is that the cultures that reject technology end up forcing human beings to get their water, grind their grain, and even to clean their "dry latrines."

Aldous Huxley was a distant devotee of Mahatma Gandhi, a promoter of Buddhism, and a pioneer of contemporary environmentalism. He blamed Christianity for the ecological crisis of the modern world. He believed that technology developed in the West because, according to the Bible, God commanded human beings to establish their dominion as stewards over the earth.

Huxley's viewpoint began to be taken seriously after Lynn White Jr., a professor of history at Stanford, Princeton, and the University of California–Los Angeles, endorsed it in an article in *Science* magazine.[1] White's historical research was impeccable. His interpretation of the sociology of technology seems right. He makes a valid criticism that Western civilization, including the church, has often affirmed man's value at the expense of nature's value.

Nevertheless, it is usually the case that pollution kills far more people in technologically less advanced, nonbiblical* cultures. Cultures that can't pump water into their homes can't flush their toilets. In India, the lack of running water led to a shameful Hindu practice

---

* The use of "biblical" or "nonbiblical culture" throughout this book does not refer to ancient Israelite culture; rather, it refers to a culture informed by a biblical worldview.

that embarrassed Mahatma Gandhi (but is still practiced): forcing untouchables to carry others' excreta in a container on their heads.

Critics who blame a Judeo-Christian worldview for the technology-created ecological problems such as global warming may be wrong about science, but at least they are right about history. Technology is a fruit of a biblical worldview. The Bible itself defends at least one aspect of their critique of technology: that the human heart and mind have been corrupted by sin. Therefore, some of our choices are destructive. Even choices made in good faith can turn out to be harmful to nature and ourselves. The fact of sin makes human authority dangerous in all spheres: familial, social, intellectual, political, religious, as well as environmental. Yet, you can't have creativity without authority. Every creator has authority over his creation. Every creator can delegate that authority to his children—even if they have the potential to abuse it.

There is no doubt the human creativity that results in technology has been abused. In most cultures, the ruling elite patronized technology if it made them stronger than their enemies, internal or external. They welcomed technology for war, pleasure, prestigious monuments, and the oppression of their people. Only one culture has promoted technology for general welfare and for liberating and empowering the weak—slaves, women, children, the handicapped, and the poor. Professor Lynn White Jr. thoroughly documented that humanizing technology came out of biblical theology:

> The humanitarian technology that our modern world has inherited from the Middle Ages was not rooted in economic necessity; for this necessity is inherent in every society, yet has found inventive expression only in the Occident [that is, the West], nurtured in the activist or voluntarist tradition of Western theology. It is ideas which make necessity conscious. The labor-saving power-machines of the later Middle Ages were produced by the implicit theological assumption of the infinite worth of even the most degraded human personality, by an instinctive repugnance towards subjecting any man to a monotonous drudgery which seems less than human in that it requires the exercise neither of intelligence nor of choice.[2]

Professor David Landes studied clock making in China and concluded that the development of technology is not merely a matter of ingenuity. The Chinese had technical ability, yet clock making did not become an industry, nor did it become a source of continuing and growing technological innovations in China as it did in Europe. Why? The Chinese were keen neither to know time nor to organize their lives accordingly.[3]

The development of the watermill illustrates that culture is as important for the development of technology as ingenuity is. In 1935, Marc Bloch published his finding that the watermill had been invented at least a century before Christ.[4] Later, its usefulness for grinding grain was known in Afghanistan, on the border of geographic India. Almost everyone needed to grind grain, yet the use of the watermill never spread in Hindu, Buddhist, or (later) Islamic cultures.* Christian monks in Europe were the first to begin the widespread use of the watermill for grinding and for developing power machinery.

What Accelerated Western Technological Progress in the Western Middle Ages?

The above question was the topic of a 1961 Oxford Symposium on Scientific Change, spearheaded by Alistair Crombie. The best answer was given by Marburg historian Ernst Benz, who published a seminal essay in 1964, *"Fondamenti Christiani della Tecnica Occidentale."* It demonstrated that "Christian beliefs provided the rationale, and faith the motive energy for western technology."[5] Benz had studied and experienced Buddhism in Japan. The antitechnological impulses in Zen led him to explore whether Europe's technological advances were somehow rooted in Christian beliefs and attitudes. His research led him to the conclusion that the biblical worldview was indeed the key to understanding Western technology.

Christendom pioneered technological creativity because the Bible

---

* When Ruth and I moved into a village in 1976, we discovered that the women were still using grinding stones to grind grain. One of our friends, whom we trained as a Village Health Worker, became the first person to install an electric flour mill.

presented a God who was a Creator, neither a dreamer nor a dancer, as Indian sages believed. God was the *architect* of the cosmos. He shaped man out of clay as a potter does, making man in his own creative image and commanding him to rule the world creatively.

Jesus Christ's incarnation in a physical body and his bodily resurrection instilled into Christian philosophers the unique idea that matter was created for a spiritual purpose. Adam was created to take care of the earth, not to despise it or try to transcend it.[6] Benz realized that the Judeo-Christian view of reality and destiny produced and nurtured technology in four ways: *First*, the Bible emphasized intelligent craftsmanship in the world's design. *Second*, the Bible suggested that human beings participate in divine workmanship by being good artisans themselves. *Third*, the Bible taught that we follow divine example when we use the physical universe for righteous ends. And *fourth*, the Bible challenged the West to use time wisely, because each moment is a valuable, one-time opportunity.[7]

Many scholars have reinforced, expanded, and qualified this thesis. For example, Robert Forbes of Leyden and Samuel Sambursky of Jerusalem pointed out as early as 1956 that technology arose because Christianity destroyed classical animism. The biblical cosmos was "enchanted." The Bible affirmed the existence of spirits, demons, and angels. It "secularized" the physical universe, however, by teaching that human beings, not spirits, were meant to rule over nature. That worldview made it possible for the West to use nature rationally for human ends—though it is true that many in the West have abused technology to exploit nature in unjust or irresponsible ways.

Biblical cosmology was not the only force behind the rise of the West's humanitarian technology. Christian compassion was an equally important factor. Christian spirituality has emphasized compassion, service, and liberation far more than the need to establish human dominion over creation.

Scholars have qualified Benz's thesis because not all versions of Christianity developed equally strong traditions of technology. Technology found a more fertile soil in the Western Latin church than in Eastern Greek Christianity. Some have suggested that the difference was that the Greek church tended to see humanity's problem as ignorance and therefore saw salvation as illumination. This view encouraged Greek saints to become contemplatives. Western saints, by contrast, tended to be activists, because they saw sin as vice—rebellion. The biblical idea of new birth included a reorientation of the will to do good works. This moral activism combined with a strong biblical work ethic proved conducive to promoting humanizing and liberating technology. This became especially true after the Protestant reformers took the biblical worldview out of the cloister to the people.

The question is, *why did Christian monks develop technology?* Why didn't Buddhist monks? The Buddhist monks did not lack creative genius. In Afghanistan they excelled in architectural feats, such as constructing the enormous statues of the Buddha at Bamiyan, which lasted for a millennium before the Taliban destroyed them.

The Buddhist and Christian monks shared one problem in common: they could not take wives to grind their grain. A crucial difference between the two was that Buddhism required monks to beg for their food, whereas the Bible required Christians to work for theirs. The apostle Paul wrote that a person who did not work should not eat.[8] St. Benedict, who made the European monastic movement different from other religious traditions, paraphrased Paul, saying, "Idleness is an enemy of the soul."[9] To work was to be like God, because the Bible's God was a worker. He worked for six days to create the world and rested on the seventh.[10]

Benedict's followers accepted the dictum that work is prayer, but they also felt a tension. They had come to the monastery to pray, not to grind grain. The theological factor that resolved their tension and drove technology was that the Bible distinguished "work" from "toil." To work was to be like God, but toil was a curse on human sin.[11] Toil was mindless, repetitive, dehumanizing labor. This distinction enabled Christian monks* to realize that human beings should not have to do what wind, water, or horses can do. People must do what

---

* Not Christian ascetics, but the Benedictine monks who took vows of personal poverty, yet believed that work and economic productivity were a divine obligation.

other species and natural forces cannot do—use creative reason to liberate human beings from the curse of toil. Lynn White Jr. summed up the biblical roots of Western technology:

> The study of medieval technology is therefore far more than an aspect of economic history: it reveals a chapter in the conquest of freedom. More than that, it is a part of the history of religion . . . It has often been remarked that the [monasteries in] Latin Middle Ages first discovered the dignity and spiritual value of labor—that to labor is to pray. But the Middle Ages went further: they gradually and very slowly began to explore the practical implications of an essentially Christian paradox: that just as the Heavenly Jerusalem contains no temple, so the goal of labor is to end labor.[12]

"APPLIED SCIENCE" OR "APPLIED THEOLOGY"?

The popular misconception that "technology is applied science" keeps people from understanding that "humanizing" technology is a peculiar product of the Bible. White wrote, "It is astonishing to our twentieth century minds how little impact Galileo and his circle had upon the technology either of their own time or of the following two hundred years. Until the seventeenth century, European technology had been both more sophisticated than European science and little related to that science."[13]

Historian Jacques Barzun tells us that science and technology merged only in AD 1890, after chemist Sir Alfred Mond persuaded a group of businessmen to take advantage of what we now call R&D (Research and Development). Only then did industry begin hiring scientists to find processes that engineers could embody in machines and appliances.[14]

Western technology is not a result of the eighteenth-century Industrial Revolution. The Industrial Revolution was a result of the Western "invention of invention." Also, Western technology predates Western science by at least five centuries. The West became the global technological leader long before the birth of modern science:

The chief glory of the later Middle Ages was not its cathedrals or its epics or its scholasticism: it was the building for the first time in history of a complex civilization which rested not on the backs of sweating slaves or coolies but primarily on nonhuman power.[15]

The collapse of the Roman Empire led to the "Dark Ages," with political disintegration, economic depression, the debasement of religion, and a marked decline in literary, philosophical, and scientific pursuits. It was in the midst of that very darkness, however, that Christianity began revitalizing the human spirit. One expression of this renewal was the origin of liberating technology. Its uninterrupted development has been traced from the eighth (possibly sixth) century to our day.[16] By contrast, the philosophical foundations of modern science were laid only in the fourteenth century, and science took off only in the sixteenth. Technological innovations, as we shall see, took place in Christian monasteries, whereas science grew in Christian universities.

It is true that the Christian West used its technological superiority to colonize much of the world, and that technology has created serious dangers for the environment as well as for humanity. Nevertheless, it is ideological blindness to ignore the fact that technology functioning within a biblical framework has been one of the chief instruments of human emancipation. Let me illustrate the point with a few examples.

THE FORE-AND-AFT RIG (LATEEN SAIL)

The "Dark Ages" were dark from the point of view of literature. Therefore, we have little information on who invented the fore-and-aft rig to sail against the wind. Some historians think the technique may have originated as early as the second century after Christ. What we do know, however, is that this invention eliminated the galley and slave labor. We also know that the Bible was the intellectual and moral force that made slavery abhorrent. Is it a coincidence that the oldest picture of the lateen sail is found in a pre-Islamic church at Al-Auja in southern Palestine?[17]

Admittedly, no firm historical conclusions can be drawn from a painting in a church. We do know, however, that in the succeeding centuries the Bible played the most important role in promoting technology that liberated slaves. We also know that, back then, secularism did not exist. And neither pagan philosophers nor temples promoted or celebrated technology that emancipated slaves. The Bible, in contrast, began to be written because God heard the cries of Hebrew slaves. Rodney Stark explains that most of the ancient philosophers supported slavery because they had "no concept of sin to put teeth in their judgments and no revelation from which to begin" critiquing slavery. Stark continues:

> Although it has been fashionable to deny it, antislavery doctrines began to appear in Christian theology soon after the decline of Rome and were accompanied by the eventual disappearance of slavery in all but the fringes of Christian Europe.[18]

There were good economic reasons for using the lateen sail. It increased the average speed of the ship, lowered the costs, reduced the size of the crew, and enabled ships to go farther. As my experience in Jinja demonstrates, however, our materialistic age overestimates the power of economics. A culture will not invest in wheelbarrows or pumps if its decision makers feel that there is a surplus of time and woman- or manpower. Only a society with a theological climate that values human dignity begins using technology as a force for human emancipation and empowerment.

THE WHEELED PLOW AND THE HORSE

The Chinese were using iron plows while Europeans were still using wooden ones. Yet they continued using iron long after Europe had graduated to steel. Clearly, something was renewing the spirit of European peasants even while its post-Roman literary culture was still mired in the Dark Ages. The peasants' humble wheeled plow generated the economic strength that helped save Europe from colonization by Islam.

During the Middle Ages, Islamic forces were able to invade Europe almost at will. Muslims conquered southern Spain and Portugal and invaded France in the eighth century. In the ninth century, they conquered Sicily and invaded Italy, sacking Ostia and Rome in 846. By 1237, they had begun to conquer Russia. Constantinople was captured in 1453, and the battles of 1526 in Hungary and 1529 in Vienna suggested that it was merely a matter of time before mullahs, caliphs, and sheikhs would rule cities like Rome, Vienna, and Florence.

Equipped with a coulter, a horizontal share, and a moldboard, Europe's new plow increased productivity by tilling rich, heavy, and badly drained river-bottom soil. This heavy plow needed as many as eight pairs of oxen, and consequently, it birthed cooperative farming, which eventually led to the manor house. By the eighth century, the new plow made the three-field system of cultivating possible, leading to better rotation of crop and fallow, less labor, and more produce. Improved productivity made it possible to replace oxen with costlier but more powerful horses. That led to still greater productivity. The net result was the gradual elimination of starvation, the improved health of the people, and a strengthening of the economic foundations of the West relative to Islam.

Environmentalists condemn the heavy plow for "violently" breaking and turning over hard soil. Economists credit it for saving labor by making cross plowing unnecessary. Social historians recognize that the development and cultural acceptance of the new plow required a mindset that saw human dominion over the earth as a divine mandate. Therefore, all three—environmentalists (such as Huxley), economists (such as Landes), and historians (such as White)—agree that the Bible created Europe's theological outlook, which justified human management of the environment and began revitalizing Europe's economy during the Dark Ages.

The horse is not native to Europe, so historians puzzle over why it was European peasants who first multiplied the life and strength of their horses with three simple technologies: the horseshoe, the horse collar, and the tandem harness. These three inventions solved three long-standing problems. First, broken hooves soon rendered horses useless. Second, the yoke harness system, quite suitable for oxen, was extremely inefficient for faster horses. The yoke's front strap pressed on a horse's windpipe. The harder a horse pulled, the closer it came to strangulation. That system also made it impossible to harness one horse in front of another. Third, since animal power was technically unavailable in sufficient quantities to pull great weights, all cultures relied on gangs of slaves for large projects.

To solve the first problem, Europeans invented the horseshoe, which protected a horse's feet and greatly lengthened its working life. To solve the second problem, they invented the modern harness, which rests on a horse's shoulders, permitting it to breathe freely and use its full strength to pull three to four times more weight than before. To solve the third problem, they attached lateral traces to the new harness. This made it possible to attach several horses behind each other, greatly increasing the horsepower available and making slave labor unnecessary. After the stirrup (dating much earlier) was added to these three inventions, the horse turned European armies into a dreadful force. Despite being in the Dark Ages, Europe pushed technology much further than the Greco-Roman civilization ever did.

From our point of view, the important fact is that the oldest information regarding these important technical developments comes from a painting in the Cathedral of Bayeux, France, which depicts a horse being used for agriculture. A Christian artist could celebrate these innovations in a church because they reflected biblical values.

THE WATER MILL, THE WINDMILL, AND THE CRANK

The modern world uses many technologies to generate energy from water, wind, coal, petroleum, natural gas, biogas, and the sun, and to utilize geothermal, tidal, and nuclear power. The first of these, the water-driven mill, seems to have appeared simultaneously during the first century BC in Jutland (Denmark), northern Anatolia (Turkey), and China. The windmill apparently developed in Tibet to rotate Buddhist prayer cylinders around a vertical axle, perhaps as early as the sixth century. From there, this technology spread to China where it was used for pumping and hauling canal boats over lock slides. Using windmills for grinding grain was tried in eastern Iran and Afghanistan in the tenth century.

The idea of harnessing water and wind energy for human emancipation from the drudgery of toil, however, did not take hold in either the Islamic or the Buddhist world. But the West was different. The first recorded use of the watermill came from a sixth-century abbot, Gregory of Tours (538–94). This Gallic bishop and historian was deeply troubled by the sight of his monks grinding grain in querns (primitive grain mills). So he encouraged the invention, or reinvention, of the watermill to relieve them of this odious duty. Following him, European monasteries and communities began using the watermill in the tenth and eleventh centuries and the windmill in the twelfth century to power labor-saving devices.

One important force behind this development was St. Bernard of Clairvaux (1090–1153), who brought the Order of the Knights Templar under the Rule of St. Benedict. In 1136, Abbot Arnold of Bonneval chronicled the life of St. Bernard, describing the rebuilding of Clairvaux. Interestingly, he made no mention of the Church but gave a delighted account of the abbey's water-powered machines for milling, tanning, blacksmithing, and other industries. An independent description of the monastic life at Clairvaux in that period enthusiastically describes the automatic flour sifter attached to the flour mill. The narrator "thanks God that such machines can alleviate the oppressive labors of both man and beast"[19] and gives a long list of tasks that can be accomplished by waterpower.

Water mills and windmills became useful to power machinery by the invention of the crank, the most important invention after the wheel. By uniting rotary and reciprocal motions, the crank enabled machines to replace the human arm. Beginning perhaps with hand-querns and rotary grindstones, the crank became almost as common as the wheel, liberating human beings for more creative tasks. At the peak of their cultural development, the ancient Greeks and Romans knew nothing about the crank. They used women and slaves for chores that power machinery began to do for Christian monks and peasants in the eighth century AD.

THE WHEELBARROW AND THE FLYWHEEL

The wheelbarrow may have been a Chinese invention. If so, why did China's Hindu and Muslim neighbors fail to see its socioeconomic potential, cutting in half the number of laborers needed for hauling small loads by substituting a wheel for the front man of the handbarrow? It was not until the later part of the thirteenth century that the use of the wheelbarrow became popular in Western Europe. Ever since then, wheels have been displacing men everywhere, except in cultures where some human beings—women, children, slaves, servants, minorities, and lower castes—are deemed less human than others.

Whereas the wheelbarrow replaces a laborer, the flywheel multiplies the power of a laborer. A flywheel stores rotational momentum, which makes better use of fluctuating energy. It makes it possible, for example, to pedal a bicycle once and get the wheel to rotate many times. This ingenious invention first appeared in a book called *De diversis artibus* (1122–23) by Theophilus, a technologically oriented theologian and Benedictine monk. His book was motivated by his faith. It codifies the skills needed to embellish a great church for the glory of God. These skills that became the key to the economic success of the West came out of religious motivations.

Some people express their opposition to machines for pragmatic reasons; for example, new machines produce unforeseen consequences, such as causing unemployment or damage to nature. However, often the suspicion also has a philosophical dimension. What is the ultimate meaning of technology (or music or art)? Innovating for economic reasons is a relatively new phenomenon. Most inventors remain poor even today. Inventing new technologies requires tremendous dedication, intense labor, and many failures and frustrations. Why bother? The Bible solved this problem for Theophilus. He did with technology what Augustine did with music. Technology was not just useful for him; it was also meaningful. Its purpose was to use human creativity for the glory of God and for the service of the weak. The absence of that worldview prevented Indian monks from developing technology.

THE PIPE ORGAN AND THE MECHANICAL CLOCK

The mechanical clock provided the nursery of mechanical engineering in the West. Nonbiblical cultures did not create mechanical clocks partly because they did not value time in the same way as cultures shaped by the Bible did. Before the clock's appearance, the pipe organ was the most complex machine in use, dedicated to the glory of God. Historians find it interesting that during the time the Latin church was embracing technology to aid spirituality, the Greek church forbade the use of music in its liturgy. It is likely Islam influenced the latter more than the Bible. It insisted that the unaccompanied human voice alone could worthily praise God. This theological dispute may sound trivial, but historians think that such little choices played key roles in the West's technological development and the relative stagnation of Eastern Christian civilizations.

An interesting fact about the clock is that the core idea seems to have come from the Indian mathematician Bhaskaracharya's view of perpetual motion described in *Siddhanta Shiromani* (AD 1150). Muslim scholars discussed his compelling thesis for five decades after him, and then Europe's intellectual leadership discussed it for an additional fifty years. Finally, in his influential work *De Universo Creaturarum*, William of Auvergne, bishop of Paris from 1228–49, put forward the suggestion to make a clock by putting these abstract mathematical notions to a practical use.

Why would a religious leader take such a keen interest in developing an instrument as mundane as the clock? In his fascinating study *Revolution in Time*, David Landes argues that clocks were invented because monks needed them. We have already seen that Cistercian monasteries, such as the one in Clairvaux, were gigantic economic enterprises, at the cutting edge of technological innovation. Monks joined monasteries, however, primarily to pray.

One factor that drove them to the monastery was the worldliness in the established church. The monks gathered for communal prayers seven times a day, including before sunrise and after sunset, when the sundial was of little use. Communal prayer required everyone to know and keep the same time. Hence the clock became a key instrument. Time management was a practical as well as a religious necessity.

Practically, the monks needed to work and also to save time to pray. *Religiously*, they needed to work as a body, supplying one another with what was needed at a given time. They were also required to follow the divine pattern of finishing their work on time and resting on days mandated for rest. The Bible-shaped culture made time management an aspect of establishing human dominion over the physical universe because the Bible saw time as a part of physical reality. By contrast, in Indian culture, time was perceived either as an eternal but terrible god (*Kal*) or as a part of the cosmic illusion (*maya*).[20]

Like Europe, my country had religious communes and genius inventors. Why, then, did we fail to develop clocks or an indigenous tradition of mechanical engineering? What we lacked was the biblical worldview. We did not see the universe as an intelligent creation. We saw it either as divine or as a dream, but not as a real creative product of intellect, will, and work. Because of this worldview, our monks did not spend intellectual energy to master and manage time. They spent their years finding ways to escape the endless wheel of time (*Samsara*) through mind-emptying meditation. Their goal was to escape work, not to make it easier. They did not need clocks because they were seeking escape from social obligations; they were not seeking salvation from the curse of toil through communally synchronized economic enterprise.

Eyeglasses

Eyeglasses turned clock making and repairing into a revolution, speeding up mechanical engineering. Eyeglasses were invented in the 1280s near Pisa or Lucca. Our first information about the invention comes from a sermon on repentance preached at Santa Maria Novella in Florence on February 23, 1306, by Dominican Fra Giordano of Pisa. As in the case of clocks, the monks were the main patrons of eyeglasses. They needed them to study, especially to study the Bible. An interesting aspect of Giordano's sermon is that it describes not only the invention of eyeglasses but also the recent invention of the invention itself. Eyeglasses practically doubled the productive life of Western scholars and craftsmen. Because of eyeglasses, Christian monks in the West were able to spend their mature years poring over and improving texts and technologies, giving birth to the movement we call the Renaissance.

The opposite happened in my part of the world. Our monks did not develop technical aids to improve their eyesight. They took pride in closing even perfectly good eyes in meditation. Even today our yogis "fly" to distant galaxies in "out-of-body" experiences. The Maharishi Mahesh Yogi, the promoter of Transcendental Meditation in the West, popularized one of the yogic techniques of levitation through meditation in corporate America. Why would anyone invent airplanes if he can fly using daydreams?

Christian monks were different because the Bible gave them a different worldview. Eilmer of Wiltshire Abbey in Malmesbury, England, was a Benedictine monk who may have been the first European to attempt to fly in the eleventh century. This learned monk* made a glider, flew from an eighty-foot-high tower for six hundred feet, fell, broke his legs, and blamed it on his faulty design—he had neglected to make a tail! Eventually the West succeeded in developing the technology to fly, while our monks have continued to try to meditate, levitate, and fly.

GOD MADE ADAM A *LIVING SOUL*

Technology is integrating mind and muscles. It is breathing reflection (soul) into physical action (matter). That, according to the Bible, is the essence of man. Adam became a living soul when God breathed his Spirit into a material body.[21] Technology develops when people who use their muscles are also allowed to develop their minds and have the leisure to use them. This means that Benz's thesis has to be qualified. Medieval technology did not develop in the ivory towers of universities, but in the humdrum of the economic life of Christian monasteries.**

* Some suggest that he may have become a monk after his attempted flight. For good reasons Lynn White believes he was already a monk.
** During the Middle Ages the only university department to take an interest in machines was that of medical astrology.

Why?

Monasticism (as distinct from earlier asceticism) began as a reaction against the corrupting influence of Greco-Roman thought in the Christian church, especially the attitude that manual work was "low class." Although this corruption eventually crept into the monasteries, too, initially the monastic movement was a quest for authentic, biblical Christianity. It followed the Bible in exalting the virtue of manual labor, as well as in cultivating a love for God's Word.

The Greco-Roman world was not alone in looking down upon manual work. That attitude was common throughout the ancient world. The God who liberated the Jews worked for six days and commanded human beings to do the same. That is the opposite of Hindu tradition, which conceives of God as a meditator or *Yogeshwar* ("god of Yoga"). It is virtually impossible to find a Brahmin guru in traditional India who resembles the apostle Paul—a rabbi who made tents for a living.[22] Brahmins said that manual work was the duty of lower castes, a result of bad karma from their previous births. Mahatma Gandhi was the first Indian leader who used a spinning wheel to try to import the Pauline work ethic into India: "No work, no food."[23]

The German monk whose biblical outlook effectively freed Christendom from the dichotomy of hand and head was Theophilus—a skilled metallurgist, a general craftsman, a stylish writer, a nimble exegete of Scriptures, and an up-to-date theologian. His 1122–23 work, *De diversis artibus*, which explains the flywheel, is the first major document on the history of technology. Prior to him, craftsmen in most cultures did not know how to write because none were trained as scholars. Those who wrote were not interested in technical issues.

The chief concern of Theophilus's book is the place of technology in the spiritual life of a monk. He cared only for the praise of God and nothing about the world beyond the cloister. At first this isolation from the "secular" world seems odd for a man with such practical gifts, until one realizes that it was this very isolation from the world that enabled him to become more biblical and less worldly—that is, less influenced by the antilabor, antitechnological snobbishness of classical Greco-Roman Europe and the corrupted Latin church. A passion for the glory of God kept technology from becoming an idol, a false and destructive god.

The Renaissance's return to classical Greco-Roman literature helped to create a cultural climate that delayed the development of Western technology. For until the eighteenth century, Western universities taught theology, philosophy, law, medicine, and mathematics (science), but not technology. The intellectual foundations for Western technology that had been laid in the monasteries by monks such as Hugh of Saint Victor in Paris (1096–1141) continued to influence culture outside the university. A contemporary of Theophilus, Hugh was a noted French philosopher and theologian. In the 1120s, he prepared *Didascalicon*, an educational guide for novices. It was the first book ever to teach mechanical arts in formal education.

Hugh believed that, according to the Bible, human beings have three basic defects: in *Mind*—therefore we must learn truth through a study of theology and philosophy; in *Virtue*—therefore novices must be taught ethics; and in *Body*—therefore those who enter the monastery must study technology to supplement their physical weaknesses. Hugh of St. Victor was studied for three centuries. That enabled the West to develop biblical cultural values dramatically different from the world-views promoted by Greco-Roman literature, Hinduism, and Buddhism.

If modern technology was a force for humanization, then why do some postmodern critics condemn technology as a dehumanizing force? During the previous millennium, biblical Christianity replaced a pagan world ruled by spirits, with a "secular" world stewarded by human ingenuity and technology. Today, many in the post-Christian West view machines as evil spirits. Hollywood, for example, is producing a whole genre of movies inspired by the idea that the human problem is not a conflict between good and evil, but between humanity and machines. Among the most popular of such movies are the *Matrix* trilogy, the *Terminator* series, and several episodes of *Star Trek*. Films such as *Crouching Tiger, Hidden Dragon* exalt the magic of Buddhist meditation rather than technological innovation. They ignore the fact that the historically proven wonder of the mind is technology, not meditation that empties one's mind.

Trying to impress me with the fact that he respected India, my host in Jinja took me to the Gandhi Memorial on the banks of the Nile. The industrial company that pumped water and an Indian bank in the city had paid for the monument. My host asked what I thought of Mahatma Gandhi. I politely commented that Jinja seemed to be following Mahatma Gandhi's antitechnology stance, but it would be better off following the Indian industrialist and the banker.

Gandhi's idea that technology was evil and that a simple, natural life was morally superior came from British idealists like John Ruskin. Sensitive people like him had become critical of England's Industrial Revolution because of the exploitation, oppression, and other evils associated with its "dark satanic mills." Mahatma Gandhi brought this opposition to technology to India. Fortunately, Gandhi's younger follower Pandit Jawaharlal Nehru, who also studied in England and became India's first prime minister, knew that nonindustrial societies can be just as wicked as their industrial counterparts. Evil is in our hearts, not in technology.

Nehru also knew that England's Christian conscience had struggled to minimize the evils of the Industrial Revolution. It turned industry into a blessing rather than a curse. Nehru led India away from Gandhi's emphasis on handlooms to mechanization and industrialization.* In 2003, the Indian government approved a manned mission to the moon. Wise or unwise, successful or disastrous, the mission will be a symbolic climax of a national decision to overturn Gandhi's rejection of technology. But without the moral and social values of the Bible, it could become an exercise in building a Taj Mahal in outer space.

LESSONS FROM THE TAJ MAHAL

Just as the pyramids symbolize the glory of Egypt, the Taj Mahal in Agra epitomizes premodern India's finest achievement. No photograph can convey its grandeur. One has to see it to experience its

---

* Unfortunately, Nehru's secular Fabian socialism created problems of its own, holding India back while small nations like Japan, South Korea, and Singapore pressed ahead. Nehru's emphasis on technical education is, however, now becoming one of India's greatest economic assets.

magnificence. The Mogul emperor Shah Jahan started building the Taj Mahal in 1631. The same year a British traveler named Peter Mundy traveled from Surat (north of Bombay) to Agra (south of Delhi), a distance of 1,083 kilometers, to see the emperor. His eyewitness accounts are among our important sources of information on the construction of the Taj Mahal:

> From Surat to this place all the highway was stowed with dead people, our noses never free from the stink of them . . . women were seen to roast their children . . . a man or a woman no sooner dead but they were cut in pieces to be eaten.[24]

The monsoon had failed[*] and people had nothing to eat. Why was Indian agriculture so dependent on rains? Northern India has many perennial rivers fed by Himalayan glaciers. Couldn't the people who built the Taj Mahal build dams and canals for peasants? Why didn't seventeenth-century India store food in warehouses as a buffer for drought years? After all, almost four thousand years prior to Shah Jahan, a Hebrew slave-turned-administrator, Joseph, built warehouses on the banks of the river Nile to survive a seven-year famine. The pre-Aryan Indus Valley civilization had access to warehousing technology at least fifteen hundred years before Christ. Moreover, this was not the first year that the monsoon had failed. Why weren't people producing surplus and saving for emergencies such as the one they faced in AD 1631?

My seventeenth-century ancestors did not starve because they were stupid, lazy, or unproductive. A people need more than ingenuity to develop their lands and technology, to increase productivity and save for emergencies. They need wise leadership, political stability, just laws, fair taxation, and economic security. Shah Jahan's grandfather Akbar tried to give some justice to his subjects for a few years, but by the 1620s, India was being governed as usual. Taxes (the

---

* Most of the Indian subcontinent gets its rain during the summer monsoon months from June to September. Some years the monsoon fails to bring enough precipitation.

"king's share") had risen from one-half to two-thirds of one's produce. Beyond this, the tax collectors collected their income from the
peasants. They had to resort to extortion because they were not paid
salaries. The peasants were left with no more than 18 to 20 percent of
what they produced. That was a huge incentive against being creative
and productive. The only way to make money was to join the exploit-
ers. Hindu, Buddhist, and Muslim kingdoms did not exist to serve
people. The people existed for the glory of their rulers, not for the
glory of God.* Historian Stanley Wolpert's description of the daily
routine of senior administrators during Shah Jahan's reign helps us
understand the nature of nonbiblical leadership:

> Unless required elsewhere on urgent business, all principal *mansab-
> dars* (administrators) mustered twice daily before the emperor at his
> Hall of Public Audience (*Diwan-i-Am*), while lesser officials stood
> somewhat more remote, yet still within call should they be needed.
> The virtues of humility, obedience, patience, and loyalty were thus
> instilled in all of the mighty generals and civil administrators, at the
> cost of intellectual initiative, independence of mind, self-sufficiency,
> integrity, and courage. Bullied and treated like children by their
> emperor, it was hardly surprising to find such "nobles" behaving
> in turn as petulant petty tyrants to their servants, bearers, soldiers,
> and peasants. The whole system was a pyramid of power designed
> to perpetuate its imperial pinnacle, whether through ruthless vio-
> lence, extortion, harem intrigue, bribery, or sheer terror. The formal
> gardens, marble mausoleums, and Persian miniatures were as nec-
> tar squeezed from a subcontinent crushed into obedience, milked
> of its riches by the few, who had reason to lyricize in Persian cou-
> plets carved into the ornate walls of Delhi's Hall of Private Audience
> (*Diwan-I Khas*), "If there be Paradise on earth, It is Here, It is Here,
> It is Here!"[25]

---

* The secular idea that individuals could exist for their own glory is philosophically unstable.
The notion does not work because individuals can find meaning for themselves only by relating
themselves to a universal—animals, race, church, state, ideology, nature, or God.

The famine of 1631 was a massive tragedy because India's leadership had been busy exploiting their subjects to build grand monuments such as the Red Fort in Delhi, the Taj Mahal in Agra, and artifacts such as the Peacock Throne*—thanks to which, it was said, the world had "run short of gold."

Asia and Africa did not lack ability. But ability alone does not produce liberating technology. Jesus said that people are like sheep, in need of good shepherds. Without shepherds, slavery will remain the norm—from the women in Jinja to the untouchables in India. Nonbiblical cultures need more than technology; they need a philosophy that values people. Technology is indeed secular: a person of any faith or no faith can develop it and use it. But secularism does not liberate, as Professor Stark has shown in his research on slavery and its abolition:

> A virtual Who's Who of "Enlightenment" figures fully accepted slavery . . . It was not philosophers or secular intellectuals who assembled the moral indictment of slavery, but the very people they held in such contempt: men and women having intense Christian faith, who opposed slavery because it was sin . . .
>
> The larger point is that abolitionists, whether popes or evangelists, spoke almost exclusively in the language of Christian faith . . . Although many Southern clergy [in America] proposed theological defences of slavery, pro-slavery rhetoric was overwhelmingly secular—references were made to "liberty" and "states' rights," not to "sin" or "salvation."[26]

Biblical theology abolished slavery because it considered slavery to be sinful. Slavery means toil, and the Bible said that toil was a consequence of sin. God loved sinners enough to send his son to take their sin upon himself. The curse of sin was nailed upon the cross of Calvary, precisely to redeem humanity from this slavery. Hunger and poverty, according to the Bible, are not secular subjects. They are

_____
* The Persian invader, Nadir Shah, carried off the Peacock Throne from India in 1739.

consequences of sin. Biblical salvation, therefore, includes freedom from oppressive poverty. That was my message in Jinja.

Technology, however, is not enough for challenging a culture of slavery. The task calls for a heroic spirit. Therefore, next we shall examine how the Bible created modern heroism.

Part IV

THE MILLENNIUM'S REVOLUTION

Then Jesus told his disciples, "If anyone would come after me, let him deny himself and take up his cross and follow me. For whoever would save his life will lose it, but whoever loses his life for my sake will find it."

—MATTHEW 16:24–25

But far be it from me to boast except in the cross of our Lord Jesus Christ, by which the world has been crucified to me, and I to the world.

—THE APOSTLE PAUL, GALATIANS 6:14

HEROISM

How Did a Defeated Messiah Conquer Rome?

W hat defines a hero? Is a hero the man who dies while saving people from a burning building? Or the person who dies while blowing up a building filled with ordinary people? Jonathan Swift (1667–1745) explained, "Whoe'er excels in what we prize, appears a hero in our eyes."[1] What is heroic in a given culture depends on what is valued by that culture.

This chapter will examine how the Bible changed the European idea of a hero during the last millennium. A thousand years ago, "Christian" Europe's idea of heroism was expressed in the first international conflict of the second millennium. It was a crusade in which Christian soldiers tried to purge the Muslims from the holy city of Jerusalem.* The last major conflict of the second millennium was Operation Desert Storm in Kuwait, in which Western soldiers risked their lives to liberate Kuwaiti Muslims from Iraqi Muslims. Petroleum was indeed an underlying motivation behind the American action, but the fact remains that while Iraq invaded Kuwait for oil, America did not and could not stay in Kuwait to loot oil. How is it that during the last thousand years there has been such a global paradigm shift

---

* When the first crusaders finally stormed the "Holy City" Jerusalem on July 15, 1099, they "purified" it by killing virtually every inhabitant.

that today few can imagine the world's sole superpower electing an Alexander the Great to colonize other nations?

That is not to say American or European Foreign Policy is not governed by their national self-interest. The question is, *why do we expect and demand "civilized" nations to send their troops only to liberate the oppressed, but not to exploit them? What changed us?* The answer is that we expect America to follow not Alexander, Augustus, or Adolf Hitler, but the Bible and its definition of heroism. Its defeated Messiah conquered the classical and medieval ideas of heroism to create the modern world, which values self-sacrifice more highly than world conquest or knightly prowess.

The original Crusades were military expeditions undertaken by European Christians between 1095 and 1270 to recover Jerusalem and other sites in the Holy Land from Muslim control. The pope usually requested these campaigns, which originated in a desire to stop Muslims from taking over Christian lands. They offered "remission of sins" (indulgences) to Christians who would fight. The Church played an important role in these military adventures because at that time Christendom was united more around the Church than around an empire. Often the state functioned as the police or the military arm of the Church. Not just the Crusades but many public initiatives, as well, came from the Church, partly because most kings were weaker than the pope and some ambitious Church leaders wanted to extend their political and religious power.

The Church had business partners who saw new opportunities in the Crusades. One of their motives was to keep troublesome European "heroes"—knights and noblemen—out of sight. If they were going to fight and die, it was better they did so in distant lands. There they would be immortalized at least in songs, if not also in heaven, as guaranteed by some popes. In short, whatever their justification, the Crusades became religious barbarism.

There is substance in the argument, made by eminent scholars such as Jacques Ellul (1912–94), that the Crusades represented the Islamization of Christianity.[2] At the dawn of the second millennium, Islamic civilization was superior to European Christendom in many ways. Europe learned many things from the Islamic world, one of them being the idea of using the sword to promote religion. The Bible would allow a theologian to make a case for "just war." But no one could learn from Jesus or his apostles the use of the sword to coerce Christianity.*

From the Crusades, the Christian millennium moved to conquistadors. The Roman Catholic kings of Spain, Portugal, and France sent their soldiers along with priests to South America and the Caribbean islands in search of gold. The priests would plant a cross on the beach, claiming the land for Christ before the soldiers would go in—often to kill, rape, and plunder. Some of the stories are horrific. A "Christian" soldier snatched a baby from his mother's breast, dashed him on the rocks, and fed him to his dog![3] The natives were often viewed as subhuman. The Crusades, at least, had some historical, political, and strategic justification. In contrast, notwithstanding the heroic adventures of men like Columbus, little besides greed drove most of the conquistadors.

On the heels of the conquistadors, the ideology of colonialism began dominating the global scene. Primacy was usurped by Protestant nations like England, which were empowered by the technology, education, freedom, and science that the Bible had produced. The evil of colonialism came to be symbolized by the first fourteen years of British rule in Bengal, eastern India, which were marked by corruption and administrative chaos (1757–70). Their devastating impact on the local economy has been best gauged by the fact that the failure of monsoon rains to fall led to the starvation of about ten million people. Lord Curzon, a later British viceroy in India, noted,

> Throughout the summer of that year [1770] it is on record that the husbandmen sold their cattle; they sold their implements of agriculture; they sold their sons and daughters, till at length no buyer of children could be found; they ate the leaves of trees and the grass of

---

* The New Testament justifies the use of the sword by the state to restrain evil. See, for example, Romans 13:1–5.

the field; and when the height of the summer was reached, the living were feeding on the dead. The streets of the cities were blocked up with promiscuous heaps of the dead and the dying; even the dogs and the jackals could not accomplish their revolting work.[4]

During the nineteenth century, the British evangelicals succeeded in turning the evil of colonialism into a blessing for my country.[5] There can be no dispute, however, that colonialism itself—one nation ruling over another nation*—was an evil.

How can a millennium that began with the Crusades and progressed through conquistadors to colonialism end with Kuwait and Kosovo—with (ex)Christian nations sending their armies to liberate Kuwaiti Muslims from Iraqi Muslims, and Muslims in Kosovo from Orthodox Christians? Why is it that at the dawn of the third millennium, any American president—whether admired or hated—cannot even think** of ruling Afghanistan?

The answer is that the Bible replaced the classical idea of the hero as a world conqueror and the medieval idea of the hero as a courageous knight with the idea of a hero as someone who sacrifices himself for the good of others. Let me begin with a personal story.

A Different Kind of Hero

In 1982, Ruth and I were leaving on a short sabbatical for a lecture-and-study tour of Europe. That very night, unknown to us, two men attacked my father and stepmother in their farmhouse, four miles from our farm. They beat up my parents, tied my father to a chair, raped the young woman living with them, and helped themselves to valuables. One of the robbers then pulled out a sharp knife and started to gouge out my father's eyes. He stopped only because Papa promised to empty out his bank account the next day and give them his life's savings.

---

* Of course, India was a thousand petty kingdoms when the East Indian Company colonized it. The idea of India as one nation came (indirectly) from the Bible during the colonial era.

** He may feel that colonization is the only way to bless Afghanistan, but for now he cannot say this to even his trusted friends. The idea is morally unthinkable.

My father had taken an early retirement and had come to help us in our rapidly growing rural development work. He knew how stressful our work had been, and had therefore encouraged me to take two months off to lecture, study, and finish writing my book *Truth and Social Reform*.[6] He volunteered to manage the projects while Ruth's parents in Bareilly, in the state of Uttar Pradesh, India, looked after our daughters.

Papa kept his promise to the robbers. He went to the police only after paying the money at the agreed-upon location. The police, however, would not even register the case, and Papa began to suspect that this might have been more than a mere robbery—that the "powers that be" were using the criminals to attack our work. In that case, I would be the real target, and the attack on him merely a trial run—a message for his son.

The indifference of the police made it impossible for my parents to continue living in their isolated and vulnerable farmhouse. So they moved to a guesthouse in the city, near the Christian hospital, a few hundred feet from the home of Papa's cousin, a retired physician. But instead of solace, their relocation brought a shock more devastating than the initial attack on them. Within a few days, my aunt and her husband were found murdered. Some men had gotten in, tied them up, looted them, and then stabbed them dozens of times. The forensic experts said the murderers seemed to have taken pleasure in their brutality.

Barely a fortnight had passed since their murder when one of our field-workers brought an almost-dead volunteer, Ashraf, to Dr. Mategaonker at the hospital. The field-worker and Ashraf, a Muslim, were serving drought victims in a town called Nagod. They had been sleeping in separate quarters, about thirty feet apart. At two o'clock in the morning, Ashraf had heard a knock. When he opened the door, two men attacked him with axes. He picked up a wooden stool and tried in vain to shield himself. They knocked him down and left him for dead, walking away with his belongings.

The cumulative impact of these and other relatively minor incidents was to convince our community that the politicians, police, and criminals may have joined forces to eliminate us or to drive us away from the area. Our chief opponent, the politician referred to in chapter 2, feared our growing clout. He may have been encouraged by some Hindu religious leaders who feared that our work might eventually lead to many people becoming followers of Jesus Christ.

Why did they not counter our influence with service work of their own, helping the poor and hungry? All the resources of the Indian government lay at their disposal. Yet the Block Development Office, through which they had to work, was considered one of the most corrupt governmental departments. Officials and elected leaders, in the habit of misusing development funds, could not be asked to become honest simply to counteract our influence. Our opponents' other difficulty was that they considered a significant proportion of the needy people we served to be *untouchables*. To follow the commandment "Love thy neighbor as thyself" required more than material resources. To serve untouchables, they would need a source of spiritual power to transcend their cultural prejudices and to risk quarrels at home and excommunication from their own caste.

Ruth and I returned to India two months after the attack on my father. He and Dr. Mategaonker, the chairman of our organization, sent three young men to New Delhi to prevent us from returning to the area. They suspected that I might be stubborn and insisted that at least Ruth must not court danger. They felt that Ruth might agree to put the security of our two daughters first, above our service.* Recounting the horrible events of the previous months, our three friends proposed that it would be safer for us to start a fresh work in the slums of Delhi.

I wanted conclusive evidence, not just reasonable guesses, that the highest officials had plotted to use criminals to put an end to our work. No one, including me, had any doubts that the most important local politician hated us. No one doubted that he was linked to known criminals. His power over the police had already sent me to jail. Yet, I wanted evidence that we were up against an organized plan backed by the highest authorities, political as well as civic. In the absence of

---

* Nivedit and Anandit were then five and three years old.

concrete evidence, I argued that the conspiracy could be diabolical, that is, supernatural. What else could produce such spiritual blindness and twisted conscience? We lacked the physical resources to fight our opponents, but if the evil opposing us was spiritual, then we were in a battle that didn't depend on weapons. I reasoned with my friends that God had given us adequate resources in *prayer* and *faith* to overcome this conspiracy. In any case, hadn't Jesus called us to take up our crosses and follow him?[7]

My course was clear to me, but I decided not to influence Ruth's decision. It would have been absurd to suggest that the threat to her or our daughters was hypothetical. Jesus Christ himself knew that faith was not insurance against death; it sometimes brings martyrdom. Ruth decided to think and pray over the matter. She had to choose not merely for herself, but for her two little girls as well. She knew her husband had nothing but faith. Experience, facts, and votes were against me. The next day she announced her decision: "There is no point in following Jesus halfheartedly. If we are going to follow him, we might as well trust him and go all the way. I will come with you even if our friends decide to stay in Delhi."

Within minutes of her decision, the phone rang. It was Liz Brattle. She had returned from Australia as a volunteer with InterServe. In 1976, she had typed my book *The World of Gurus*. Now, years later, in the fall of 1982, without any correspondence with us, Liz had come back to India unannounced, to serve as my secretary! She called because she had heard that Ruth would not be returning to the village. She wanted confirmation, because if that were the case, InterServe would not allow her to risk her life either.

Minutes after we finished talking with Liz, there was another call. It was Kay Kudart,* someone we did not know. Kay said that she was a student from America. She was part of the HNGR (Human Needs and Global Resources) program at Wheaton College in Illinois, which required her to do a six-month internship in a developing country. She had not been able to contact us in the village because we did not

---

* Now, Kay Holler.

have a phone. Her professor had advised her to just show up, as our community accepted almost everyone who came. After arriving in Delhi she heard the scary stories, but her faith was as crazy as ours. She was fortunate that her guide in Delhi was equally radical in his faith; nevertheless, he had a responsibility. He told her that he could not allow her to risk her life if Ruth were not going.

The countryside was stunned when we arrived back on the battle-field with three young women and two little girls. For our neighbors and opponents, heroism implied the ability to fight back—to find our enemies and take revenge. They assumed that we must have imported secret weapons from the West.[8] It did not occur to them that someone might choose to serve his enemies and sacrifice his life for them. For us this was a spiritual warfare. And we had a secret weapon—prayer. In hindsight, I think Liz and Kay were a part of the answer to our prayers. They became an effective shield. The district authorities must have feared that harming them would internationalize our situation, so they reined in those spearheading the opposition.* Was Ruth's decision to return to Chhatarpur heroic or foolish? Was it wise to risk rape and murder to continue serving God among poor peasants? Our choice was based upon our beliefs. It went against the classical and medieval concepts of heroism.

THE CLASSICAL HERO

The classical Greco-Roman world would have never offered the Nobel Prize for Peace to Jimmy Carter, a defeated president. To be a classical hero he would have needed to strategize, forge alliances, plot assassinations, and bounce back to power. A hero was a person who had the power to conquer and rule over others. The Greek model was Alexander the Great (356–323 BC), one of history's most ruthless conquerors, who marched from Greece to India. He considered himself divine, as did his contemporaries, and he ordered Greek cities

---

* My father died a few months later, and then we heard that those who had robbed him died in an accident involving the motorcycle they had bought with his money.

to worship him as god. He left his empire, in his own words, "to the strongest," unlike Jesus, who said that the poor and the meek would inherit the kingdom of God that he was ushering in. Alexander's invitation to the strongest ensured conflicts among his lieutenants, and they tore his kingdom apart within half a century.

Augustus Caesar (63 BC–AD 14) was the ideal Roman hero. He consolidated his power by killing three hundred senators and two hundred knights, including the aging orator Cicero. Augustus made himself and his successors gods on earth. The classical idea of heroism became so deeply embedded in Western consciousness that Napoleon Bonaparte (1769–1821) tried to revive the Roman Empire, modeling his rule on that of Augustus. Napoleon's quest for power and glory plunged Europe into terrible and mindless wars. William Blake (1757–1827) lamented, "The strongest poison ever known came from Caesar's laurel crown."[9]

This classical understanding of a hero as a person with power is almost universal. It is the core of the Hindu idea of a hero. That is why most Hindu gods and goddesses are depicted with weapons in their many hands. That also explains why well-known criminals can win democratic elections in India. Once they win, their guilt is written off. Hinduism requires that a spiritual hero must also conquer his own body by controlling his eating, drinking, sexuality, and involuntary actions such as breathing. An Islamic hero is also an individual with power, as long as it is coupled with piety and prayer. That is the chief reason why a terrorist can be a devout Muslim and a hero in the eyes of orthodox clergy.

The Medieval Hero

The Roman Catholic Church inherited the classical understanding of heroism as well as the culture of Germanic barbarians and Frankish aristocrats. These cultures prized personal bravery, physical strength, and skill in the use of arms. Prowess—the ability to beat other men in battle—became the chivalric virtue. The sociopolitical chaos that followed the collapse of the Roman Empire in the fifth century recurred after the collapse of the Carolingian dynasty (751–987). Without a central authority or institutions of justice enforcing contracts, Europe's feudal society would have entirely collapsed, had not the virtue of loyalty risen to preeminence. A knight was now considered a hero if he had prowess *and* if he was loyal to his lord.

Loyalty as a virtue was cultivated by wandering minstrels who composed and circulated epic tales of knightly deeds. Along with the knights, they depended on the generosity (largesse) of the courts. It was the minstrels' interest also to exalt generosity as a high virtue. Generosity merited an important place in their songs. Great heroes were the ones who gave the most.

The favorite pastime of aristocratic patrons of minstrels and troubadours was to win favors from court ladies. This called for courtesy. If courtesy were to be a virtue, it had to be extended also to fellow knights. So courtly love and courtesy were added to prowess, loyalty, and generosity as medieval virtues.

A medieval hero's ultimate goal in life was to find glory, that is, his prestige won in battle was glorified in songs and stories. He also looted goods from his foes, and, of course, wanted women. Tournaments were a substitute for wars. By the twelfth century, tournaments had become a flourishing institution in northern France, spreading to other areas soon afterward.

Feudal Europe did not have a standing army to keep these knights under discipline. Nor did it have a legal mechanism to ensure that the knights' aspiration for heroism did not interfere with the society's need for law and order, peace and stability. For centuries, Europe lacked a political order that could civilize knightly heroism.* That vacuum was filled by the Church.

In 1027, the Roman Catholic Church initiated a movement called the "Truce and Peace of God." It issued a decree restricting the pursuit of private warfare. The ordinance was based upon an earlier canon law forbidding hostilities between Saturday night and Monday morning. The Church now extended that prohibition to ban all types of

---

* The Church sent knights on crusades to liberate Jerusalem partly because at home they were nuisances.

private warfare. In about 1040, the ban was applied between sunset on Wednesday and sunrise on Monday. Later the seasons of Advent, Christmas, and Lent were included. The penalty for violating the truce was excommunication from the Church. This was an extremely potent threat in that nonsecular era. It meant losing one's social security in this life and in the next.

The Church's actual success may not have been huge, but the Church acted because the civil authorities had already failed. The Church's attempt to protect the defenseless against the lawless nobility in a period of feudal anarchy was noble. The "Truce of God" soon spread throughout France, Italy, and Germany. The Ecumenical Council of 1179 applied it throughout Western Christendom.

Formal bans and excommunications were not the only weapons the Church used against medieval heroes. In his authoritative work, *French Chivalry*, Sidney Painter pointed out that "the largest volume of criticism of chivalric ideas and practices came from the pens of ecclesiastics."[10] For example, the greatest Roman Catholic theologian, Thomas Aquinas (1225–74), condemned chivalry on the grounds that the knights who sought "glory" through homicide and rapine sought "vainglory." In 1128, Galbert of Bruges argued in his writings that a desire for fame was worthy, but for a nobleman to kill for the sole purpose of winning glory was sin. St. Bernard of Clairvaux (1090–1153), John of Salisbury (1115–80), and a famous preacher named Jacques de Vitry were among the fiercest critics of chivalry.

As a result of these writings, the Council of Clermont (1130) prohibited tournaments, labeling them as homicidal contests. It resolved that no one killed in tournaments could be buried in consecrated grounds. The Lateran Councils of 1139 and 1179 confirmed the ban, and the ban became a part of canon law among the decretals of Pope Gregory IX (1147–1241).

RELIGIOUS CHIVALRY

While leading Catholic writers launched a frontal attack on the medieval concept and practice of heroism, the church adopted another strategy to bring chivalry under its moral authority. It ritualized it. In the thirteenth century, the church asked the esquire to dedicate his armor on an altar. He stayed up the entire night praying and fasting. Before donning his armor, he took a ritual bath. Elaborate rituals were designed to turn loose cannons into "knights of God." These were meant to give them a sense of responsibility to serve God and the Church, and to take care of the weak and vulnerable.

In medieval English, this culminated in *Sir Gawain and the Green Knight*. This alliterative poem is our most important source of information on the court of the semi-legendary King Arthur. The poem exalts the heroic spirit as a key to the renewal of society. It defines heroic courtesy as *gentilesse*—dedication of a gentleman's (a knight's) superior strength to the honor or service of those with less worldly power. The poem places the code of courtesy among the glorious accomplishments of Europe's medieval civilization. Through courtesy, all people, including the lowliest, could practice heroic virtue.

The Church's attempt to bring chivalry under its moral authority had notable results. One of the outcomes was the founding of the Order of the Knights Templar. Two French knights began this order in 1119 as a small military band in Jerusalem. Their aim was to protect pilgrims visiting the Holy Land after the First Crusade. Military in nature from the beginning, the order soon received papal sanction. The Council of Troyes gave them an austere role patterned after the Cistercians. The Knights Templar began to be called upon regularly to transport money from Europe to the Holy Land. Consequently, they developed an efficient banking system upon which the European rulers and nobility came to rely. Gradually the Templars became bankers for a large part of Europe and amassed wealth; however, power and wealth brought corruption and trouble. Philip IV of France and Pope Clement V suppressed and looted them, labeling them a satanic cult.

The Teutonic Knights of St. Mary's Hospital at Jerusalem are another example of modified chivalry. They were a religious military order formed by German crusaders in 1190–91, in Acre Palestine, and by 1199 they received papal recognition. The members were German knights of noble birth. By 1329 they held the entire Baltic region as a papal fief.* They exist today as a charitable and nursing order, head-quartered in Vienna.

Notwithstanding such notable examples, the fact remains that the idea of Christian chivalry could not be sustained. It had no biblical foundations. It demanded "noble birth," and it glorified physical prowess, skill in arms, and killing. These were values contrary to the spirit of Christ and his apostles. The idea of the knights of Christ began to be undermined by *Devotio Moderna*, a movement of spiritual reform centered in the Netherlands, stressing the moral example of Christ. A classic representative of this movement is the devotional treatise, *Imitation of Christ*, written by the German monk Thomas à Kempis (1379–1471).**

Strictly speaking, à Kempis's book is not about imitating the Christ of the Gospels. The book's title comes from the old tradition of using the first phrase of a book as its title. The book's significance lies in the fact that it emphasizes the internal, spiritual nature of Christian discipleship, whereas the idea of religious knighthood had focused on external acts. *Imitation of Christ* became a bridge from the medieval to the modern idea of Christian spirituality as understood by Desiderius Erasmus and Martin Luther.

Modern Heroism

Roland Bainton, Martin Luther's biographer, gave us a vignette of the modern hero. The Council of Constance (1417), which burned John Huss at the stake, had suppressed the reform movement initiated by John Wycliffe. A century later a monk and professor at the University of Wittenberg, Martin Luther, picked up the Reformers' baton. Knowing the context will help us appreciate Luther's heroism.

In 1516 Albert of Brandenburg borrowed a substantial sum from German bankers to buy the archbishopric of Mainz from Pope Leo X. Albert was very young, yet he was already the bishop of both

---

* Land or property held under the feudal system of "ownership."
** Some scholars dispute that Thomas à Kempis was the author of this particular volume, though it does represent his understanding of Christian spirituality.

Halberstadt and Magdeburg. Powerful dynasties had a vested interest in keeping the Church as a family business. Being the archbishop of Mainz would make Albert the primate* of Germany. But occupying three bishoprics was irregular. It required the unusually high price of ten thousand gold coins (ducats). Albert knew that money would speak. The pope was in need.

The pope authorized Albert to sell indulgences (certificates of remission of sins) to raise money. Half of the money was to go to the pope for rebuilding St. Peter's Cathedral in Rome, and the rest was for Albert to repay the money borrowed to bribe the pope. Luther had been reading the Greek-Latin New Testament, recently translated by Erasmus. Recognized as the greatest humanist scholar of his time, Erasmus was then teaching in Cambridge. Through his translation and the marginal notes that explained why his translation differed at some crucial points with the earlier one called the Vulgate, Luther learned that Jesus had already paid the price required for a person's salvation. Jesus was the Lamb of God, sacrificed on the cross as our substitute. He had taken upon himself the full penalty of our sin. There was nothing human beings could pay to buy salvation. All that we needed was to repent of our sin and accept the free gift of God by faith.

Selling indulgences, Luther realized, was exploiting the masses in the name of religion. As a priest, Luther was responsible to educate his flock and protect them from ravenous wolves. In this case, the wolves happened to be his superiors, whom he had taken vows to obey. But he was also a professor with certain academic freedoms; he had a right to express his opinions for his peers' scrutiny. On October 31, 1517, Luther nailed his famous ninety-five theses on the doors of the Castle Church of Wittenberg. This was a call for an academic debate. It stated that the Church was in error and that the selling of indulgences was a corrupt exploitation of the poor masses. His challenge was so sensational that immediately copies began to be made. A gauntlet had been thrown down at a thousand-year-old civilization.

---

* The highest ranking bishop of a province.

In December 1520, Luther was asked whether he would be willing to appear before Emperor Charles to be tried for heresy. Jan Hus (1369–1415), the Czech reformer, and others of Luther's predecessors had been burned at the stake in spite of the Church's assurance of a safe passage. Luther had not yet been given such assurance. Here is how he answered:

> You ask me what I shall do if I am called by the emperor. I will go even if I am too sick to stand on my feet. If Caesar calls me, God calls me. If violence is used, as it may well be, I commend my cause to God. He lives and reigns who saved the three youths from the fiery furnace of the king of Babylon, and if He will not save me, my head is worth nothing compared with Christ. This is no time to think of safety. I must take care that the gospel is not brought into contempt by our fear to confess and seal our teaching with our blood.[11]

Fortunately, Frederick, the duke of Saxony and patron of Luther's university, obtained an assurance of safe passage. Luther faced the trial in the city of Worms. The authorities intended either to intimidate him into submission or eliminate the threat that he posed to the status quo. It is hard to improve upon Bainton's prose:

> The scene lends itself to dramatic portrayal. Here was Charles, heir of a long line of Catholic sovereigns—of Maximilian the romantic, of Ferdinand the Catholic, of Isabella the orthodox—scion of the house of Hapsburg, lord of Austria, Burgundy, the Low Countries, Spain and Naples, Holy Roman Emperor, ruling over a vaster domain than any save Charlemagne, symbol of the medieval unities, incarnation of a glorious if vanishing heritage; and here before him a simple monk, a miner's son, with nothing to sustain him save his own faith in the Word of God. Here the past and the future were met. Some would see at this point the beginning of modern times. . . . What overpowered him [Luther] was not so much that he stood in the presence of the emperor as this, that he and the emperor alike were called upon to answer before Almighty God.[12]

Luther was not seeking to be a hero. He was being obedient to his conscience, which he claimed was captive to the Word of God. He did not know that he was inaugurating a new era, unleashing a new source of power, redefining heroism, or contending for a new source of civilizational authority.

THE BIBLE REDEFINES HEROISM

The Roman Catholic Church made a splendid beginning in transforming the Western idea of the hero. Yet, notwithstanding the exceptions,* the modern hero did not emerge until after the Bible began shaping Western consciousness. John Milton's (1608–74) epic *Paradise Lost*, for example, was a paradigm-altering force. The hero (or anti-hero) of this Puritan epic is Lucifer (Satan), who won when human beings fell in sin, losing Paradise. Lucifer reveals the character of his heroism when he says it is "better to reign in hell, than serve in heav'n." An implication is that classical heroism is diabolical. In its quest to rule, it makes our world hellish.

Classical heroism clashed with the Bible because while the former valued power, Christ's heroism prized truth. Other kingdoms fostered heroic deeds by cultivating racial, geographic, linguistic, religious, class, or caste pride and hatred. Jesus made *love* the supreme value of the kingdom of God. This love was not sentimentalism. It went beyond loving one's neighbors as oneself. Its supreme manifestation was the cross: sacrificing oneself for others, including one's enemies.

Jesus' heroism replaced brutality with love, pride with meekness, and domination over others with self-sacrificing service. He exemplified this when he humbled himself, took a basin of water and a servant's towel, and started washing his disciples' feet. This, he said, is what the kingdom of God is all about. He was the King of kings and the Lord of lords. All power in heaven and on earth, he claimed, was his. But he had come not to be served, but to serve, not to kill but to give eternal life. These were not homilies delivered by a guru who

---

* St. Patrick is a good exception. See Cahill's *How the Irish Saved Civilization*.

sat on a golden throne. These teachings changed history because they emanated from a life lived in the public arena.

I became aware of the gospel's power to transform when I heard our first prime minister, Pandit Jawaharlal Nehru, in 1963. He began, "Fellow citizens, I have come to you as your *first servant*, because that is what the term *prime minister* literally means." It amazed me because even as a young boy I knew that no ruler in India's long history had ever seen himself as a servant. Pandit Nehru did so because the Bible had been transforming Allahabad, where both of us grew up. From Allahabad he went to England to study. Britain's political system had been brought under the authority of the Word of God through long spiritual struggles. Many heroes died to take power from kings and give it to servants (ministers). As a result, the *first servant* became more important than the king. Jesus began this revolution when he taught, "and whoever would be first among you must be your slave, even as the Son of Man came not to be served but to serve, and to give his life as a ransom for many."[13]

How did the kingdom of Lucifer, which worshipped power, come to accept a humiliated and crucified Christ as the Almighty God?

The church saw the cross of Christ as the only way to salvation. The apostle Paul wrote that Jews were looking for a demonstration of miraculous powers and that the Greeks considered his gospel foolishness because they sought knowledge. He was, however, determined to preach nothing but the cross of Christ, because the weakness of God on Calvary's cross was more powerful than the mightiest man. The foolishness of the gospel was wiser than all the wisdom of Greek philosophers.[14]

Following the New Testament's emphasis on the cross, the preachers preached about the cross, the painters painted it, the poets wrote poems about it, and the singers sang about the glories of the "old rugged cross." Carpenters and masons made so many crosses that the cross became the very motif of Christian civilization. Architects placed the cross as the centerpiece of the stained glass windows of their churches and cathedrals. As masses sat meditating on the meaning of the cross, it changed Western consciousness from within. A brutal, triumphant knight could no longer be an inspiring Christian hero. He was the very opposite of a crucified, humiliated Messiah who died so that others may live.

The Bible ensured that heroism took on a new meaning. Heroism now meant a robust faith that refuses to bow before evil and falsehood. A faith that triumphs over Satan's ultimate weapon, the fear of death.[15] It involves a surrender to God that authorizes God to sacrifice you for others' benefit.[16] This was the heroism of Wycliffe, Hus, Luther, Tyndale, Calvin, Knox, and those who followed them to create the modern world.

These were not supermen. They were people like us—fallible, with feet of clay. They made their mistakes. Luther justified crushing the peasants' revolt. Many Lutherans did not tolerate the Anabaptists. They were children of an intolerant and brutal medieval age. Yet, they became the pioneers of the modern world because they also transcended their age. They ushered in the greatest revolution of the second millennium—a revolution that, among other things, turned heroes into self-sacrificing servants.

Chapter Nine

REVOLUTION

WHAT MADE TRANSLATORS WORLD CHANGERS?

Villiam Tyndale (1492–1536) should not have been shocked, but he was. Bishop Tunstall had burned copies of his New Testament, the first attempt ever to print the Bible in English.* The bishop did not act impulsively. On October 24, 1526, he preached his first sermon against Tyndale's New Testament at the magnificent St. Paul's Cathedral in London.** He then proceeded with a public Bible bonfire. Then, in the summer of 1529, he bought up the entire available stock in Antwerp, across the English Channel, to burn Bibles in a bigger bonfire. Not long afterward, the bishop of Cambrai presided over Tyndale's trial, which led to burning the Bible translator himself.

The ferocity of this opposition should not have surprised Tyndale because Bishops Fisher and Wolsey had already been burning Martin Luther's German New Testament imported into England. And similar burnings had been going on in continental Europe where Tyndale was hiding as a fugitive, refusing to repent of sharing the opinions of the heretic Martin Luther.

---

* The earlier translation, inspired by John Wycliffe, preceded the invention of the printing press in the West.
** The present cathedral was built by Sir Christopher Wren in the seventeenth century. Four earlier churches/cathedrals had been built on the same site since AD 604.

His crime? He was strangled and burned as a heretic, though he also was guilty of leaving England without permission and illegally translating the Bible into English. The "Constitutions of [Archbishop] Arundale" had outlawed translating the Bible into English in 1408 in response to the earlier work by John Wycliffe (1330–84) and his associates in Oxford.

Tyndale knew that English bishops had been burning all the available manuscripts and fragments of the Wycliffe Bible for more than a century. The bishops had also been burning people alive who possessed even fragments of its copies. To own a few pages of an English Bible was evidence* that one was a Lollard—a follower of John Wycliffe. That distinguished Oxford professor had been declared a "heretic" posthumously at the Council of Constance in 1417. His bones were dug out of the cemetery and burned, and the ashes were thrown into the river Avon.

Why would bishops burn Bibles, Bible translators, and Bible buyers?

The charge of "heresy" was a proverbial fig leaf. The Bible was burned because the Bible translators had begun a battle for the soul of Europe. They were transforming Europe's thousand-year-old civilization from medieval to modern. They were revolutionaries who sought to make the pope's authority subject to the Word of God.

Every civilization is tied together by a final source of authority that gives meaning and ultimate intellectual, moral, and social justification to its culture. For Marxists it may be *Das Capital* or the Communist Party. For Muslims it could be the Qur'an or the caliphate. Rome created the core of what we call today the West. From the fall of Rome to the Reformation, the papacy had been the principal authority for Western Christians. To the present time, Western civilization has had at least five different sources of cultural authority: Rome, the pope, the Bible, human reason, and the current individualistic nihilism whose future will be determined by quasi-democratic culture wars. This chapter tells the story of the reformers who replaced the pope's authority with that of the Bible.

---

* In theory, it was possible to own a copy legally, after obtaining a bishop's permission. In practice, the permission was never given. Nevertheless, two hundred manuscripts of the Wycliffe Bible are still in existence.

THE ROMAN PHASE

Rome's influence on the West lasted from the rise of Caesar Augustus about 27 BC to the sacking of Rome in AD 410. Prior to Augustus, Rome was a republic, run by a few powerful families who kept each other's ambition in check. After the Senate murdered Julius Caesar in 44 BC, his nephew, Augustus, made himself the ultimate source of authority in the Roman Empire. That took nearly two decades of bloody civil war. Caesar was already a military leader, but he made himself the sole political and religious authority—the "Lord." His authority rested on the power of the sword. Philosophers and poets, artists and architects, mythmakers and priests rallied round Caesar's brute power to build an entire civilization. After Augustus, each successive Caesar would usually begin his reign by deifying his predecessor.

The Augustan age accepted the sword as mightier than the pen because the Romans knew that philosophers, storytellers, and writers did not know the truth. Poets such as Virgil used religious myths to write aesthetically superb propaganda that justified Augustus's use of the sword in making himself the divine Lord. This disregard for truth made the pen powerless. Writers, poets, philosophers, and orators acquired patronage but lost legitimacy. For example, Cicero, one of the greatest Roman orators and philosophers, supported Augustus in his initial power struggle. The duplicitous Augustus repaid him by ordering his murder soon afterward!

Into this story-based, politically oppressive culture came Jesus, who unleashed the power of truth. The Roman governor Pontius Pilate was baffled when Jesus claimed that he was not another religious myth-maker. He had come to bear witness to truth.[1] For centuries, no one had invoked truth's authority. Jesus did not merely claim that he knew God because he was God's unique, "only begotten," son. He claimed that his words were God's words, and that he embodied truth.[2] Pilate threatened him with crucifixion when Jesus challenged Caesar's lordship and Rome's truthless totalitarianism. His dictum, "Render to Caesar the things that are Caesar's, and to God the things that are God's"[3] meant that Caesar had no right to claim the allegiance that belonged to God. Jesus' belief that the kingdom of this world ought to belong to God began the long conflict between the sword and Jesus' followers, the followers of the truth.

Those who followed Jesus were tired of men's stories and their kingdoms. They were seeking God's kingdom, a kingdom that did not derive its legitimacy from the sword, philosophy, or myths, but from truth. Therefore, while Jesus' followers honored civic authority as divinely ordained, their commitment to truth empowered them to resist the sword when demanded that they bend the knee before false-hood. Christians did not see themselves as "revolutionaries." They were not seeking to usurp Caesar's throne. It was their commitment to truth that forbade ascribing divinity to Caesar or submitting to brute force exercised apart from goodness.

The Roman Empire was pluralistic. It tolerated all stories and reli-gions. What it refused to tolerate was a rejection of the finality of its own authority. Large numbers of Christ followers were burned alive by emperors from Nero (AD 37–68) to Diocletian (AD 284-305) because their commitment to the true God was a threat to Rome's absolutism.

Jesus' statement that those who live by the sword, shall die by the sword[4] turned out to be prophetic for Rome. Alaric the Visigoth led German barbarians to a shocking triumph over Rome in AD 410. This defeat dealt a death blow to the myth that Caesar was Lord. That hastened the end not just of an empire but of a civilization built on story, poetry, and power. In place of Caesar and his myth, the barbar-ians brought chaos—leaving a large vacuum.

THE PAPAL PHASE

Rome's fall caused bureaucrats to flee from their posts with whatever they could grab. They had good reasons to fear the people they had looted with the backing of the imperial army. In most cases, the only official who remained to help the people was the bishop or priest. During the first five centuries after Christ, the local bishop was the people's elder and often was chosen by them. His authority came from his track record of community service, leadership, wisdom, and integrity.

Jesus had described a leader's role as that of a shepherd to his flock. The good shepherd, as Jesus taught by word and deed, lays down his life for his sheep. St. Cyprian (ca. 200–258), the aristocratic bishop of Carthage, exemplified Jesus' view of leadership. St. Cyprian described his democratic style of servant leadership: "From the beginning of my episcopate, I decided to do nothing of my own opinion privately without your advice and the consent of the people."[5] Unfortunately, after the fifth century, that style became the exception.*

Times of turmoil are poor breeding grounds for literacy and education.** In the chaos following the collapse of Rome, a bishop often remained the only literate person in a region. Democracy, which depends on a well-informed electorate, began to disappear from the church. Illiterate chiefs backed by local gangs filled the administrative vacuum left by the absence of centrally appointed secular authorities. Bishops became mentors to the chiefs. In turbulent times, people tend to bow to whoever promises security, stability, and justice. Neither the bishops nor the chiefs objected to increasing their powers at the people's expense.

In addition to being educated, the local bishop was connected to a larger organization, headquartered in the imperial city of Rome. The Church of Rome was the only entity that retained the Roman genius for organization and grandeur. Its bishop claimed to have God on his side, empowering him to confer divine legitimacy on civil authorities. Therefore, it became in the rulers' best interest to defend the bishop's authority.

A particular ruler might be more powerful than a bishop or a pope, but Christendom had only one pope,*** and he could always count on the support of a ruler's rivals who wanted to extend their

---

* The term "democratic" in this context is used in contrast to the hierarchic nature of the Church government as it developed in the Roman Catholic Church, not in the modern sense of democratic church government as developed by the Presbyterians after the Protestant Reformation.
** See the story of John Amos Comenius in chapter 12 as a splendid exception.
*** Wycliffe's era was an exception. Two rival popes fought bitterly. For a brief period, a third pope made the waters muddier. Their rivalry was an important factor in saving Wycliffe from being burned at the stake as a heretic. He died in his home and was declared a heretic almost two decades later. Then his bones were dug out and burned, and the ashes were thrown in the Swift River.

little kingdoms. Because popes claimed for themselves the power to remit sins and free souls from purgatory, anyone wishing to rule in Christendom had to turn to this one Church to receive divine legitimacy. Popes first used this power to mobilize Christians against Muslims via the Crusades. Then they began using it to mobilize Christians against those Christian rulers who displeased the Church hierarchy.[6]

Thus, over time, the Roman Catholic Church filled the vacuum created by Rome's demise. The papacy became the ultimate source of authority. Western civilization became "Christendom" as the bishop of Rome pontificated as the infallible voice of God, the ultimate arbiter in all matters. He decided whether or not the sun revolved around the earth, whether Henry VIII could divorce his wife, or whether the Bible could be translated into English.

This power need not have made the church a hierarchical, authoritarian structure. The hierarchy could have submitted itself to God's Word, which made all God's children a "royal priesthood."[7] But ignorant of the Word of God, bishops and priests made themselves accountable not to God's people but to the pope. It helped that the Church owned virtually all the centers of learning.* These centers could have been used to educate the people of God, but it became in the Church's vested interest to keep even literate people ignorant of the Bible.

The Church had acquired its power in the name of truth through dedicated service, commitment to wisdom, and disciplined organizational labor. This reputation was largely legitimate; it was unnecessary for the Church to reinforce that power through forgery, deception, and magic, coupled with shrewd diplomacy, wars, or assassinations. A famous forgery that gave the Church secular power was the *Donation of Constantine*. This eighth-century document purported to have been written by a fourth-century emperor, Constantine, conferring temporal powers upon Pope Sylvester, who baptized him. It was not

---

* Universities, like monasteries and other religious orders, had a degree of autonomy as "trade unions" of either students (Bologna) or the faculty (Oxford). As such, they governed themselves, but under the church's overall authority. The bishop licensed professors, and the Church could burn any of them for heresy.

until the Renaissance that a devout philologist and writer named Lorenzo Valla (1405–1457) exposed the forgery.[8]

By Tyndale's time Christ's church of piety had become Rome's church of power. Power so blinded the Church's hierarchy that it began persecuting the pious followers of Jesus Christ just as Roman emperors had done a thousand years earlier. Bishops' palaces became torture chambers for dedicated Christians. For example, painter Edward Freese was imprisoned at the bishop's house at Fulham. His crime? On a cloth for the new inn in Colchester, he had painted "certain sentences of Scripture [in English]: and by that he was plainly known to be one of them that they call heretics."[9]

THE BIBLICAL PHASE

THE REFORMATION'S MORNING STAR

These "heretics" were not atheists or agnostics. They were radical Reformers.* They questioned whether ultimate authority belonged to the Church. Voices for practical reforms had never been absent, however. They were often heard and often enjoyed financial support, employment, and even protection by bishops and other church officials. Lorenzo Valla, for example, was a papal secretary. The new Reformers were punished as heretics because they replaced the authority of the pope with the authority of God's Word. John Wycliffe was not the first such Reformer, but as one of the greatest scholars of his time, he took up his pen against the pope's sword (usually wielded via secular forces). He raised the question of ultimate authority, challenging the very foundations of a church governed by sinful, and at times, foolish men. Here, in Wycliffe's own words, is the heart of the matter:

> We ought to believe in the authority of no man unless he say the Word of God. It is impossible that any word or deed of man should be of equal authority with the Holy Scripture. . . . Believers should

---

* Reform and Reformers with a capital *R* refer to the pioneers and leaders of the Protestant Reformation, including Luther's predecessors, such as Wycliffe and Hus.

ascertain for themselves what are the true matters of their faith, by having the Scriptures in a language which all may understand. For the laws made by prelates are not to be received as matters of faith, nor are we to confide in their public instructions, nor in any of their words, but as they are founded in Holy Writ, since the Scriptures contain the whole truth.... It is the pride of Lucifer, and even greater pride than his, to say that the teachers of man's traditions, made of sinful fools, are more profitable and needful to Christian people than the preachers of the Gospel.[10]

People revered and followed the Reformers because they were not promoting themselves. They were learned and godly men who risked their lives for the public good, including the good of the Church. They wanted to liberate and empower the masses by giving to them the knowledge and authority of the truth by translating the Scriptures into the vernaculars.

At times, secular rulers also supported and defended those Reformers who pointed out that, according to the Bible, God had given certain authority to secular rulers and that it was wrong for the Church to usurp power that belonged to the state. Such, for example, was the context of Wycliffe's entry into the public arena, outside the academic life of Oxford. Incited by the French king, the pope had demanded that Edward III should pay (along with the arrears) the annual tribute earlier imposed by the disreputable Pope Innocent III. England had discontinued its payment of that unjust tribute long before.

The people of England resented the demand. Parliament voted against it in 1366. But it was unsafe to disobey the pope. France would have loved to go on a Holy War in support of the pope. One critic of Parliament's decision directed his attack against Wycliffe, whom he considered the brain behind Parliament's policy. Wycliffe had been ordained and been appointed parish priest of several small hold-ings—Lutterworth from 1374 to 1384 being the most well-known. What right had he to go against the Church? Did anyone have the right to disagree with the pope, God's voice on earth? The attacks raised the question whether ultimate authority rested with the pope or in the Scriptures.

That attack stirred Wycliffe's mighty pen, which began a revolution because it wrestled with the issues of truth. At first, Wycliffe's writings made him the champion of a national cause. After his death, the same writings earned him the label "heretic." Many devout Catholics had been speaking against corruption in the Church. What made Reformers like Wycliffe revolutionaries was that they introduced a foundational change—Scriptures were to be held above men, including the popes.

Wycliffe's followers began translating the Bible into English so that people could read God's Word for themselves and discover truth. Wycliffe's translation (made before the invention of the printing press) was copied and studied. It exposed many of the deceptions that lay at the root of Church's claim to power. Grasping the social implications of translating the Bible in Wycliffe's day will help us understand why he is called "the Reformation's Morning Star," and why translating the Bible birthed the modern world.

During Wycliffe's time, England was a three-tiered literary hierarchy. Like the rest of Europe's elites, England's intellectual elite spoke Latin. The Bible was *their* book. Translated by Saint Jerome (347–419), this Latin "Vulgate" held sway for a thousand years. Church leaders, including Wycliffe, were a part of this exclusive club. Below them were the nobility, who spoke French or its Anglo-Norman dialect. They had some portions of the Scriptures available to them in their declining dialect. At the bottom of the social ladder were the illiterate peasants, who spoke primitive English. Hardly anyone thought of enlightening them. Literary efforts in English, such as Chaucer's (1343–1400) *Canterbury Tales*, came after Wycliffe. Most of Wycliffe's contemporaries scorned the idea that the Bible could be translated into a rustic dialect like English.

Elitism keeps others down. It uses everything, including language, education, and religion to suppress the masses. The Bible could be used to oppose the Church because caring for the poor and the oppressed is a key biblical value.[11] Moses began writing the Torah after liberating the Hebrews from their slavery in Egypt. The New Testament was born in the context of Rome's colonization of the Jews. The Bible is a philosophy of freedom. It is very different from the speculations of the upper-caste philosophers and sages in my country, who taught that those who suffered in ignorance, poverty, and powerlessness did so because of their poor karma in previous lives. The Bible translators began what the Marxists later tried to duplicate—the creation of a classless society. Oxford historian Alister McGrath wrote that by encouraging the translation of the Bible into English,

> Wycliffe threatened to destroy the whole edifice of clerical domination in matters of theology and church life. The translation of the Bible into English would be a social leveler on a hitherto unknown scale. All would be able to read Christendom's sacred text, and judge both the lifestyle and teachings of the medieval church on its basis. The very idea sent shockwaves throughout the complacent church establishment of the day.[12]

Some people ridicule the Protestant Reformers but relish the notion of human equality. They do not know that the Reformers paid with their lives to make the biblical idea of equality a foundational principle of the modern world. Today, we take it for granted that uplifting the downtrodden is a noble virtue. In Wycliffe's England, the idea of raising peasants to the status of aristocracy was abhorrent. Henry Knighton, one of those Wycliffe-haters, put on paper the elitist reaction to Wycliffe's radical effort to uplift peasants, women, and other "swine":

> John Wycliffe translated the gospel, which Christ had entrusted to clerics and doctors of the church, so that they might administer it conveniently to the laity . . . Wycliffe translated it from Latin into English—not the angelic language. As a result, what was previously known only by learned clerics and those of good understanding has become common, and available to the laity—in fact, even to women who can read. As a result, the pearls of the gospel have been scattered and spread before swine.[13]

Most people fail to realize that the modern world was birthed in those theological controversies that now seem trivial to us. In Wycliffe's hands, the biblical doctrine of predestination and the controversy over transubstantiation became the "bomb that rocked the papacy."[14] He used the Bible's teaching on predestination to argue that God, not the Church, chooses the saved. The Church consists both of saints and sinners. It is possible that even a pope may not be predestined to salvation. Likewise, his mocking the idea of transubstantiation robbed the priests of their magical power to turn ordinary bread and wine into the very body and blood of Jesus Christ. Such writings threw England into turmoil.

Wycliffe was suspected of stirring a revolution when the social unrest of his time culminated in the peasants' revolt of 1381. Mobs of frustrated laborers marched on London. The instigators justified their act by invoking the authority of Wycliffe's scholarship. Christopher de Hamel, manuscript scholar from Oxford and Cambridge, summarized the situation by saying, "English was the language of peasants. Therefore, in proposing that the Bible should be translated, Wycliffe was touching on issues of class prejudice which still confound society in England but which were then of exceptional sensitivity."[15]

Wycliffe was a hero who disowned his class and sided with the "swine," the underdogs. Why? Not because he was trying to win a democratic election. Democracy followed in his trail. Rather, Wycliffe was following Moses, who "chose to be mistreated along with the people of God rather than to enjoy the pleasures of sin for a short time."[16] He followed Jesus, who preached the good news to the poor.[17] It was neither pursuit of career nor political correctness but commitment to truth that inspired Wycliffe to begin translating the Bible into English. The same commitment empowered people to copy by hand that banned translation at the risk of their lives. Even reading that translation required special permission, and anyone caught with a copy could be tried for heresy and burned at the stake.

DESIDERIUS ERASMUS

A powerful plea for translating the Scriptures came a century later from Desiderius Erasmus (1466?–1536), a leading Renaissance writer.

This Dutch writer, scholar, and humanist interpreted intellectual currents of the Italian Renaissance for northern Europe. Patrons of high culture acknowledged him as the foremost humanist scholar. Popes and bishops courted him. Erasmus accepted their benefaction but criticized their corruption. He called for moral reform, especially after 1513, when Pope Leo X called for a new Crusade against the Turks. The pope offered the crusaders plenary remissions of all sins and reconciliation with the Most High. Erasmus was the pope's friend, but he wrote a passionate *Complaint of Peace.* He argued that the Lord Jesus had asked the Church to give the world the gospel, not the sword.

Erasmus had traveled throughout Europe, witnessing her strife and pain. He had mastered all the Greek and Roman wisdom available, including what came into Latin via Muslim scholars, but he found nothing except the Bible that could bring reform and peace. He advocated that the Bible be translated and made accessible to peasants and even to women:

> Christ wishes his mysteries published as openly as possible. I would that even the lowliest women read the Gospels and the Pauline Epistles. And I would that they were translated into all languages so that they could be read and understood not only by Scots and Irish but also by Turks and Saracens . . . Would that, as a result, the farmer sing some portion of them at the plow, the weaver hum some parts of them to the movement of his shuttle, the traveler lighten the weariness of the journey with stories of this kind! Let all the conversations of every Christian be drawn from this source.[18]

Erasmus undertook to bring out a fresh Latin translation of the New Testament. He used the best available Greek manuscripts and corrected mistakes made by Jerome eleven hundred years earlier. One "minor" correction became foundational to the Reformation and also one of the most disputed biblical phrases of the sixteenth century. Christ's predecessor, John the Baptist, had called his first-century listeners to repent. St. Jerome had translated repentance as *penitentiam agite,* which means "do penance."

Erasmus proposed that the correct Latin equivalent would be *Resipiscite,* "be penitent." Erasmus's concern was to render an accurate translation. He had no idea that his translation would undermine a large part of the superstructure of medieval religiosity: Christians going on pilgrimages, buying indulgences, and doing penance to earn spiritual merit and God's grace. As Martin Luther saw it, Erasmus's rediscovery of a simple biblical truth freed people from economic exploitation in the name of religion.

MARTIN LUTHER

Luther followed Erasmus's advice regarding Bible translation. Many feared that Luther would be destroyed as a heretic after his heroic stand at the trial at Worms.* But Frederick, his university's patron, ordered some of his trusted soldiers to "kidnap," hide, and protect Luther. They hid him at the castle of Wartburg. Though they thought Luther had been killed, his friends started receiving letters and writings from him that laid much of the foundation for the Reformation.

Luther hated his confinement. It gave him insomnia and psychosomatic illnesses. Besides writing letters and books, he also used the time to translate the New Testament into German. That became the foundation for reforming German-speaking Europe. The masses, who did not know Greek or Latin, began reading or hearing God's Word in a language they understood. This democratized truth, enabling simple people (future voters) to make up their own minds in controversies between the church-state establishment and the Reformers. Luther's New Testament had hundreds of print runs,[19] including several pirated editions. It established the standard language for modern German.

WILLIAM TYNDALE

For the English-speaking people, William Tyndale picked up Luther's baton. After graduating from Oxford, William Tyndale is believed to have spent some time in Cambridge. Since the Cam River opens into the sea, smugglers found it easier to bring Luther's banned

---

* See chapter 8 on heroism.

books into Cambridge than into Oxford. Some students were deeply concerned with the state of affairs in the Church and the nation. They were devout students, but they defied the official ban, frequenting pubs to secretly read smuggled books of Luther's subversive literature. This made Cambridge England's gateway to Reformation ideas.

Secrecy was the hallmark of pre-democratic, hierarchic Europe. But juicy secrets have a way of leaking out. Some of these were as disturbing as they were titillating. According to historian John F. D'Amico, although vows of chastity were compulsory for the clergy, concubinage and prostitution were thriving institutions in Rome. Almost all the clergy, including the popes, participated in this corruption.[20] And there were plenty of stories about *simony*—buying and selling of power in the Church.

Albert buying his archbishopric from the pope was one example. But not all bishops sold indulgences to pay back their debts. Some took the faster route of extorting money from their priests. For example, Pope Alexander VI arrested Cardinal Orsini on dubious charges. The cardinal conveniently died shortly after his arrest, allowing the pope to confiscate his considerable estate.[21] Stories like these caused students to ask questions. Oxford and Cambridge were Church institutions, and most of their students were preparing to serve God. Did serving the Church equal serving God? Many students agreed with Luther that reform was the need of the hour.

Several factors convinced Tyndale that biblical illiteracy was an important source of Europe's corruption. Professor David Daniell, one of the world's foremost authorities on Tyndale, explained that some priests who knew little Latin "would be glossing and allegorizing a few texts of Scripture, twisting them into curious shapes that the Church's centuries-old tradition of exegesis expected—and using Latin Scriptures, of course, which in places differed markedly (and conveniently) from the Greek originals."[22]

Priests often twisted and disobeyed God's Word, including the Ten Commandments. Many priests did not even know the Ten Commandments. In 1551, three decades after Tyndale's New Testament, a reforming Bishop Hooper discovered that in Gloucestershire, one of the godliest places in England, "[o]f the unsatisfactory clergy, nine did not know how many commandments there were, 33 did not know where they appeared in the Bible (the gospel of Matthew was a favourite guess) and 168 could not repeat them."[23]

Tyndale first announced his resolve to make the Word of God available to the masses when a priest advised him that "we were better be without God's law than the pope's." Tyndale retorted, "If God spare my life ere many years, I will cause a boy that driveth the plough, shall know more of the scriptures than thou dost."[24] That was an echo of the wish that Erasmus had expressed when he pondered the question of how to reform Christendom.

Tyndale sought permission from Bishop Tunstall of London to translate the Bible into English. Tunstall had personally helped Erasmus with his Latin translation, but he refused to allow a translation into English. He looked upon Tyndale as another position seeker, anxious to display his literary talents. It is also likely that the bishop did not want to produce another Wycliffe or an English Luther.

Tyndale spent another year in London exploring all his options for translating the Bible legally. Finally he realized that no one in England would allow him to do the one thing that was needed to reform his nation—translate the Bible into English. The mission to give God's Word to his people required him to risk his life. He slipped out of England, hoping to find support on the Continent, where Luther's Reformation had already begun. This "fugitive" needed only a few secret supporters to give us what became the greatest book in the English language and culture.

The bishops perceived Tyndale's translation as a threat because it transferred power from the leaders to the people, and it implied that the Roman Catholic hierarchy was more Roman than Christian. For example, Tyndale deliberately decided not to translate the Greek word *ekklesia* as "church." Jesus had used *ekklesia* to describe the community of followers that he was going to leave behind him. Thanks to Renaissance philologists, Tyndale knew that the word had originally meant a democratic "assembly" or "congregation." In the words of twentieth-century theologian William Barclay,

The *ecclesia* [*ekklesia*] was the convened assembly of the people [in Greek city-states]. It consisted of all the citizens of the city who had not lost their civic rights. Apart from the fact that its decisions must conform to the laws of the State, its powers were to all intents and purposes unlimited. . . . Two other things are interesting to note: first all its meetings began with prayer and a sacrifice. Second, it was a true democracy. Its two great watchwords were "equality" (*isonomia*) and "freedom" (*eleutheria*). It was an assembly where everyone had an equal right and an equal duty to take part.[25]

Tyndale's other renderings had powerful implications too. For example, the New Testament taught that every believer was a priest; therefore, Tyndale used the term *priest* only for the Old Testament Jewish priests. Christian leaders were "presbyters"—pastors, shepherds, elders, or bishops of the people—who derived their earthly authority from the congregation, not from a hierarchy with an ultimate seat in Rome.

The democratic ethos of Tyndale's New Testament was a threat, not merely to the Roman Catholic Church, but also to the monarchy. Consequently, England's kings began to take an active interest in overseeing Bible translations.

Tyndale was arrested, tried, and condemned. His martyrdom marked the death of the medieval world and the beginning of the modern. Although we do not have the details of his martyrdom, the scene can be re-created based on the accounts of similar deaths:

On the morning of October 6, 1536, at Vilvorde, Belgium, a large crowd gathers behind a barricade. In the middle of the circular space, two great beams are raised in the form of a cross, with iron chains and a rope of hemp passing through holes in the beams at the top. Brushwood, straw, and logs are heaped ready nearby. The Procurator General (the emperor's attorney) and his colleagues are seated on specially prepared high chairs within the circle. Outside of the circle, on a tall platform, some bishops are seated. A priest in chains is brought to the bishops. The prosecutor condemns him as *"William Tyndale—arch-heretic."*

As evidence of his guilt, a copy of Tyndale's New Testament is given to the presiding bishop. Articles of guilt are read. The anointing oil is symbolically scraped from Tyndale's hands; the bread and wine of the Mass are placed on his hands and quickly removed. His priestly vestments are ceremonially stripped away. As Tyndale is handed over to the guards, the bishop begins to turn the pages of the New Testament.

The crowd is parted to let the guards bring the prisoner through the barricade. As they approach the cross, the prisoner is allowed to pray. A last appeal is made for him to recant. Then he alone moves to the cross. The guards kneel to tie his feet to the bottom of the cross. Around his neck the chain is passed, with the hempen noose hanging slack. The brushwood, straw, and logs are packed close round the prisoner, making a sort of hut with him inside. The executioner goes to stand behind the cross, and looks at the Procurator General. Tyndale cries out a loud prayer: "Lord, open the king of England's eyes!"

The Procurator General gives the signal. The executioner quickly tightens the hempen noose, strangling Tyndale. The Procurator General watches Tyndale die, then reaches for a lighted wax torch being held near him. He takes it and hands it to the executioner, who touches off the straw and brushwood.

As Tyndale's body burns, the crowd cheers. The bishop walks to the fire and throws the New Testament into it. Little does he realize that Tyndale's prayer has been heard.

The eyes of the king of England were opened shortly after Tyndale's execution. Tyndale's words, incorporated into various versions of the Bible, were read in English churches and around the world. Their authority superseded the authority of the popes. Tyndale's words shaped the language of Shakespeare, sparked revolutions in England and America, democratized nations, and ushered in a new civilization where right became superior to might.

THE GENEVA BIBLE

Tyndale's translation of the Bible threatened the hierarchical organization of medieval society. That threat became particularly potent a few decades later after the Geneva Bible incorporated much of Tyndale's translation.

King Edward VI, who reigned from 1547 to 1553, was sympathetic to Protestantism and appointed reformers like Martin Bucer to Cambridge and Oxford. Upon the king's death in 1553, Mary Tudor, who became known as "Bloody Mary," reigned from 1553 to 1558. She reversed the official policy and brought England back under the papacy. She married Philip II, the king of Spain, in 1554 and began persecution of Protestants in England. Mary had approximately three hundred Protestants murdered.

Some who escaped ended up in Geneva, an independent city-state under John Calvin's teaching and moral influence. Among these refugees were William Whittingham, who later married John Calvin's sister; Anthony Gilby; Thomas Sampson; Miles Coverdale; John Knox; and Laurence Tomson. These scholars produced the first Protestant Study Bible, the Geneva Bible, in 1560. It incorporated most of Tyndale's labor. It excelled as an accurate translation with illustrations, maps, prefaces, and study notes that explained the "hard places."

By 1600, the Geneva Bible had become the Bible of choice for English-speaking Protestants. It posed a greater threat to monarchy than Tyndale's New Testament, because it not only followed his tradition but also added marginal notes. Tyndale had explanatory notes in the margins of his first New Testament, but his first attempt to publish that translation with notes had to be aborted after printing the first twenty-two chapters of the gospel of Matthew. Tyndale narrowly escaped getting caught.

In his second and successful attempt to print the New Testament, Tyndale deleted notes to keep the edition small—easier for smuggling across the channel into England. The Geneva Bible reintroduced notes—some were Tyndale's, but most were authored by Geneva Reformers, including the prominent John Knox—to expound the

Bible's nonhierarchical, egalitarian ethos of freedom. Dr. McGrath explained the significance of the Geneva Bible:

> [O]fficial opposition to the Geneva Bible could not prevent it from becoming the most widely read Bible of the Elizabethan, and subsequently the Jacobean, era. It may never have secured official sanction, yet it needed no such endorsement by the political or religious establishment to gain enthusiastic and widespread acceptance. Even though the book initially had to be imported from Geneva—English printings of the work having been prohibited by nervous bishops—it still outsold its rivals.[26]

For more than a hundred years, the Geneva Bible dominated the English-speaking world. It was the Bible used by Shakespeare. The King James Bible was published in 1611, but it took fifty years for it to supplant the Geneva Bible. The Pilgrims and Puritans carried the Geneva Bible to the shores of the New World, where American colonists were reared on it.[27]

THE KING JAMES BIBLE

King James I opposed the Puritans who championed the Geneva Bible. He upheld the doctrine of the divine right of kings, which the Geneva Bible challenged. His beliefs clashed with the biblical idea of human equality, promoted by the Reformers. Before becoming the king of England, James reigned in Scotland, and during a heated encounter, a leader of the Scottish Reformation, Andrew Melville, physically took

> hold of James, and accused him of being "God's silly vassal." Melville pointedly declared that while they would support James as king in public, in private they all knew perfectly well that Christ was the true king in Scotland, and his kingdom was the kirk—a kingdom in which James was a mere member, not a lord or head. James was shaken by this physical and verbal assault, not least because it suggested that Melville and his allies posed a significant threat to the Scottish throne.[28]

James had opposed Puritanism before becoming the king of England. In 1598 he wrote two books defending the divine right of kings, *The True Law of Free Monarchs* and *Basilikon Doron*. In Alister McGrath's words,

> James I held that kings had been ordained of God to rule the nations of the world, to promote justice, and to dispense wisdom. It was, therefore, imperative that kings should be respected and obeyed unconditionally and in all circumstances. The ample notes provided by the Geneva Bible taught otherwise. Tyrannical kings should not be obeyed; indeed, there were excellent reason for suggesting that they should be overthrown.[29]

For example, the margin notes for Daniel 6:22 imply that the commands of kings are to be disobeyed if they conflict with the law of God.

> For he [Daniel] disobeyed the king's wicked commandment in order to obey God, and so he did no injury to the king, who ought to command nothing by which God would be dishonored.[30]

The notes for Daniel 11:36 indicate that the days of oppressive tyrants are numbered. The Puritans were suffering for their sins, but their suffering would not last forever.

> So long the tyrants will prevail as God has appointed to punish his people: but he shows that it is but for a time.[31]

McGrath wrote: "Notice also how the Genevan notes regularly use the word 'tyrant' to refer to kings; the King James Bible *never* uses this word—a fact noted with approval as much as relief by many royalists at this point."[32]

King James authorized a fresh translation of the Bible to undermine the republican implications of the Geneva Bible. That version is famous as the King James Version of the Bible. It incorporated about 90 percent of Tyndale's New Testament and as much of the Old Testament that Tyndale had translated before getting caught.

Biblical reforms did not stop in the West. As the church started studying the Bible, many realized that God wanted to bless all the nations of the earth that suffer because they do not know the truth.[33] Believers who wanted to serve God resolved to make the Bible available to everyone in their native language. They believed that as people came to know the truth, the truth would set them free.[34] At the dawn of the nineteenth century, that belief inspired history's greatest movement to translate and publish the Bible in every language of the world. The translators had to turn oral dialects into literary languages. In the process, these linguists built the intellectual bridges over which modern ideas could travel from the West to the rest of the world. That is what we now call "globalization"—the subject of the next chapter.

What the Church did to oppose the Bible was terrible. But although most of the Church is no longer a persecutor, opposition to the Bible has not ended. The previous two centuries have seen equally fierce attacks on the Bible, and not just in Marxist, Muslim, or Hindu countries. This book began in response to one such attack by Arun Shourie. The Bible remains a threat to those who want man's authority to supersede God's, to those who want to preserve oppressive cultures based on falsehood and sin. Mr. Shourie was right in seeing the Bible as the most dangerous intellectual challenge to Hindutva. Western intellectuals who want man to be the measure of all things are also right in seeing the Bible as a threat. The Bible claims to be God's Word. And that implies that words, values, and beliefs will harm us if they are not in alignment with what our heavenly Father has said is true and good.

Part V

THE INTELLECTUAL REVOLUTION

In Lincoln's Community of Protestants the supremacy of the Bible as the book of daily life encouraged acquiring basic reading skills . . . Words and ideas were inseparable in a nation in which the Bible dominated. It was given full currency as the source of the dominant belief system. It was also the great book of illustrative stories, illuminating references, and pithy maxims for everyday conduct. More than any other glue, it held the society together . . . As six-year-old Abraham Lincoln began to learn to read, his household text was the Bible.

—FRED KAPLAN, *Lincoln: The Biography of a Writer*

Chapter Ten

LANGUAGES

How Was Intellectual
Power Democratized?

B ritish prime minister Margaret Thatcher was too conserva-
tive to endear herself to the mainstream media. The following
statement from a speech in 1988 illustrates how politically
incorrect she was. The truth of her comments began to be considered
only after British-born and -educated terrorists began to threaten
Britain. Speaking with a humility unusual for heads of state, she said,

> We are a nation whose ideals were founded on the Bible. Also it is
> quite impossible to understand our literature without grasping this
> fact. *That* is the strong practical case for ensuring that children at
> school are given adequate instruction in the part which the Judaeo-
> Christian tradition has played in moulding our laws, manners and
> institutions. How can you make sense of Shakespeare and Sir Walter
> Scott, or of the constitutional conflicts of the seventeenth century in
> both Scotland and England, without such fundamental knowledge?
> But I would go further than this. The truths of the Judaeo-Christian
> tradition are infinitely precious, not only, as I believe, because they
> are true, but also because they provide the moral impulse which
> alone can lead to that peace, in the true meaning of the word, for
> which we all long . . . there is little hope for democracy if the hearts

of men and women in democratic societies cannot be touched by a call to something greater than themselves. Political structures, state institutions, collective ideals are not enough . . . [Democracy requires] the life of faith . . . as much to the temporal as to the spiritual welfare of the nation.[1]

What role did the Bible play in creating English language, literature, and culture, including the very notions of nation, nation-state, and nationalism?

Americans still tolerate patriotism, but *nationalism* is a dirty word for most people who graduated from a secular college during the previous three decades. Whether it is a virtue or a vice, it is helpful to understand that on the world stage the issue of nationalism is a recent phenomenon. If the British prime minister died in office, would the British people ask the French, the Germans, or the Dutch to send them a prime minister? That would be inconceivable even though Britain is a part of the European Union. Like other nations, the British want one of their own people to lead them.

At different points in their history, however, the British invited a Dutch monarch, William III, and a German aristocrat, George I, to become their kings. Why would they have even allowed—let alone requested—a foreign monarch to take power? Because Europe was an empire—Christendom—and religion was more important than nationalism. The interests of an international fraternity of clerics and aristocrats superseded those of individual nations. In the wake of the Reformation, it was the Bible that reorganized Europe as modern nation-states. Developing vernaculars through Bible translation was only the first step toward linguistic nation-states. The Bible also provided the theological justification for fighting to build independent nation-states such as Holland.

Latin

Jesus was a Jew and taught mostly to Jews. Yet, according to most biblical scholars, his public speeches were not in Hebrew, then a sacred but dead language. He taught in Aramaic, which had been the language of the people living in Palestine since the Babylonian exile.

When his disciples wrote the New Testament, they followed the principle of using the vernacular—that is, the native language of the people they were trying to reach. They wrote the Scriptures in *Koine* (common Greek), a trade language spoken throughout the Roman Empire. Two centuries earlier, seventy Jewish scholars had made the Septuagint Greek translation of the Hebrew Scriptures.

Gradually, Latin replaced Greek as the vernacular of the empire. Following Jesus and his apostles, the Christian scholar St. Jerome undertook the arduous task of translating the entire Bible from Hebrew and Greek into Latin. He believed it was essential for people to have the Scriptures in their own language. He finished the project in AD 405, and his translation became known as the Vulgate because it was written in the "vulgar" or common language of the people.

Soon afterward, the Roman Empire collapsed and gradually Latin became a dead language. The languages of the European peoples continued to change through conquest, migration, mingling, and linguistic evolution. But for a thousand years, nobody after Jerome bothered to translate the Bible into the dialects of the people of England.

A lack of economic patronage for vernacular literacy reinforced Latin's monopoly. A more important reason, however, was the snobbery of the educated. They believed that vernaculars of the common men were of little value and that serious study, jurisprudence, and literature could only happen in Latin. Why should anyone learn to read a language in which no one writes? As a consequence, in order to read, one had to learn Latin.

This meant that only the aristocracy or the clergy could become educated. The time and expense required to educate people in Latin was prohibitive for most families. Printing did not exist and students had to copy their own textbooks on expensive parchment paper. Finding teachers was not easy either. Most men and women who were capable of teaching Latin had taken monastic or clerical orders in the Church. Their spiritual, scholastic, and ecclesiastical duties did not leave time for teaching. This linguistic caste system strengthened the Church's power over Europe, but it kept Europe weak.

The intellectual and religious elite did not believe that a profound book such as the Bible could be translated into the dialects of peasants. In any case, the peasants were illiterate, and their dialects had no written form. These were some of the factors that made translators such as Luther and Tyndale revolutionary reformers. They democratized language. Taking knowledge that belonged only to the elite, they gave it to the masses. Their revolution went on to transform the way Europeans understood the role of the nation-state and the role of the masses in government affairs.

These translator-reformers followed Jesus' example in using the languages of the people. They fostered an environment in which Europe's modern languages could develop and flourish. Translating the Bible into vernaculars of German, French, and English, they dug the intellectual tunnel through which spiritual and secular knowledge could flow. It empowered people who had been ignored and oppressed by the Latin-speaking elite.

When Europeans became literate, the only book most families owned was the Bible, and it became the source of their language and their worldview. The idea of "government of the people, for the people, by the people" became possible only because the people's mother tongue became the language of learning and governing. The common man, who formerly had no knowledge of government and legal affairs, could now participate in national debates and decision making. Likewise, the modern free-market economy, which allows everyone to freely contribute their potential for everyone's good, became possible because the languages of the people became strong enough to be the languages of law, technology, and the marketplace.

Transforming India—a Brief Case Study

My personal interest in the Bible and its translation into the vernacular did not come from what it accomplished in Europe, but from what it accomplished in India. I grew up in the heart of Hindi-land, in

Allahabad, barely fifty miles from Kashi, where Tulsidas wrote North India's most important religious epic, *Ramcharitmanas*. I was always told that my mother tongue, Hindi, came out of his great epic. When I started reading the classic, I was puzzled because I couldn't understand a single sentence. The author's "Hindi" was completely different from mine, and it caused me to ponder: *Where exactly did my mother tongue—our national language—come from?*

I was surprised to discover that two hundred years earlier, when the British began to rule North India, our court language was neither Hindi nor Urdu. Before the British, Muslims had ruled our land and they were not interested in our dialects. Nor were they interested in the primitive language of the thirteenth-century Muslim poet Amir Khusro. They thought he had corrupted their classical languages, Arabic and Persian, by mixing in dialects around Delhi. It took the labors of a British Bible translator, Rev. Henry Martyn (1781–1812), to forge those dialects into a literary language, modern Urdu. For a while it served as the official language of my state of Uttar Pradesh before retreating to become the national language of Pakistan.

Likewise, Hindu scholars did not develop India's national language, Hindi. Bible translators such as Reverend Gilchrist and missionary-linguists such as Reverend Kellogg made the dialect of poet Tulsidas (AD 1532–1623) the base for developing modern Hindi as a literary language.

Sanskrit could have been the court language of pre-British India, but it wasn't. Sanskrit *is* India's national treasure. But those who had the key to the intellectual treasure would not share it even with their own women, let alone with non-Brahmin males. The Brahmins' religion required them to treat their neighbors as untouchables. Sanskrit was used as a means to keep people at a distance from knowledge that was power.

Ashoka (304–232 BC), India's greatest Buddhist ruler, used the Pali language and Brahmi script to spread his wisdom throughout India. It became the language of Buddhist learning. Yet, at the dawn of the nineteenth century, India did not have even one scholar who could read a single sentence inscribed on the Ashoka pillars found throughout India. Worse—the antihistoric nature of Hinduism had ensured that for centuries no Indian had even heard Ashoka's name until the 1830s when an Anglo-India scholar, James Prinsep, found the key to reading Brahmi script on the pillars.

Ashoka's efforts to unify geographic India by promoting one script, language, and wisdom were magnificent. Why did they fail? Persecution by the Brahmins was a factor, but that does not explain why Brahmi script became extinct. Ashoka's religious philosophy worked against his social agenda that could have made India a great, unified nation built by great literature.

The Buddha, as we have seen, taught that the Ultimate Reality was Silence, or *Shoonyta*. The human mind was a product of *Avidhya* (Primeval Ignorance). It was not made in the image of God; human language, logic, and words had no correlation with Truth. The way to Enlightenment was through emptying one's mind of all words and thoughts. The goal was to reach absolute Silence. Therefore, the Buddhist monks barely studied their own scriptures. They had no religious motivation to take the trouble to turn their neighbors' dialects into literary languages to make the Buddha's thought accessible to everyone. The monks' mission was to propagate meditation techniques to *empty* everyone's minds of all thought. They were not out to fill minds with great ideas.

I was utterly surprised to learn that when the British Raj (the British Indian Empire) began in North India, our court language was Persian! Mogul emperor Humayun had won back his father's kingdom with the help of fourteen thousand Persian soldiers. His son Akbar (AD 1556–1605), the greatest Mogul emperor, patronized Indian artists and writers, including those who wrote in old Hindi. He also promoted his religious language, Arabic, but he realized there was no language that he could use to govern India. He kept Persian as his court language. Persian did for Moguls what Sanskrit did for Brahmins. It excluded most Indians from power. One way to keep government of the rulers, for the rulers, and by the rulers is to run it in a language not understood by the ruled.

In the eighteenth century, when the British started governing

India, they faced this same communication problem. Their situation was worse, because unlike the Moguls who had settled in India, individual English rulers came to India for the short term. The East India Company, which ruled the subcontinent, was a commercial company. Its governors were interested in cutting expenses, not wasting money on noncommercial projects like developing dialects. Colonialism did not cultivate the vernaculars.

The British East India Company needed Indian servants who spoke a little English. A few Englishmen, called Classists, promoted Sanskrit, Arabic, and Persian. Neither Classists nor the Company had an interest in educating a class of Indians who would enrich Indian vernaculars, educate the masses, and prepare India for liberty and self-government. That was the agenda of the followers of Jesus Christ who sought to obey the command to love their neighbors as themselves. One only needs to read the writings of British member of parliament Charles Grant (1792); neo-Hindu reformer Raja Rammohun Roy (1823); Scottish missionary Alexander Duff (1830); and British civil servants Charles Trevelyan (1834 and '38) and his brother-in-law Lord Macaulay (1835) to realize that these men opposed the Classists and championed English only as the best means to enrich Indian vernaculars.

Hindu intellectuals who have only read excerpts from Rammohun Roy and Lord Macaulay assume that these men promoted English to colonize, not liberate, the Indian mind.* But Mahatma Gandhi (a British-educated Gujarati) and Rabindranath Tagore (a Bengali-speaking scholar of English) understood Macaulay and Christian missionaries. The two of them met together in the 1920s and decided that Hindi, not Sanskrit, not English, had to be India's future.

In order to give us our national language, missionaries struggled against the East India Company's commercial interests. Rev. John Borthwick Gilchrist (1759–1841) worked for the company at Fort William College, Calcutta, India. He developed "Tables and Principles" of Hindustani in his spare time and submitted them to the

---

* For example, this is one of Arun Shourie's misinformed attacks on Macaulay.

college council for publication on June 6, 1802. On June 14 the council not only returned his work but prohibited him from publishing it. Gilchrist persisted in promoting the cause of Hindustani at great personal cost.

Hindustani is the root of Hindi as well as Urdu. Rev. Claudius Buchanan (1766–1815), the vice-provost of the Fort William College, recorded the pioneering effort of Rev. Henry Martyn in enhancing Hindustani to the position that it could give to India and Pakistan our national languages:

> The Rev. Henry Martyn, B.D. Fellow of St. John's College, Cambridge, went out to India about five years ago . . . After acquiring the highest academical honours in science, and a just celebrity for classical knowledge, he devoted himself to the acquirement of the Arabic and Hindostanee Languages . . . the grand work which had chiefly engaged the attention of this Oriental Scholar, during the last four years, is his Translation of the whole Bible into the Hindostanee Language . . . His chief difficulty is in settling the orthography of the language, and in ascertaining what proportion of words ought to be admitted from the Persian and Arabic fountains; for the Hindostanee is yet in its infancy, as a written and grammatical tongue; and it is probable that Mr. Martyn's work will contribute much to fix its standard.[2]

Decades of sacrificial service by Bible translators made it possible for the British government to agree to making Hindustani their court language at the lower levels of administration. This meant that a peasant could now go to a British court in North India and understand the prosecutor, witnesses, and lawyers who argued his case and the judge who passed down the ruling. Bible translators' labor also made it possible for a gifted Indian writer to write in a language that ordinary Indians could understand.

Gandhi and Tagore were not the first to see that India's future lay in Hindi. British bureaucracy preferred Urdu for decades because, even at the end of the nineteenth century, "Hindi" was not one language. Every North Indian city spoke a different dialect. People in my hometown Allahabad did not understand Tulsidas's "Hindi," although he lived in the next city—Benaras. This problematic literary situation only changed after Rev. S. H. Kellogg, an American missionary in Allahabad, coalesced more than a dozen dialects to help create today's Hindi. He entitled his Hindi Grammar (still in use) as, *A Grammar of the Hindi Language: In Which Are Treated the High Hindi, Braj, and the Eastern Hindi of the Ramayan of Tulsi Das, also the Colloquial Dialects of Rajputana, Kumaon, Avadh, Riwa, Bhojpur, Magadh, Maithila etc.*

In spite of the best efforts of translators and administrators, doubts about the viability of Hindi as a national language persisted into the twentieth century. It was the labor of the Kashi Nagari Pracharini Sabha[3] that made it possible for our national leaders to have the confidence that Hindi could become our national language. Most Indians do not know that the key figure behind the work of the Sabha was the American missionary Rev. E. Greaves in Benaras. Dr. Shyam Sunder Das, the editor of the Sabha's landmark Hindi *Shabd Sagar,* recorded the following tribute to Greaves in his preface:

> On 23 August 1907, the Society's best wisher [not "well-wisher"] and enthusiastic member, Revd E. Greaves, proposed in the Managing Committee Meeting that the Society should accept the responsibility of producing a comprehensive Hindi dictionary . . . He also showed us how this could be accomplished.[4]

Bible translators and missionaries did not merely give me my mother tongue, Hindi. Every living literary language in India is a testimony to their labor. In 2005 a Malyalee scholar from Mumbai, Dr. Babu Verghese, submitted a seven-hundred-page doctoral thesis to the University of Nagpur.[*] It demonstrated that Bible translators, using the dialects of mostly illiterate Indians, created seventy-three modern literary languages. These include the national languages of India (Hindi), Pakistan (Urdu), and Bangladesh (Bengali). Five Brahmin scholars examined Dr. Verghese's thesis and awarded him a PhD in 2008. They

---

[*] *The Impact of Bible Translation on Indian Languages—A Study.*

also unanimously recommended that his thesis, when published as a book, should be required reading for students of Indian linguistics.

Three English missionaries—William Carey, Joshua Marshman, and William Ward—began the work of learning hundreds of dialects spoken by illiterate Indians in order to turn them into seventy-three literary languages and to create their grammars and dictionaries. The impact in creating modern South Asia was best summarized by historian Hugh Tinker:

> And so in Serampore, on the banks of the Hooghly, soon after 1800, the principal elements in modern South Asia—popular linguistic identification ("linguism"), the press, the university, social consciousness—all came to light. The West and South Asia were about to come to grips with each other in terms not merely of power and profit, but also of ideas and principles.[5]

The Serampore Trio, as the missionaries were known, began with Bible translation and then established the college that grew into Serampore University. They chose to use Bengali, rather than English, as the medium of instruction in their college, because the missionaries noticed that Indian families wanted their children to learn only enough English to get a job with the East India Company. The missionaries had not dedicated their lives to producing good English-speaking servants for the British Raj. They wanted Indians to come to their college to begin cultivating their minds and their spirits, to question the socioeconomic darkness around them, to inquire and find the truth that liberates individuals and builds great nations. The Bible teaches that the Creator gave us the gift of language because he loved us. *Love includes communication, and the communication of great ideas requires great language.*

THE BIBLE AND NATIONALISM

The Bible did far more than create the modern English, German, Dutch, Hindi, Urdu, and Bengali languages. It also created the modern idea of the nation-state and the value that we call *nationalism.*

Nationalism has acquired a bad name because of the atrocities it inspired during the twentieth century. The German nationalism that led to two world wars was a secularized perversion of a biblical value. Devout Roman Catholics who hate secular nationalism but do not appreciate biblical nationalism have fueled the recent reaction against nationalism and the yearning for a united continent in Europe.

Appreciating nationalism is easier for us in India and Pakistan because all our lives we have witnessed Shia-Sunni riots. Why do some Muslims occasionally kill their own countrymen as a religious duty? Each riot is apparently triggered by a petty incident, but the underlying reason is that loyalty to one's nation and fellow citizens is not an Islamic virtue. For Sunnis, the authority is Mecca; for Shiites, the authority—the Caliphate—is in Persia.

In Britain some Muslims believe there is no Qur'anic warrant to value British nationalism. In fact, their religious duty is to bring England under Sharia law. This threat was part of the social context of Mrs. Thatcher's speech quoted at the beginning of this chapter. There should be no doubt that her fear is legitimate. Without the Bible her universities have no philosophical foundations for believing in the very idea of nation-states. On the other hand, they have very good historical reasons for despising (secular) nationalism and reasonable pragmatic grounds for transferring federal sovereignty to a European Union.

The Reformation broke up the Holy Roman Empire into modern nation-states, often defined by language. Beginning with Genesis 11, the Bible teaches that nations are an invention of the sovereign God. Although all human beings came from one set of parents, they were separated into different linguistic communities as a result of human sinfulness. Living in a particular nation can be hellish, but sovereign nation-states serve as a barrier to global totalitarianism. The apostle Paul said to the Athenians,

> And he made from one man every nation of mankind to live on all the face of the earth, having determined allotted periods and the boundaries of their dwelling place, that they should seek God.[6]

Just as Jesus, Peter, and Paul experienced the oppressive nature of Europe's (Roman) imperialism, so did the reformers such as Wycliffe, Hus, Luther, and Tyndale. It was easy for them to recognize the significance of the Bible's teaching regarding national identity. This concept plays a pivotal role in the Bible's narrative from Genesis all the way to the last book of Revelation.

The narrative begins with God's promise to make Abraham a great nation. The promise included descendants, ownership of a particular land, authority to govern, and economic prosperity subject to his people obeying God's law.[7] God's promise became the basis for his descendants' attachment to the promised land and its history. It made nationalism a special Jewish value.

The Old Testament is the history of twelve tribes becoming one nation, under a common law overseen by elders, with or without a king. The king's primary responsibility was their common defense. Priests and prophets helped elders keep a check on the king that he lived and operated under God's law. When these twelve people-groups bound themselves together to obey God's authority, they flourished. When tribalism overrode national identity under one God and one law, they went into slavery. The Old Testament inspired Hebrew tribes to live as a unified nation following the principles of divine justice. It taught them to transcend tribal loyalties and worship the one true God together, inviting all the nations—in fact, all creation—to join in worshipping him.

Jewish nationalism, which inspired English and Indian poets, became an explicit part of biblical poetry after the southern tribes (Judah) were taken to Babylon as captives. One cannot understand the influence of English poets like Tennyson, Cowper, and Blake without understanding Jewish nationalism, expressed in these psalms:

> You will arise and have pity on Zion [Jerusalem];
> it is the time to favor her;
> the appointed time has come.
> For your servants hold her stones dear
> and have pity on her dust.[8]

By the waters of Babylon,
there we sat down and wept,
when we remembered Zion.
If I forget you, O Jerusalem,
let my right hand forget its skill!
Let my tongue stick to the roof of my mouth,
if I do not remember you,
if I do not set Jerusalem
above my highest joy![9]

By virtue of being the temple-city, Jerusalem became sacred for the Jews—God's city.[10]

Being God's city, however, required that its inhabitants live by God's law. The failure to do so brought forth the prophets' condemnation and God's judgment. This gave a peculiar flavor to biblical patriotism—loving one's people and land was a reflection of God's own loving heart for his people. Biblical nationalism was different from Germany's secular nationalism. The former was God-centered rather than culture- or race-centered. Being a product of God's promise and law, it had to remain self-critical and repentant. Old Testament characters like Moses, Daniel, Nehemiah, and several of the prophets powerfully exhibited this peculiar, repentant nationalism.

Chapters 6 and 9 of the book of Daniel are the best examples of repentant nationalism. Daniel loved his nation enough to fast and pray for its rebuilding. He risked being thrown into the lions' den to pray for Jerusalem's restoration. The Babylonians had destroyed his holy city, but he never cursed them. In fact, he devoted his life to serving Nebuchadnezzar, the very king who razed Jerusalem to the ground.

The prophet Jeremiah, an eyewitness to Jerusalem's destruction, shaped Daniel's nationalism, telling Daniel to serve his nation's "enemies." Jeremiah's advice to Daniel's fellow captives in Babylon was the opposite of what some mosques today teach in Britain. Jeremiah asked Jewish exiles to "seek the welfare of the city [Babylon] where I have sent you into exile, and pray to the Lord on its behalf, for in its welfare you will find your welfare."[11]

Daniel's nationalism was not an exception. Nehemiah also loved his people, his land, and his ruined city enough to risk his life to rebuild the physical, psychological, and moral ruins of his nation. It was this kind of biblical nationalism that inspired English poets. They were deeply critical of England's sins and yet they yearned to see it rebuilt as a new Jerusalem. In his poem "England," William Cowper (1731–1800) wrote: "England, with all thy faults, I love thee still." William Blake's (1757–1827) poem "Jerusalem" is still sung in English churches. He condemned England's "dark satanic mills" but concluded his poem with a resolve that came directly from the book of Nehemiah:

> *I will not cease from mental fight,*
> *Nor shall my sword sleep in my hand,*
> *Till we have built Jerusalem*
> *In England's green and pleasant land.*

Nineteenth-century Europe secularized biblical nationalism. That led to avoidable bloodshed and made *nationalism* a dirty word. Abraham's great-grandson Joseph learned through his life experiences that God chose him (as an individual) and his people to bless all the nations of the world. His future generations had to fight bloody wars to take their promised land and consolidate their freedom. (The British, the Americans, and Mahatma Gandhi's followers also fought to win or preserve their freedom.) But once Abraham's descendants obtained their land, their nationalism was no threat to other nations. They believed in God's sovereignty and that, just as God had given their land to them, he had also given lands to the Edomites, Moabites, Ishmaelites, and Assyrians. And Abraham's descendants believed they had been chosen to bless other nations, to serve them as God's light.

By contrast, Germany's secular nationalism became a threat to all the nations of Europe because it was not based on a belief in God's sovereignty as expressed in Paul's teaching in Acts 17:26–27. Albert Einstein, a German Jew, called nationalism a deadly disease of infant nations because he experienced arrogant nationalism that killed six million of his people. His denunciation of nationalism applies to the counterfeit, secularized version. It neglects the fact that the Bible, which inspired the English national identity, also inspired international human solidarity.

The Jewish prophets knew that God's promise to bless their nation was contingent upon their people obeying God's law. Their love for their nation enabled them to critique their own culture and rulers in the light of God's higher moral law. Jewish rulers killed many of their prophets, and they even crucified their Messiah. But the Old Testament helped the West to become a self-critical culture in a healthy way. It taught Western governments to respect the freedoms of their "prophets" or writers who expose corruption and call for reform. Nonbiblical cultures pay only lip service to a free press.

The British presence in India showed that British nationalism, when it was anchored in God's sovereignty, was the source of a healthy balance between love for one's nation and international concern.

Jesus demonstrated this balance. While he came first to "the lost sheep of the house of Israel,"[12] he also asked his disciples to go to every nation as missionaries, beginning with their capital, Jerusalem.[13] This teaching inspired Englishmen like William Carey to come to India to serve, educate, and liberate Indians by introducing the biblical-European ideas of nation-state and nationalism.

Indian polytheism assumed that each tribe and caste had a distinct god. Therefore, each caste had its own *dharma*, or religious duty. They could not be united as equals before one law from one God that applied equally to every people group. Like most other cultures, India's religious culture produced neither nationalism nor internationalism. It had no sense of a global mission. In contrast, the Bible taught monotheism, the idea that there is only one God for the whole universe and that he loves the whole world. He chose Abraham and his descendants as his special people, but only in order to bless "all the nations of the earth" through them.[14]

For Bible translators such as William Carey, this balance between nationalism and internationalism meant that they could love both their own nation and the country to which they were called to serve.

In nineteenth-century India, it meant that while the employees of the East India Company made their money and went back to England, missionaries such as William Carey spent their lives and wealth in service to India.

Polytheism divides people from one another according to their gods and goddesses. Geographic India became vulnerable to colonization, first by Muslims and then by the Europeans, because Hinduism weakened the Hindus. It did not embrace all Hindus as equal citizens of India. The non-Aryans were categorized as *dasa, dasyu, asura, rakshasa, malichha* (slaves, servants, demons, monsters, untouchables, etc.).

Bible translators such as Carey, Buchanan, Martyn, and Gilchrist began to create a new national identity for modern India. The Bible's humble, repentant nationalism, balanced with a sense of international responsibility, attracted Hindu writers such as Madhusudan Dutt to Christ and to England. After coming to Christ in 1843, Dutt became fluent in ten European and Indian languages. He read Milton, Homer, Virgil, Dante, and Tasso in their original languages. Later, under the influence of his missionary friends, Dutt realized that even though his poetic hero Milton was the minister for Latin in Oliver Cromwell's government, he wrote his poetry for the people in their still under-developed language, English.

Dutt realized that if he really wanted to follow Milton, he would need to write in Bengali. One day, on a sudden impulse and encouraged by some of his friends' enthusiasm for Bengali drama, he turned his hand to writing in his mother tongue, giving up English as a vehicle for literary expression for good—although with great reluctance.

Dutt's turn to his vernacular ushered in the Bengali nationalist movement. He used his poetry to give voice to his love for Bengal. "Light up Bengal, India's jewel may she bide!"[15] he prayed, applying the spirit of English poetry to India. Through his poetry, Bengal did go on to become India's jewel, giving lead to the Indian Renaissance. Bengal became the birthplace of Indian nationalism, revivalism, and reformism. It produced most of India's early reformers, litterateurs, nationalists, and intellectuals. "Why has Providence given this queenly, this majestic land for a prey and a spoil to the Anglo-Saxon?" asked Dutt. And he answered, because "it is the mission of the Anglo-Saxon to renovate, to regenerate, to Christianize the Hindu—to churn this vast ocean that it may restore the things of beauty now buried in its liquid wilderness."[16]

As my nation's linguistic engagement with Christian nations illustrates, nationalism need not be a disease. When yoked to the reforming power of the Bible, it can become a powerful redemptive force. India suffered under Muslim and European domination for nine centuries, but in that entire time no one united us with a sense of national identity. Nor did anyone unleash the energy to overcome foreign domination. India did not produce a Gandhi under the Moguls. Hindu military generals sustained the Mogul empire. Only when Bible translators began developing our languages did biblical ideas begin sweeping through our land.

As it did in Europe, the Bible empowered our people by cultivating a nationalist consciousness. Our national leaders, such as Gandhi and Nehru, provided leadership to the nationalist movement, but they would have had no "nation" to lead without the biblical idea of nation that came to us through the linguistic revolution initiated by Bible translation and English literature introduced by Christian education.

Before examining how the Bible created modern education, let us review its impact on literature.

Chapter Eleven

LITERATURE

WHY DID PILGRIMS BUILD NATIONS?

K hushwant Singh (b. 1915) is a secular Sikh and one of India's best-known writers. For decades he also taught English literature at Delhi University. He has often said that he reads at least two chapters of the Bible every day, because no one can understand English literature without first reading the Bible.

The Bible is just as necessary to understand the literature written during the nineteenth and early twentieth centuries in India, a period often referred to as the "Indian Renaissance." One could, for example, read any poem from *Gitanjali* in a Christian church without anyone suspecting that the Bengali poet, Nobel laureate Rabindranath Tagore (1861–1941), was not a Christian. The Indian Renaissance triggered various reform movements and beginning with Madhusudan Dutt created Indian nationalism.

As a part of Europe, England inherited great books, epics, and myths from the Greco-Roman era. But arguably, none of this literature exerted the same influence on English writers as did the Bible—an Asian book. The Bible's direct and indirect influence on English literature outstrips Homer's influence on the development of Greek and Latin literature. Ruth apRoberts, a Canadian expert on Victorian literature, agreed with Khushwant Singh when she said, "Virtually all writers of English draw on the Bible, and the more memorable ones are the great recyclers of biblical elements."[1]

Homer's heroes were exciting. They were terrifying when armed with weapons. They were entertaining, but readers could not follow these heroes in efforts to build great and free nations. In contrast, Bunyan's faltering Pilgrim started out with nothing but the burden of sin on his back and a Bible in his hands. Thousands of preachers talked about him. Hundreds of millions of readers meditated on him and sang about his quest, and many became pilgrims themselves.

The Bible has exercised unique authority over European literature because it is different from all other stories. First of all, it has a ring of truth. Tradition ascribes Moses as the principal author of Genesis, the first book of the Bible. But Moses was born around four hundred years after Joseph, whose narrative concludes Genesis. The author did not know the people he wrote about. He talked to no eyewitnesses. He had no primary sources that we know of to examine. And he makes no claim resembling the Prophet Muhammad's that an angel appeared to him in a prophetic trance and revealed the stories to him. Therefore, the heroes and events described in Genesis could be called "legends" handed down from generation to generation.

This oral tradition had plenty of time for gifted storytellers to embellish it. Yet no one turned them into anything like Indian or Greek epics. Brilliant editors could have used those centuries to refine and polish the narratives, for Genesis is superbly crafted. Why didn't a storyteller turn his ancestors Abraham, Isaac, Jacob, and Joseph into heroes like Achilles or Odysseus?

Abraham did fight and win one battle against four kings who had beaten five kings and taken his nephew captive. Yet Genesis says nothing about his bravery, prowess, military strategy, or skill with arms. Nor does it say anything about God performing a miracle to help him win that battle. The narrative appears mundane. Its point is to show Abraham's loyalty to his rather selfish nephew and his integrity in refusing to keep his neighbors' goods that he recovered in battle. One-tenth was given to the king of Salem (later Jerusalem), who fed his men, and the rest was returned to its rightful owners.

The Bible suggests that Abraham's heroism consisted of being a simple, fearful man who believed God's promise and obeyed him. When I first read Genesis as an adult, I was shocked by the timidity of Abraham and his son Isaac. They were so afraid of lawless men around them that they described their wives as their "sisters." One petty king, Abimelech, took Abraham's word at face value and herded Abraham's beautiful "sister" into his harem! Abraham did nothing of the sort that Ram, the divine hero of India's religious epic, the *Ramayana*, did to Ravana, after he had taken Ram's wife Sita into his harem. Ram organized an army of monkeys, built a bridge across the ocean, burned Sri Lanka, brought his wife back in a flying machine, and inspired James Cameron's *Avatar*. Abimelech, on the other hand, returned Abraham's wife because God rebuked him in a dream.[2]

Aren't divine interventions in the domestic affairs of an insignificant nomad reasonable grounds for dismissing the Bible as myth? Quite the contrary. Their shocking simplicity inspires confidence that the Bible records reality. The Bible's narratives are true, not myths. Its realism is neither an artist's creation, nor contrived. Far from being an aesthetic goal, the Bible's realism is a means of conveying the message of our Creator caring for his creation. He intervenes in our personal and national histories in response to humble faith. These narratives carry within them a stamp of authority absent in classical legends.

The German philologist, literary critic, and comparative scholar Erich Auerbach compared Homer's Odysseus to Abraham in the account of Abraham's sacrifice of Isaac. He concluded that although no historical evidence is available for the biblical narrative, its literary character is the opposite of Greek myths.

> [The biblical narrator] . . . had to believe in the objective truth of the story of Abraham's sacrifice—the existence of the sacred ordinances of life rested upon the truth of this and similar stories. He had to believe in it passionately; or else (as many rationalistic interpreters believed and perhaps still believe) he had to be a conscious liar—no harmless liar like Homer, who lied to give pleasure, but a political

liar with a definite end in view, lying in the interest of a claim to absolute authority.[3]

Indian myths, like Greco-Roman myths, are about aristocrats—the ruling elite and sages. The heroes of Genesis, by contrast, are ordinary people with feet of clay. Abraham and Sarah were elderly nomads who could not even bear a baby until God visited them. He blessed them for their hospitality to strangers and promised to bless all the nations of the earth through their descendants.[4]

Homer wouldn't pick any of us as heroes. But all of us can be like Abraham and Isaac, Jacob and Joseph. If extraordinary things can happen to simple people, if through the obedience of faith we can become a blessing to our neighbors and to the nations of the earth, then all of us can be heroes.

The Bible's message that God is a compassionate Savior is another distinctive that made the Bible a source of nation-building literature. God does incredible things through ordinary people because he is committed to blessing his children.

Another feature that contributed to its unique power was that the Bible enabled thinkers in different cultures at different times to make sense of their world. The Bible's narrative begins at the beginning, takes a realistic look at evil—its causes, terrible consequences, and cure—and concludes by projecting a prophetic glimpse into a glorious future. The biblical history thus offered an unfolding worldview. That enabled big-picture writers like John Milton and J. R. R. Tolkien to make sense of the mess in our world, while allowing Shakespeare to find meaning in the ordinary, tragic struggles of young lovers like Romeo and Juliet.

Transformation and development of character is an important feature of the Bible that has had enormous impact on modern writing. Homer's heroes don't change. But Jacob does. He begins his career by deceiving his father, stealing his brother's blessings, and cheating his father-in-law. His experiences with God transform him into a very different person. He then blesses his children and grandchildren with a prophetic faith in the future. Moses is an archetypal reluctant hero, who has greatly influenced Hollywood's idea of a hero. Simon, who denied his Lord three times, is transformed into Peter—the rock. Saul of Tarsus begins his career as a persecutor of the church but becomes Paul, an apostle who suffers for the truth.

Biblical characters change as God calls individuals to follow him rather than culture. God asks Noah to build a boat—an act of prophetic judgment on the corruption of his times. God asks of Abraham: "Go from your country and your kindred and your father's house to the land that I will show you."[5] God chooses Abraham for his friend: "I *am* Almighty God; walk before Me and be blameless. And I will make My covenant between Me and you."[6] God implies that we are to walk with Him, not follow the traditions and counsel of rebellious men. To make a difference one must live differently.

Biblical narratives of individual transformation that impacted history became an essential feature of modern literature and art. The Bible produced writers who were world changers. This was dramatically different from the avatars of Indian epics, like Rama and Krishna, who preserved *dharma*—the status quo. They posed a problem for Indian novelists. Meenakshi Mukherjee, a literary critic teaching English at Delhi's Jawaharlal Nehru University, best captured this tension:

> The picaresque tradition in the European novel has achieved one main purpose—it had liberated the protagonist from the rigidity of a static society into being a free agent who could to some extent shape his own destiny. *Robinson Crusoe* (1719), *Moll Flanders* (1722), *Pamela* (1740), three early examples of the English novel, show how the central character is in each case an active rather than a passive agent challenging his or her fate. The Indian novelist had to operate in a tradition-bound society where neither a man's profession nor his marriage was his personal affair. His life was mapped out by his family or his community or his caste. In the rigidly hierarchical familial and social structure of nineteenth-century India, individualism was not an easy quality to render in literature.[7]

The Bible exercised a unique authority over creative writers by presenting an unfolding view of the world and life that claimed to be true. This claim demanded that our literature and culture confront and conform to God's revealed will. Since our world is so different from the Bible's world of shepherds, sowers, and tax collectors, writers found plenty of room to be imaginative in making our world more biblical. As Auerbach put it: "Far from seeking, like Homer, merely to make us forget our own reality for a few hours, it [the Bible] seeks to overcome our reality: we are to fit our own life into its world, feel ourselves to be elements in its structure of universal history."[8]

In contrast to Homeric poems, the Bible presents itself as our sole authority with truth that explains history while giving ultimate meaning. Far from stifling thought, its claim enabled believers to interpret and apply it to their ever-changing world. This made it possible for creative writers to anchor on the rock of timeless truth while allowing their imaginations to fly with and beyond their times.

As T. S. Eliot put it, the "Bible has had a *literary* influence upon English literature not because it has been considered as literature, but because it has been considered as the report of the Word of God. And the fact that men of letters now discuss it as 'literature' probably indicates the *end* of its 'literary' influence."[9]

The Bible's influence on English literature is illustrated throughout its history.

EARLY ENGLISH LITERATURE

Vernacular dialects became Old English in the seventh and eighth centuries AD. Monasteries were thriving in Europe. From Italy to England, Ireland to Spain, monasteries used Latin. But in England some of them began writing English literature. Among England's earliest chronologists, the Venerable Bede (AD 673–735) told of the shepherd Caedmon in a seventh-century monastery. One night the illiterate Caedmon miraculously received a gift for poetic verse in his vernacular Anglo-Saxon (a Germanic forebearer of Old English). When the abbess in charge heard Caedmon's gift, she had him study the Bible. He then paraphrased biblical narratives into vernacular poetry understandable by even the roughest-hewn English peasant. [10]

While Caedmon is exceptional, Old English poetry has a consistently biblical flavor, from "The Dream of the Rood," about Christ's victory over sin on the cross (rood), to *Beowulf*, an epic poem interspersed with biblical comments on merits or demerits of the narrative. Anglo-Saxon poets consistently heeded the Bible's vernacular literature.

RENAISSANCE ENGLISH LITERATURE

This biblical consciousness became conspicuous in England's sixteenth- and seventeenth-century Renaissance literature. Dr. Louise Cowan, editor of *Invitation to the Classics*, was an English department chairman and graduate school dean. Although her university education had demolished her childhood faith, teaching *Hamlet* began to open her eyes to biblical faith and heroism. Hamlet's friend Horatio cautions him to call off his duel. But Hamlet's faith overcomes this warning. "There is special providence in the fall of a sparrow," Hamlet declares, alluding to Jesus comforting his worried disciples that not even a sparrow falls to the ground without his Father's will.[11] Hamlet places his life in God's hands, affirming God's sovereignty: "If it be now, 'tis not to come; if it be not to come, it will be now. If it be not now, yet it will come. The readiness is all."[12]

Cowan's professors and scholarly authorities made Shakespeare a nonbeliever—a free thinker. They described Shakespeare as a genius writing for money, not art. His comedies were but bits of froth, his tragedies nihilistic. Shakespeare, they believed, summed up his secular outlook in *King Lear*:

> *As flies to wanton boys are we to gods;*
> *They kill us for their sport.*[13]

Reading Shakespeare to her class forced Cowan to reconsider:

This mention of providence struck me as being in marked contrast with Hamlet's earlier anguished irony. It took on the aura of something momentous. What did Shakespeare intend his readers to think of so radical a turnabout? Did it not in fact imply that the author himself saw and understood the change wrought in Hamlet by faith? . . . I pored over *Hamlet* several times during the ensuing months, each time finding further evidence of Shakespeare's spiritual outlook. And gradually it became apparent that his perspective was not simply spiritual, but overtly Christian. Sacrificial love was evident everywhere in his dramas. *Grace* was one of his key words; *evil* was its darker counterpart. His comedies in particular were virtual illustrations of themes and passages from Scripture. By today, of course, several scholars have come to acknowledge and even explore Shakespeare's Christian faith; but at that time my discovery seemed monumental. It meant recognizing the secularism of our day and discerning the bias of most scholars.[14]

THE CLASSICAL INFLUENCE OF GREEK AND ROME

Pre-Christian Greek and Roman literature enormously influenced Christian Europe. Highlighting the Bible's foundational role in the West's rich literary tradition is not to say that ancient literatures are without merit and influence. Classical Greeks and Romans produced some of the West's best literature. Poets like Æschylus, Virgil, Homer, and Seneca skillfully crafted stories. They delved into psychology and critically explored culture, setting them apart from most world literature. Yet, for all their genius, they failed to find a foundation for positive cultural change. Their worldview was infused with fatalism under petty gods. It gave no basis for faith to move mountains. Their vicious, unpredictable gods inflict suffering on the good and bad alike. Why, then, choose good, if compromise makes life easier?

Playwrights like Æschylus defended Athens' democracy, but people used it for personal gain over the *polis*'s good. Prominent Athenian politicians were frequently exiled by political gamesmanship. This democracy executed Socrates for castigating its self-indulgence. The great poet Virgil (70–19 BC) wrote the *Aeneid* as propaganda that all mythology and history culminated in Caesar Augustus's reign.

A persistent Western theme is the centrality of journeys in developing plot. Homer's *Odyssey* followed Odysseus's long journey home from the Trojan War. Written in an age of never-ending war, returning to one's wife and home was the climax of heroism. Virgil's hero, Aeneas, left his home in Troy to found the imperial city of Rome. In his *Aeneid*, Virgil skillfully plies the power of poetic diction to this journey motif.*

Rome's Christians had to grapple with the purpose of pagan poets. Virgil's Rome was but grand literary fantasy. Caesar's real Rome tortured, crucified, and burned them alive. The martyrs' experience confirmed the biblical worldview that sinful humans are incapable of building a just city without divine help.

In his classic *The City of God*, St. Augustine (AD 354–430) brought this tension into focus. For Jews, Jerusalem was the city of God. But Christians viewed themselves as "strangers and pilgrims in this world."[15] They sought "for a city whose designer and builder is God."[16] The Bible's last book, Revelation, reveals the New Jerusalem—a heavenly paradise for God's people. Augustine embedded this biblical goal deep into Europe's subconscious.

Dante Alighieri (1265–1321) used this journey of Christian faith in *The Divine Comedy*, rivaled only by John Milton's *Paradise Lost*. While Dante chose Virgil as the guide through hell and purgatory, he did not deify his Latin forebearer. Instead, he explored contemporary religious battles navigating the spheres of hell (the *Inferno*), purgatory** (the *Purgatorio*), and heaven (the *Paradiso*). His cosmic journey ends with a vision of the triune Godhead:

> *In the profundity of the clear substance*
> *Of the deep light, appeared to me three circles*
> *Of three colours and equal circumference;*

---

* A *motif* is an element in a story that appears repeatedly and meaningfully, as with the messiah motif in the *Matrix* trilogy. In this case, the journey is a motif that appears in a number of different works, not simply many times in one work.

** In Catholic theology, purgatory is an intermediate place between heaven and hell where baptized Christians suffer as penance for their sins while on earth before ascending to heaven. Protestants reject this doctrine as having no biblical basis.

And the first seemed to be reflected by the second,
As a rainbow by a rainbow, and the third
Seemed like a flame breathed equally from both ...
O eternal light, existing in yourself alone,
Alone knowing yourself; and who, known to yourself
And knowing, love and smile upon yourself![17]

Dante's profound journey serves as a divine metaphor for the values necessary to develop the city of God on earth. Just as the Father, Son, and Holy Spirit are "of three colours and equal circumference," humans, too—who find their "effigy" in the face of the Trinity—ought to function as individuals while retaining collective goals and institutions. The only force that can effect this unity, Dante believed, is divine love. Without that love people act like the damned in Dante's hell—they abuse, insult, and cannibalize one another with no check on their destructive behavior.

Mimicking the city of God while on earth became the driving vision for history's most famous journeying sects: the American Pilgrims. Those sailing from England to America on the *Mayflower* knew that they were going away from Jerusalem's "holy land." Why, then, did they call themselves "pilgrims"? Because they were looking for a New Jerusalem, a place for God's will to be done "on earth as it is [done] in heaven."[18] They sought a land where God's law and grace would rule in place of human oppression and wickedness. The forerunners of the Pilgrims, poets, and writers were nurtured on this biblical idea of a New Jerusalem.

This idea of the heavenly Jerusalem inspired great literary works such as *Pilgrim's Progress* (1678) by John Bunyan (1628–88), which drove biblical spirituality deep into the soul of Western civilization. Unlike Homer's hero, Bunyan's pilgrim is not returning home. Bunyan wrote, "I saw a man . . . with his face [turned away] from His own House, a Book in his hand, and a great burden upon his back."[19] Nor did Pilgrim follow Virgil's hero to found another imperial city. Pilgrim set his face on a journey to the celestial city, the City of God. His weapon was not a sword, but a book—the Bible. His goal was not to battle the proud and impose his law upon the conquered. His first goal was deliverance from his own burden of sin and overcoming overpowering temptations.

Bunyan's hero is poles apart from Homer's heroes, Achilles and Odysseus. Achilles is huge, swift, immortally beautiful, and the "most terrifying of all men." Odysseus is a trickster, a master of disguises and artful deceptions, who is able to endure countless hardships to cleave to his one virtuous purpose—to return home to his family. But in England, Bunyan's vision of the hero as a pilgrim won out. For four centuries following Bunyan, English-speaking Christians have sung the heroism of pilgrimage into the subconscious of their culture:

> *Who would true valour see,*
> *Let him come hither,*
> *One here will constant be,*
> *Come wind, come weather,*
> *There's no discouragement*
> *Shall make him once relent*
> *His first avow'd intent*
> *To be a pilgrim.*[20]

Bunyan was thrown in prison for three months for refusing to follow an Elizabethan Act against religious freedom. He ended up spending a total of twelve years in prison on different counts and occasions, giving him time to write sixty books. *Pilgrim's Progress* was translated into Dutch, French, and Welsh within his lifetime. Since then it has been translated into more than two hundred languages. After the Bible, it is the second most translated and published book. It was through this book that Puritanism entered the mainstream of English religious life.

Bunyan's pilgrims succeeded where Homer's and Virgil's heroes could not, as Bunyan's pilgrims built cities and nations that were clean outside because they emphasized cleanliness inside—in the inner life of the spirit. But this literary revolution went far beyond clean cities. In "Puritans as Democrats," historian Jacques Barzun concludes that the socio-economic-political reforms that our age ascribes to the Enlightenment actually came from writers expounding the Bible:

> That the English wrapped up every idea and attitude in religious language and used precedents from Scriptures as their best author-ity gives the period an aura of a struggle about obsolete causes. But these causes were double, and the ideas hidden by the pious language were . . . pregnant for the future. The sects and leaders classed as Puritans, Presbyterians, Independents, were social and political reformers. They differed mainly in the degree of their radicalism.[21]

If Barzun is right, then have secular universities deceived several generations into believing that the great ideas that built the mod-ern world came from secular Enlightenment? John Lilburne's career (1614–57) could help us understand the answer.

Lilburne was a member of the revolution Barzun is talking about. A contemporary of John Milton and John Bunyan, as a pamphleteer John Lilburne became one of the most radical Puritan writers of that time. He applied the Bible to social, economic, and political issues, helping to lay the foundations of our modern world. His challenge to the leadership and institutions of his day was so profound that he was arrested time and again. He narrowly escaped martyrdom more than once. Barzun wrote,

> Lilburne deserves more fame than he has been granted by poster-ity. Plumb in the middle of the 17C here is a writer who declares and demands the rights of man. His program was the one that has made the glory of the 18C theorists and his behavior has become standard policy for revolutionists down to the present. His handicap is that although he invokes the law of nature, his argument is full of biblicisms.[22]

Barzun points out that what Lilburne carried whole in his mind, dozens of his fellow Puritan pamphleteers advocated piecemeal. Many called for a republic, the vote for all, the abolition of rank and privilege, equality before law, free trade, and a better distribution of property. A few urged toleration. All of them, however, justified these goals out of Scripture. Because of their "bias," modern historians trace these ideas to secular sources rather than to the Puritan writings in which they originated. They prefer to source free trade from Adam Smith rather than Lilburne's discussion of the parable of the talents. With their bias, they would rather credit John Locke than an obscure Anabaptist preacher for the principle that all men are born free and equal.

The preacher quoted St. Paul, who said that God has "no respect of persons" and that there is "no difference between Jew and Gentile."[23] Other Puritans insisted that God's grace is free—all share in it as they share in Adam's sin. Hence superior rank has no warrants; the only superiority is that of spirit. To rationalists, this was no way to argue.

LITERATURE IN THE SECULAR WEST

Not until 1900 did secular literature outsell religious literature in England—though much "secular" Western literature was a byproduct of the Bible. One example is England's poet laureate Alfred, Lord Tennyson (1809–92), son of clergyman Dr. George Clayton Tennyson. Tennyson is classified as a secular writer, but his entire corpus is imbued with a religious sensibility. Henry Van Dyke's analysis of Tennyson includes a forty-seven-page-long list of biblical quotations and allusions that appear in the poet's works.[24]

Similarly, just the index of Bible references in the writings of John Ruskin (1819–1900)—who had a great impact on Mahatma Gandhi—runs to more than three hundred pages. Ruskin was not a theologian or Bible teacher. He was the Slade Professor of Art at Oxford and wrote on art and architecture, rebelling against the aesthetically numbing and socially debasing effects of the Industrial Revolution, and exploring the domestic, social, moral, and spiritual effects of art and architecture.[25]

Though dominated by secular humanism, the twentieth-century elite failed to weaken the power of biblical narrative in literature.

Secular humanism rejects the biblical worldview of a personal, rational, meaningful universe with good triumphing over evil, providing the hope of redemption. Jean Paul Sartre (1905–80) masterfully expressed the atheistic existential wasteland in *Nausea* (1938). In Sartre's world, every aspect of human existence is ludicrous. Even the torturous rape and murder of a young girl is trivialized as just one more meaningless event in an empty universe. Sartre's solution to this dilemma is to escape our absurd existence by creating something (in this case a jazz recording) that exists independent of ourselves.

In *The Stranger*, Albert Camus (1913–60) similarly explores the bumbling life of a degenerate, who—for no apparent reason whatsoever—murders a stranger on an Algerian beach. While a well-wrought piece of literature, it provides no basis for the moral reforms that Camus sought. It may resonate with people dragged into depression by their belief in the meaninglessness of life. Yet it provides no impetus for them to lift themselves back out of their existential angst and make their world better.

The stories that inspired us, that fired our imaginations and called for social reform—even in the secular twentieth century—have often been inspired by the biblical worldview. *East of Eden* (1952) by Nobel Prize–winner John Steinbeck (1902–68) is a modern retelling of the rivalry between Cain and Abel from Genesis. In contrast to Eastern fatalism, the Bible teaches that humans have genuine freedom. The premise of Steinbeck's novel stands or falls on the translation of the Hebrew word *timshel* in Genesis 4:7. The overarching message is that humans are slaves neither of fate nor of forces beyond their control, such as the stars. Rather, we have freedom, the ability to choose. *Timshel*, according to Steinbeck, means that people can overcome sin.

The Bible's influence on literature continues unabated to this day. For example, the hero in Stephen King's *The Green Mile* is a Christ figure. King explained:

Not long after I began *The Green Mile* and realized that my main character was an innocent man likely to be executed for the crime of another, I decided to give him the initials J.C., after the most famous innocent man of all time. I first saw this done in *Light in August* (still my favorite Faulkner novel), where the sacrificial lamb is named Joe Christmas. Thus death-row inmate John Bowes became John Coffey. I wasn't sure, right up to the end of the book, if my J.C. would live or die.[26]

Another of King's stories, *Black House* (2001), has a strong biblical redemption theme. After the hero, Jack Sawyer, saves a Wisconsin town from a serial killer and in the process liberates multitudes of children of every race and language from an evil, other-dimensional force, he is shot repeatedly by a crazed woman. Before slumping down, he holds up his bloody hand pierced by a bullet and looks at her with forgiveness in his eyes. He is then whisked away to a parallel universe where "the Carpenter-God" has more work for him to accomplish.

But King's concept of redemptive transcendent reality contrasts sharply with the trend in contemporary literature. Today's Western literature is adept in using aesthetic forms to analyze and diagnose the problems in Western culture. Writers such as Don DeLillo, Umberto Eco, José Saramago, and Julian Barnes—masters of form and the aesthetic pleasures—have done significant work to point out where the West urgently needs improvement. They have been much less successful, however, in offering a positive source of reform for Western culture.

Western writers since the 1960s have found meaning in their racial or ethnic traditions, in the praxes of the various feminisms, in the customs of sexual identity groups, and in the traditions of their geographic regions. While these writers have located many important centers of cultural activity and identity, few have been willing to take the next step in asserting that their personal center could solve the West's malaise *in general*. They assume that we as human beings cannot locate any source of meaning outside our local identity groups—that there is no source of transcendent authority from which to call for broad social and institutional reform.

The other dominant school of Western writers advocates living lives of "free play." It believes that if we continually reinvent ourselves in the midst of our fluctuating social, psychological, and economic environments, we will be able to meet our immediate needs. In practical, if not theoretical Darwinian terms, they assume that nothing exists outside the moment. To meet the needs of each moment is the best one can hope for.

This has some truth in that we act and speak according to our context. Yet this concept of free play has lost any sense of a unifying force holding together the disparate elements of modern life. Proponents of this free play reject Dante's trinitarian view that, amid the diversity and fragmentation of our individual lives, a unity can emerge to give breadth, depth, and meaning to our different experiences.

Without a trinitarian God, most postmodern writers are left with little choice but to immerse themselves in the moment in an attempt to forget their very real need for transcendence. In their perpetual search for personal soul, they exacerbated the West's loss of its collective soul.

The Bible's impact on literature made it the West's source of cultural authority. A rejection of the Bible is resulting in moral and intellectual anarchy. Second-generation Muslims are therefore reexamining Islam in their search for a way to fill the vacuum created by secular education. Let us next consider the Bible's influence on education.

Chapter Twelve

UNIVERSITY

Why Educate Your Subjects?

W hy did my university in Allahabad have a church,* but not a Hindu temple or a Muslim mosque? Because the university was invented and established by Christians.

Neither colonialism nor commerce spread modern education around the world. Soldiers and merchants do not educate. Education was a Christian missionary enterprise. It was integral to Christian missions because modern education is a fruit of the Bible. The biblical Reformation, born in European universities, took education out of the cloister and spread it around the globe.

In chapter 3 I told of how the university shook my teenage faith, and why I decided to test if the Bible's prediction—that all nations would be blessed through Abraham's descendants—was being fulfilled. I was astonished to discover that the Bible was the source of practically everything good in my hometown, even the secular university that undermined the Bible.

At the confluence of the "holy" rivers Ganges, Yamuna, and the mythical** Saraswati, Allahabad is revered as one of India's holiest places. Rivers were natural highways for people and cargo before the

---

* The Holy Trinity Church was a part of the University of Allahabad until a few decades ago.
** There is no Saraswati now, though there may have been an underground stream at some point in history.

British built our roads and railways. The Ganges and Yamuna enabled people to travel north to the Himalayas and southeast to the Bay of Bengal. Consequently Allahabad hosts the world's largest assembly, the Kumbh Mela, every twelve years.

Akbar, the greatest Mogul emperor,* built a massive fort in 1583 at our town's strategic confluence, renaming it the "abode of Allah." An Ashoka pillar (232 BC)** commemorates the Buddha's first sermon at nearby Sarnath.

Around 263 BC Ashoka had converted to Buddhism in reaction to the horrors of war prompted by his remarkable imperial expansion. He erected these ornate pillars, often as tall as fifty feet, to commemorate notable points on a Buddhist pilgrimage he undertook around the year 253 BC. Most of the pillars are inscribed with imperial edicts and the reason that the particular location of a pillar is a notable one. Subsequent rulers of India have occasionally transcribed their own histories upon these pillars.

Annual festivals drew every important Hindu religious, political, economic, and intellectual leader to this confluence in the last two millennia. The money pilgrims donated is incalculable. Yet the Hindu, Buddhist, and Muslim civilizations did not establish a single significant institution of learning in this center of Gangetic civilization.

Some "holy men" near Allahabad's confluence were at least as brilliant and dedicated as the friars who founded Oxford and Cambridge. They failed to establish a university because of their religious quest to "kill" their minds. They lay on nails, buried themselves, or sat covered only with ashes and cow dung, smoking drugs, and seeking enlightenment. Their path to enlightenment was Jnana Marg—the path of knowledge of Self, God, or oneness of everything. Yet they had no interest in the material world, for they thought it *maya* or illusion.

---

* The Moguls were a Muslim dynasty that conquered and ruled large parts of India from 1526 to about 1761. They built some of India's finest buildings, such as the Taj Mahal, Red Fort, and Jama Masjid. Akbar, the greatest of the Moguls, patronized some of our best poets, artists, and musicians.

** Ashoka pillars are a series of monuments raised by the Mauryan emperor Ashoka (ruled ca. 271 BC to 233 BC).

Their philosophy gave no motivation to accumulate partial, piecemeal worldly knowledge that is the hallmark of modern education. By contrast, the biblical view made modern science possible by enabling the Christian mind to be content with partial and finite knowledge, which grows incrementally through coordinated efforts over generations.

In Allahabad, the few Hindu educational institutions of the twentieth century were in response to the Christian initiatives. These imitations were not inspired by the Hindu worldview. Generally, Hindu learning was taught to young Brahmin men, not in institutions but in their gurus' homes.* In places like Nalanda and Takshila, the Buddhists built religious education centers.** By the second millennium, however, these centers were in decline. They disappeared completely with the Muslim conquest of India.

Takshila was about forty miles west of modern Rawalpindi in Pakistan. It was never as well organized as Nalanda.

Mogul India was one of the largest Muslim empires.*** But Muslims developed no noteworthy educational institutions in India. Historian Michael Edwardes summed up India's pre-British education:

> The type of education the British had found when they arrived
> in India was almost entirely religious, and higher education for
> Hindus and Muslims was purely literary. Hindu higher education
> was almost a Brahmin monopoly. Brahmins, the priestly caste,
> spent their time [in schools called Tols] studying religious texts in
> a dead language, Sanskrit. There were a number of schools [called
> Pathshalas], using living languages, but few Brahmins sent their
> children to such schools, where the main subject taught was the
> preparation of account. Muslim higher education was conducted

---

* guru: a personal religious teacher and spiritual guide in Hinduism. Hindu centers of learning, such as Varanasi, Ujjain, or Kanchi had learned gurus but did not have educational institutions comparable to a university.

** Nalanda, near Patna in Bihar, began as a major center of Buddhist learning during the Gupta period in the fifth century after Christ. By the twelfth century, it was in total ruins.

*** It included Pakistan and Bangladesh.

[in madrasas*] in a living language—Arabic, which was not spoken in India. But there were also schools which taught Persian** and some secular subjects. The state—as distinct from individual rulers—accepted no responsibility for education.[1]

It made sense for Akbar to fortify Allahabad to consolidate his Islamic rule. But it makes no sense to most people for British imperialists to build universities to educate their subjects for self-rule. Why? British evangelicals forced colonial rulers to educate Indians for freedom.[2] They founded our University of Allahabad as Muir Central College (1873) after its chief patron, Sir William Muir (1819–1905). Though lieutenant governor of the United Provinces, Muir was the greatest Christian apologist vis-à-vis Islam. By 1887, the college grew into the fourth Indo-British university in India after Calcutta, Madras, and Bombay. (Serampore was Dutch.)

Michael Edwardes explained the motive behind the Christian educational mission:

> The decision to concentrate on providing Western education in the English language was made from other motives than economy. . . . Education had moral, political, and commercial overtones in the eyes of such men as Macaulay. He, and those who thought like him, were following Evangelical rather than Utilitarian principles. It was Charles Grant who was the prophet of English education in India, not James Mill. Indeed, Mill was highly sceptical about the effectiveness of *any* [emphasis in the original] form of education in India. The moral overtones were, of course, Christian in character . . . Macaulay and others looked forward to a future in which Indians, having acquired a taste for "European civilization," might demand European institutions and even independence from Britain.[3]

---

* madrasa: a school where people go to learn about the religion of Islam.
** Persian was Mogul India's official language until 1837.

CHARLES GRANT (1746–1823)

The Indian government's educational records begin with extensive quotations from Charles Grant. He arrived in Bengal (1768) just as the devastating famine of 1769–70 killed millions. That famine motivated Grant to reform British administration to transform the Indian mind, agriculture, industry, and economy. Those secular goals, acceptable to non-Christians, were inspired by Grant's biblical worldview. He saw education as a foundation for his goals because India's "secular" problems emanated from its religious worldviews. Transforming India's economic culture required transforming its religious presuppositions.

Grant came to India as a secular, penniless young man to make money. He saw the corruption and misrule that enriched some Englishmen but destroyed Bengal's economy. Within this corruption, Grant saw Richard Bechner, his Christian boss, feed up to seven thousand people every day in Murshidabad, exerting "every nerve to alleviate the sufferings of the famine-stricken people." Later, in Calcutta, a personal tragedy—the deaths of his two daughters—forced Grant to address the questions of life and eternity. He became a Christian and met with two other men to study the Bible and pray. The Bible did not give him philosophical speculations or an absentee, distant Creator. Rather, it revealed a God intimately involved in human history. Jesus' mission to inaugurate God's kingdom for the poor was radically different from Grant's and his company's mission in India.

Studying the Bible enabled Grant to make God's mission his own. God's Word, as Grant concluded, required realigning the British mission with God's purposes for India. On September 17, 1787, Grant sent his famous appeal for missions to fourteen public figures in Britain.[4] The only positive response came from Charles Simeon (1759–1836) of Cambridge. Simeon was the vicar of Holy Trinity Church and a fellow of King's College. This influential preacher, sometimes called the father of modern evangelicalism, challenged students to serve India.

In 1790, Grant returned to England disappointed that his appeal for mission seemed to have gone unheeded. Then through amazing circumstances, he became a friend of William Wilberforce, an evangelical member of Parliament. Wilberforce had received Grant's appeal for India when he was sick. With his encouragement, Grant wrote his rationale for missions: *Observations on the State of Society among the Asiatic Subjects of Great Britain, particularly with respect to Morals and on the Means of Improving it. Written Chiefly in the Year 1792.*

Though not formally published until 1797, Grant's book was the acknowledged background of Parliament's 1793 debate on missions. In 1812, Parliament ordered it published as a state paper, as the best source of information on India. Grant's arguments for mission and education were inseparably intertwined. (Legal walls separating church and state in education were not in place yet.) His arguments triggered a movement that enabled India to become one of the world's leading centers for education.

Grant addressed his book to British leaders who knew how the Bible and Christian universities had helped reform British society, politics, and economy. He advocated the same blessing for India:

> The true cure for darkness, is the introduction of light. The Hindoos [*sic*] err, because they are ignorant; and their errors have never fairly been laid before them. The communication of our light and knowledge to them, would prove the best remedy for their disorders . . . it is perfectly in the power of this country, by degrees to impart to the Hindoos our language; and afterwards through that medium, to make them acquainted with our easy literary compositions, upon a variety of subjects . . . our arts, our philosophy and religion . . . With our language, much of our useful literature might, and would, in time be communicated . . . the Hindoos would see the great use we make of reason on all subjects, and in all affairs; they also would learn to reason, they would become acquainted with the history of their own species . . . their affections would gradually become interested in various engaging works, composed to recommend virtue, and to deter from vice; the general mass of their opinions would be rectified; and above all, they would see a better system of principles and morals. New views of duty as rational creatures would open upon them; and that mental bondage in which they have long

been holden [*sic*] would gradually dissolve . . . perhaps no acquisition in natural philosophy [science] would so effectually enlighten the mass of the people, as the introduction of the principles of mechanics [technology], and their application to agriculture and the useful arts . . . At present it is wonderful to see how entirely they resign themselves to precedent: custom is the strongest law to them.[5]

WILLIAM WILBERFORCE (1759–1833)

Every twentieth year, the British East India Company had to renew its charter with Parliament. In 1793, William Wilberforce used this renewal application to present Grant's case for missions to Parliament. Wilberforce placed Grant's resolution before the House of Commons. They contended that it was immoral to leave India to the mercy of traders and soldiers. According to the Bible, Britain as a Christian nation had an obligation before Providence. Therefore, Parliament should ask the East India Company to allow missionary-educators to serve India.*

Wilberforce won the vote in the House of Commons but lost it in the House of Lords. He was opposed by the lucrative African slave trade conducted by the British Company. Many Lords and MPs (members of Parliament) owned stock in African and Indian companies. They wanted no missionaries to interfere with their economic interests. After his defeat in Parliament, Wilberforce wrote to a friend: "It is a shocking idea that we should leave sixty millions of our fellow subjects, nay of our tenants (for we collect about seventeen million sterling from the rent of their lands), to remain in a state of barbarism and ignorance, the slaves of most cruel and degrading superstitions."[6]

Wilberforce's parliamentary battle continued for twenty years. Grant became a member of Wilberforce's inner circle, the Clapham Sect. That helped him become a director and then the chairman of the East India Company. From this position Grant started sending

---

* In the eighteenth century, education was inseparable from missions because the church provided both religious and secular education. India had no teachers for the company to hire.

Simeon's Cambridge protégés as company chaplains to India. These Cambridge men included some of history's greatest Bible translators and promoters.

Henry Martyn (1781–1812) found his place in history by translating the New Testament into Urdu and Persian. His Urdu work founded the development of my mother tongue, Hindi. Martyn also revised the Arabic Bible. Claudius Buchanan (1766–1815) served as vice-provost of India's first British college, Fort William. There he oversaw and promoted the development of India's modern languages via Bible translation. Later, Grant became a member of Parliament. Their parliamentary battle for missions was finally won in 1813. The Crown conditioned the company's charter on allowing missionaries to function in India and to invest from its annual profits one hundred thousand rupees to educate Indians.

WILLIAM CAREY (1761–1834)

In 1792, while Grant sought to awaken Parliament and church, William Carey, a young cobbler turned linguist, published what became the manifesto of modern Western Protestant missions: "An Enquiry into the Obligation of Christians to Use Means for the Conversion of the Heathen." He inquired whether Jesus' ancient command was still binding on his followers—to go into all the world, make disciples of all nations, and teach them to obey all that God had commanded.[7] Carey focused on the missionary obligation, not on India, per se. He was writing for common Christians, not parliamentarians. Thus, his arguments were explicitly biblical. As Grant, Cary advocated teaching the gospel to transform the uncivilized world.

In 1793 Carey left for India to become the father of vernacular education. Run by Joshua Marshman, the mission's 1818 college[8] at Serampore was India's first vernacular college. Carey, the mission's leader, taught half of each week at Serampore and the rest at Calcutta's Fort William. One of history's greatest Bible translators, Carey became a model for countless missionary-educators. Besides his linguistic work, Carey regularly lectured on science and astronomy, and he excelled in botany, gardening, forestry, and agriculture. Floods have since washed away his garden. The stone specimens he collected from across India, however, are still on display at his college, reminding us that India's scientific interest began with the Bible's arrival. Carey's influence on Indian reformers like Raja Rammohun Roy triggered India's Renaissance.

Raja Rammohun Roy (1772–1833)

The 100,000 rupees that Parliament required the East India Company to spend on education started India's "language controversy."* Everyone familiar with Europe's Reformation agreed that the Indian mind could not progress in secular matters without developing her vernaculars. But neither Hindu pundits nor Muslim mullahs wanted to develop vernaculars.[9] The Orientalist British scholars lobbied for promoting India's classical languages: Sanskrit for the Hindus; Arabic and Persian for the Muslims. The company agreed to start a Sanskrit college.** The fiercest opposition came from the renowned Sanskrit scholar, Raja Rammohun Roy, who saw it would keep India in perpetual darkness. In 1832, he wrote a powerful letter to the British government, arguing that

> [funding] the Sangscrit system of education would be the best calculated to keep this country in darkness, if such had been the policy of the British Legislature. But as the improvement of the native population is the object of the Government, it consequently ought to promote a more liberal and enlightened system of instruction, embracing mathematics, natural philosophy, chemistry and anatomy, with other useful sciences which may be accomplished with the sum proposed by employing a few gentlemen of talents and learning educated in Europe, and providing a college furnished with the necessary books, instruments and other apparatus.[10]

---

* Serampore College did not qualify for the grant because it was a private college run by the Baptist mission in a Danish settlement, outside the British jurisdiction.
** The Company was already funding a Sanskrit college in Benaras.

Roy's proposal echoed Grant's view and was championed by the "Anglicists," against the Orientalists. The Anglicists believed that the best way to strengthen India's vernaculars was to educate a class of Indians who knew English and could translate European knowledge into living Indian languages. Alexander Duff (1806–78), a Scottish missionary, started an English medium college in Calcutta in 1830. He became the most important Anglicist. His college, founded with William Carey's blessing, had been an instant hit with Indians.

Duff's teachers and students had an advantage over Carey; they did not need English books translated before teaching and learning. Indians who knew English could study science, literature, history, philosophy, and economics. Adam Smith's capitalism became immensely popular, even though it undermined the economic philosophy inherent in the Hindu caste system. Duff's successful experiment became official British policy, largely due to his young evangelical friend Charles Trevelyan.

CHARLES TREVELYAN (1807–86)

Trevelyan, a British East India Company civil servant, spelled out unequivocally that the aim of the evangelicals' educational mission was to end the British rule in India. His influential book *On the Education of the People of India* (1838) was blunt:

> The existing connection between two such distant countries as England and India, cannot, in the nature of things be permanent: no effort of policy can prevent the natives from ultimately regaining their independence. But there are two ways of arriving at this point. One of these is through the medium of revolution; the other? through that of reform. . . . [Revolution] must end in the complete alienation of mind and separation of interests between ourselves and the natives; the other [reform] in a permanent alliance, founded on mutual benefit and goodwill. . . . we shall exchange profitable subjects for still more profitable allies . . . trained by us to happiness and independence, and endowed with our learning and political

institutions, India will remain the proudest monument of British benevolence.[11]

How could a civil servant be so daring as to advocate Britain educating India to end British rule and expect Britain's parliament to endorse his passion? Trevelyan was married to the sister of Thomas Babington, Lord Macaulay—a member of the Supreme Council that governed India. Lord Macaulay lived with Charles and Hannah. Macaulay had already argued the case for India's liberty before Parliament in London—five years before Trevelyan penned those amazing lines.

LORD MACAULAY (1800–59)

Wilberforce and Grant passed the torch for India's emancipation on to their successors in Parliament, Lord Macaulay and Charles Grant Jr. These young men grew up as the Clapham Sect's children. Wilberforce's long parliamentary battle against the slave trade was finally won by Macaulay's speech in 1833. That was also a renewal year for the East India Company's charter.

Macaulay served as the secretary to the East India Company's board. Charles Grant Jr. was the company's chairman. Grant drafted the new charter, and Macaulay helped Parliament to accept the implications of the missionary enterprise via education. His rhetoric was at its noblest. His appeals to the path of "duty," "wisdom," and "national honor" make sense only in the context of a shared worldview shaped by the Bible. No other invader in India—Aryan, Greek, or Muslim—ever had a similar sense of duty.

> Are we to keep the people of India, ignorant in order that we may keep them submissive? Or do we think that we can give them knowledge without awakening ambition? Or do we mean to awaken ambition and to provide it with no legitimate vent? . . . The path of duty is plain before us: and it is also the path of wisdom, of national prosperity, of national honor. . . . The destinies of our Indian empire

are covered with thick darkness. It is difficult to form any conjecture as to the fate reserved for a state which resembles no other in history, and which forms by itself a separate class of political phenomena. The laws which regulate its growth and its decay are still unknown to us. It may be that the public mind of India may expand under our system till it has outgrown that system; that by good government we may educate our subjects into a capacity for better government; that, having become instructed in European knowledge, they may, in some future age, demand European institutions. Whether such a day will come, I know not. But never will I attempt to avert it or to retard it. Whenever it comes, it will be the proudest day in English history.[12]

Why would Parliament accept such a radical mission? Not everyone was motivated by Macaulay's moral ideals. After Wilberforce's four-decade-long "culture war," however, few had the courage to defend slavery. The debate on Indian policy occurred against the backdrop of the American Revolution, which ended British rule. Just as the Bible had liberated England, it had been the moral force behind the Great Awakening, which launched the American Revolution. Macaulay's audience in Parliament may have disliked his ideas, yet they knew they could not prevent Indians from getting the Bible, and that the Bible would fuel the fires of freedom.

One year after delivering his historic speech, Macaulay came to India to help the company implement his recommendations. As the governing council's legal member, he was asked to resolve the language controversy. Macaulay listened to all sides and ruled on February 2, 1835, that English would better serve Indian vernaculars than Sanskrit, Arabic, or Persian. Therefore, he recommended that public funds impart English education to Indians, who could enrich vernaculars. Macaulay wrote in his famous "Minute," which has been more condemned than read in India:

[I]t is impossible for us, with our limited means, to attempt to educate the body of the people. We must at present do our best to form a class who may be interpreters between us and millions whom we govern; a class of persons, Indian in blood and colour, but English in taste, in opinions, in morals, and in intellect. To that class we may leave it to refine the vernacular dialects of the country, to enrich those dialects with terms of science borrowed from the Western nomenclature, and to render them by degrees fit vehicles for conveying knowledge to the great mass of the population.[13]

The 1833 charter, which Macaulay and Grant Jr. piloted through Parliament, asked the East India Company to appoint Indians at the highest levels of administration. Yet by 1853 the company had not yet hired any Indians, not because of prejudice but because India had no qualified graduates. By this time, veterans like Duff, Macaulay, and Trevelyan were back in Britain. They proposed the solution: India should have universities.

In spite of opposition from company heavyweights such as philosopher John Stuart Mill (1806–73), the Christian campaign for education won the day. A devout evangelical, Sir Charles Wood, headed the committee that wrote the "Educational Despatch" [sic] of 1854. That led to the establishment of the first three universities in India in 1857. Allahabad University was born three decades later.

Hindu and Muslim soldiers in the British army revolted against the Raj in the great Indian mutiny of 1857. To drive out the British from Indian soil, they massacred English men, women, and children. The British retaliated with brutal force and suppressed the mutiny. Due to the mutiny, the company's monopoly rule was ended and the British crown assumed direct responsibility for governing India. That gave liberal Protestants (who gradually turned into secular humanists) an opportunity to take over the state-funded education.

The liberal Christians were able to blame the evangelicals for igniting the fire for India's freedom. The charge had credible grounds. India's freedom had been a stated goal of the evangelicals and their descendants. They had upset Indians by opposing traditional beliefs and practices, such as widow burning, infanticide, untouchability, temple prostitution, polygamy, and idolatry. Evangelicals had held important positions in the East India Company for decades and had supported the conversion of Hindus and Muslims to Christ. At the final triumph of their educational campaign, Bible-believing Christians lost their power to mold the institution they had created.

Once liberal Protestants gained control of the university movement, they undermined the spiritual essence of the Bible, promoting only its intellectual and social fruit. They doubted the Bible's reliability but championed its principles of human dignity, equality, and rights; its morality and rationality, which Grant had desired for India; its ideas of nationalism, civility, and justice, which William Carey said needed to be spread; and its ideas of freedom under law as championed by Macaulay and Trevelyan.

The question is, *why did the Bible promote education with such secular goals?* The Bible has a uniquely "this world" spirituality. It teaches that God created Adam and Eve to live in an earthly paradise. Even after our fall into sin, God wants to "walk" with us during our earthly sojourn. The sorrows, "thorns and thistles," on earth are a result of human sin. Fear of God, wisdom, and righteousness exalt nations. Jesus promised that the meek shall inherit the earth.[14]

By 1885, this watered-down biblical education had created a class of educated Indians. The retired British civil servant Allan Octavian Hume (1829–1912) inspired them to establish the Indian National Congress. That congress led the movement for India's independence. Graduates from Calcutta and Bombay started it, but Allahabad eclipsed them in importance for India's liberation. Its educational and political culture forged by its municipality, High Court, university, press, and a strategic location gave India five of her first seven prime ministers.*

This story of India's educational revolution is merely illustrative. During the nineteenth and twentieth centuries, Western missions repeated this process throughout most of the non-Western world. They birthed, financed, and nurtured hundreds of universities, thousands of colleges, and tens of thousands of schools. They educated

---

* Pandit Jawaharlal Nehru, Lal Bahadur Shastri, Mrs. Indira Gandhi, Chandra Shekhar, and V. P. Singh had important family and political roots in Allahabad, though not all of them studied at Allahabad University.

millions and transformed nations. This gigantic, global mission was inspired and sustained by one book—the Bible. In return, poorly informed gentlemen, such as Arun Shourie, have attacked the Bible and Western missions.

THE BIBLE AND EUROPEAN EDUCATION

Just as Islamic invasions ended India's Buddhist learning in the second millennium, the barbarian conquests virtually ended Europe's classical education in the first. Though never completely lost, education was so depressed that the fifth to the ninth centuries are sometimes called Europe's "Dark Ages." Illiteracy was the norm in most of the world, until the missionary movement began transforming our world.

Secular scholars fondly claim that Greeks and Romans first invented universities. But historians like Charles Haskins point out that although Greeks and Romans had brilliant writers and teachers, they established no permanent institutions, no libraries, and no scholarly guilds.[15]

During the medieval era, learning survived in Europe in isolated Christian monasteries before cathedrals started schools to train men to meet the needs of Christian institutions. Influenced by visionaries such as St. Augustine, bishop of Hippo (AD 354–430), Flavius Magnus Aurelius Cassiodorus (AD 490–585), and Anicius Manlius Severinus Boethius (AD 480–524), some monasteries and cathedral schools grew into universities.

The most influential syllabus for medieval education was St. Augustine's treatise on Christian learning, *De Doctrina Christiana*. He taught that all the sciences known to pagan philosophers were useful for interpreting the Bible. Therefore, students ought to be taught languages, history, grammar, logic, and sciences. These studies brought students to the door of a rich country of spiritual truth found in the Bible. The ultimate goal of scholarship was to dig into the scriptural mine of knowledge. "The work of interpretation was a scientific labor, not a matter of lucky inspiration,"[16] even if the interpretation was conveyed in allegory and imagery. The fruit of such biblical scholarship had to be conveyed to the world; therefore, every student needed to study the art of rhetoric, taught by masters such as Cicero.

Cassidorus (AD 485–585) developed an alternative syllabus in his treatise *Divine and Secular Learning*. He "adopted Augustine's view of the unity of secular sciences in the service of the Biblical interpretation."[17] But the way he organized his syllabus made it possible for students and teachers to focus either on secular or sacred learning without focusing on their relationship to each other, without integrating them into a worldview. Therefore its popularity gradually declined.

Boethius (AD 480–ca. 524/525) was the third influential author. Just as the sun was setting over the Roman Empire, he attempted to translate all of Greek learning into Latin. His works influenced the intellectual life of the eleventh-century church and promoted Aristotle. Thanks to reinforcement by Muslim scholars, Aristotle became immensely popular during the thirteenth and fourteenth centuries. But in spite of many positive contributions, Aristotle's authoritarian influence prevented Europe from experiencing the power of the Bible until the sixteenth-century Reformation.

Europe's intellectual life, obviously, was more complex than can be discussed here. Oxford historian Sir Richard William Southern (1912–2001) observed that "the eleventh-century monastic scholar wrote his works in the intervals between church services which were laden with readings from the Bible."[18] In the twelfth century, however, Bible reading declined, being replaced by special lessons for a large number of saints' days. Archbishop Thomas Cranmer (1489–1556) complained that the Bible was replaced by "Stories, and Legends, with multitudes of Responds, Verses, vain Repitions, Commemorations, and Synodals."[19]

In schools, Bible commentaries left little time to read the Bible itself. Nevertheless, studying the Bible's interpretations remained central to all schooling. Southern wrote:

> It was in the Schools that the Biblical interpretation of the Fathers were collected together in a convenient form and attached to the relevant section of the text. The *Ordinary Gloss*, the earliest of all

the twelfth-century works consolidating past learning, was one of the indispensable hand-books for study. Everywhere the Biblical text was commented on, and became the starting point for discussions of many kinds—grammatical, dialectical, theological and historical. The twelfth-century schools were not centers of research into the mystical senses of Scriptures of the kind which St. Augustine had urged scholars to undertake. But they made the Biblical text in all its many meanings more familiar than ever before . . . They made the Bible . . . [a] part of the idiom of both secular and divine literature.[20]

Again, the question is, *why did the Bible, an Asian book, retain its hold over the Western mind even after most of Greek, Roman, and Islamic literature became available?* Two factors are important:

1. MEDIEVAL EDUCATION WAS A RELIGIOUS ENTERPRISE.

Virtually all education was Church education. H. G. Wells grudgingly admitted,

The Catholic Church provided what the Roman Republic had lacked, a system of popular teaching, a number of universities and methods of intellectual communication. By this achievement it opened the way to the new possibilities of human government . . . possibilities that are still being apprehended and worked out . . . But though it is certain that the Catholic Church, through its propaganda, its popular appeals, its schools and universities opened up the prospect of the modern educational state in Europe, it is equally certain that the Catholic Church never intended to do anything of the sort. It did not send out knowledge with its blessings; it let it loose inadvertently.[21]

How, why, and when did the Church-owned education become available to everyone? In a moment we will see the role Reformers such as Martin Luther and John Amos Comenius played in transforming medieval education into modern. First, we need to comprehend why the Bible remained central to education even after theologians became fascinated with Aristotle and Bible reading declined in schools and churches.

2. THE BIBLE IS A UNIQUE LIBRARY.

The Bible remained key to education because it is a library—a unique collection of books selected with extreme care. The sixty-six books of the traditional Bible were written by at least forty authors, over sixteen hundred years, in three different languages, yet they tell one story.* This metanarrative begins with creation and ends with re-creation.

An amazing feature of this library is that its books give an expanding, progressive, yet coherent view of life and the world. It presents a consistent yet unfolding worldview that explains reality and the human situation. It gives purpose to an absurd-looking life, meaning to the human quest for morals, and hope in the face of awful evil. It inspires faith in God, in a universe that seems to be governed by random chance, if not capricious fate or fortune. Monks did not study or teach because they were looking for jobs. They studied because the Bible asked them to seek the knowledge of truth.

THE REFORMATION OF EDUCATION

THE CALL FOR REFORM: MARTIN LUTHER

Modern education began with Martin Luther's call for a complete overhaul of medieval education. He made his passionate plea in 1520 in "An Open Letter to the Christian Nobility." "I believe," said Luther to German aristocracy, "that there is no work more worthy of pope or emperor than a thorough reform of the universities. And on the other hand, nothing could be more devilish or disastrous than unreformed universities."[22] Luther observed that Church-owned-and-operated Renaissance universities were becoming "places for training of youth in the fashions of Greek culture." They were institutions "where loose living is practiced, where little is taught of the Holy Scriptures and Christian faith, and where only the blind, heathen teacher Aristotle rules far more than Christ."[23]

---

* One ground for rejecting other Jewish or Christian books as noncanonical was that some of their teachings diverged from the ones known to be authoritative.

Luther knew and taught Aristotle. Luther believed that for reform to happen, "Aristotle's *Physics, Metaphysics, Concerning the Soul*, and *Ethics*, which hitherto have been thought to be his best books, should be completely discarded along with all the rest of his books that boast about nature, although nothing can be learned from them either about nature or the Spirit."[24] Luther would only keep Aristotle's *Logic, Rhetoric*, and *Poetics*—without commentaries.[25]

Luther next threw out the entire course on canon (or Church) law, "from the first letter to the last,"[26] because "more than enough is written in the Bible about how we should behave in all circumstances. The study of canon law only hinders the study of the Holy Scriptures."[27] Then he called for a drastic pruning of secular law, which "has become a wilderness."[28] Life would be a lot easier if the legal jungle was made a carefully trimmed garden. Fewer laws, with "wise rulers, side by side with Holy Scripture, would be law enough."[29]

Luther left medical reform to experts but targeted theology. "Our dear theologians have saved themselves worry and work. They just let the Bible alone and lecture on sentences."[30] Reform would turn this upside down. "The number of books on theology must be reduced . . . It is not many books that make men learned, nor even reading. But it is a good book frequently read, no matter how small it is, that makes a man learned in the Scriptures and godly."[31]

In short, Luther argued that to reform the university, the Bible would have to be put at the center of its curriculum. His appeal to Christian nobility was itself a historic move. For better or for worse, it began to transfer educational authority from the Church to the state. It brought non-Church money—taxes from people and gifts from merchants and other wealthy people—into education. Luther was not advocating political control over our minds. In his scheme, the Word of God, not the state, the donor, or the Church, had ultimate authority over our minds. The university, the Church, and the state were subject to the Bible. Nevertheless, right or wrong, Luther began the trend of holding the state responsible for education, not just the Church.

Luther's initiative led to civic leadership becoming involved with higher education as well as mass literacy. The Reformation required lay Christians to read the Bible and judge whether the Catholic Church or the reformers were right. It was not enough for Luther and Tyndale to make the Bible available to people in German or English. People needed to read in their own languages. That could not be done merely through cathedral schools. Every parish needed to educate every child. The desire to read the Bible became the fuel that drove the engine of Europe's literacy. This is why John Dewey, who perhaps did more than anyone else to secularize American education, advised secularists to move slowly in attacking Christianity. He noted,

> These persons [evangelical Christians] form the backbone of phil-
> anthropic social interest, of social reform through political action,
> of pacifism, of popular education. They embody and express the
> spirit of kindly goodwill toward classes which are at an economic
> disadvantage and toward other nations; especially when the latter
> show any disposition toward a republican form of government ... It
> has been the element responsive to appeals for the square deal and
> more nearly equal opportunities for all, as it has understood equality
> of opportunity. It followed Lincoln in the abolition of slavery, and it
> followed Roosevelt in his denunciation of "bad" corporations and
> aggregations of wealth.[32]

Dewey's depiction of America is true for most countries. In Kerala, India's second most literate state,* the word for school is *pallikudam*— "[the building] next to the church."

John Amos Comenius (1592–1670)
Martin Luther called for reforming the university but was consumed with reforming the Church, therefore, many consider John Amos Comenius (Jan Amos Komensky) to be the father of modern education. Comenius was born March 28, 1592, in Nivnice, Moravia,

---

* According to *India Today* (July 5, 1999), Mizoram, India's most Christian state (98 percent) has also become India's most literate state (95 percent) while literacy in Kerala is 93 percent. Kerala has the oldest Christian community in India, tracing its origin to the apostle Thomas in the first century after Christ.

now in the Czech Republic. He died November 15, 1670, after serving the Moravian Brethren as a bishop, writing nearly ninety books on education, demonstrating his educational philosophy in several countries, inspiring the birth of the Royal Society of Science in England, and helping establish the first modern university at Halle, Germany. Halle University later merged with Luther's to form Wittenberg-Halle University.

As a young man, Comenius thought that the medieval schools were the "slaughterhouses of the mind." He strove to make them "happy workshops of humanity," an "imitation of heaven." Comenius built upon the educational ideas advocated by the German Wolfgang Ratke (1571–1635), ideas that were in turn based on those of the British philosopher Francis Bacon. These began with principles such as proceeding from things to names, from the particular to the general, and from the mother tongue to foreign languages. After studying philosophy and theology, Comenius returned to his native Bohemia as a preacher and teacher. His innovative school quickly became well-known. During the thirty years of religious wars (1618–48), his country fell to the Catholic forces (1620). He could have kept his school by converting to Catholicism, but he chose freedom and fled as a refugee.

Comenius knew war, hunger, disease, the death of his wife and children, the burning of his school and books, political treachery, and disappointments at the hands of politicians and rulers. Some of his books were written under the political patronage of kings, others while hiding in cold and dangerous woods. The Buddha saw suffering secondhand. Comenius experienced it firsthand. He chose to be a "suffering servant" of Christ, following the martyred Messiah. He sought for more than inner bliss; he wanted to see Europe liberated from the kingdom of Satan.

Comenius believed that discipling the next generation through education would create a new world. Comenius saw education as a means of forming again God's image in humanity. He called his biblical philosophy *Pansophia*, integrating all wisdom, secular and sacred, into a biblical framework.[33]

Secular historians have yet to compute Comenius's contributions to the modern world. This father of modern education is often ignored because he rarely made a statement without justifying it from the Bible. All the characters reviewed in this chapter—men like Grant, Wilberforce, Carey, Roy, Duff, Trevelyan, Macaulay, and Muir—were following Comenius, even if some of them were not conscious of it. Not only modern India, but also modern America was shaped by Comenius's vision. The difference is that the pioneers of American education knew the debt they owed Comenius. They invited him to come to the new world to head up their new college, Harvard, in New England. Comenius's optimism through education had such a profound impact on some Puritan settlers in America that they chose to become an educational community before becoming a commercial or industrial nation.[34]

In the absence of a coherent worldview, secular education is fragmenting knowledge. Unrelated bits of information give no basis to grasp a vision like Comenius's to change the world through education. The secular university knows no Messiah that promises a kingdom to the poor, the weak, the sick, and the sorrowing destitute.

TURKEY

In 1871, the American Board of Commissioners for Foreign Missions sent Mary Mills Patrick (1850–1940) as a missionary to Turkey. In 1875, she was transferred to Scutari (Üsküdar), an Asiatic suburb of Constantinople, to teach at the American High School for Girls, also known as "Home School." With the help of American philanthropist Caroline Borden, she turned the school into the modern Constantinople Women's College. It required heroic strength to keep it open through the Balkan Wars, the Turkish revolution, and World War I. Through those struggles it evolved from a school primarily for minority Greek, Armenian, and Bulgarian Christian women into a leading center of higher education for Turkish women teaching all sorts of useful trades, including dentistry and medicine. The Women's College still exists as part of Roberts College, serving both men and women.

KOREA

The world's largest women's university is Ewha in Seoul, South Korea. It boasts of 140,000 graduates, 21,000 students, 14 colleges, and 13 graduate schools. Not much more than a century ago, South Korea's oppressive feudal social order was governed by the Chosun dynasty. Its polite culture mocked the idea of teaching anything to women beyond caring for their husbands and sons. The Korean peninsula was little more than skirmish ground between Asia's two giants, China and Japan. Even missionary societies had little interest in the killing fields of Korea. Its destiny changed with a discussion in the small town of Ravenna, Ohio, in 1883.

While the Women's Foreign Missionary Society of the Methodist Episcopal Church discussed missionary plans for Japan and China, an elderly woman beseeched her peers not to overlook the little kingdom nestled between the two Asian giants on the Korean peninsula. Three years later, on May 31, 1886, Mary F. Scranton (1832–1909), a fifty-two-year-old Methodist missionary, began Korea's first school for women in a house located in what is now the Chong-dong district of Seoul. It was not easy for her to find female students. The only student willing to risk social disapproval was the king's concubine. By 1887, Mary had seven students, and Korean emperor Gojong's wife, Minbee, named the new school Ewha Hagdang or "Pear Blossom School." Labors such as hers helped turn that little kingdom into one of Asia's greatest countries.

BEYOND THE ELITE

The snobbery of the English class system is mocked in films and books. Few know that the Bible inspired history's most effective challenge to that snobbery through the Sunday school movement launched by Robert Raikes (1735–1811).

Raikes, the crusading editor of the *Gloucester Journal*, became frustrated with inefficient jail reforms. He concluded "vice could be better prevented than cured." A visit to the slums of his city opened his eyes to the distressing corruption of children. He shared the problem with Reverend Thomas Stock in the village of Ashbury, Berkshire. Together they conceived of a school that could be run by volunteers on Sundays, when children from poor homes were not forced to work. Most writers wrote for the rich, who had the money to buy books and the leisure to read. But Jesus had said that he had come to preach good news to the poor. Raikes and Stock chose God's Word as their curriculum, and committed to reaching even street children.

This Sunday school movement began in July 1780, with Mrs. Meredith conducting a school in her home on Souty Alley. Older boys were trained to coach younger ones. Raikes wrote four textbooks around the Bible core. Gradually girls were allowed to attend. Raikes shouldered most of the financial burden. Other schools opened in and around Gloucester. Though Raikes died in 1811, by 1831 about 25 percent of the 1.25 million British children were attending Sunday schools. England was on its way to becoming a literate society, educated by God's Word, not by the state.

RESTORING HUMAN DIGNITY TO THE DEAF AND THE BLIND

The Greeks often used blind boys as galley slaves and blind girls as prostitutes. Jesus, however, restored their sight. By the fourth century, Christians began opening asylums for the blind. In AD 630, some Christians started a typholocomium (typholos = blind + komeo = take care of) in Jerusalem. In the thirteenth century, Louis IX built the Hospice des Quinze-Vingts for the blind in Paris. By the sixteenth century, Christians had begun to teach the blind to read, using raised letters on wax or wood. Education for the blind seriously began after 1834, when Louis Braille, a blind Church organist, invented the six-dot system of embossing letters. The Christian missionary movement carried his invention around the globe, challenging traditional neglect and contempt for the blind, inspiring secular establishments to imbibe some of Christ's spirit.

Darwin's secular "survival of the fittest" philosophy would never pay for developing an education to humanize the handicapped. Every traditional culture left them to their fate or karma. Some deliberately exposed handicapped infants to death. The Bible alone presents a compassionate God who has come to this earth to save us from our sin and its consequences—including sickness and death. Jesus restored sight to the blind. He opened the ears of the deaf and the mouths of the dumb. He gave his disciples the power to love the unlovely. Christians began to understand that education plays a central role in restoring the dignity of the handicapped.

Formal education for the deaf began with Charles-Michel de l'Épée (1712–89). It came to America through Thomas Gallaudet (1787–1851). Épée, a priest in Paris, developed the sign language for the deaf. In 1754, he financed and founded in Paris the first public deaf school, the "Institution Nationale des Sourds-Muets à Paris" (National Deaf-Dumb Institute). His sign language enabled French deaf people to communicate words and concepts. It influenced other European sign languages and became the basis for American Sign Language through Gallaudet, a graduate of Yale and Andover Theological Seminary. Gallaudet brought this innovation to the United States in 1817 to help the deaf to "hear" Christ's gospel. He founded the American School for the Deaf at Hartford, which led to the formation of Gallaudet University for the Deaf in Washington DC.

SECULAR EDUCATION

Harvard University is one of the most compelling examples of the symbiosis between the Bible and education. The Puritans established this college within the first decade of arriving in America, before they built any industry. The Bible directly inspired the first 123 colleges and universities in America that taught secular subjects. The Bible did so because God commanded human beings to establish their dominion over the earth. The story of the secularization of American universities is well presented by George Marsden in *The Soul of the American University: From Protestant Establishment to Established Nonbelief.*[35]

What will be the results of a self-consciously antibiblical education?

A worldview such as the Bible's turned information into meaningful knowledge and wisdom. It gave education a purpose that went beyond equipping young people for jobs. Secular philosophers rejected the Bible but found no alternative to their grasping the big picture of truth. They now know that, by itself, the human mind cannot find answers to the meaning and purpose of life or the universe. Thus secularism is but a transitory phase, like its earlier incarnation, deism.

Christian education (especially Bible-based science, discussed in the next chapter) developed knowledge in small increments, like a puzzle, because God had already given us the big picture. Secular universities have survived because the larger culture had retained the biblical outlook. Now having rejected the Bible, the West is trying to find meaning through myths. It is following Joseph Campbell, George Lucas, and James Cameron and inventing and selling myths, as Greece did after it realized that a finite mind cannot know universal truth. Britain gave universities to India to set us free. The West is now giving its youth myths that can only enslave them. This is ironic because it was the West's quest for truth that birthed science. To science, therefore, we must turn next.

Chapter Thirteen

SCIENCE

WHAT IS ITS SOURCE?

A round the time I was born, my parents bought a farm about fifty miles northwest of the diamond mines of Panna. My cousin, uncle, brother, I, and then my father farmed it for nearly forty years. None of us, however, ever tried to dig for diamonds. Why not? Because no one had ever found such wealth in our district. People only toil for treasures if they *believe* that such labor might lead to rich rewards. Faith makes a difference.

A culture may have capable individuals, but they don't look for "laws of nature" if they believe that nature is enchanted and ruled by millions of little deities like a rain god, a river goddess, or a rat *deva*. If the planets themselves are gods, then why should they follow established laws? Cultures that worship nature often use magic to manipulate the unseen powers governing nature. They don't develop science and technology to establish "dominion" over nature. Some "magic" may seem to "work," but magicians don't seek a systematic, coherent understanding of nature.

- Ancient India produced great surgeons like Sushruta. Why didn't his tradition develop into scientific medicine?
- As early as the fifth century, Aryabhata suggested that the earth rotates on its axis and revolves around the sun. Indian

astrologers knew of his theory, but it didn't change their practices.

- Ancient and medieval India's genius for mathematics is widely recognized. An unknown Indian mathematician introduced zero. Mathematicians Brahmagupta (seventh century), Mahavira (ninth century), and Bhaskara (twelfth century) were eons ahead of the West.

Why didn't Indian mathematics become the language of science? Consider growing up in a culture that believed that the world you see and touch is unreal—*maya*, an illusion, a dream. Would you devote your life to study that "unreal" world? Wouldn't you seek to escape the world? To meditate inwardly—"go within" your consciousness—to try and find "reality" there?

The Chinese monks and Hindu sages did not lack ability. They lacked the philosophical motivation. They looked for a psychological paradise, for bliss within their consciousness. Until the sixteenth century, the Western Christian mind also looked for a psychological or spiritual salvation. *It was only when a major portion of Christendom could read the Bible and take it at face value that it began to understand the loss of Eden as a loss of earthly paradise.*

The West's passion for science began when the Bible inspired Christians to devote their lives to recovering God's forgotten mandate for humans to take dominion over nature.[1] The first historian of the Royal Society of Science, Thomas Sprat (1635–1713), explained that the society's objective was to enable mankind to reestablish "Dominion over Things."[2] It was this religio-scientific exercise that collected the data that showed the apparent design in nature. Darwin later theorized that this design may have resulted from random natural selection.

During the twentieth century, science became increasingly intertwined with technology and industry. However, until the nineteenth century, science was "natural philosophy" or "natural history," a subdivision of theology: "natural theology" or "general revelation." The scientific method of studying nature grew out of theology, out of a particular way of viewing the material world based on the Bible. This way assumed that the physical universe was *real*. It was neither a Platonic "shadow" nor a Hindu *maya* (illusion).

The pioneers of science believed that the material realm was real, not magical, enchanted, or governed by spirits and demons. They assumed it was understandable because God created it as *rational*, *ordered*, and regulated by *natural laws*. Those pioneers invested their time, effort, resources, and their lives studying the physical universe because they believed that God created it *good*.[3] It was not the creation of a malevolent deity to entrap pure souls in impure matter. The scientific pursuit started with the assumption that people were created as stewards of creation, not that fate or gods bound human beings. By understanding nature, we could manage and control it to benefit our future and us.

This scientific outlook was born in a critique of Aristotelian rationalism. The scientific method assumes that human logic has validity, but it must be subservient to observed facts, because man is finite, fallen, and fallible. Scientists use logic to make sense of facts. They *theorize* to explain the world. But for a theory to be scientific, it must make *quantitative predictions* that are empirically verifiable, or at least falsifiable. A theory is modified or replaced if it doesn't fit observed facts, or if later observations don't match its predictions.

Science rests on a paradox. Science must have the confidence that human beings can *transcend* nature (understand it, master it, and change it). Yet, science requires humility—accepting that humans are not divine but finite and fallen—prone to sin, error, and hubris. Therefore, science needs more than Aristotelian logic or individual enlightenment. It needs objectivity, observed facts, peer review, and constant skeptical testing. "As iron sharpens iron, so one man sharpens another."[4] Accumulating knowledge with collection, modeling, and correction, requires the organized effort not just of schools and then universities, but also of a scientific community—the association and competitive yet cooperative network of people developing science.

Science had to reject two opposing beliefs: 1) The reductionistic idea that man was merely a part of nature—a cog in the machine, incapable of transcending it; and 2) the science-precluding notion that the human self was the Divine Self and could be enlightened only by insight or mystical experience; that it could become infinite, knowing everything, needing no correction.

The global spread of Western education made this scientific way of seeing nature so common that most educated people do not realize that the scientific outlook is a peculiar way of observing the world—an objective ("secular") method molded by a biblical worldview. Science uses objective methods to observe, organize, and understand the natural world.*

But this perspective is neither "natural," "universal," nor "common sense." It is a peculiar way of viewing things. Europe did not stumble upon the scientific method through random trial, error, and chance. Some individuals in the ancient world may have looked at nature with a scientific outlook, but their perspective did not become a part of their intellectual culture.

The scientific perspective flowered in Europe as an outworking of medieval biblical theology nurtured by the Church. Theologians pursued science for biblical reasons. Their scientific spirit germinated during the thirteenth and fourteenth centuries and blossomed after the sixteenth-century Reformation—after Europe became a more literate place, where people could read the Bible themselves and become consciously biblical.

My intellectual upbringing gave me confusing information about how the Bible and science relate. In *The Tao of Physics*, physicist-turned-mystic Fritjof Capra observed:

> The notion of fundamental laws of nature was derived from the belief
> in a divine lawgiver which was deeply rooted in the Judaeo-Christian

---

* Some scientists, unaware of the theological roots of modern science, try to define science as an exclusively materialistic understanding of nature, explicitly excluding any possibility that God exists, or can create or interact with nature (philosophical materialism). However, the Creator's existence cannot be excluded a priori without universal knowledge of the entire universe and how it originated. The consequences of God's creation and intervention should be objectively observable and thus subject to rational science.

tradition. In the words of Thomas Aquinas: "There is a certain eternal law, to wit, Reason, existing in the mind of God and governing the whole universe."

This notion of an eternal, divine law of nature greatly influenced Western philosophy and science. Descartes wrote about the six laws which God has put into nature, and Newton believed that the highest aim of his scientific work was to give evidence of the six laws impressed upon nature by God.[5]

Capra and people familiar with Aldous Huxley blamed the Bible for creating an ecological mess by producing science and technology. Others claimed the Bible and science were incompatible and that science arose from the Renaissance rediscovery of Greek learning.

Since both opinions—that the Bible was incompatible with science *and* that it was the source book of science—could not be true, I investigated the matter. I found that those who blamed the Bible for birthing modern science at least had their history right. For better or worse, the Bible created and underpinned the scientific outlook. Bible-believing scientists launched the "scientific revolution" of the sixteenth and seventeenth centuries. Capra's observation that belief in the laws of nature came from the Bible has been validated by careful research of Francis Oakley.[6]

The Bible inspired the pioneers of science to embark on the road to discover the laws of nature—a long, tedious, demanding, multigenerational journey. The Bible taught that God "gave the sea its boundary so the waters would not overstep his command."[7] This Lawgiver established "the laws of Nature."[8] These laws can be understood because we were created in God's image to understand and manage nature.[9]

Capra merely affirmed what scientists and scholars had concluded before him. Chatterjee, my atheist friend at Allahabad University, followed Bertrand Russell into believing that atheism was the source of science. He rejected Hindu polytheism and pantheism as equally antithetical to science. One cannot simultaneously worship Mother Earth yet rule her by dissecting, understanding, controlling, managing, and changing her. Scientists had to assume that the cosmos is an inanimate, natural (or "secular") object. They had to assume that in some aspects man could take care of nature by understanding and then managing or "ruling over" it.

Chatterjee also rejected Hindu pantheism—that everything is one (Brahma). That makes the universe either *maya* or the "dance" of God—not God's "handiwork" or craftsmanship. A painting or a machine is crafted. It reflects the painter or the engineer but is distinct from its creator. By contrast, dance and the dancer are one. If God and nature are one, then nature has no Lawgiver, nor are there "laws of nature" to be discovered.

Pantheism may say that nature is a living organism—Gaia or "Mother Earth." Nature's "order" is but the rhythm of its dance—unpredictable with no mathematical laws to be quantified. Chatterjee argued that if the earth is a goddess, then her will—not mandatory, scientific laws—governs her.

Russell's atheism, however, raised a problem: Why didn't China produce science? Some of China's elite prided themselves in following a universal essence, or principle, called the Tao; others believed in "yin and yang." If Russell's atheism was the presupposition of science, then China ought to have developed science before Europe. Though baffled by the gap between his belief and reality, Russell had the chutzpah to assert that since Chinese civilization did not have the Bible's God who intervenes in nature, its science would soon surpass the West's.

No one in our university told us that Russel's coauthor, Alfred North Whitehead, considered his arguments carefully then shocked Western intellectuals in his Harvard Lowell Lectures (1925). Whitehead declared that Western science had sprung from the Bible's teaching that the cosmos was the product of "the intelligible rationality of a personal being [God]." The implication was that personal beings—humans—could understand the cosmos. Whitehead elaborated:

> I do not think, however, that I have even yet brought out the greatest contribution of medievalism to the formation of the scientific

movement. I mean the inexpugnable belief that every detailed occurrence can be correlated with its antecedents in a perfectly definite manner, exemplifying general principles. Without this belief the incredible labours of scientists would be without hope. It is this instinctive conviction, vividly poised before the imagination, which is the motive power of research—that there is a secret, a secret which can be unveiled. How has this conviction been so vividly implanted in the European mind?

When we compare this tone of thought in Europe with the attitude of other civilizations when left to themselves, there seems but one source of its origin. It must come from the medieval insistence on the rationality of God, conceived as with the personal energy of Jehovah.[10]

Whitehead concluded that China failed to develop science because for much of its history it did not have a firm conviction in an almighty Creator.* Joseph Needham (1900–95), a Marxist historian who spent his life investigating Chinese science and civilization, confirmed Whitehead's views. Needham searched for materialistic explanations for China's failure. Finally, his integrity overcame his ideology. He concluded that there were no good geographical, racial, political, or economic reasons that explained the Chinese failure to develop science. The Chinese did not develop science because it never occurred to them that science was *possible*. They did not have science because "the conception of a divine celestial law-giver imposing ordinances on non-human nature never developed in China."[11]

Premodern Greeks, Egyptians, Chinese, Indians, and Muslims had many insights into nature; they observed facts, noted information, developed skills, accumulated wisdom, and passed on their knowledge to others. We have good reasons to marvel at the accuracy with which Greek mathematician, astronomer, geographer, and poet Eratosthenes (ca. 276 BC–ca.196 BC) measured the circumference of the earth. He determined astronomically the difference in latitude

---

* There is some evidence that the early Chinese did believe in one almighty Creator.

between Syene (now Aswan) and Alexandria, Egypt, where he was the librarian. Our principle of floating bodies is named after Archimedes (287–212 BC), who also studied in Alexandria. His mathematical principles of the lever, pulley, and screw are impressive. Hipparchus (ca. 190–120 BC), who greatly influenced Ptolemy, calculated the solar year to within six minutes and fourteen seconds. His lunar month was off only by one second.

Despite their impressive achievements, the ancients did not develop a culture of science. While they observed accurately, they did not model the world. They made no effort to empirically verify their explanations. Not even Copernicus (1473–1543) formed a preliminary heliocentric theory. It was deeply Christian Isaac Newton (1642–1727) who modeled planetary orbits due to gravity. Without explanation, one can have facts but not science. As Charles Darwin noted:

> About thirty years ago there was much talk that geologists ought to observe and not theorize; and I well remember someone saying that at that rate a man might as well go into a gravel-pit and count the pebbles and describe the colours. How odd it is that anyone should not see that all observation must be for or against some view if it is to be of any service.[12]

When the ancients tried to explain the world, they used intuition,* logic, mythmaking, mysticism, or rationalism—detached from empirical observation. For example, Aristotle's (384–322 BC) intuition-based logic posited that if you drop two stones from a cliff, then a twice-as-heavy stone would fall twice as fast as the lighter stone. No Aristotelian scholar—Greek, Egyptian, Roman, Christian, or Muslim—ever actually tested Aristotle's theory by dropping two stones. Finally, biblically grounded Galileo Galilei (AD 1564–1642) actually tested and

---

* Before Democritus in Greece, Indian philosopher Pakudha Katyayana, a sixth century BC contemporary of the Buddha, taught that the world was made up of atoms. Some Indian atomic theories of physical universe are brilliant and agree with modern physics. However, they were based on intuition and logic with no experimental science.

disproved Aristotle's assumption by showing that two balls of differing mass landed together.*

Intuition, logic, observation, experimentation, information, techniques, speculation, and the study of authoritative texts existed before the sixteenth century. By themselves these do not constitute sustainable science. If one insists that ancient discoveries prove that science predates the Bible, then one has to admit that nonbiblical cultures stifled and killed that commendable beginning. Only in Europe did astrology turn into astronomy, alchemy into chemistry, and mathematics into the language of science. Then only in the sixteenth and seventeenth centuries—after the Western Christian mind took seriously God's command: "Be fruitful, and multiply, and replenish the earth, and subdue it: and have dominion over the fish of the sea, and over the fowl of the air, and over every living thing that moveth upon the earth."[13]

The command to rule over the earth had been in the Bible for a few thousand years. Why was there no sustainable science until the sixteenth century? Professor Harrison said science started when Christians began to read the Bible literally:

> Only when the story of creation was divested of its symbolic elements could God's command to Adam be related to worldly activities. If the Garden of Eden were but a lofty allegory, as Philo, Origen, and later Hugh of St. Victor had suggested, there would be little point in attempting to re-establish a paradise on earth. If God's command to Adam to tend the garden had primarily symbolic significance, as Augustine had believed, then the idea that man was to re-establish paradise through gardening and agriculture would simply not have presented itself so strongly to the seventeenth-century mind.[14]

The Church persecuted some individuals, like Galileo, who were scientists. But the Church is far more guilty of burning Bibles, Bible translators, and theologians, than of banning science books or

---

* Galileo pioneered experimental science. He disproved Aristotle by reportedly dropping a cannonball and musket ball from a tower in Pisa and showing both landed together—or by dropping the balls from a ship's crow's nest.

harassing scientists. Is Christianity thus opposed to theology or not responsible for compiling, preserving, and propagating the Bible?

Religious leaders in my country, India, never persecuted a Galileo. Does that give me a right to boast? Well into the nineteenth century our teachers taught—in a British-funded college—that the earth sat on the back of a great tortoise![15] We never persecuted a Galileo because the Hindu, Buddhist, or animist India never produced one. Those who have no children never experience conflict with their teenagers.

The Church didn't execute scientists for their science. The conflicts ("heresies") were theological, moral, social, personal, political, or administrative. Science was born in the university—an institution invented by the Church. Almost all early scientists worked in Church-related universities, under bishops. Many of them were theologians and biblical exegetes. Giordano Bruno (1548–1600) is often held up as a scientist killed by the Church. The Church saw him as a renegade monk and a Hermetic sorcerer, who did a bit of astronomy but made no contribution to science. Bruno taught a speculative, immanentist philosophy* of a world soul with an infinite number of worlds. His immanentism, from Greece and Islam, hindered science.

Yes, the medieval church and state failed to invent an independent judiciary to which convicts could appeal for justice. One can criticize them for not respecting human rights. That would also apply to every other culture. That doesn't demonstrate that the Church opposed science per se. Many universities and industries treat their scientists and nonscientists unjustly. Except for an independent judiciary—itself a fruit of the Bible—today's institutions would be just as oppressive as medieval ones.[16] Persecuting a subordinate is abuse of power, not opposition to science.

Galileo was revolutionary, brilliant, and popular—but abrasive. He was investigated (1616), yet feted in Rome by cardinals and assured by Pope Paul V of his goodwill and support. Though warned to stick to

---

* This is the idea that the laws of nature are inherent or immanent in things, not imposed by the Creator.

science and treat Copernicus as a hypothesis, Galileo wrote his *Letter to Castelli*, his overzealous student, arguing Copernicus's heliocentric system was consistent with the Bible. Aristotelian professors were jealous of Galileo's popularity and hurt by his insults. The Inquisition first dismissed their accusation that Galileo's *Letter* contradicted the Bible.

In *Dialogue on the Two Great World Systems* (1632), Galileo belittled the Aristotelians and advocated Copernicus as a thesis rather than hypothesis. After *Dialogue* was printed with permission, the Liga accused Galileo of having the fool Simplicio spout Pope Urban's views on cosmology. Galileo was Pope Urban VIII's personal friend; however, mocking his protector and rejecting advice proved too much. Summoned again, Galileo returned to Rome, though Venice offered him asylum and Germany could have sheltered him.* The Inquisition (1633) found little theologically wrong, but banned Galileo's *Dialogue* and sentenced him for breaching unpublished conditions from 1616.

Bible translators like Tyndale were hanged and burned. Galileo, the scientist, had his sentence commuted to house arrest, hosted by the archbishop of Siena. He returned to his own villa at Arceti under supervision, allowing him to finish his *Two New Sciences* (1638). The Vatican allowed Galileo's *Dialogue* to be printed in 1743 and formally lifted its ban in 1822.

Leo XIII (1891) said: "[T]he Church and her Pastors are not opposed to true and solid science ... but that they embrace it, encourage it, and promote it with the fullest possible dedication. . . . Truth cannot contradict truth, and we may be sure that some mistake has been made either in the interpretation of the sacred words, or in the polemical discussion itself.'"

Pope John Paul II (1992) said: "Galileo, a sincere believer, showed himself to be more perceptive [on Bible interpretation] than the theologians who opposed him." "If Scripture cannot err," he wrote to

---

* Luther scorned Copernicus's model, but Lutheran friends published Copernicus's book. Copernicus's heliocentric system lacked a theoretical base and Galileo's experiment on Venus.

Benedetto Castelli, "certain of its interpreters and commentators can and do so in many ways." He affirmed that "Galileo . . . understood why only the Sun could function as the centre of the . . . planetary system."[17]

Power corrupts, and the Church abused its power. That doesn't prove the Bible is against science. Is government opposed to justice and human rights because kings, presidents, dictators, and courts have perverted justice and violated human rights? To repeat: Science was born in universities governed by the Church. It blossomed under the Church's patronage and nowhere else.

Controversies such as the clash between evolution, design, and creation are not conflicts between science and religion. Evolution began as a brilliantly imaginative theory to explain the origin of species without appealing to God. While there is some objective support for "microevolution" or variations within a species, the primary controversy is over the feasibility of macroevolution—and science's philosophical presuppositions. Philosophical atheism has hijacked Darwin's elegant but unproved theory as a weapon in its ideological crusade. Geneticist Richard Lewontin epitomized modern evolutionary science in reviewing Carl Sagan:

> We take the side of science in spite of the patent absurdity of some of its constructs, *in spite* of its failure to fulfill many of its extravagant promises of health and life, *in spite* of the tolerance of the scientific community for unsubstantiated just-so stories, because we have a prior commitment, a commitment to materialism. It is not that the methods and institutions of science somehow compel us to accept a material explanation of the phenomenal world, but, on the contrary, that we are forced by our *a priori* adherence to material causes to create an apparatus of investigation and a set of concepts that produce material explanations, no matter how counter-intuitive, no matter how mystifying to the uninitiated. Moreover, that materialism is an absolute, for we cannot allow a Divine Foot in the door.[18]

In his book *For the Glory of God: How Monotheism Led to Reformations, Science, Witch-Hunts and the End of Slavery,* Rodney Stark shows how Darwinism, once a brilliant and plausible theory, has become "arrogant occultism"[19]—a secular bigotry. Contemporary high priests of academia propagate the theory of macroevolution as "fact"; yet, one and a half centuries after Darwin, scientists still have no quantitative explanation for how major biological groups originated, nor for the Origin Of Life (OOL).

How can unintelligent "chance" produce new organisms with previously nonexistent organs? For example, through intelligent breeding we can produce big cats or small cats, brown cats or black cats—but not flying cats. Scientists had hoped to find fossil evidence for macroevolution. Yet fossil records show biological taxa appearing fully formed and continuing virtually unchanged to the present or until they become extinct.

Evolutionary biologists have stridently insisted that macroevolution is unquestionable. But they face rapidly mounting evidence of incredible biochemical complexity and genomic information. Biochemist Michael Behe evaluated mutation rates and found that two required mutations are all that random mutation can achieve under earthlike conditions.[20] Quantitative evolutionary population dynamics shows increasing mutation loads. *Mendel's Accountant* now enables even high school students to quickly evaluate and visualize these trends.[21] The consequent probabilities of macroevolution from prebiotic chemical soup are so astronomically small as to require great faith.

Some Christians blindly oppose evolution. Others assume God used evolution. But many scientists who are Christians maintain that both the strengths and weaknesses of micro- and macroevolution should be studied and taught objectively as a theory. Mathematician William Dembski and molecular biologist Jonathan Wells explore biological systems from the viewpoint of Intelligent Design as a scientific theory.[22] Scientists need to objectively evaluate all available facts to discover if they support intelligent design in biochemistry or show that life and species could have originated through neo-Darwinian mechanisms.

SHADOWS AND THE BIRTH OF THE
SCIENTIFIC REVOLUTION

The Bible is not a European book. Between the fifth and eleventh centuries, European scholars tended to view nature through the lens of the European philosopher Plato. He taught that the realm of Ideas was the real world and the material world was merely its shadow.

For example, one house may be completely different from another. Why, then, are both of them called a "house"? Plato might answer: Because they are both shadows of the same "Idea"—of the ideal "house" that exists in the *real* nonmaterial or spiritual realm of ideas. The material world is but its shadow. Each *real* object can have an infinite number of shadows, depending on the source, distance, and angle of the light. A study of shadows throws some light on their source. Medieval scholars studied the *shadow* nature primarily to understand the spiritual *reality.*˙

Thus some European church fathers saw the physical universe merely as an inferior, transient, and decaying image of an eternal, spiritual realm. They also saw nature as a *hieroglyph*—a holy book written in a script that uses pictures of natural objects, for example, animals, birds, trees, and mountains. Nature was deemed to be a pictorial book written by God for our moral and religious edification. European church fathers believed that God infused the created world with symbols to lead us to the superior world of spiritual realities. For example, when we see an ant, we ought to learn virtues such as industry, diligence, social organization, and foresight. They saw no value in studying ants for their own sake.

Since we can learn many different lessons from ants, the European church fathers, such as Origen (AD 185–254), adopted the Greek *allegorical* method of interpreting texts. Greek philosophers had developed the allegorical method (hermeneutics) of interpreting their poems, legends, and myths to sanitize morally problematic stories.

---

* Platonic metaphysics was not the only hindrance to science. Some held the pagan idea that a lesser, malevolent deity created the world and that matter was inherently evil. Others believed the Gnostics, that matter was unreal.

For example, regarding Homer, Heraclitus said: "If everything he wrote is not an allegory, [then] everything is an impiety."[23] Philo, the Alexandrian Jew, adopted this allegorical approach to find Greek philosophy in Hebrew Scriptures—the Old Testament—thus bringing it into Jewish culture.*

Like Philo, Alexandrian Christians were immersed in Hellenistic thought. They adopted the Greek allegorical method of reading both the book of God's *words* (the Bible) and the (hieroglyphic) book of God's *works* (nature). They thought that each creature was a divinely made symbol to teach us a lesson. This attitude short-circuited an understanding of nature. Science was born after the Church started reading the Bible literally, not allegorically. That is, when Christendom started to read a text (book or nature) objectively or inductively to see what it taught, instead of seeing what they wanted or thought they should find in it.

Peter Harrison, professor of Humanities and Social Sciences at Bond University, Australia, has amassed evidence** that science became a "revolution" because Protestant reformers insisted that God's word in the Bible and in nature ought to be read literally, not allegorically.

> The emergence of "proper" natural history . . . was due largely to the efforts of Protestant reformers . . . It is commonly supposed that when in the early modern period individuals began to look at the world in a different way, they could no longer believe what they read in the Bible. In this book I shall suggest that the reverse is the case: that when in the sixteenth century people began to read the Bible in a different way, they found themselves forced to jettison traditional conceptions of the world. The Bible—its contents, the controversies it generated, its varying fortunes as an authority, and most importantly, the new way in which it was read by Protestants—played a central role in the emergence of natural science in the seventeenth century.[24]

---

* See chapter 6, "Rationality."
** Harrison amasses evidence that the Bible is the sourcebook of science but believes that the Bible created science indirectly. What was the direct cause? His answer is: the literal way in which the Protestant reformers read the Bible.

Catholic theologians had laid the foundations of science in the thirteenth and fourteenth centuries.[25] The Reformation's success in establishing the Bible's intellectual authority unleashed in the popular culture the Bible's teaching about God, creation, man, sin, salvation, knowledge, education, and the priesthood of all believers. These biblical ideas, as we shall see, were crucial to the birth of what we now call the scientific revolution.

Several recent studies have explored the Bible's role in launching modern science. For nonspecialists, an excellent starting point is Rodney Stark's book *For the Glory of God*. Stark, who taught sociology at the University of Washington, became deeply interested in history. He drew up a "Roster of Scientific Stars," a list of the fifty-two most important scientists who pioneered the scientific revolution, beginning with the publication of Copernicus's *De revolutionibus* in 1543. Stark reviewed all the information available on their personal beliefs and discovered that all but two were Christians. Only Edmund Halley and Paracelsus could be called skeptics.

Sixty percent of the men who created science were "devout" Christians—Catholic and Protestant—who did science "for the glory of God." The rest were "conventional" Christians. Although their piety did not stand out, it was entirely satisfactory to their religious associates.[26] Elaine Howard Ecklund's statistics[27] may be better. Specialists are squabbling over Stark's list and will probably contest Ecklund's statistics. What is incontestable about Stark's thesis is that devout Christians who pioneered modern science include people like Robert Boyle (1627–91), who "expended a considerable portion of his limited funds to have the Bible translated into various languages."[28] Boyle's friend Sir Isaac Newton "was as interested in theology and Bible prophecy as in physics—he left more than a million words on these topics."[29] These men promoted the Bible because they saw it as the sourcebook of science.

INFERENCE OR PRESUPPOSITION?

Some scientists think that "God"—an intelligent creative agent behind the cosmos—is a necessary *inference* from what we know about the universe. Historically, the biblical idea of God is not the inference but the *presupposition*, or source, of science. This will be easier to understand by discussing why Islam could not develop science.

Islam appropriated Greek knowledge via the Eastern Church, which had preserved and copied Greek manuscripts. Islamic scholars translated those manuscripts into Arabic and improved on Greek knowledge. They brought Greek manuscripts or translations into Europe. Why, then, did Islam fail to develop empirical science? Scholars are studying that question. One factor is the failure of Muslim scholars to critique the foundations of Greek thought, especially its cosmology and rationalism. During the twelfth and thirteenth centuries, Greco-Islamic pseudo-science almost trapped the West. For reasons discussed in the Appendix, Europe read and believed the Bible as God's revealed truth. That saved it from the Greek worldview that was incompatible with the Bible.

Islam had an almighty, personal Creator; what it lacked was the Bible. Though Muhammad declared the Bible was divinely inspired, Muslims read it only to critique it. The compilers of the Islamic *Rasa'il, the Encyclopedia of Brethren of Purity* (around the tenth century), embraced the Greek idea that the world was *Gaia*, a huge conscious living organism with its own intellect and soul. This opened the way for pantheistic, cyclic, animistic, and magical ideas to permeate the Islamic worldview. It infected Islam with the critical problem of Greek Platonic perspective, that the world was intelligible through eternal "forms" for its objects. For Greeks, to *know* something was to perceive those forms. Once the mind understood these forms, it grasped the essence—the inherent, necessary, immanent logic—of things. That knowledge was final. It could not be challenged or changed by experience.

This Aristotelian and Islamic "metaphysical Necessitarianism"[30] made empirical verification of "true knowledge" unnecessary. This outlook caused Muslim philosophers, such as Avicenna (980–1037) and Averröes or Ibn Rushd (1128–98), to become doctrinaire and intransigent followers of Aristotle. They believed that Aristotle's physics was complete and infallible. Consequently, if an observation contradicted Aristotle, then the problem was with the observation—it must be incorrect or an illusion.

European theologians studied all the great books. They were open to receiving knowledge from the Greeks, including via Muslim scholars, translators, and interpreters. However, they were committed to the Bible. The biblical worldview both improved upon Aristotle and opposed the Greek cosmological worldview.

The Bible cleansed Aristotle's confidence in human reason from the contaminating influence of animism. It strengthened it by grounding it in the image of God. In his seminal essay, "Christian Theology and Modern Science of Nature," M. B. Foster explained:

> The first great contribution of Christian theology to the development of modern natural science was the reinforcement which it supplied to the scientific element in Aristotle himself; in particular it supplied a justification for the faith, which for Aristotle had been an ungrounded assumption, that there is reason in nature discoverable by the exercise of reason in man.
>
> The "rationalist" element of Aristotle's philosophy of nature was inconsistent with the "animism" which he maintained side by side with it. The latter element was utterly incompatible with Christian doctrine, and had to be quite eliminated from any theory of nature which should be consistent with a Christian theology.[31]

Foster's insight is important: Alexander the Great's conquests spread Greek ideas as far as India. But in most cultures, animism, gnosticism, and mysticism overshadowed reason and evidence. The Bible reinforced the Greek confidence in the human mind, and even more importantly it removed the irrationalism inherent in animism.

Foster explains that for the birth of science, disagreement with Aristotle was more important than the agreement over the usefulness of reason. He calls these disagreements the "un-Greek" elements of the Bible. They were critically responsible for science.

> What is the [historical] source of the un-Greek elements which were imported into philosophy by the post-Reformation philosophers, and which constitute the modernity of modern philosophy? . . .

What is the source of those un-Greek elements in the modern theory of nature by which the peculiar character of the modern science of nature was to be determined? The answer to the first question is: The Christian revelation [the Bible], and the answer to the second: The Christian doctrine of creation.[32]

What were these "un-Greek" teachings of the Bible that became foundational for science? The Bible begins with: "In the beginning God created the heavens and the earth." Consequently, the cosmos was not eternal, nor was God a part of the cosmos. God was free and he existed before the cosmos. He was free to create whatever kind of cosmos he wanted to create. There were no eternal forms, no necessary preexisting logic to bind God. St. Albertus Magnus (Albert the Great, or *doctor universalis,* ca. AD 1206–80) introduced Greek and Arabic science and philosophy to the medieval world and critiqued it. Medieval Catholic theologians realized that Aristotle's "necessitarianism" contradicted the freedom and omnipotence of the biblical God.

Consequently, the bishop of Paris, Etienne Tempier, and the archbishop of Canterbury, Robert Kilwardby, convened the 1277 Church Council. It formally rejected the Greco-Islamic idea that logic dictated what God could or could not do. They learned from the Bible that God was free. Therefore, neither the cosmos nor human logic could bind him. This was one cornerstone of the scientific principle: we need to empirically *observe* what God has done, not presume what he could or could not do based on our intuition and logic. If the essence of the Greek "forms" were knowable, logic would be able to deduce the properties of objects without empirical observation.

John Locke later restated this biblical objection to Aristotle by declaring that the "Real Essence" of natural objects was unknowable.

Not every statement of the 1277 Council was helpful. But the council clarified issues and triggered intense reflection. The strongest criticism of Greco-Islamic natural philosophy (or science) came from the nominalist Franciscan theologians. William of Ockham (1285–ca. 1349), the most prominent nominalist, studied and taught at the University of Oxford (1309–19). Known as *Doctor Invincibilis* ("unconquerable doctor") and *Venerabilis Inceptor* ("worthy initiator"), he formulated "Ockham's razor." He turned the Islamic/ Aristotelian perspective down, grounding natural law and all ethical values on the will of God rather than in metaphysical necessity or ideal forms. Ockham distinguished between God's absolute power (*agistrat absoluta*), by which he could do anything, and his ordained power (*agistrat agistra*), by which he condescends to work within the natural and moral law that he established.

Pope John XXII denounced some moral implications of Ockham's teachings, placing him in house detention from 1324 to 1328. However, many influential Catholic theologians advanced his teachings. Among Ockham's advocates were French Scholastic philosopher Jean Buridan (1300–58) of the University of Paris, and his renowned successors Pierre d'Ailly (1350–1420) and Jean Gerson (1363–1429), both chancellors of the University of Paris. D'Ailly in turn influenced Martin Luther and Zwingli, bringing Ockham's perspective on the Bible into the Protestant Reformation and stimulating empirical science.

Professor Willis B. Glover summarized:

> The biblical doctrine of creation is unique; no religion other than those developed out of the biblical tradition contains anything like it. In the biblical doctrine God is in any ontological sense completely discontinuous with the world. The world on the other hand is completely dependent on God; it continues to exist for his continuing will for it to exist. Its unity is in his will or purpose and not an intrinsic property. Its order is, therefore, in no way binding on God. The complete freedom of God with respect to the whole creation was a fundamental influence on late medieval thought. Since God's creative acts are subject to no eternal truths, knowledge of the world could not be derived deductively from philosophy but must come through actual observation. It could not, moreover, be certain knowledge because no one could know for sure what God might do next. There thus entered into Western philosophy, especially into

---

* Refined as "Einstein's razor" to ~ *Make things as simple as possible, but not simpler.*

its empirical tradition, that kind of relative skepticism which recognizes that human knowledge is not without a kind of validity, but yet sees it as partial and only approximate.[33]

GOD'S TWO BOOKS

Francis Bacon (1561–1626) and Galileo Galilei (1564–1642) are considered founders of the scientific method—the reliance on empirical observation over human logic or authority.[34] Both held to the truth of both of God's two books—the book of nature and the book of God's Word, the Bible. Both books had to be studied to better understand God. In 1603, Francis Bacon, Lord Chancellor of England and a founder of the Royal Society, wrote, quoting Jesus:

For our Saviour saith, "You err, not knowing the Scriptures, nor the power of God," [Matthew 22:29 KJV] laying before us two books or volumes to study, if we will be secured from error: first the Scriptures, revealing the will of God, and then the creatures [natural science] expressing his power, whereof the latter is a key unto the former: not only opening our understanding to conceive the true sense of the Scriptures by the general notions of reason and rules of speech, but chiefly opening our belief, in drawing us into a due meditation of the omnipotency of God, which is chiefly signed and engraven upon His works.[35]

Similarly, in 1615 Galileo wrote:

For the Holy Bible and the phenomena of nature proceed alike from the divine word the former as the dictate of the Holy Ghost and the latter as the observant executrix of God's command.[36]

In 1776, the American colonists founded the United States of America on these "laws of nature and of nature's God."[37] Many secularists associate the Bible with dogmatism, and science with skepticism or open-mindedness. Thus, it is worth repeating that the West's intellectual openness, which set it apart from Islam and Plato, is a result of biblical theology. It began with the epistemology of medieval nominalists who realized that the biblical doctrine of God does more than make logic subservient to empirical observation. As Glover put it:

> The nominalists avoided the Averroistic heresy of thinking that God acted in accordance with some necessity of his own nature. Because creation was a completely free act of God, its very existence was not necessary. And because God was completely free to establish any order of creation he pleased, the order that he did in fact establish cannot be known by deduction from any principles whatsoever but only by observation or revelation. So far as the physical world was concerned, knowledge of its objects and of the relationships that existed between them could be known only empirically ... The contingency of the world on the absolute freedom of God had skeptical implications. God could do anything he pleased free of any rational order which might guide human mind in its predictions; nothing, therefore, was predictable in any absolute sense. If one insisted with Aristotle that only what could be known with certainty was valid knowledge, then all physical science was a vain undertaking.[38]

Why, then, should we study science? Philosophers like Plato and Aristotle looked at nature to discover universal and metaphysical truths, including the meaning and purpose of existence. They proceeded abstractly and deductively. But their conclusions became the a priori assumptions of future generations, and these assumptions chained the European mind. Europe could not develop the scientific method until these chains were broken by the biblical doctrine of divine freedom. As Professor Glover pointed out, the Bible did not lead them merely to question the Aristotelian/Islamic idea of absolute knowledge, but

> it also impressed upon them the reality and worth of the material creation . . . They accepted the significance of what conditional

knowledge of the world was possible to them. The historical fact is that scientific interest was stimulated in them.[39]

Science is an objective ("secular") study of the laws of nature *because* of its biblical inspiration as God's creation, not in spite of that. Science was not founded on a presupposition of God-less materialism.

Many philosophers and scientists today expect that no answers to the "big questions" are possible, and that we can only have knowledge that is discovered by science. This attitude leads to nihilism. Almost all founders of science thought differently. They were willing to concentrate on studying small, specific questions because they believed that the Creator had already answered the big questions in the Bible. They believed it was their duty and privilege to discover what had not been revealed, but which was written in nature. Francis Bacon explicitly cited the Bible to give meaning to in-depth inquiries into details of creation: "It is the glory of God to conceal a matter; to search out a matter is the glory of kings."[40] Glover said this implied that:

> [t]he purpose which informed creation was inscrutable (except insofar as God had revealed it); it was God's purpose and was not inherent in created objects. Final causation was thus banished from physics; the aim of physics was to discover the efficient causation that operated in the order that God had established for physical objects in the world. This was a crucial step from ancient physics to the physics of the modern world . . . they were free to make the limited, piecemeal studies of the physical world which have been the hallmark of modern science and the way to its great accomplishments.[41]

SIN AND SCIENCE

The Bible's teaching on creation was a key factor behind the birth of modern science. Biblical perspectives on sin, the curse, and salvation were equally important.

The premodern world did not deal with diseases, hunger, and

starvation or cope with natural calamities and social injustices as we do. As Thomas Hobbes noted, life was tragically "solitary, poor, nasty, brutish, and short." For sages like the Buddha, the fact of suffering was the first inescapable or "Noble" truth. This suffering made the Gnostics think that the material world was evil. Therefore, they believed that God could not have incarnated in a material body.

Christians lived in the same world as everyone else—filled with inexplicable suffering. Jesus' closest friend, John, refuted Gnostic teaching as demonic heresy[42] because he and others were eyewitnesses of the bodily life, death, resurrection, and ascension of Jesus. For those disciples, the physical incarnation, resurrection, and ascension of Jesus were the ultimate proof that matter was good.[43] It existed for God's glory.[44]

Some philosophies, such as Christian Science and the New Age's *A Course in Miracles*, see physical problems as illusory. The Bible deals with real problems in the physical world. Were they intrinsic to nature, a result of the Creator's poor craftsmanship? No, the Bible shows our suffering as an abnormality that God hates. It came as a curse upon the rebellion of Adam and Eve (called "the fall" into sin).[45] The Bible teaches "when the crown of creation had fallen, his dominions had fallen with him."[46] According to the Bible, sin seriously hinders human attempts to establish dominion over the earth.[47]

The "good news," according to the Bible, is that Jesus Christ came to save us from our sin.[48] He took our sin and its curse upon himself on the cross.[49] Jesus died for our sin.[50] Therefore, he is able to forgive us when we repent for our sin and ask for forgiveness.[51] Old Testament readers knew that God's gift of salvation includes healing for the land,[52] which the New Testament affirms:

> For the creation waits with eager longing for the revealing of the sons of God. For the creation was subjected to futility, not willingly, but because of him who subjected it, in hope that the creation itself will be set free from its bondage to decay and obtain the freedom of the glory of the children of God. For we know that the whole creation has been groaning together in the pains of childbirth until now. And

not only the creation, but we ourselves, who have the first fruits of the Spirit, groan inwardly as we wait eagerly for adoption as sons, the redemption of our bodies.[53]

Francis Bacon, the "father of the scientific method," expressed the relationship of sin to science in these famous words:

> For man by the Fall fell both from his state of innocence and his dominion over creation. Both of these, however, can even in this life be made good; the former by religion and faith, the latter by arts and sciences.[54]

GOD'S BOOK OF NATURE

In my country, the Hindu ashrams and Buddhist monasteries did not teach science. Why did Christian universities in Europe—equally religious institutions—begin developing and teaching science? Bible scholars learned that reading the "book of nature" was more important than reading Greek and Latin books. The latter were written by men, but the former was written by God. Paracelsus wrote that before we study Galen, Avicenna, and Aristotle, we should study the book of nature, which is a library of books that "God himself wrote, made, and bound."[55]

Some theologians even advocated that the study of nature should precede the study of Scriptures because, as English author and physician Sir Thomas Browne (1605–82) put it, nature was God's "universall and publick Manuscript."[56] Tertullian, the second-century theologian, taught that God wrote the book of nature long before the Scriptures had been compiled.[57]

As European theologians began studying the Bible seriously, they came to realize that Adam and Eve knew nature before the fall. One result of the fall was losing that knowledge of nature. To recover the Creator's image required being renewed in our minds. By knowing the world, people could begin to restore things to their original unity, which they had possessed with the divine mind. By controlling and subduing the world, human beings themselves could begin to be restored to their original position as God's viceroys on earth.

During the Middle Ages, many Christians thought that redemption meant a flight from the world, mastery over one's lusts, and a mystical absorption into God. But this fresh study of the Bible suggested that redemption meant not mystical absorption into God, but the restoration of God's likeness, including the recovery of his creative and ordered knowledge of the natural world and power over it.

This new understanding of biblical salvation is often associated with Francis Bacon. However, it was a growing understanding that began centuries before him. Adelard of Bath (d. post-1142) said, "If anyone born or educated in the residence of this world neglects learning the plan underlying its marvelous beauty, upon attaining the age of discretion, he is unworthy and, were it possible, deserves to be cast out of it."[58]

The Protestant Reformation awakened popular interest in discovering and knowing truth, and that boosted science. The Reformers took Christ's exhortation seriously that knowledge of truth would liberate.[59] Luther emphasized the biblical idea of the priesthood of all believers.[60] Consequently, all human beings should do everything for the glory of God.[61] Since everything exists for the glory of God,[62] and the heavens declare his glory,[63] it is right for God's people to study all things, including the heavens. Thus almost all the pioneers of science were Christians and a majority of them were devout Christians. They were laboring for the glory of God.

Part VI

WHAT MADE THE WEST THE BEST?

*For the individual person [in the West] this myth of original sin
and redemption is turned into the ritual of confessing the guilt. The
confession of guilt not only relieves the confessor of the burden of guilt;
it also purifies him. If the confessing individual proves to be innocent,
but nevertheless takes on the burden of collective guilt, he sanctifies
his own mundane individuality, he performs Christomimesis
and—as a political leader—partakes of the charisma of the hero.
Thus the European ritual of confessing guilt for sins of the past relies
on a mythology that remains even if the political representatives
performing the ritual are utterly secularized individuals who ignore
the cultural origin of their actions.*

—BERNHARD GIESEN

Chapter Fourteen

MORALITY

WHY ARE SOME LESS CORRUPT?

In films such as *Wall Street: Money Never Sleeps* and *Social Network*, Hollywood is showing secular capitalism changing America's motto to "In Greed We Trust." In the summer of 2010, the US Congress passed a twenty-three-hundred-page act to regulate the financial sector. This act is an admission of the massive corruption in that sector of the economy. Wall Street's corruption, however, has yet to become a part of Main Street. Growing immorality has, once again, begun to hurt the church's credibility. Nevertheless, the traditional morality of the West, easily evident in small towns and villages, is incomprehensible to most non-Western visitors.

For example, in 1982, I was traveling to England for a conference on economic development. Leaving New Delhi after midnight, I was sleepy, but the Sikh gentleman next to me talked nonstop. He was returning to England after visiting his parents in a Punjab village in northwest India. He could not comprehend why I was living in poverty, serving the poor. He took it as his mission to persuade me to settle in England. Doing business in England, he argued, was easy and profitable. After being harassed for more than an hour, I began to lose my patience. But something intrigued me. He could not speak a single sentence without making a mistake. How could someone who spoke such poor English succeed as a businessman in England? So I asked, "Tell me, sir, why is business so easy in England?"

"Because everyone trusts you there," he answered, without pausing for a moment. Having not yet ventured into a business, I did not grasp how important trust was to success in business. I pushed back my seat and went to sleep. After the conference, Mr. Jan van Barneveld hosted me in his home at Doorn Holland.

One afternoon Jan said to me, "Come let us get some milk." We walked between gorgeous moss-covered trees to a dairy farm. I had never seen anything like this: a neat and tidy dairy farm with about one hundred cows but no human beings. The cows were milked automatically, and the milk was pumped into a large boiler-like tank.

We entered the milk room, where Jan opened the tap and filled his jug. Then he reached out to a windowsill and pulled down a bowl full of cash. He took out his wallet, drew a twenty-guilder note, and put it into the bowl. He helped himself to the change from the bowl, put it into his wallet, picked up the jug, and started to walk out. I couldn't believe my eyes. "Man," I said, "if you were an Indian, you would take the milk and the money!" Jan laughed. But in that instant, I understood what that Sikh businessman had been trying to tell me.

If this were India and I walked out with the money and the milk, the dairy owner would need to hire a cashier. Who would pay for the cashier? I, the consumer, would; and the price of milk would go up. But if the consumer were corrupt, why should the dairy owner be honest? He would add water to the milk to make more money. I would then be paying more for adulterated milk. I would complain, "The milk is adulterated; the government must appoint inspectors."

Who would pay for the inspectors? I, the taxpayer, would. But if the consumer, producer, and the supplier were corrupt, why should the inspectors be honest? They would extract bribes from the supplier. If he did not bribe them, the inspectors would delay the supply and ensure that the milk curdled before it got to me.*

Who would pay for the bribe? Again, I, the consumer, would pay

---

* Much of the world does not have refrigerated vans and storage facilities for milk.

the additional cost. By the time I paid for the milk, the cashier, the water, the inspector, and the bribe, I would have little money left to buy chocolate for the milk—so my children would not drink the milk and would be weaker than the Dutch children. Having spent extra money on the milk, I would not be able to take my children out for ice cream. The cashier, water, bribe, and inspector add no value to the milk. The ice-cream industry does. My corruption keeps me from patronizing a value-adding business. That reduces our economy's capacity to create jobs.

Some years ago I shared this story in a conference in Indonesia. An Egyptian participant laughed the most. As all eyes turned to him, he explained, "We Egyptians are cleverer than these Indians. If no one was watching, we would take the milk, the money, and the cows." The gentleman was too charitable toward us Indians.

CYNICISM IN INDIA

Many years after my trip to Holland, I heard "uncle" Emmanuel* complain that they were getting highly adulterated milk in Mussoorie. I told him that Ruth had finally found an honest milkman and that we were getting pure milk. After I had spent half an hour trying to persuade the uncle that they should buy milk from our milkman, he got tired and dismissed me as utterly naïve. "It's impossible to get pure milk in Mussoorie," he said. "Your milkman must be very clever. He must be adding something other than water to the milk, something that you haven't figured out as yet."

Taking the hint, I changed the conversation to the question of corruption. Uncle, a retired railway engine driver, told me that he had just heard from a friend of his (also a retired driver) that his son had spent nine months and thirty thousand Indian rupees in bribes and still had not gotten a job with the railways. This was in spite of the policy that after an employee retires, one of his children will be given preference in recruitment. Then uncle described at length how he became employed in the 1940s. Here's the abridged version.

---

* Father-in-law to my older brother and younger sister.

The British were ruling India. The recruiting officer examined his certificates, ordered an immediate in-house physical checkup, offered him a cup of tea, looked at the doctor's report, and ordered that an appointment letter be given to him the next day. The following morning the clerk issued the appointment letter with another cup of tea! No bribes, no strings pulled, and no delays.

Recruitment was a clean, prompt, and professional affair, based solely on merit. The consequence was competent employees who were loyal to the enterprise, proud of their work, and respectful of law, authority, and the government. That era, the uncle lamented, had gone for good. Fifty years of independence offered no hope for the future.

THE EFFECT OF CORRUPTION

Transparency International (TI), a German nongovernmental organization, has long recognized the correlation between corruption and poverty. Each year TI publishes a Global Corruption Perceptions Index (CPI) that ranks countries from the least corrupt to the most corrupt. The index for 2009 ranks 180 countries, with 10 points allotted for a totally clean country. No country, of course, gets 10 points; a majority of the countries receive fewer than 5 points—meaning that they are more corrupt than clean. Here are extracts from the 2009 rankings:

Rank	Country	CPI 2009 Score (out of 10 points)
1	New Zealand	9.4
2	Denmark	9.3
3	Singapore	9.2
17	United Kingdom	7.7
19	United States	7.5
79	China	3.6
84	India	3.4
146	Russia	2.2
176	Iraq	1.5
179	Afghanistan	1.3
180	Somalia	1.1

Does poverty cause corruption? Or does corruption cause poverty? Whether the chicken comes first or the egg is an interesting but theoretical question. Peter Eigen, TI chairman in 2002, emphasized the role corruption plays in keeping countries poor:

> Political elites and their cronies continue to take kickbacks at every opportunity. Hand in glove with corrupt business people, they are trapping whole nations in poverty and hampering sustainable development. Corruption is perceived to be dangerously high in poor parts of the world, but also in many countries whose firms invest in developing nations . . . Politicians *increasingly* [emphasis added] pay lip service to the fight against corruption but they fail to act on the clear message of TI's CPI: that they must clamp down on corruption to break the vicious cycle of poverty and graft . . . Corrupt political elites in the developing world, working hand-in-hand with greedy business people and unscrupulous investors, are putting private gain before the welfare of citizens and the economic development of their countries.[1]

Eigen considers corruption to be a major roadblock to development. He blames it on the political and economic elite—not on the poor. TI has released such CPIs for many years now. They are finding that hypocrisy (lip service) and corruption are increasing in many parts of the world. Eigen appeals to political leaders in the developing world to exert political force to eradicate corruption, but he complains that such appeals aren't working.

An important finding of the CPI is that the least corrupt countries are the Protestant countries—that is, secular nations whose cultures were shaped decisively by the Bible. The only exception is Singapore, a tiny city-state.*

---

* Like Hong Kong, Singapore was also a British colony. It has a rapidly growing and highly influential church. It is estimated that of the citizens who matter in government, for example, university students and graduates, approximately 33 percent are already Christian. That statistic notwithstanding, Singapore is an example that under certain circumstances, dictatorship or political force can help eradicate corruption.

Let us ignore the results of British administration and assume that even though dictatorship usually increases corruption, at least in Singapore it has uprooted some of the corruption. The Singapore experiment raises these questions:

- Will Singapore remain corruption-free after the dictators are gone?
- Could the methods of a city-state be used in large countries where an individual cannot oversee the overall administration?
- Does Singapore's dictatorship demonstrate that when you rely exclusively on force to eradicate corruption, you free a people from freedom as well as from corruption?

How did ordinary people of Holland become so different from our people in India and Egypt? The answer is simple. The Bible taught the people of Holland that even though no human being may be watching us in that dairy farm, God, our ultimate judge, is watching to see if we obey his commands to neither covet nor steal. According to the Bible, "Nothing in all creation is hidden from God's sight. Everything is uncovered and laid bare before the eyes of him to whom we must give account."[2]

How was this Bible teaching instilled in Holland's culture? Following the sixteenth-century Reformation, the Heidelberg Catechism played perhaps the most important role in shaping Holland's moral culture. This 1563 German catechism was translated into Dutch in 1566. Four Dutch synods approved it for use in Dutch churches. Finally the Synod of Dort (1618–19) adopted it officially as the second of the Three Forms of Unity. The synod made it obligatory that ministers teach the catechism every Sunday. The catechism played the same role in Holland as Moses' "ark of the covenant" played in Israel. The catechism expounds the eighth commandment, "You shall not steal," as follows:

Question 110: What does God forbid in the eighth commandment?

Answer: God forbids not only those thefts and robberies that are punishable by the courts; but he includes under the name of "stealing" all deceitful tricks and devices, whereby we design to appropriate to ourselves anything belonging to our neighbor—whether it be by force or under the appearance of right, as by unjust weights, inaccurate measurements, false reckoning of time spent in service, fraudulent merchandise, false coins, exorbitant interest, or by any other means forbidden by God. God is forbidding covetousness as well as all abuse as waste of a person's gifts.

Question 111: But what does God require in this commandment?

Answer: That I seek the advantage of my neighbor rather than my own every instance I can and deal with my neighbor as I desire to be dealt with by others. Further, that I faithfully labor and generously give, so that I may be able to care for the hurting and relieve the needy.

The command against stealing sounds simple, so why was the catechism reading all these extra things into it? The catechism did not inject anything into the Ten Commandments that the Bible itself did not teach. The Bible said that God's people who did not give a tenth of their income to God were robbing God.[3] A tiny nation such as Holland had surplus money to give to India, Egypt, and Indonesia because the Bible taught its people to work hard and give tithes and offerings to God. The people obeyed the Bible, which commanded, "Let the thief no longer steal, but rather let him labor, doing honest work with his own hands, so that he may have something to share with anyone in need."[4]

The CPI confirms what I saw in Holland—that the Bible is the only force known to history that has freed entire nations from corruption while simultaneously giving them political freedom. The most secular nations—that is, the ex-communist, atheistic nations, which teach that when no man or machine is watching you, then no one is watching you—are among the most corrupt nations, not too different from Hindu, Buddhist, and Muslim nations.

What the Indian businessman told me on the plane to London about England's culture of trust intrigued me because as students in India we always heard that Robert Clive, who won Bengal for the British, took a huge bribe to install his puppet as the *Nawab* (ruler) of Bengal. Following Clive's example, the employees and soldiers of the British East India Company began a reign of amazingly overt corruption. No British historian disputes that verdict. Lord Macaulay, who spent many years in India, catalogued and explained this corruption. His conclusion was that during its early phase, the British rule in India was a "government of an evil genii, rather than the government of human tyrants."[5]

How was England transformed? What changed the moral character of British administration in India? Was it the Ten Commandments? Or is there some power greater than the law?

In the plane I was too sleepy to discuss this with the Sikh gentleman, but during the conference I was delighted when an American author, Miriam Adeney, showed me Ian Bradley's book *The Call to Seriousness: The Evangelical Impact on the Victorians.*[6] I grabbed it. Bradley started me on a course of study that resulted in two of my books,[7] describing how the Bible transformed British administration in India from the rule of an evil genie to a "civil service." I learned that Macaulay played a crucial role in that transformation.

THE GOSPEL'S POWER TO SAVE US FROM OUR SIN

The empirical data says that countries most influenced by the Bible are the least corrupt. Why would that be the case? The apostle Paul experienced the gospel's power to change his life and those of his followers. He said that the gospel—the incident of Jesus' shameful death on the cross—that sounds like foolishness to the philosophical Greeks and weakness to the Jews was in fact the wisdom and the power of God for our salvation.[8] Paul succinctly summed up the gospel: "Christ died for our sins in accordance with the Scriptures, that he was buried, that he was raised on the third day in accordance with the Scriptures."[9]

What is so powerful about this theological jargon? Even if it actually happened in history, how could repeating such a story deliver entire nations from corruption? True or false, the gospel is anything but mumbo jumbo. It is a straightforward eyewitness account. To say that Jesus died for our sins is to say that the eyewitnesses who saw Jesus hanging on the cross understood that Jesus was carrying the sin of the world on it. That is, they saw with their naked eyes that it was not the justice of the world that was hanging upon the cross of Calvary, but injustice, cruelty, and brutality.

Both judges who tried Jesus—Pilate and Herod—found him not guilty. Why, then, was he hanging on the cross? It was the envy, jealousy, hatred, and fear of the then Jewish leadership that crucified him. It was the greed of his disciple Judas who betrayed him for thirty pieces of silver. It was the moral cowardice of Jesus' followers and the Jewish masses. The sin of the world, in other words, was visible to the naked eye of every witness—whether a follower of Christ, his opponent, or an indifferent passerby. The cross was a demonstration that even if sin yields some good results—silver, in the case of Judas—the ultimate consequence of sin is terrible. It is death.

The other part of the gospel is an equally straightforward eyewitness statement. The followers of Jesus Christ, who saw him dead and buried, later saw that his tomb was empty. Jesus did not reincarnate into another body. He was resurrected in the same, although transformed, body. The disciples saw him, talked with him, touched him, and ate with him—not in a state of trance or meditation, but in full possession of their skeptical senses.

At least one of the disciples, Thomas, did not believe the multiple reports of the resurrection. But then, the man who had died stood in front of Thomas, inviting him to verify that he was the same person whose hands were pierced with the nails that hung him upon the cross. Thomas chose to accept the fact and modify his worldview. The historical fact of Christ's crucifixion and resurrection had profound philosophical implications.

Those who saw the resurrected Jesus had empirical grounds for believing that death was not the end of human existence. Resurrection

meant that we continue to exist beyond our death and remain accountable to God. Just as the consequence of sin was death, the consequence
of faith and obedience was resurrection life. The death and resurrection of Jesus became good news—the gospel—because they were
more than historical events. They were a demonstration of God's
redemptive intervention in our history. They implied, among other
things, that morality was more than a social construct or the law of
the land.

A tyrant may be above the law; a politician, civil servant, or well-
connected businessman may belong to a brutal system that operates
above the law. He may ignore the law and rob people in broad daylight
by forcing them to pay bribes. It may be impossible to bring corrupt
officials to justice in this world. Yet, if moral law is God's law, no
one will be able to escape it. Everyone will stand before the judgment
seat of God and give an account of his life.[10] He will have to take the
consequence of his sin—unless, of course, he repents for his sin and
accepts the forgiveness and eternal life that Jesus offers. Jesus can forgive because he became the sacrificial Lamb of God and took the sin
of the world upon himself.

This was the good news, the gospel. It cleaned up America when
Jonathan Edwards (1703–58), America's first philosopher, began
preaching it in sermons like "Sinners in the Hands of an Angry God."

The risen Jesus appeared to John when he was imprisoned on the
island of Patmos and said, "Behold, I stand at the door and knock.
If anyone hears my voice and opens the door, I will come in to him
and eat with him, and he with me."[11] When the light comes in and
begins to dwell in us, our inner darkness will be driven out. In other
words, Jesus does what no dictator can do. A dictator could punish
me for taking a bribe, but Jesus deals with the greed in my heart that
prompts me to covet other people's money. A dictator could punish
me for abusing my wife. Jesus, if he dwells in my heart, convicts and
asks me to repent. He also gives me his power to love. When I invite
Jesus to come into my heart by his Spirit, then I am born again into a
new spiritual life.

Islam and Christianity share in common the idea of moral absolutes.

The difference is that Allah is too majestic to come into a dirty manger or into a filthy heart. If God does not come into this world to save sinners, then other sinners—dictators and tyrants—have to do the dirty work of restraining our sinfulness. But by cleaning us from the inside, Jesus makes possible inner self-government, socio-political freedom, and clean public life.

Is the gospel merely religious rhetoric? The testimony of history is that Christendom was as corrupt as any other part of the world until it recovered this biblical gospel during the Reformation. That created the moral climate and trustworthiness in England, witnessed first-hand by my fellow passenger on the airplane.

ENGLAND BEFORE AND AFTER JOHN WESLEY

Ian Bradley's book began helping me understand England and the power of the gospel that transformed its colonies in Africa and Asia. A few years later, a lecture by Donald Drew given at L'Abri Fellowship in England helped me connect the dots that Bradley had already drawn. The lecture was on the founder of Methodism, John Wesley (1703–91), and his impact on England. Following are the main points of Drew's lecture.[12]

In 1738, two centuries after the Reformation, Bishop Berkeley declared that religion and morality in Britain had collapsed "to a degree that was never before known in any Christian country." The important reasons for the degeneration of Protestant England were the restoration of the monarchy and the supremacy of the Anglican Church at the end of the seventeenth century. Once the Anglican Church came back to power, it began to oppress the Puritans and expelled more than four hundred conscientious Anglican clergymen. They had become priests to serve God, and therefore they refused the oath of allegiance to William of Orange.

The combined impact of these developments was to leave the church bereft of prophets. Matters were made worse by the decree prohibiting Anglican bishops and clergy from meeting together to deliberate on ecclesiastical matters. With little correction, encouragement, or accountability, the moral life of the priests degenerated, lowering the standards for the whole nation.

The rise of the Enlightenment, toward the end of the seventeenth century and through the eighteenth century, made the situation hopeless. Deism, or "natural religion," taught that God is not involved in the affairs of the world. He has given no law. He is neither watching over you, nor will he judge, punish, or reward you. God is just an uninvolved creator. That belief took away the fear of God. The Bible was still available, but it was not the Word of God. It was just another book about wisdom and virtue.

A national church publicly muzzled, with its prophetic and priestly wings clipped, could not refute deists and skeptics. Deism progressed to rationalism, skepticism, atheism, and finally cynicism. Once biblical truth was undermined, biblical morality began to lose ground. The corruption of the clergy of the Church of England spread from top to bottom. A succession of archbishops and bishops lived luxuriously, neglecting their duties, unashamedly soliciting bishoprics and deaneries for themselves and their families. Parish clergy followed suit.

Beginning with Queen Anne, the royalty began to fill their courts with courtiers who flaunted levity and practiced vice. Serious Christians began staying away from Oxford and Cambridge, where dons busied themselves in their books while undergraduates immersed themselves in wine and women, sport and song.

A corrupt church with closed Scriptures darkened most aspects of English life. By the treaty of Utrecht in 1713, England had wrung from France and Spain the monopoly of the slave trade. The slave trade bred and fed financial greed. It brutalized masters' and slaves' lives, making labor undignified. That became a curse on the economic and political life of the eighteenth century.

The Industrial Revolution was gradually spreading, and the attitudes of the slave traders influenced many owners of mines, factories, and mills in the treatment of their workers. The barbarities practiced in industry were bad enough, but those carried out on slave ships and then in plantations chill one's blood. It is estimated that during that century the number of Africans carried into slavery, largely in British ships and largely from West Africa to America, ran into the millions. There was some slavery in England too. And because of the enormous sums of money involved in the slave trade, there were repeated financial scandals, leading to loss and ruin, the chief of which was the South Sea Bubble of 1720 that virtually wrecked the national economy. Dishonesty fortified more dishonesty.

Corruption spreads like cancer. Nepotism, place seeking, and bribery became the order of the day in politics, especially at election times. For the first half of the century, the prime minister, Robert Walpole, epitomized corruption. His politics were not about public service but about managing men, means, money, and the manipulation of laws, their administration, and the penal system in the interest of the ruling classes.

Britain at this time, more than at any other, was a nation divided between the rich and the poor. The laws were devised largely to keep the poor in their place and under control. Thus to steal a sheep, to snare a rabbit, to break a young tree, to pick a pocket for more than one shilling, and to grab goods from someone's hand and run away with them were hanging offenses. Executions at Tyburn in London were known as "hanging shows." They occurred regularly and drew huge crowds. As for the prisoners' existence in jails; the transportation to Australia of men, women, and children; the flogging of women; the pillory; and branding on the hand—such horrors continued unabated.

The strangulation of biblical Christianity had further inhumane consequences in the treatment and mortality of children. Their death rates tell a terrible tale, though authentic statistics are only available for London. These show that between 1730 and 1750, three out of every four children born to all classes died before their fifth birthday. James Hanway, the Christian friend of "parish and pauper children," produced scores of statistics and pamphlets, preserved in the British Museum library, revealing his investigations into the treatment and death rate of the parish infants. Death occurred time after time because of murder and the practice of exposing newly born babies to perish in the streets, as well as the placing of unhappy foundlings with heartless nurses, who let them starve or turned them into the streets to beg or steal.

The eighteenth century in England is known as the "Gin Age." Horrible child abuse was often the result of drinking strong, fiery, poisonous gin, which outrivaled beer as the national beverage. Irish historian William Lecky defined the national gin-drinker's drunkenness as *the* "master-curse of English life between 1720–1750." The inevitable evils of alcoholism followed—poverty, violence, prostitution, and murder. The liquor trade, with its daily disruption of the nation's life, was the cardinal cause of social disintegration and degeneration during those thirty years.

The moral darkness of the age expressed itself in a perverted conception of sport, which, like alcohol, brought attendant evils in its train, such as further coarsening of the personality, cruelty, and gambling. The baiting of bulls, bears, badgers, and dogs—with fireworks attached to them—was typical of the third and fourth decades of this century. Most of those tortures took place in public house grounds, in a village green, in village church grounds, or in cathedral closes. The animals were often baited to death to provide greater excitement.

Another "sport" was cockfighting with metal spurs. Many eighteenth-century clergymen bred fighting cocks and sometimes had church bells rung to honor a local winner. The setting of trained dogs on ducks in lakes was another favorite recreation, as was fox hunting. Cudgel play and pugilism—boxing without gloves—for men and women, which sometimes went on for hours, was another sport, while prize fights between famous male bruisers who battled bare-fisted attracted mobs of twelve thousand or more.

Gambling was a national obsession for all classes, bringing appalling ruin to thousands. In London and other big cities, promiscuity became a sport, from court masquerades to fornication in daylight on the village green, or selling one's wife by auction at a cattle market. There was an abundance of openly pornographic literature. Donald Drew quotes Irish historian Lecky: "The profligacy of the theatre during the generation that followed the Restoration, can hardly be exaggerated." Likewise, a judge remarked that "no sooner is a playhouse opened in any part of the kingdom, than it at once becomes surrounded by a halo of brothels."

The Bible became a closed book, and the result was ignorance, lawlessness, and savagery. Until the advent of the Sunday school movement toward the end of the century, little or no provision was made for the free education of the poor, except the church system of charity schools. They were invariably a farce, most teachers being half-literate. Millions of English people at this time had never set foot in any kind of school, but young people of school-leaving age were usually apprenticed, often sold to masters, and frequently viciously treated.

As for lawlessness, thieves, robbers, and highwaymen, Horace Walpole observed in 1751, "One is forced to travel, even at noon, as if one were going to battle." Savagery showed itself in the plundering of shipwrecked vessels, lured by false signals onto rocks, and in the indifference shown to the drowning sailors. This was a regular activity along the entire coastline of the British Isles.

Into this spiritual and moral quagmire stepped John Wesley. He was born the same year as Jonathan Edwards, on June 28, 1703, in a Lincolnshire country rectory. One of nineteen children, he narrowly escaped death as a little boy when one night the rectory caught fire and was burned to the ground. He went to Charterhouse School and on to Oxford, where his intellectual gifts led to his being elected a fellow and tutor of Lincoln College. Devoutly religious, he and others ministered as best they could to the poor and downtrodden, but their peers despised them for it.

After a few years, John was ordained in the Church of England, along with his brother Charles, and then sailed to the United States. On returning to England much heart searching ensued. It was not until he talked with some Moravians in London that he realized he was a Christian in name only. It was in a Moravian service on May 24, 1738, that Wesley repented of his sin and found the salvation that Jesus offers. Wesley wrote, "[I] felt my heart strangely warmed. I felt I did trust Christ, Christ died for my salvation and an assurance was given me that he had taken away my sins, even mine . . . I testified openly to all there what I now . . . felt in my heart."[13]

John Wesley experienced what Jesus called being "born again." It began to warm his heart, unify his personality, multiply his sympathies, sharpen his critical faculties, and clarify his life's purpose. He at once began to declare the "glad tidings of salvation" in prisons, workhouses, and wherever churches would open their pulpits to him. But they were few and far between.

On April 2, 1739, in response to George Whitefield's invitation, Wesley arrived in Bristol. Whitefield convinced him of the need for field preaching as the most likely means of reaching the greatest number of people, especially the working class, who were then virtually untouched by the established church. The following day, despite his misgivings but encouraged by Whitefield's example, Wesley, aged thirty-six, preached his first open-air sermon, expounding the Bible to the unchurched. The Great Awakening, the evangelical revival, was born. It was to be reared for many years in an atmosphere of insolence, contempt, abuse, and violence.

For three decades, magistrates, squires, and clergy turned a blind eye to the continual drunken and brutal attacks by mobs and gangs on Wesley and his supporters. Wesley endured physical assault with missiles of various kinds. Frequently bulls would be driven into the midst of congregations or musical instruments blared to drown out the preacher's voice.

Time after time, the Wesleys and Whitefield narrowly escaped death, while several of their fellow itinerant preachers were attacked and their houses set on fire. Hundreds of antirevival publications appeared, as did regular, inaccurate, and scurrilous newspaper reports and articles. And the most virulent attacks, not surprisingly, came from the priests, who referred to Wesley as "that Methodist," "that enthusiast," "that mystery of iniquity," "a diabolical seducer, and impostor and fanatic."

After a few years, wanting to set out his wares in plain, rational, and scriptural terms, Wesley wrote a pamphlet in which he declared, "It is the plain old Christianity that I teach." His paramount purpose was to make men and women conscious of God. He was fully aware of the many and varied powers of evil and corruption, including within the organized and established religion. He believed that God's purpose for him was to open the Word of God for his nation, pointing men and women to God through Christ. This, in turn, would reclaim their homes, towns, and country from paganism and corruption.

Wesley's central understanding of Christianity was that individual redemption leads to social regeneration. He believed that the main purpose of the Bible is to show sinners their way back to God by the sacrifice of Christ. This is what he preached, but he also understood that social changes are an inevitable by-product and a useful piece of evidence of conversion. Because of the preaching of the gospel, the high moral principles set forth in Scriptures slowly began to take root in people's minds. Wesley believed that God's Word calls for the salvation of individual souls. It also gives us firm ordinances for national existence and a common social life under God—these were his goals, and he never lost sight of them.

Converted people joined other converted people in what Wesley called "Societies." He regarded all his services as supplementary to regular Church of England services. He remained a Church of England clergyman for most of his life—his brother Charles for all of his. John Wesley's break with the Church of England occurred much later, when he began to ordain ministers in what became known as the Methodist Church.

John Wesley's life was a triumph of God's grace. Under physical and verbal attack thousands of times, never once did he lose his temper. He was prepared to endure a blow if the dealing of it would diffuse the hysteria. When struck by a stone or cudgel, he would wipe away the blood and carry on preaching. He loved his enemies, and do what they would, they could not make him discourteous or angry.

It is no exaggeration to say that Wesley—and all these things were true of Charles and Whitefield also—instilled into the British people a new and biblical concept of courage and heroism. His tranquil dignity, the absence of malice and anger, and above all, the evidence of God's Spirit working in his life, eventually disarmed his enemies and won them for Christ. Soldiers, sailors, miners, fishermen, smugglers, industrial workers, thieves, vagabonds, men, women, and children listened intently, in apt reverent attention, gradually removed their hats and knelt, often emotionally overcome, as he pointed these thousands upon thousands to God's grace. For more than fifty years, Wesley fed the Bible, the Word of Life, to drink-sodden, brutalized, and neglected multitudes.

In May 1739, the cornerstone of the first Methodist preaching house was laid in Bristol. Soon Kingswood School and the London foundry were opened. The foundry became the hub of many social service projects, such as an employment bureau, loans for the poor, and a free medical dispensary. These initiatives were followed by houses for preaching the Bible, which started springing up all over Britain, as well as in Scotland and Ireland. Meanwhile, in America, the progress of the evangelical revival was phenomenal, led by Jonathan Edwards and by George Whitefield, who courageously crossed the Atlantic thirteen times before he died in 1770.

From 1739 to his death in 1791, Wesley was indefatigable. His energy was prodigious. He got up each morning at four and preached his first sermon most mornings at five. He and his itinerant preachers divided each day into three equal parts—eight hours for sleeping and eating; eight for meditation, prayer and study; and eight for preaching, visiting, and social labors. He organized hundreds of local Methodist societies in the places he visited, established and kept an eye on Kingswood School, opened the first free medical dispensary for the poor and a rheumatism clinic, wrote a treatise on medicine, and prepared and preached at least forty-five thousand sermons on the Bible.

Wesley traveled a quarter of a million miles on horseback, in all weather, night and day, up and down and across England, on roads that were often dangerous and sometimes impassable. During these travels he composed his commentary on the Bible verse by verse, wrote hundreds of letters, kept a daily journal from 1735 to the year before his death in 1791, and wrote some of the 330 books that were published in his lifetime. He composed English, French, Latin, Greek, and Hebrew grammars. He edited many books for the general education of his preachers and congregations, which became the fifty volumes of his famous Christian library.*

---

* Republished by the Wesley Center Online.

This cultured man, keen theologian, and esteemed intellectual warned his preachers that one could "never be a deep preacher without extensive reading, *any more than a thorough Christian.*" Every preacher was made a distributor and seller of books and was expected to have mastered his contents. The *Encyclopedia Britannica* says of Wesley in this regard that "no man in the eighteenth century did so much to create a taste for good reading and to supply it with books, at the lowest prices."

Wesley's book *Rules for a Helper* gives a sampling of the cultural influences he diffused in Britain: "Never be unemployed for a moment; believe evil of no one; speak evil of no one; a preacher of the Gospel is the servant of all; be ashamed of nothing but sin; be punctual; you will need all the (common) sense you have to have your wits about you."

Wesley understood the Bible demands that individual conversion should lead to changes in society, and this was hammered home in different ways. Thirteen years before the Abolition Committee was formed to end the slave trade, he published his *Thoughts upon Slavery*, a graphic, vehement, and penetrating treatise denouncing this "horrid trade" as a national disgrace. He kept up his attack on slavery until the end of his life, the last letter he wrote being to William Wilberforce, an evangelical member of Parliament who led a lifelong campaign to abolish the slave trade.

By the same token, Wesley deplored the stupidity and futility of war, especially Britain's war with the American colonies. He frequently wrote and spoke about the use and abuse of money and privilege. He wore inexpensive clothes and dined on the plainest fare, not spending more than thirty pounds a year on his personal needs. But his clothes were spotless, his shoes were always shined, and he never wore a wig. He publicly and repeatedly questioned why food was so expensive and himself gave the answer: immense quantities of corn were consumed in distilling. On humanitarian and social grounds, he pleaded for the abolition of alcoholic liquors for use as beverages.

Wesley supported fair prices, a living wage, and honest and healthy employment for all. There is no question but that he was more familiar with the life of the poor than any other public figure of his age. Constantly moving all over Britain, he could and did sense the mind of the people as no king or statesman was able to do. He ceaselessly called upon the rich to help the poor, and he gave this warning to his thousands of followers: "Give none that asks relief an ill word or an ill look. Do not hurt them."

As Charles Dickens after him, Wesley put certain aspects of the law "in the stocks," holding them up to public ridicule. In this regard, he attacked smuggling but considered that in most cases the representatives of the law were more criminal than the imprisoned smuggler. He strongly campaigned against bribery and corruption at election times, and against the scandal of pluralities* and sinecures** in the Church of England. He fearlessly criticized aspects of the penal system and prisons (paving the way for reformers John Howard and Elizabeth Fry), depicting prisons as "nurseries of all manner of wickedness." He campaigned against the near-medieval methods of medicine and agitated for funeral reform.

We have already noted Wesley's wide interests, concerns, and activities. The list, however, would be incomplete without mentioning his practical interest in electricity; vocational training for the unemployed; the raising of money to clothe and feed prisoners, to buy food, medicine, fuel, and tools for the helpless and the aged; and the founding of a Benevolent Loan Fund and Stranger's Friend Society. He preached heaven but he believed that nature was God's gift to us, and therefore work was noble and science was essential.

The biblical revival caused England to sing. John Wesley's poet brother Charles, whose fame as a preacher is still overshadowed by his fame as a hymn writer, wrote between eight and nine thousand poems, of which eight thousand became hymns. John taught the people to sing. Many hymns were set to popular tunes of the day. They paved the way for the sermon and pressed home its message. And hundreds of thousands of those who sang his hymn, "My chains

---

* pluralities: holding of two or more church benefices at the same time.
** sinecures: holding an office that provides an income but requires no work.

fell off, my heart was free," were singing not only about their salvation but also the chains of alcohol, abuse, hunger, and poverty.

The Great Awakening gave to the entire English-speaking world its richest ever heritage of poetical and sacred songs and an understanding of hymns as literature, as history, as theology. Other fine poets and hymn writers also emerged during this period and during the nineteenth century: William Cowper, Isaac Watts, John Newton, Augustus Toplady, Bishop Heber, Horatious Bonar, Mrs. Alexander, and Frances Havergal. But Charles's hymns, praise, and prayer—like the metrical version of the Psalms of David in Scotland—sank deep into the subconscious life of England.

Wesley, Whitefield, and their associates revitalized and reinforced the truths of biblical Christianity. This was an enormously important contribution. The Bible, which during the early eighteenth century had been a closed book to Englishmen as much as it had been in Chaucer's day, became the Book of books. Britain was saved from lapsing into infidelity.

John Wesley died as he had lived since his conversion. For fifty-three years, he faithfully preached that men need and are saved only by *faith* in Christ, but the corollary was that they would be judged by *works*—by how they lived. He often prayed, "Let me wear out, not rust out. Let me not live to be useless."

Until a week before his death, when fever incapacitated and forced him to take to his bed, he had, in his eighty-eighth year, continued to preach, write, supervise, and encourage. He died on the morning of March 2, 1791. Those who had come to rejoice with him "burst into an anthem of praise." No coach or hearse was needed for his funeral, for he had given instructions that six poor men, in need of employment, be given a pound each to carry his body to the grave.

It is given to few people, as it was to John Wesley, to see the reward of their labors. In the first decades of his service, his arrival and that of his followers in any town and village was the signal for a violent popular uprising. But for the last ten of his eighty-eight years, it is no exaggeration to say that Wesley was the most respected and beloved figure in Britain. After his death he was immortalized in thousands of portraits, his likeness on teapots and crockery and busts in every conceivable medium.

We have seen something of what England was like before Wesley. Now briefly, let us look at what it was like after him. The Great Awakening was a source from which issued many streams.

The first thing to note is that before Wesley, the devout and evangelical clergy were a tiny remnant in the Church of England. After him, at the close of the eighteenth century, their number increased, and they became the dominant religious influence inside and outside the Church of England. Under the influence of biblical revival, religious nonconformity that transforms culture became a power in the land. This was even more so in Scotland, especially under Whitefield's influence.

A further fruit of Wesley's work were the conversions of William Wilberforce, Lord Shaftesbury, and others, and the development of what is called the Clapham Sect. This was a group of devout evangelicals who lived around Clapham Common, southeast of London. This community of Christians included businessmen, bankers, politicians, colonial governors, and members of Parliament, whose ceaseless, sacrificial labors benefited millions of their fellows at home and abroad—especially in Africa and India.

Restoration of the authority of the Bible in the English world amounted to a civilization finding its soul. Writings of a number of literary men and women give evidence of their recovering a biblical perspective. Poets such as William Blake, William Wordsworth, Robert Browning, Lord Tennyson, and later Rudyard Kipling and John Masefield; novelists like Sir Walter Scott, Charles Dickens, William Thackeray, the Brontë sisters, Robert Louis Stevenson*—all these and others owed much to the purging and ennobling influence of the biblical revival.

---

* This is not to suggest that everyone was fully biblical in this worldview, or that no other belief-system shaped their mind-set.

To the degree their writings were shaped by the Bible's worldview, they held in check the logical consequences of the Enlightenment's rejection of revelation, discussed in a previous chapter.

The impact of the Bible via Wesley's work is evident in the lives and labors of the social emancipators during the nineteenth century. Wilberforce and Clarkson fought against the slave trade; Lord Shaftesbury and Sadler championed industrial emancipation; Elizabeth Fry and John Howard reformed prisons; Plimsoll focused on ships' safety regulations; Hannah More and Robert Raikes launched Sunday schools; and many more were to follow.

The biblical revival resulted in the nineteenth-century preaching tradition. Finny, Moody, Spurgeon, Nicholson, Ryle, Moule, James, Danny, Chavass, and others were popular preachers who expounded on the Bible rather than telling man-made stories. The Great Awakening, as we saw in an earlier chapter, opened up the intelligent study of the Bible to the masses. It restored the Bible's position as the Book of books of the Anglo-Saxon peoples. Their biblical revival held in check the character-destroying consequences of atheism that corrupted other European nations like France.

Charles Simeon, a fellow of King's College, Cambridge, was vicar of Holy Trinity Church for more than fifty years. Wesley's ministry made it possible for him to introduce biblical Christianity back into university life, in spite of sustained opposition. His training of young men as preachers made a valuable contribution to evangelical worship in the nineteenth century. He established what has proved to be a lasting evangelical tradition in Cambridge. His protégés carried out or supported splendid global missionary endeavors that took modernity to remote parts of the world. Some well-known names are Coke, Asbury, Livingstone, Moffat, Martyn, Morrison, Paton, and Slessor.

When the work of the biblical revival had become established, many missionary societies were formed, all within a few years of each other—the Baptist Missionary Society, the London Missionary Society, the Wesleyan Mission Society, the Church Missionary Society, the British and Foreign Bible Society, and the China Inland Mission.

That missionary spirit stirred up hundreds of thousands of Christian young men and women to go to the uttermost parts of the world, often at great personal cost and sacrifice, and serve people who could not repay them in earthly terms. That same missionary spirit also moved millions of people who could not go overseas personally to assume a moral obligation upon themselves for the welfare of others, to pray, and to give generously.

The biblical revival affected the lives of politicians. Edmund Burke and William Pitt were better men because of their Bible-believing friends. They helped redefine the civilized world as those parts of the world where morality plays as significant a role in state policy and administration as do pragmatic politics and practical economics. Perceval, Lord Liverpool, Abraham Lincoln, Gladstone, and the Prince Consort, among others, acknowledged the influence of the Great Awakening. The biblical revival, beginning among the outcast masses, was the midwife of the spirit and character values that have created and sustained free institutions throughout the English-speaking world. England after Wesley saw many of his century's evils eradicated, because hundreds of thousands became Christians. Their hearts were changed, as were their minds and attitudes, and so society—the public realm—was affected.

The following improvements came in a direct line of descent from the Wesleyan revival. First was the abolition of slavery and the emancipation of the industrial workers in England. Then came factory schools, ragged schools, the humanizing of the prison system, the reform of the penal code, the forming of the Salvation Army, the Religious Tract Society, the Pastoral Aid Society, the London City Mission, Müller's Homes, Fegan's Homes, the National Children's Home and Orphanages, the forming of evening classes and polytechnics, Agnes Weston's Soldiers' and Sailors' Rest, YMCAs, Barnardo's Homes, the NSPCC, the Boy Scouts, Girl Guides, the Royal Society of Prevention of Cruelty to Animals, and the list goes on.

Ninety-nine out of a hundred people behind these movements were Christians. All these movements grew out of the revival of biblical spirituality, the result of John Wesley and his associates opening up the Bible that led to the Great Awakening of hearts, minds, consciences, and wills.

Wesley's purpose under God had been achieved: to attack the root cause of spiritual atrophy and moral decay and purge the nation's soul. One cannot explain nineteenth-century Britain until one understands Wesley and the Bible. The same applies to nineteenth-century America. Indeed, there were mistakes, misunderstandings, friction, and discord, and people were hurt. It has been argued that Wesley's social achievements were purely palliative and that he pointed to another world as the only God-given remedy for the ills of this life. But this criticism comes from a failure to understand the gospel, explained in the early part of this chapter.

Transformation of a nation is an intergenerational task. Ian Bradley's book is but one of the studies that detail the reforms that followed in England, Africa, and India during the post-Wesleyan generation. My books, such as *India: The Grand Experiment*, tell the story of how the Bible created a relatively corruption-free India during the nineteenth century.

John Wesley's life under God refutes the idea that history is bound to go down toward corruption, or that it is "made" by material conditions and institutions. The biblical revival changed history by transforming the character, words, thoughts, and deeds of men and women. It prevented a French-style bloody revolution in England that seemed inevitable given the harshness of eighteenth century English social, political, and religious life.

Although John Benjamin Wesley was a spiritual and intellectual giant during the eighteenth century, the real enlightening power did not lie in the human instrument at all. It resided in the Scriptures, whose power was unleashed for all who would come to them to drink the water of life. Mr. Singh, my fellow traveler in the plane, had tasted the fruits of biblical spirituality. But apparently, no one in England had explained to him the roots of its moral transformation—that is, the role that the biblical idea of family played in shaping and transmitting the moral character first forged in the fires of a religious experience.

Chapter Fifteen

FAMILY

Why Did America Surge Ahead of Europe?

I n 1831–1832, four decades after the failed French Revolution, a French magistrate came to the United States of America on an official visit. He used the occasion for an unofficial investigation into the success and consequence of American democracy. He published his findings in a two-volume classic: *Democracy in America*. Toward the end, Alexis de Tocqueville wrote:

> I have recorded so many considerable achievements of the Americans, if anyone asks me what I think the chief cause of the extraordinary prosperity and growing power of this nation, I should answer that it is due to the superiority of their women.[1]

Simply stated, Tocqueville believed America was prospering because the American women were superior. But, why? Didn't American women have the same genes as European women?* Tocqueville continued:

> In almost all Protestant nations girls are much more in control of their own behavior than among Catholic ones. This independence is even greater in those Protestant countries, such as England, which

---

* That is, the Anglo-Saxon women that Tocqueville was talking about.

+ 274 +

have kept or gained the right of self-government. In such cases both political habits and religious beliefs infuse a spirit of liberty into the family. In the United States, Protestant teaching is combined with a very free constitution and a very democratic society, and in no other country is a girl left so soon or so completely to look after herself.[2]

The strength of the traditional American character and culture cannot be understood without understanding the Bible's teaching on gender roles, sex, marriage, and family life. Up until the 1980s, America was almost the only nation in the world where these biblical teachings were so thoroughly ingrained in the public conscience that a candidate for a high political office had to get out of the race if it was discovered that he had cheated on his wife.[3] As Tocqueville put it,

> Certainly of all countries in the world, America is one in which the marriage tie is most respected and where the highest and truest conception of conjugal happiness has been conceived.[4]

Tocqueville was not oblivious of the natural, historical, political, legal, and educational factors that made America strong. In fact, the family is a minor topic in his massive study. Nonetheless, he correctly noted that it was a significant factor with profound consequences for the broader society. The Bible was the source of the American expectations of marriage.

Building on the Old Testament account of creation and opposition to adultery and divorce, the New Testament suggested that God's intention for humans was monogamy—a one-man, one-woman lifelong and exclusive relationship. Jesus explained that God, "who created them from the beginning made them male and female . . . said, 'Therefore a man shall leave his father and his mother and hold fast to his wife, and the two shall become one flesh'? So they are no longer two but one flesh. What therefore God has joined together, let not man separate."[5]

Monogamy was not the Jewish, Hindu, Buddhist, or Islamic

conception of marriage. It was a peculiarly Christian idea. It spread around the world in the nineteenth century, mainly through the Western missionary movement.

What did the biblical idea of marriage and family do for the status of women and for civilization?

As mentioned in chapter 2, we began our service to the poor in village Gatheora in 1976 by training Village Health Workers (VHWs). Dr. Mategaonker and his staff would come to our farm twice a week to teach village folk how to stay healthy, prevent diseases, and cure simple ailments. The village families wouldn't allow women to attend these classes,* so we had to begin by training young men. After a few months, after we had bonded and become free with each other, the VHWs conveyed to us their considered opinion: "You Christians are very immoral."

"What do you mean?" I was taken aback, since the jury had reached this verdict after due deliberation. "How are we immoral?"

"You walk with your wives holding their hands," they explained. "Our wives walk at least ten feet behind us. You take your sister-in-law to the market on your scooter. Our wives are too modest to sit behind our bicycles, and they cover their faces in front of our fathers, uncles, and older brothers."

I had no clue how to answer my accusers. But Vinay, my older brother, had lived there longer than I. He responded with brutal frankness: "Come on, you guys! You know perfectly well that the truth is exactly the opposite. You do not allow your wives to uncover their faces in front of your fathers and brothers because you trust neither your father nor your brothers nor your wives. I allow my wife to go to the market with my brother because I trust her and I trust my brother. Our wives can walk in the fields with us and visit you in your homes because of higher moral standards. You chain your wives to your kitchens and imprison them behind their veils because *you* are immoral."

To my utter amazement, every one of the VHWs agreed with Vinay without a whisper of protest. They may have remained skeptical about

---

* The only women who went to other people's farms were landless laborers from untouchable castes.

our morality, but they knew firsthand their own moral standards. I was grateful for Vinay's insight, for I had never seen the connections of morality to liberty, liberty to the status of women, and the status of women to the strength of a society. I should have known better because our village was less than twenty miles from Khajuraho, where every imaginable sexual act had been carved in stone to adorn Hindu temples. My ancestors' religion of "sacred sex" had enslaved our women just as it did in the pre-Christian Greco-Roman civilization.

Our neighbors could not even refer to their wives by their names. A wife was *Bhitarwali*—the one who belongs indoors. Women's enslavement was then sold as traditional morality. The consequence? Not one girl in our village had gone beyond the fifth grade because the nearest middle school was three miles away. It was too risky to send a girl so far out of sight. It took time for the VHWs to recognize that what they considered morality was, in fact, our women's slavery. Morality is meant to liberate. *Morality without liberty is slavery. Liberty without morality is destructive.*

Why did the women's liberation movement begin in America and not in a Muslim nation under regimes like the Taliban? Was it because American women were more oppressed than their Muslim counterparts? Clearly, the opposite is true. An anemic body cannot fight disease. One has to build up strength in order to fight germs. Women's lib began in America because the American women were simultaneously empowered and discriminated against.

The Bible is a patriarchal book. Its teachings have been held responsible for women's subordinate status in traditional Western homes, churches, and society. Is it possible that the Bible was also the force that empowered women in the West and enabled them to fight for their liberation? One factor was obvious to Tocqueville: American Christians believed in practical, social, and temporary hierarchy of husbands and wives while affirming their inherent, intrinsic, or metaphysical equality.

Most cultures have believed that women are intrinsically inferior to men. For example, Rousseau—one of the fathers of secular Enlightenment and a champion of liberty—believed that woman was unfinished man. Hindu sages taught that a soul with poor karma incarnated as a female to serve males. Tocqueville noted that following European Christendom, America "allowed *social* inferiority of women to continue."[6] It is not difficult at the present time to find American churches that believe women can lecture in the nation's Congress but not in their local congregations; women can serve coffee after the worship service but not communion during the worship; women can play the piano in a church service but not pray the pastoral prayer.

Most Christians who practice social or temporary inequality, however, agree that the Bible teaches that men and women were created equal as the image of God;[7] social inequality—that is, the husband's headship in the home—came as a part of the curse upon human sin.[8] They agree that Jesus came to deliver us from sin and its curse. This distinction between the essential metaphysical equality and temporary social inequality due to sin was not a theological juggling act. It ensured that the quest for equal dignity became an aspect of seeking salvation from the consequences of sin.

Tocqueville witnessed the "social inequality"—suffering and sadness—in the eyes of the very women he admired. These were educated women who, in submission to their husbands, left city life for unsettled territories. They sacrificed themselves for their children and the dreams of their husbands. In a moving appendix Tocqueville described a visit to a typical pioneer couple who had moved from New England to the West, cleared a patch in a dense forest, and started farming. I find it moving, first, because he could well have been describing my wife and me in 1976, except that we moved to a social, not a physical, wilderness. And second, because the passage explains America's economic success to those who have been infected by the socialist prejudice that America's wealth came from exploiting other nations.

> We went into the log house; the inside was quite unlike that of the
> cottages of European peasants; there [were] . . . fewer necessities . . .
> on a shelf formed from a roughly hewn plank, a few books: the Bible,
> the first six cantos of Milton, and two plays of Shakespeare . . . the

master of this dwelling . . . was clearly not born in the solitude in which we found him . . . his earlier years were spent in a society that used its brain and that he belonged to that restless, calculating, and adventurous race of men who do with the utmost coolness things which can only be accounted for by the ardor of passion, and who endure for a time the life of a savage in order to conquer and civilize the backwoods. . . .

A woman was sitting on the other side of the hearth, rocking a small child on her knees. She nodded to us without disturbing herself. Like the pioneer, this woman was in the prime of life; her appearance seemed superior to her condition, and her apparel even betrayed a lingering taste for dress; but her delicate limbs were wasted, her features worn, and her eyes gentle and serious; her whole physiognomy bore marks of religious resignation, a deep peace free from passions, and some sort of natural, quiet determination which would face all the ills of life without fear and without defiance.[9]

Tocqueville is describing the kind of heroic strength that shows itself in submission, sacrifice, and endurance—qualities often twisted into ropes used to oppress women. In the biblical, democratic culture of America, Tocqueville maintains, these qualities became the source of women's liberty and national strength. It will be easier to understand his point if we see American culture in the light of other traditions.

Veiled Women

The Prophet Muhammad made a visit to Zaid—his highly esteemed adopted son. Zaid was the third convert to Islam and totally loyal to his foster father. His beautiful wife, Zaynab bint Jahash, was the Prophet's cousin. Zaid was not at home, and the lightly clad Zaynab opened the door, inviting her cousin to come in. Smitten by her beauty, the Prophet exclaimed, "Gracious Lord! Good heavens! How you do turn the hearts of men." The Prophet hesitated and then declined to enter the house.

Zaynab narrated the incident to her husband, who promptly went to the Prophet and dutifully offered to divorce his wife for him. Magnanimously, Muhammad declined. "Keep your wife and fear God." But in many parts of the world, it is dangerous to deny the powerful what their heart desires, despite what they may say. Apparently the Prophet's compliments had grabbed Zaynab's heart, and the devoted son divorced his wife.

The Prophet hesitated in marrying Zaynab since marrying his son's wife would be considered incest. A new revelation rescued him from his scruples. With his wife Aisha—whom he had married when she was only six years old—sitting next to him, Muhammad went into one of his prophetic swoons. Coming out of it, he asked, "Who will go and congratulate Zaynab and say that the Lord has joined her to me in marriage?" Then flowed the Qur'anic Sura 33.2–33.7, laying down the law that the adopted sons should go by their own father's name and that marrying the wives of adopted sons should not be considered a crime among the faithful. God assured the Prophet, "When Zaid had settled concerning her to divorce her, We married her to you."

Muslim apologists defend Muhammad by arguing that the marriage was contracted for political reasons. Aisha, however, had a wittier remark: "Truly your God seems to have been very quick in fulfilling your prayers." Whether the prophecy was a divine revelation or a product of the subconscious mind, the Islamic world learned that it was safer to cover your women's beauty than to be sorry.[10]

The Ten Commandments had already made it a sin to covet your neighbor's spouse. Jesus offered a more radical solution—one that demanded not merely modesty from women but also self-discipline and inner holiness from men. He asked his followers to deal with the spiritual problem of adultery in their hearts and the lust in their eyes. He told them not to divorce their wives except for marital unfaithfulness and not to marry women divorced in circumstances that mock marriage and camouflage adultery—circumstances that use divorce and marriage as a veneer for breaking up families.[11]

At the beginning of the second millennium, when the Khajuraho temples were being built in central India, Islam began conquering Northwest India. Today, many "westernized" Hindus, proud of Khajuraho, *Kama Sutra*, and Tantric sexuality,[12] think that free sex equals liberty. They claim that Islam brought the veil and the enslavement of women to India. Even if that were true, the fact remains that during the eight hundred years of Islamic influence, Tantra, Yoga,* and goddess worship did nothing to liberate Indian woman.[13] The emancipation of Asian women began in the nineteenth century when the Western missionary movement[14] brought to us the biblical worldview, spirituality, and morality—what Tocqueville called "mores" or the "habits of the heart."[15]

Keshab Chandra Sen (1838–84), the Bengali philosopher and social reformer, grasped what Tocqueville had seen. In the 1870s he became the first Indian to demand that polygamy should be banned and monogamy made the legal definition of marriage. The British rulers in India chose not to challenge Hindu and Muslim polygamy. They made monogamy the law only for Indian Christians and for those Hindus who joined Sen's sect—the Prarthana Samaj. A few generations after Sen, in 1949, Pandit Jawaharlal Nehru, India's first prime minister, also tried to make monogamy part of India's Constitution; he wanted it to be binding on all Hindus. But he failed.

Monogamy only entered the Hindu marital law in 1956. Yet, in the mid-1990s, we still had a member of Parliament who had forty-nine wives! Many men with more than one wife have occupied high elected offices in India. It is no problem for the mistress of a popular elected leader to contest and win an election. I am not trying to condemn specific individuals. But I do want to drive home the point that our culture has had ethical foundations very different from those of America. I believe the habits of India's hearts (habits gaining ground in America since the 1960s) have been at the root of the enslavement of our women and the stagnation of Indian civilization.

_____

* Yoga began as a Hindu technique to suppress all activity of body, mind, and will in order that the self may realize its distinction from them (in Samkhya philosophy) or its oneness with the infinite (in Monism), in order to attain liberation.

POLYGAMY TO CELIBACY

Christianity arose in Rome's promiscuous, polygamous culture—a culture not unlike Khajuraho's. Many historians have noticed what the New Testament suggests, that Christianity conquered Rome because, as we shall see below, it attracted and empowered women. It is important to understand how polygamy weakens and enslaves women.

A domestic incident in the Prophet Muhammad's harem illustrates one problem with polygamy. A Muslim is allowed no more than four wives at a time. The Prophet, however, had received revelations permitting him as many as thirteen. To prevent jealousy, he spent one night with each of them in turn. One day it was his wife Hafsa's turn. She was away visiting her father but then returned unexpectedly. She was furious to find the Prophet in bed with Mary, the Coptic maid and concubine. Hafsa reproached him bitterly, threatening to tell other wives. Muhammad promised to stay away from the hated Mary if she would keep quiet. Hafsa, however, confided in Aisha, who also hated Mary.

The scandal spread and Muhammad found himself ostracized by his own harem. Another revelation—Sura 66.15[16]—absolved him from keeping his promise to stay away from the attractive maid. The revelation required that he reprimand his wives, hinting to them that he would divorce them all, replacing them with submissive wives. The Prophet was prompt in obeying the angel's word that liberated him from his obligation to keep his promise. He spent a month with Mary away from his wives. The wives were terrified by his obedience to the revelation. They fell in line. Aisha's father, Abu Bakr, and others pleaded with the Prophet to forgive the foolish wives.

Although many of our contemporaries have argued that the right to easy divorce is necessary for a woman's liberty and happiness, the experience of easy divorce in Islam and the accumulated wisdom of the ages suggest that divorce and polygamy weaken women. They undermine a wife's ability to fight for her rights and dignity. Ironically, celibacy could become the opposite end of the spectrum.

The Bible presents it as a rare calling for leaders who need to give all their time to service in special circumstances.[17] But some Christian scholars misinterpreted the Bible to imply that a marriage relationship with a woman was polluting. During the middle ages, the Catholic Church began to promote the idea that celibacy was spiritually superior to marriage. The Bible enabled sixteenth-century reformers to restore the honorable status of marriage. Before discussing that controversy, however, we need to note the Bible's contribution to women's emancipation through the Catholic Church.

ROMAN CATHOLICISM AND THE EMANCIPATION OF WOMEN

Rodney Stark, in his authoritative study *The Rise of Christianity: A Sociologist Reconsiders History*,[18] discusses the rise of Christianity in its early pagan Greco-Roman setting. Among other things, he explores the impact of the Bible's commands concerning adultery, rape, murder, divorce, love for wives, care for widows, and so forth, on womanhood in general. The following is from a section entitled "Wives, Widows, and Brides":

> First of all, a major aspect of women's improved status in the Christian subculture is that Christians did not condone female infanticide[19] . . . the more favorable Christian view of women is also demonstrated in their condemnation of divorce,[20] incest,[21] marital infidelity,[22] and polygamy.[23] As Fox put it, "fidelity, without divorce, was expected of every Christian." . . . Like pagans, early Christians prized female chastity, but unlike pagans, they rejected the double standard that gave pagan men so much sexual license. Christian men were urged to remain virgins until marriage, and extramarital sex was condemned as adultery. Chadwick noted that Christianity "regarded unchastity in a husband as no less serious a breach of loyalty and trust than unfaithfulness in a wife."[24]

Stark pointed out that Christian widows enjoyed substantial advantages over pagan widows, who faced great social pressure to remarry. Augustus Caesar, for example, fined widows who failed to remarry within two years. When a widow remarried, she lost all her inheritance—it became the property of her new husband. In contrast, the New Testament required Christians to respect and care for widows.[25] Well-to-do Christian widows kept their husbands' estates, and the church sustained the poorer ones, giving them a choice whether or not to remarry.

Christians also expressed their respect for women by raising the age of marriage. Roman law established twelve as the minimum age at which girls could marry. But the law was nothing more than a recommendation. It carried no penalties and was routinely ignored. The best available studies show that in the Roman Empire the pagans' daughters were three times more likely than Christians to marry before they were thirteen. By age eleven, 10 percent were wed. Nearly half (44 percent) of the pagan girls were married off by the time they were fourteen, compared with 20 percent of the Christians. In contrast, nearly half (48 percent) of the Christian females did not marry before they were eighteen.[26]

Stark reported that in 1955, French historian Durry published his findings that Roman marriages involving child brides were consummated even if the bride had not achieved puberty. Durry thought that this was not the norm. However, substantial literary evidence has since emerged that consummation of these marriages was taken for granted.[27] Pagan writers like Plutarch called this custom cruel and contrary to nature because it filled girls with hatred and fear. Christians, in contrast, could delay their daughters' marriages because the New Testament gave them different moral standards—the same standard for men and women. The Bible's sexual ethic gave Christian girls the time to grow up and become better wives and mothers.

SEX AND MARRIAGE

Rome's classical culture did not see sex merely as secular pleasure. Like the Tantric sects in India, many Roman temples were packed with prostitutes—female as well as male. An 1889 study found that quite a few married women of high-ranking families in the Roman Empire had "asked to have their names entered amongst the public prostitutes, in order that they might not be punished for adultery."[28]

Adultery was a crime with serious consequences because it was an *economic* offense, taking another man's property (wife)—not because it was a matter of sexual impurity, a disruption of the holy union of husband and wife or a violation of sacred vows. In fact, extramarital sex with a temple prostitute was considered a purifying, god-pleasing, religious event, if not the very means of Gnostic enlightenment. Even today, many Hindu gurus and Yoga teachers have sex with their female and male devotees on the pretext of "purifying chakras"—the psychic centers in one's body.

Religious and aristocratic promotion of extramarital sex had colossal consequences. Easy availability of sex without commitment took away men's motivation to be married. Dislike for marriage had become evident as early as 131 BC, when the Roman censor Quintus Metellus Macedonicus proposed that marriage must be made mandatory. Too many men preferred to remain single, leading the censor to concede: "If we could get on without a wife . . . we would all avoid that annoyance."

Metellus continued, however, stating that men needed to take into account the long-term welfare of the state: "But since nature has ordained that we can neither live very comfortably with them nor at all without them, we must take thought for our lasting well-being rather than for the pleasure of the moment."[29] More than a century later, Augustus Caesar quoted this passage to the Senate to justify his own legislation on behalf of marriage. The need was obvious, the argument was compelling, but the legislation was not greeted with any greater enthusiasm the second time around. Historian Beryl Rawson wrote: "[O]ne theme that recurs in Latin literature is that wives are difficult and therefore men do not care much for marriage."[30]

Another cumulative result of promiscuity, child marriage, mistreatment of women, divorce, and fear of marriage was that Rome's pagan population began to decline during the final years of the empire. Unwed mothers and insecure wives (who feared divorce) chose abortion and infanticide even if their natural instincts were for nurture and care. Toward the end of the second century AD, Minucius Felix charged in *Octavius* that religious mythology encouraged murder through infanticide and abortion:

> I see your newly born sons exposed by you to wild beasts and birds of prey, or cruelly strangled to death. There are also women among you who, by taking certain drugs, destroy the beginnings of the future human being while it is still in the womb and are guilty of infanticide before they are mothers. These practices have certainly come down to you from your gods.[31]

The long-term consequence of prostitution, permissiveness, singleness, divorce, abortion, infanticide, and decline of population was that Roman towns began to shrink in numbers and size. Eventually the empire had to depend on a constant influx of "barbarian" settlers. As early as the second century, Marcus Aurelius had to draft slaves and gladiators and hire Germans and Scythians in order to fill the ranks of the army. Consequently, Rome became vulnerable. The main challenge to this depressing trend came from the Church, which followed the biblical injunction to Adam and Eve to "be fruitful and multiply."

Compared to the pagans, the Christians' commitment to marriage resulted in more secure women and a higher fertility rate. Likewise, Christian opposition to infanticide and abortion resulted in a lower mortality rate. Together the Christian population naturally grew faster than that of Rome's pagans. Christians' choices in favor of sexual purity, stable marriage, and care for children, orphans, and widows aided civilization but were not caused by concerns for civilization. Their motive was to please God by obeying his Word.

During the first millennium AD, the Roman Catholic Church was the greatest force for the emancipation of women. In the beginning of the second millennium, however, the "cult of Virgin Mary"* and

---

* The Reformers saw it as a "cult," since there was no biblical basis for praying to Mary or for

the idea of earning salvation through religiosity led to an unbiblical exaltation of celibacy. The idea of "salvation by works" often leads to denial of comforts—certain foods, drinks, sleep, sex, marriage, etc. This mind-set—the denial of pleasure and the achievement of righteousness by pious works—caused people to view sex, marriage, family, and economically productive labor (necessary to sustain a family) as concessions for the spiritually inferior. The renunciation of marriage and the pleasures (and responsibilities) of family life were held up as pious virtues. Celibacy became public proof of spiritual superiority. Joining a monastery became the surest way to heaven. This spiritual pride led to gross prejudice against women.

For example, the popular *Hammer Against the Witches* (AD 1487) seduced Inquisitors to think that women were sexually insatiable hyenas and a constant danger to men and their society.[32] Tantric sexual permissiveness resulted in similar reactions in mainstream Hinduism—exaltation of asceticism and celibacy (*Brahmacharya*) with a degrading view of women as temptresses. The Hindu reaction went further than European exaltation of celibacy by considering physical matter, the human body, and sex as inherently evil, in contrast to spirit, which was good. For example, Swami Sivananda, the founder of the Divine Life Society and a pioneer of the modern guru movement, wrote statements such as:

> Sex-pleasure is the most devitalizing and demoralizing of pleasures. Sexual pleasure is no pleasure at all. It is a mental delusion. It is false, utterly worthless, and extremely harmful.[33]

Thankfully for the West, the sixteenth-century Reformation began restoring biblical norms for sexual mores. Reformers like Martin Luther argued that, according to God's Word, sex and marriage were a means to holiness. The family, not the monastery, was the divinely ordained school of character. Acclaimed author and historian Roland

---

assuming that she had remained a virgin after Jesus' birth. There is biblical evidence that she had normal marital relations and children with her husband (Matthew 13:55–56; Mark 6:3; Galatians 1:19).

Bainton wrote: "Luther who got married to testify to his faith . . . did more than any other person to determine the tone of German [and Protestant] domestic relations for the next four centuries."[34] Luther's home in Wittenberg became the first Christian vicarage after centuries. The biblical norms for family life that Luther taught remained virtually unchallenged until the end of the twentieth century.

Martin Luther's attack on the Catholic idea of celibacy and his advocacy of the biblical idea of marriage did more to promote the Reformation than his attack on indulgences. He taught that according to the Bible some individuals are called to a celibate life. However, God's normal plan for human beings is marriage. The doctrine that marriage is spiritually inferior or undesirable is "teaching of the demons."[35] Luther taught that the family, not the monastery, is God's school of character; celibacy has become the devil's trap to lure priests and monks into sin.

Initially, from 1517 to 1521, to ordinary Europeans the Reformation appeared as a matter of theological disputes between experts. Ordinary people woke up to it when priests began to marry as a result of Luther's little book *The Babylonian Captivity*. Luther argued that the laws of men could not annul the command of God to marry. God ordained marriage for men before sin entered the world. Sex was a part of the material world that the Creator declared "very good."[36] Luther noted that the Scripture informs us: "Then the LORD God said, 'It is not good that the man should be alone; I will make him a helper fit for him.'"[37] In other words, God made Eve for Adam. She is good and necessary for him—a perfect gift planned by divine wisdom. God made only one woman for a man—the two of them to "become one flesh."[38]

Luther followed up his iconoclastic book with an *Address to the Nobility*. This presented the practical rationale for priests (not monks) to marry: A priest had to have a housekeeper; to put a man and a woman together was like bringing fire to straw and expecting nothing to happen. The unchaste chastity in the Church needed to be brought to an end. Priests had to be set free to marry. The natural, divinely ordained sexual drive needed to be recognized as a necessary, good, and honorable impulse.

Luther—a monk—was still hiding in the castle of Wartburg to avoid being burned as a heretic, when three priests affirmed the rightness of his teaching by getting married. Archbishop Albert of Mainz arrested them. Luther sent a stern protest. Albert decided to consult the University of Wittenberg. Luther's senior colleague and a highly respected scholar, Andreas Carlstadt, answered the bishop's query by writing a book against celibacy. He concluded that, according to the Bible, a priest not only *might* marry but that he *must* marry and father a family. In place of obligatory celibacy, Carlstadt substituted obligatory matrimony and paternity. He went on to confirm his Bible study by setting a personal example. He got married.

Luther was delighted by Carlstadt's bold decision. He was uncomfortable, however, with Carlstadt's proposal that even monks should marry. Luther felt that the case for monks, like him, was different from that of priests. Monks had taken voluntary vows to remain celibate. It would be wrong to break those vows. That raised a new question: Did God enjoin the vows of celibacy? Luther's answer helped create the modern concept of marriage as well as the modern politico-economic world.

The question forced Luther to go back to the Scriptures. He found the monk's vow against marrying unscriptural and in conflict with charity and liberty. He sent his theses back to the university: "*Marriage is good, virginity is better, but liberty is best.*" From the Bible Luther concluded that monastic vows rested on false and arrogant assumptions that celibate Christians had a special calling or vocation, to observe the counsels of perfection, which were superior to ordinary Christians who obey ordinary moral laws. Luther's revolutionary conclusion is known as the "priesthood of all believers."[39]

Luther's exposition of the Bible began to empty out monasteries. His exposition became the basic theological factor that enabled Protestant nations to develop economically faster than Catholic countries and to build egalitarian democracies. The family is a civilization's primary engine for economic growth. If a man has no family, he might plant crops, but he is unlikely to plant and nurture trees and develop fields for coming generations. He might dig a cave or hew a tree house, but he is unlikely to build a home for his grandchildren. The family motivates parents to plan, earn, sacrifice, save, and invest for future generations—for their physical as well as social welfare.

This "priesthood of all believers" negated a priest's vocation as superior. Luther taught the cobbler was as important as the priest. All vocations had to be honored equally. Each had to be undertaken diligently as a service to God. This biblical priesthood of all believers challenged Europe's class distinctions. It birthed the modern democratic equality of all citizens—rich or poor, educated or illiterate, old or young, male or female. Luther planted seeds in Europe that yielded their best harvest in America.

On January 10, 1529, Luther preached on the second chapter of the gospel of John. The passage recounts Jesus' miracle of turning water into wine at a wedding in Cana at his widowed mother's request. Luther encapsulated the intrinsic goodness of marriage, the priesthood of all believers, the equal value of every vocation, and the family as the school of character:

> There are three estates: marriage, virginity, and widowhood. They are all good. None is to be despised. The virgin is not to be esteemed above the widow, nor the widow above the wife, anymore than the tailor is to be esteemed above the butcher. There is no estate to which the Devil is so opposed as to marriage. The clergy have not wanted to be bothered with work and worry. They have been afraid of a nagging wife, disobedient children, difficult relatives, or the dying pig or a cow. They want to lie abed until the sun shines through the window. Our ancestors knew this and would say, "Dear child, be a priest or a nun and have a good time." I have heard married people say to monks, "You have it easy, but when we get up we do not know where to find our bread." Marriage is a heavy cross because so many couples quarrel. It is the grace of God when they agree. The Holy Spirit declares there are three wonders: when brothers agree, when neighbors love each other, and when a man and a wife are at one. When I see a pair like that, I am glad as if I were in a garden of roses. It is rare.[40]

Radical feminists were not the first to see marriage as a "heavy cross"—a burden or slavery. Luther said marriage was slavery for men as much as for women. That is precisely why many men in pagan Rome preferred not to marry but to seek extramarital or homosexual relationships. Christianity made marriage harder for men by requiring that husbands remain faithful, committed, and loving to the same woman—no matter what—"until death do us part." When a husband is forbidden extramarital affairs, taking a second wife, or divorcing a difficult wife; when he is not allowed to hate or be harsh with her; when he is required to love and honor his wife; then his wife is empowered. She has the security to seek for her dignity and rights.

Marriage brings out the worst in both husbands and wives. They must choose whether to stay in that school of character or to drop out. The Bible made divorce difficult because one does not learn much by quitting a challenging school. The only way to make monogamy work is to value love above pleasure, to pursue holiness and humility rather than power and personal fulfillment, to find grace to repent rather than condemn, to learn sacrifice and patience in place of indulgence and gratification. The modern world was created by countless couples who did just that. In working to preserve their marriages and provide for their children, they invested in the future of civilization itself.

FATHERHOOD

In his book, Tocqueville discusses the consequences of biblical Christianity,[41] equality, and freedom on the American family life: on father-son, mother-daughter, parent-child, and husband-wife relationships.

In most of Europe, Christianity had become a state religion. Most people thought themselves "Christians" simply because they were baptized as infants. In contrast, biblical Christians—who encouraged, even required, children to take personal responsibility for their spiritual lives—shaped the social ethos of America. Each person had to find God and live in a personal relationship with him. Knowing God as one's heavenly Father changed the nature of family relationships on earth.

In Tocqueville's opinion, the difference between the European and American family was so great that the American family was not even a "family" in the European (Roman) sense. I find Tocqueville's following observation about America extremely interesting since I come from a patriarchal culture. In our non-nuclear, "joint families" all married sons live together with their parents. A son does not become the "man of his house" as long as his father is alive. Tocqueville wrote:

> In America the family, if one takes the word in its Roman and aristocratic sense, no longer exists. One only finds scattered traces thereof in the first years following the birth of children. The father then does, without opposition, exercise the domestic dictatorship which his son's weakness makes necessary and which is justified by both his weakness and his unquestionable superiority. But as soon as the young American begins to approach man's estate, the reins of filial obedience are daily slackened. Master of his thoughts, he soon becomes responsible for his own behavior. In America there is in truth no adolescence. At the close of boyhood he is a man and begins to trace out his own path . . .
>
> In [European and Asian] aristocracies society is, in truth, only concerned with the father. It only controls the sons through the father; it rules him and he rules them. Hence the father has not only his natural right. He is given a political right to command. . . . He is heard with deference, he is addressed always with respect, and the affection felt for him is ever mingled with fear. . . . [The father-son relationship] is always correct, ceremonious, rigid, and cold, so that natural warmth of heart can hardly be felt through the words . . . But among democratic nations every word a son addresses to his father has a tang of freedom, familiarity, and tenderness all at once.[42]

Of course, unfortunately, Tocqueville is describing "ancient" America. Today as many as 40 percent of American boys do not have fathers. They have biological fathers, but not a man who takes the moral responsibility to bring them up to responsible manhood.

America is following in the footsteps of poor nations such as Jamaica, where they say that as many as 85 percent of the children do not have fathers in the home to guide them.

This is the result of a deliberate policy adopted by slave owners. They wanted their male slaves to serve as "stud bulls"—to breed children but not to bring them up as educated, productive people. Uneducated boys and girls could only grow up to be slaves. What made the American family different? The explanation goes back to Abraham. He was chosen to teach his children to walk in God's ways.[43]

"Early" American parents did not always look after their children. At the very time when Tocqueville visited America, far too many fathers were drunkards, gamblers, and wife- and child-abusers. Revivalists, such as Charles Finney, were preaching that America needed a spiritual revival that would "turn the hearts of the fathers to the children."[44] Their preaching resulted in a mighty revival that transformed families and created a great nation.

THE AMERICAN GIRL

Tocqueville noted that even in the 1830s the French Catholics were providing their girls with a timid, withdrawn, and cloistered education, then leaving them unguided and unaided amid huge social disorder. In contrast, biblical Christians in America were systematically preparing their girls for responsible freedom—to rule their own thoughts, choices, and behavior, and to defend their chastity. *Morality bred freedom, and freedom reinforced morality.*[45]

America's (original) strict sexual mores, which produced strong women, were spelled out in laws consciously derived from the Old Testament. Adultery and rape were punishable by death. Premarital sex or fornication resulted in a fine, whipping, and/or an order to marry. Tocqueville observed, however, that "the death penalty has never been more frequently prescribed by the laws or more seldom carried out" than in America.[46] The New Covenant is a testament of grace. Under this covenant, God's Spirit writes his laws on the human heart, not on tablets of stone.

In aristocratic Europe, as in Asia, marriage was meant more to unite property than persons. Class, caste, dowry, or horoscopes determined the choice of spouses. In Protestant democracies, on the other hand, young people were encouraged to seek God's will and choose with whom they wanted to spend their lives.

Marriage as a lifelong commitment had another advantage. Tocqueville observed:

> Because in America paternal discipline is very lax and the bonds of marriage very tight, a girl is cautious and wary in agreeing thereto. Precocious weddings hardly occur. So American women only marry when their minds are experienced and mature, whereas elsewhere women usually begin to mature when they are married. . . . When the time has come to choose a husband, her cold and austere powers of reasoning, which have been educated and strengthened by a free view of the world, teach the American woman that a light and free spirit [permissiveness] within the bonds of marriage is an everlasting source of trouble, not of pleasure, that a girl's amusements cannot become the recreation of a wife, and that for a married woman the springs of happiness are inside the home.[47]

In the 1960s, American women began rejecting the Tocquevillian portrait of the ideal American woman. Now many, perhaps a majority of Americans, reject the biblical mores for family life. One reason for this rejection is the assertion that from a "natural" perspective monogamy is unnatural and that men, by nature, are polygamous. There is a lot of truth in that assertion. However, that argument overlooks that *all* morality is designed to bring our present "fallen" or sinful nature under the moral law. Wearing clothes is unnatural; stealing is natural for animals; lying is a child's natural response when he gets into trouble. Giving free rein to human nature would require abolishing all morality, not just monogamy.

History's verdict is that by defining marriage as monogamy and making extramarital sex immoral, the biblical tradition laid down a foundation for stable families, strong women, children, economy, and society. By keeping his vows to a woman, made before God and community, a man learns to keep his word in other situations. When keeping one's word becomes a strong cultural value, then trust becomes the foundation for social life. This foundation is now being shaken by the proponents of easy divorce.

THE PHILOSOPHY OF MARRIAGE

The biblical principle of marriage is based on several assumptions. One of them is that human beings are finite. I am male, not female. God made Eve because he saw that "it is not good for the man to be alone."[48] Historically, Hindu philosophy has promoted homosexuality and become foundational to the contemporary interest in Tantric or "sacred sex" because it teaches that each one of us is God, infinite and complete. Consequently, I don't need a wife because the feminine is already within me (*Shakti*). It lies dormant, coiled up as a serpent (*Kundalini*) at the base of the spine in the psychic center of sex (*Muladhara Chakra*). I don't need a wife to be complete, although I might need sexual help to awaken the feminine within me. I will transcend my finiteness as male (or female) and experience my completeness (divinity) when the feminine within me rises, travels up, and merges with the male energy (*Shiva*) in my crown (*chakra*).

The biblical philosophy of marriage is based on God being personal and triune. The family reflects God's image. The first chapter of Genesis presents the Creator as God (v. 1), his Spirit (v. 2), and his Word (v. 3). This triune God said, "Let us make man in our image, after our likeness . . . So God created man in his own image, in the image of God he created him; male and female he created them (vv. 26–27)." Every man and woman bears God's image.

Man and woman become more like God when a man and woman become one in marriage. If a marriage is biblical, then selfishness begins to be replaced by self-giving love—for God is love. Husband and wife become more like God when they have a baby and become a three-in-one—a family. Being parents helps them understand the father-heart and the mother-heart of God—the real meaning of love, sacrifice, and submission. To break that oneness through rebellion, adultery, or divorce hurts the whole family because it violates our essential nature: the image of the triune God, the personal communion of unity and diversity.

The biblical basis for family does not work unless one accepts a third assumption: that we live in a universe of hierarchy and authority. Christian civilization—Orthodox, Catholic, and Protestant—has maintained that equality does not preclude authority. A conductor and a musician are equal as human beings, but in an orchestra, the musician is under the conductor's authority. Submission to that authority does not make the musician a lesser human being; it makes him an effective musician.

According to the Bible, the husband and wife are a team of equals. But the team is no longer how it was created—sinless. Both men and women have sinned, and it is impossible for two sinners to live happily ever after. In a perfect world it *may* be possible for a team of two to function without a notion of authority. But in a "fallen" world, the only way a team of two sinners can function smoothly is for one of them to be recognized as the captain—not because the captain is the best, wisest, or always right, but because the creator and owner of the team—God—has given one of them the responsibility of leadership.

Many hate the Bible because it says that the husband is the head of his wife,[49] even though the New Testament defines leadership as servanthood. The biblical idea of marriage survived for centuries because Luther taught that the wife is to give to her husband not merely love but also honor and obedience. He is to rule with gentleness, but he is to rule.[50] This biblical teaching clashes with the contemporary concepts of equality—the ideas that equality eliminates notions of authority and different roles for men and women.

Today, Luther's understanding of the Bible's teaching on authority in the family has become unpopular.[51] The great American family is now falling apart because America is a land divided by culture wars. On one end are the feminists who believe that equality demands that twenty-year-old girls be sent as soldiers into enemy territories (where they are vulnerable to being captured, gang raped, and brutalized) in defense of feminist ideology. At the other end are conservatives who think that the biblical notion of authority prohibits women from praying in public—that the heavenly Father would be displeased if he heard his daughters pray in his sanctuary.

In my view, neither of the extremes is likely to win the culture war. The painful fact, however, will remain that quarrels paralyze and can even destroy families of sinners once the notion of authority is thrown out of the window. The Bible is not a book for ideal people. It is a handbook for sinners. No community of sinners can function without authority.

Yet, authority—however essential—is a dangerous thing in the hands of sinful persons. The Bible says that headship of a sinful, abusive, oppressive husband is not what God intended for marriage. It is a curse, a result of sin. The good news (the gospel) is that God came to this earth to take the curse of sin upon himself on the cross. The cross of Jesus Christ is the means of deliverance from sin.

As husbands and wives are sanctified from sin and become more God-like, they find ever-increasing deliverance from the curse.[52] The Christian idea of marriage does not work unless a husband and wife come to terms with the fact that they are sinners and need a savior. When they recognize their sinfulness and find God's grace and forgiveness, they can become agents of divine grace and compassion. And Christian compassion is another factor that made the West the best civilization in history. Let us examine it next.

Chapter Sixteen

COMPASSION

WHY DID CARING BECOME
MEDICAL COMMITMENT?

We were driving sixty miles an hour through downtown Minneapolis on the interstate, when we heard loud sirens behind us. The high-speed traffic came to a screeching halt. Two ambulances and a few police vehicles sped by us. Before we had an inkling of what was going on, tears welled up in Ruth's eyes.

"What have I done now?" I asked.

"How much they care for their people," Ruth said, ignoring me and trying to see if beyond the traffic there was an accident, and if someone had been hurt.

That was the year 2000. We had just come to America to write this book and to explore the possibility of making a television program. This was not Ruth's first trip to America. She had studied here for three years, 1971–74. The culture shock was still potent. Even today, Ruth sheds a tear or two when she sees traffic stop at the sight of a flashing school bus, picking up or dropping off a child. It brings back memories of her ordeal in New Delhi, when every day an adult family member had to help Anandit, our youngest daughter, get onto the school bus without coming under its wheels or getting hit by a speeding scooter.

Having been a beneficiary of the kindness and thoughtfulness of hundreds of people in America, Ruth has become America's unashamed apologist. Sometimes this gets her into controversies—especially when she talks with other Asians who have lived longer in America. Some of them condemn America's selfish individualism.

On a few such occasions, I have intervened to mediate between the opposing perceptions. I explain to Ruth's opponents that unlike them we have not lived and worked in secular America. Our impressions are based on our limited experience of America—limited mostly to interactions with the Christian community. We find that serving others at personal cost is an amazingly high value in the American church. The Indian church has many excellent institutions that serve others. Yet, in general, much of the Christian community in India lacks the spirit of service at the personal (noninstitutional) level as we experience it here in America. Knowing human nature, however, I have no doubt that behind the steering wheels of those ambulances there could be "fallen" men, who may actually hate the people they serve.

COMPASSION: A FRUIT OF THE SPIRIT

Karl Marx believed that religion is an opiate that the elite administer to the masses to keep them from revolting against oppression and exploitation. Though an unabashed critic of Christian love, compassion, and morality, German philosopher Friedrich Nietzsche disagreed with Marx. He noted that Judaism began under Moses as a slaves' revolt against their Egyptian masters.

Christianity, likewise, was the religion of a weak and crucified Galilean. It appealed to the downtrodden of the Roman Empire—women, slaves, outcasts, and the defeated. Nietzsche noted that Christianity enabled the weak to overthrow the classical civilization that celebrated strength, sensuality, and a tough-minded acceptance of death seen, for example, in gladiator games.

According to Nietzsche, the Judeo-Christian tradition was a means by which the powerless enchained the powerful, by manipulating guilt, requiring benevolence, and suppressing natural vitality. Nietzsche strongly influenced those advocating Aryan supremacy. The Nazis acted on his argument that the modern decadence—that is, the ideas of equality, emancipation of women, democracy, and so forth—came from Jews and Christians. These had "the gospel preached to the poor and the base, [leading to] the general revolt of all the downtrodden, the wretched, the failure, the less favored, against 'race.'"[1] This point of view summarizes a striking contrast between Judeo-Christian egalitarianism and the Hindu (Aryan) strategy of organizing society hierarchically based on biological breeding with the Brahmins on top and the untouchables at the bottom.

Nietzsche was not alone in condemning Christian compassion. Many Hindus cannot believe that the poor are not the victims of their own karma and that God cares for the poor. They cannot understand why the West gives so much charity to serve the poor and destitute in India. They deeply suspect Western philanthropy and dislike the fact that Christians deliberately choose to serve, educate, and empower lower castes and the marginalized. This was an underlying factor behind the Hindu enthusiasm for Dr. Arun Shourie's attack on Christian missions. Some Hindus believe that Christians serve the poor to prepare them for colonization by America.

Be that as it may, Nietzsche's critique was correct that the Bible has been the greatest humanizing force in history. It drove the movement for the abolition of slavery and promoted care for the weak, such as widows, orphans, the handicapped, and leprosy patients. From liberating and rehabilitating temple prostitutes to reforming prisons and bringing sanity and morality to wars, the biblical tradition has been the most powerful civilizing force. Today, secular ideology has taken over institutions like the Red Cross. Commercial interest has captured practices like nursing care. New Age groups have become champions of the prevention of cruelty to animals. And historians have forgotten the origin of human rights and the justification of civil disobedience. Originally these were all expressions of what the Bible calls the fruit of the Spirit: "love, joy, peace, patience, kindness, goodness, faithfulness, gentleness, self-control."[2] These efforts and institutions are the outworking of the Spirit that Jesus promised to those who believe in him,[3] the Spirit of God who is the "Father of mercies and God of all comfort."[4]

A survey of the history of the medical profession confirms the assertion of macro-historian David Landes that "culture makes almost all the difference."[5] Greek, Roman, Indian, and Islamic civilizations produced great physicians and surgeons; however, they did not develop modern medicine partly because they could not create caring cultures. For that reason, over time they lost their technical expertise and their advantage of a head start in medicine to biblical civilization. Western civilization was able to learn from preceding cultures and develop modern medicine because the Bible informed it that real sickness in human society was selfishness. Human community was intended to reflect the image of a triune God—to be a community of love—but it chose to follow the diabolical temptation to put self-interest first.

In the classical (Greco-Roman) world, medicine had a promising beginning, but it did not become a self-sustaining, ever improving science. Medical students are familiar with the Hippocratic tradition (Hippocrates of Cos ca. 460 BC–ca. 377 BC) in Greece. This first recorded practice of rational medicine relied upon critical questioning. It encouraged rationality overruling superstitions, magic, and rituals. The Hippocratic tradition introduced professionalism and ethical standards to medical practice. A physician was required to respect patients, not abuse the power he had over their bodies, maintain confidentiality, and give life not take it. The Hippocratic oath included caring for the unborn; therefore, it banned abortion. The physician took an oath to serve the poor for free when needed. This is summarized today as "First, do no harm" (*Primum non nocer*).

The Greeks thus made the first commendable start in medicine, but they could not build upon this wonderful foundation. Today, in almost every town in India we have *Unani Dawakhanas*—Greek medical houses. Mostly Muslims run these, indicating that Islam brought Greek medicine to India. They dispense "Greek" medicine, mostly herbs. These clinics survive because they help some patients. Most Indians, however, regard these practitioners as quacks because these Greek medical houses are not known for rational[6] medicine. Nor are they part of an ongoing preventive, curative, and nursing care. The medical knowledge in Greece did not produce a culture of care. In fact, the wider culture overpowered and stifled the promising beginning of rational medicine.

During the early centuries of the Christian era, Greek doctors thronged to Rome. The most illustrious of these was Galen, whose works on medicine were translated into Arabic by Islamic scholars such as Hunayn ibn Ishaq, who also translated works of Hippocrates and wrote commentaries on them. Rome, however, did not contribute much to the theory or practice of medicine except in matters of public health, in which it set a great example. Rome had an unrivaled water supply and public baths. It provided gymnasiums, domestic sanitation, adequate disposal of sewage, and even built some hospitals.

After Rome's fall, learning was no longer held in high esteem, experiment was discouraged, and originality became a dangerous asset. The ability was there, but the culture of care could not become a part of the classical world. The Roman Empire built a culture of cruelty that killed for entertainment. For example, exposing unwanted infants had been a common practice for centuries before Rome fell. Greek writers Plato and Aristotle had both recommended infanticide as a legitimate state policy. The Twelve Tables—the earliest known Roman legal code (450 BC)—permitted fathers to expose any female infants to the elements, as well as deformed or weak male infants. During excavations of a villa in the port city of Ashkelon, Lawrence E. Stager and his colleagues made

> a gruesome discovery in the sewer that ran under the bathhouse . . .
> The sewer had been clogged with refuse sometime in the sixth century A.D. When we excavated and dry-sieved the desiccated sewage, we found numerous small bones that we assumed were animal bones. Only later did we learn . . . that they were human bones—of nearly 100 little babies apparently murdered and thrown into the sewer.[7]

All of the ancient world was not selfish and pleasure seeking. Many thought that renouncing the world and its pleasures was a high and desirable ideal. What they lacked was the knowledge that God loved this sinful, rebellious world full of sickness and suffering; he loved it enough to send his son to suffer in order to save others.

"FOR GOD SO LOVED THE WORLD"

Jesus Christ was born when Emperor Augustus was self-consciously building what he thought would be the secure foundations of civilization. There would be one empire and one emperor. Wars would cease. The world would be safe for civilization. His problem was that this empire had to be built by force, which required a brutal army. But then the army had to be kept in check by force. Building an empire by force turned citizens into virtual slaves. The entire system had to be built on the backs of sweating, bleeding slaves who had no stake in it. The empire was good for the privileged few; for the rest it was so horrible a civilization that Jesus' compassion was seen as radical light in a dark age.[8]

Christ attracted the oppressed masses because he preached good news to the poor.[9] Jesus had compassion on the crowds that followed him because he saw them as "harassed and helpless, like sheep without a shepherd,"[10] exploited by heartless wolves that pretended to be their custodians. Jesus mentored his disciples to become good shepherds who would lay down their lives for their sheep.[11] At the risk of his life, Jesus stood up against the religious-political establishment of his day for the dignity and value of the insignificant, crippled, mentally deranged individuals.[12] He rebuked the callousness of his disciples when they prevented mothers from bringing little children to him to obtain his blessings.[13] Jesus infuriated the community leaders of his day by embracing social outcasts—the lepers, the tax collectors, and the "untouchable" Samaritans.[14]

Christ's brilliant apologist Justin Martyr (ca. 100–165) was converted in AD 133. In his *Apology*, Martyr explained that Jesus renounced the prestige that could have come from seeking the patronage of classical civilization. Instead, Jesus became the Messiah of the sick, the sorrowing, and the suffering. It was this that transformed his persecuted community. Martyr wrote:

> Those who formerly delighted in fornication now embrace chastity
> alone; those who formerly made use of magical arts have dedicated

themselves to the good and unbegotten God; we who once valued above everything the gaining of wealth and possessions now bring what we have into a common stock, and share with everyone in need; we who hated and destroyed one another, and would not share the same hearth with people of a different tribe on account of their different customs, now since the coming of Christ, live familiarly with them, and pray for our enemies, and try to persuade those who unjustly hate us to live according to the good advice of Christ, to the end that they may share with us the same joyful hope of a reward from God the Master of all.[15]

Obviously, the Christian church has not always lived by these high ideals. Emperor Julian (AD 331–363) inadvertently confirmed the essential validity of Justin's claim, however, when he tried to save Rome's pagan religions by persecuting Christians. He told his co-religionists that if they really wanted to prevent Christianity's growth, they would have to serve their neighbors better than Christians did.[16] One hears similar statements from militant Hindus today who hate Christian missions, yet challenge each other to serve like Christians in order to prevent people from becoming followers of Christ.[17]

Augustine, bishop of Hippo, explained the difference between Rome's kingdom of men and Christ's kingdom of God. He was a professor of rhetoric, whose books *City of God* and *Confessions* dominated the intellectual life of Europe for more than a thousand years. His mother was a Christian, but he ridiculed Christianity because he was a learned philosopher and because of his "playboy culture"—he kept a mistress since he was fifteen years old. His contempt for Christianity continued until the age of thirty, when Augustine realized that philosophy had failed both him and the ancient world. In his book, *On Nature and Grace* (AD 415), he describes the two cultures—the secular and the celestial:

That which animates secular society (*civitas terrena*) is the love of self to the point of contempt for God. That which animates divine society (*civitas caelestis*) is the love of God to the point of contempt for self. The one prides itself on itself (*amor sui*), the pride of the other is in the Lord. The one seeks for glory from men, the other counts its consciousness of God as its greatest glory (*De Civitate Dei* 14:28) . . . These desires may therefore be described respectively as greed (*avaritia*) and love (*caritas*). The one is holy, the other foul; the one social, the other selfish; the one thinks of the common advantage for the sake of the higher association, the other reduces even the common good to a possession of its own for the sake of selfish ascendancy. The one is subject to, the other a rival to God; the one is peaceful, the other turbulent; the one pacific, the other factious; the one prefers truth to the praises of the foolish, the other is greedy of praise on any terms; the one is friendly, the other envious, the one desires the same for his neighbor as himself, the other to subject his neighbor to himself, the one governs his neighbor in his neighbor's interest, the other in his own.[18]

Augustine rejected Roman civilization, which was characterized by *amor sui* (self-love). The philosophy of self-love began with an assertion of the animal right to live and find its fulfillment in a satisfaction of the demands of belly and loin. It created a community, but that was the concord espoused by thieves and pirates. This phenomenon is seen today among corrupt officials of "democratic" states. It is the lowest kind of cooperative endeavor. Corrupt officers of a hospital or police may have such a strong brotherhood that no one blows the whistle against their foul play. Theirs is a self-centered community. It covers up each other's crookedness. It matters not whether a corrupt medical "community" has taken the Hippocratic oath; it would earn the hatred of its beneficiaries were it to follow the self-love driven culture, the secular city.

Romans rejected Rome's culture because Christ confronted its cruelties with the gospel of a compassionate God. He invited the poor, the meek, the sick, the sorrowing, the hungry, the weak, and the weary to come to him for rest. He blessed children, touched lepers, healed the handicapped, delivered the demonized, ate with social outcasts, protected prostitutes, taught illiterate masses, opposed the oppressors, and reconciled rebellious sinners with their loving and forgiving heavenly Father. Christ's followers built upon this tradition of compassion for the unlovable. For example, in AD 369—a few centuries before the birth of Islam—St. Basil (AD 329–379), Orthodox bishop of Caesarea, founded the first hospital in Cappodocia (modern Anatolia) with three hundred beds.

The monasteries were the real pioneers of the Western culture of care. Hermits and ascetics had preceded the monks, but they saw spirituality as a renunciation of the world—not too different from the Hindu ascetics. St. Benedict of Nursia (ca. AD 480–547) rejected the hermitic tradition of monks withdrawing from society to cultivate their own spirituality. Realizing that God loved this world, he practiced a celibate spiritual life not for its own sake, but to serve society, especially the poor and sick. The Benedictine monks imprinted on the Western consciousness the idea of humility and service as the true means of greatness. This idea became a defining feature of Western civilization. It is the opposite of the Asian idea that lesser beings must serve the greater.

COMBINING COMPASSION WITH KNOWLEDGE

Compassion was not the only force behind the Christian contribution to medicine. Equally important was the commitment to knowledge. Christ's followers preserved, transcribed, and translated Greek medical manuscripts. Medieval Catholic monasteries absorbed Greek and Islamic medicine and enriched the tradition by accumulating knowledge, recording it in books, and carefully observing what treatment worked and what did not. Ancient philosophical, scientific, and medical classics have come down to us substantially because the monasteries had scriptoria where they copied books, multiplied knowledge, and enabled learning to survive through the Dark Ages.

Monasteries began to practice medicine, and because they were a confraternal body, they transferred their medical knowledge from one institution to another. These were translated into Latin in many medieval monasteries. The Nestorian Christians (an Eastern Church)

established a school of translators to render Greek texts into Arabic—
that became the key step to blessing the Arab world. It ensured the
survival of Greek medicine when barbarians destroyed learning in
Europe.

The Benedictine tradition not only saved ancient medical learning,
but caused it to spread by building upon it. Gradually the monasteries
decided not to spend too much time away from their main responsibilities of prayer and meditation. They began to pass some of their
medical responsibilities onto laymen. Christian monasteries began to
spread the knowledge they gained from manuscripts and experience.
Medical knowledge was thus accumulated and improved upon, even
before universities began in the thirteenth century.

Medieval universities in Europe refined and taught medical knowledge they received from Islamic and monastic sources. As already
noted, these universities were the educational arms of the church.
Secular or state-owned universities did not exist. Catholic priest
Guido de Cauliaco (ca. AD 1300–1368) wrote the first modern book
of surgery (*Chirurgia Magna*, AD 1363). Christian scholars and artists
of the Renaissance period, like Leonardo da Vinci, built on that tradition, gathering phenomenal knowledge of human anatomy.

Arabian Medicine

Muslim empires stretched from Persia to Spain. When people talk of
"Arabian medicine," they do not necessarily imply that all physicians
during the Middle Ages were Arabs or natives of Arabia or Muslims.
Some were Jews and some Christians. The overall philosophical and
medical doctrines of the "Arabic" medicine were substantially those
of Galen and Hippocrates. Some Muslim physicians made Galen's difficult writings accessible. The intellectual prodigy Avicenna (ca. AD
980–1037) was the most celebrated Islamic physician of the eleventh
century.

The greatest "Islamic" physicians—Rhazes, Avicenna, and
Avenzoar—were all heads of hospitals. They had time to study patients
and to follow the evolution of a disease. They made case histories

and kept registers of their patients. Abulcasis (Abu'l–Qasim Khalef ibn Abbas az-Zahrawi), born near Córdoba, Spain, was the medical authority most frequently consulted by physicians in medieval times. He restored surgery to its former glory and wrote a medical encyclopedia. From the ninth to the fifteenth centuries, the teaching of medicine was best organized in the schools of Baghdad, Damascus, Cairo, and Córdoba, which were connected with hospitals.

With this tremendous heritage, Islamic civilization could have gone on to develop modern medicine, because Islam also believed in a compassionate God and respected Jesus Christ as a prophet. It failed to capitalize on its assets because it preferred to follow a military hero—Muhammad—in place of a self-sacrificing savior, Christ. Consequently, the Islamic tradition could not liberate Muslims from the classical pursuit of power. It could not glorify self-giving service as a superior virtue. The Hippocratic culture did not take off in Greece, Rome, India, Arabia, or medieval Europe—not even in medieval Christian universities.

THE BIRTH OF MODERN MEDICINE

Seventeenth-century English physician, Thomas Sydenham (1624–1689), is called the "English Hippocrates" and the "father of English medicine." He began questioning the medical assumptions and practices that had been handed down. He revived rational medicine in such a way that it survived not just a few generations, but continues to grow even today.

Born in 1624 in a Puritan home, Sydenham fought in the British civil war with his father and brothers on the side of Oliver Cromwell. When Cromwell came to power, Sydenham trained as a physician. He started practicing in Westminster and began what we now call "modern medicine." Sydenham was a friend of other Puritan scientists, such as Robert Boyle, and was involved in the Royal Society of Science. These pioneers of science and medicine were not concerned merely for rational, experimental, scientific, or academic medicine. Their concern was for the glory of God and the love of human beings.

The Bible undergirded Sydenham's medical mission. He summed up his medical philosophy in the following advice to his students:

> Whoever applies himself to medicine should seriously weigh the following considerations: First that he will one day have to render an account to the Supreme Judge of the lives of sick people entrusted to his care. Next, by whatever skill or knowledge he may, by the divine favor become possessed of, should be devoted above all things to the glory of God and the welfare of the human race. Thirdly, he must remember that it is no mean or ignoble creature that he deals with. We may ascertain the worth of the human race since for its sake God's only begotten Son became man and thereby ennobled the nature that he took upon him. Finally, the physician should bear in mind that he himself is not exempt from the common lot but is subject to the same laws of mortality and disease as his fellows and he will care for the sick with more diligence and tenderness if he remembers that he himself is their fellow sufferer.[19]

While Greek, Roman, Arabian, and Indian medical traditions stagnated or died, Sydenham's tradition continues to flourish after four centuries because it was an integral part of a larger culture shaped by the Bible. The medical scene in India can help one grasp this point.

INDIAN MEDICINE

Indian medical students and doctors constitute the largest ethnic minority in many prestigious medical institutions in America. Some Indians imagine that it is due to the fact that the history of medicine in India goes back three thousand or more years. *Ayurveda*, the ancient Indian system of medicine, has been popularized in the West by Deepak Chopra and others.* But *Ayurveda* is not the only medical invention of India. The first textbooks on surgery are Sushruta's

---

* Deepak Chopra's *Ayurveda* is very different from the original Indian practice, which believed that the human body was comprised of five elements: earth, water, air, fire, and ether. Disease was believed to be caused by a disturbance in the proper equilibrium of these elements.

Samhita. These were compiled between the first century BC and the seventh century AD. Sushruta is said to have been the first to perform cataract operations at a time when even the great Hippocratic tradition does not mention it.

Plastic surgery is another Indian invention. The need for plastic surgery serves as an illustration of a culture's impact on medicine. If someone behaved shamefully in traditional India—for example, by committing adultery—then the penalty was the loss of one's nose. So many noses were cut off that as early as two thousand years ago we needed plastic surgery. No evidence exists that Greco-Roman civilizations had the idea of plastic surgery.

To *Ayurveda,* cataract operations, and plastic surgery, we could add massage and aromatherapy as examples of India's pioneering in medical expertise. But this glorious picture of medicine in ancient India has to be contrasted with the reality encapsulated in Ida Scudder's story from barely a century ago.

Ida, a young American woman, a graduate of D. L. Moody's school for young ladies at Northfield, MA, came to visit her missionary father in south India in 1892. One night a Brahmin (the highest caste Hindu) man came to her and said that his wife was ready to deliver a baby, but it was a very painful labor, so would she please come and help deliver the baby? Ida replied, "No I'm just a girl. I'm not a doctor; I know nothing about medicine. My father is the physician; you take him!" The Brahmin answered, "I can't take a man to see my wife!"

A little later, a Muslim man came and asked if she would help his wife, also experiencing a difficult labor. Ida said, "Look, I'm just a girl visiting my dad—why don't you take him?" The Muslim, echoing the Brahmin, wouldn't take a man to see his wife!

Next a man from the Mudaliar* caste came and pleaded with her to come and help deliver his wife's baby. She refused again.

By the morning, all three women were dead. That shook Ida. She believed God was saying something to her. She came back to America,

---

* Mudaliars are socially "forward" Shudras, that is, the fourth class in the Hindu caste system. They have served as bureaucrats and soldiers.

trained at Cornell Medical College, and then returned to India in 1900 to establish a one-bed clinic, which grew into the Vellore Christian Medical College.[20] Mahatma Gandhi called it the best medical college in Asia, and it became the largest in India. In some ways it may be the best in the world. The professors serve as mentors. They do not practice privately; all their time is available to students and patients. The college is also on the cutting-edge of developing medical education through distance learning.

Heroic efforts of missionaries such as Ida Scudder produced an amazing result. After a century, there are more women doctors in India than in any other country in the world. But what happened to the tremendous beginning in medicine that India had made two thousand years earlier? In the year 1900, why didn't a city have female doctors or nurses who could deliver a baby?

Several factors caused the decline and stagnation of the Indian medical tradition. One was the attitude toward knowledge. There were individuals in India with medical genius. But our culture saw knowledge as power—something to be kept secret and guarded, not disseminated. Our learned physicians trained their sons and also their students if they surrendered their minds and bodies to their gurus as their *shihyas* (disciples). Knowledge gave authority. To remain the expert, you could not allow your expertise to be questioned by your disciples. The disciples had to surrender their minds to the guru's authority.

This attitude toward knowledge could not create and sustain an academic culture where peers and students could challenge, reject, and improve the medical techniques they had received. Thus, India had intellectual giants but our religious tradition failed to build academic communities. Individual genius, knowledge, and excellence in technology are insufficient to build a medical culture. It requires community effort.

In addition, there was the problem of caste. Only the lower castes were supposed to undertake service professions that appeared dirty or degrading. Only the lowest caste women could serve as midwives. Besides, all women were second-class human beings and their health and safety were not priorities in our villages.

When Ruth and I started serving the poor in central India, one of our first priorities was the training of village health workers. We found that illiterate midwives were delivering babies in totally unhygienic ways. Tetanus was a common occurrence because they cut umbilical cords with a sickle. Then they used rags to try and stop a woman's bleeding after delivery. Washing wounds in dirty water increased infections. These elementary problems were huge issues because midwifery was seen as a dirty job to be done by the lowest caste. These cultural attitudes precluded the development of gynecological care in our culture.

Karma became another philosophical factor preventing a culture of care. A person's suffering was believed to be a result of her or his karma (deeds) in a previous life. In other words, suffering, was cosmic justice. To interfere with cosmic justice is like breaking into a jail and setting a prisoner free. If you cut short someone's suffering, you would actually add to his suffering because he would need to come back to complete his due quota of suffering. You do not help a person when you interfere with the cosmic law of justice.

As human beings we Indians have as much natural empathy as anyone else in the world, but the doctrine of karma prevented us from turning that natural empathy into institutions and traditions of caring. We had no dearth of gods, goddesses, and saints in our country, but missionaries like Ida Scudder and Mother Teresa of Calcutta[21] had to come from outside to help us see that the dying destitute on our streets were human beings, albeit with rotting bodies. While most Hindus honor the missionary spirit, those like Arun Shourie, who are anxious to preserve Hindu culture, rightly see Christian missions as their biggest threat.

Buddhism did teach *karuna* (compassion) as a high value, but Buddhist compassion could not develop into a culture of care. This was partly because Buddhism, too, believed in the doctrine of karma and partly because it taught that we must not get attached to anyone. The Buddha had to renounce his own wife and son to find enlightenment. He saw attachment as a cause of suffering. Detachment, therefore, became an important religious virtue. That turned Buddhist *karuna* into compassion without commitment to another person. Those whose commitment was to their own spiritual enlightenment did not have the motivation to develop a scientific medical tradition.

The decline of Indian medicine ought to serve as a warning to the West. Our failure demonstrates that ultimately the development of the medical profession cannot depend on technical knowledge and expertise alone. A society with medical genius could destroy the future of its medicine. In the final analysis medicine requires a caring culture that brings together the heart and mind to create and sustain appropriate values, laws, and socioeconomic systems that nurture medicine. Building a culture conducive to medicine calls for wisdom, and that has been in short supply lately in America. A prominent Hollywood documentarian-activist went as far as urging America to follow Cuba. Health care dominated the public square throughout 2009. It is likely to be a hot issue in 2011 as well.

Today, many Indian physicians are at the cutting edge of medical technology in the West. Yet, some of my Indian friends in the UK have started a "blood insurance" company for those traveling to India. They assure their clients that in an event of an emergency, medically clean blood will be flown from England within two hours. Supplying clean blood to India is understandable. It is humiliating, however, when international athletes and sports teams have to bring their own bottled water to India for drinking. We do not lack the ability or the resources to provide clean blood or water. The problem is that Indians living in the West have a hard time trusting their culture.

CULTURAL TRANSFORMATION

A small town in Maharashtra state was celebrating the fiftieth anniversary of the local Christian hospital. During the celebration, an elderly public figure narrated the following incident from the early days of the hospital.

A poor family brought a woman to the hospital for a surgery. She needed blood, but no one from her extended family would donate his or her blood. Deeply disappointed by their fear and lack of compassion, and realizing the urgency of her situation, the missionary surgeon donated his own blood and then proceeded to operate on the dying woman. The town was baffled. Why would a surgeon do such a thing? Worldviews blind people so that critics cannot begin to comprehend that the surgeon was following a Savior, who had given his own blood to give us life.

The missionary doctor was the opposite of many civil surgeons who demand bribes to operate on the poor. Hindu, Buddhist, and Muslim civilizations had ruled India during the preceding thirty-five hundred years. None of them gave us even the concept of a welfare state—a state that exists to serve the citizens. The idea that the state should pay surgeons to serve the poor came to India with the Bible.[22] Secularism hijacked the biblical idea, but it provides only the form, not the spirit. It is possible to bring a mango plant from India and grow it in Minnesota. One might even get a few crops. But under normal circumstances, the tree will not survive and certainly not reproduce in Minnesota's cold climate.

Likewise, the history of medicine shows that a few great men might have great insights, they might practice and propagate good cures, but knowledge is not enough. Medical research requires money. But a people that put their trust in greed, rather than in a crucified Savior, will find other ways to spend money than to fight economically unattractive diseases. The culture of compassion needs the transcendent, supernatural power of God's Spirit to be able to love as God loved the world. To become a continuing and growing tradition, medicine needs the transformation of the philosophical and spiritual climate.

Malcolm Muggeridge (1903–90), the late British journalist and author, noted the impact different worldviews make on their respective cultures. Like most British journalists of his day, he was a secular humanist, but he was honest. He did not say that all worldviews are the same. He said, "I've spent a number of years in India and Africa where I found much righteous endeavor undertaken by Christians of all denominations; but I never, as it happens, came across a hospital or orphanage run by the Fabian society, or a humanist leper colony."[23]

The biblical teachings on love and compassion are not matters of private piety. They are culture-shaping forces because they move believers into the public arena of social protest, civil disobedience, and positive nation building. Compassion, however, could not have built modern medical culture on its own. It also required an economic milieu.

Chapter Seventeen

TRUE WEALTH

How Did Stewardship Become Spirituality?

In chapter 5 I shared the tragic story of Sheela—the little girl starved to death by her parents. Some experts say that forty thousand children will die today from chronic malnutrition and all the diseases associated with it. Tonight around 1.2 billion people will go to bed hungry. A decade ago that was a tragedy; today it is a scandal, because for the first time in history we possess the knowledge and technology to prevent starvation.

Why are some nations so poor and others so rich? Why do you suppose most wealth is so persistently one-sided? Why do some appear selfish and others incapable of generating wealth? These questions have long divided individuals and nations along ideological fault lines. Yet, for the sake of curiosity, if not compassion and fairness, we must ask: Is there some other vision of wealth—a true inner wealth—that might be more instructive and persuasive for our future? Do cultural beliefs and values condemn whole cultures to poverty? Should the inner wealth—a culture's ability to create material wealth—be shared across cultures?

More Precious Than Diamonds?

The birth of modern industrial capitalism was celebrated in 1851 at the first World's Fair in Hyde Park, London, in a specially constructed

Crystal Palace. In part, the fair was a celebration of the fact that England was the world's first industrial nation and ruled an empire on which the sun never set. Nations such as Russia, Austria, France, and Japan—rich in art and culture—displayed their magnificent works of art. The chief exhibit from India was the Kohinoor, one of the world's largest diamonds. It was set in Queen Victoria's state crown on becoming Empress of India.

To Europeans, the United States was still the New World. They considered it uncivilized. It didn't even have a king! Americans had little wealth to display at the time. They did not even fill the space they had rented. The British press, proud of England's cultural superiority and global dominance, ridiculed the American exhibit as "the prairie ground." America's chief contributions to the fair were two humble horse-driven reapers, one invented by Cyrus McCormick and the other by Obed Hussey.[1] Cultural critics thought them rather primitive, and in 1851 the *London Times* mocked the reaper as a cross between a flying machine, a wheelbarrow, and an Astley chariot. In comparison to the fruit of older European countries, the American exhibit indeed appeared primitive and barren—even ridiculous; an expression, at best, of the Puritan preference for function over beauty.

The British public was more practical than its press. After a trial run in bad weather, an international jury estimated that McCormick's reaper was capable of harvesting twenty acres a day. The day after the trial, the American "prairie ground" was thronged by more people than was the Kohinoor diamond. The McCormick reaper quickly came to define the very shape and tempo of mechanized agriculture and free market economy. In industrialized countries 2 to 5 percent of the population now cultivates more land than was plowed when most people spent their lives growing food.

No one disputes that McCormick (along with the inventiveness of American culture) transformed agriculture and the world. What cultural factors produced such inventors? McCormick and many others like him were products of a theological, spiritual, moral, and legal climate produced by the Bible. It is not possible to explain their humanitarian inventiveness, pursuit of wealth, business practices, and commercial success without understanding their biblical worldview.

A PECULIAR SPIRITUALITY

My people in India did not lack creative genius. They erected great monuments to gods and goddesses and built palaces for kings and queens. But our worldview did not inspire these same engineering skills to be directed toward labor-saving devices. My personal interest in McCormick is rooted in the fact that his widow, Nancy McCormick, financed the building of the Allahabad Agricultural Institute in my hometown, Allahabad, on the banks of the river Yamuna. My brother studied in this institute and, for a few years, I cycled there every Sunday afternoon to study the Bible.

Between 2002 and 2006, from two to twenty thousand people—mostly Hindus—gathered there every Sunday for spiritual fellowship. This is significant because one of the holiest Hindu sites in India—the confluence of the holy rivers Ganges and Yamuna—is less than three miles from the Institute. As mentioned in chapter 12, practically every important Hindu holy man has come to this confluence during the last two thousand years; so have most politicians and wealthy merchants. Not one of them, however, ever started an institution to serve poor peasants.

The Agricultural Institute, now a Deemed University, was established by Sam Higginbottom, a professor of economics in my alma mater.* He saw the plight of the peasants, returned to America to study agriculture, forged links with McCormick's family, and returned to establish this institute. His purpose was to inject into Indian culture McCormick's spirit of loving one's neighbors enough to attempt to alleviate their suffering.

---

* In India colleges function under a university chartered by the Government. *Deemed University* is a status of autonomy granted to high performing institutes and departments of various universities in India. I did my Intermediate studies (grades 11 and 12) at Jamuna Christian College, a part of Ewing Christian College, in Higginbottom's time. Now independent, it is still located across the river from the Agricultural Institute.

Love is not a common ethical principle of all religions. No Hindu sage did anything like Sam Higginbottom did, because in order to be spiritual, the learned pundits had to separate themselves from the peasants, not serve them. The hallmark of Indian spirituality was detachment from worldly pursuits like agriculture. Therefore, the spiritually "advanced" in my country treated the toiling masses as untouchables.

McCormick's reaper reinforces the point made in an earlier chapter—that necessity is *not* "the mother of invention." All agricultural societies have needed to harvest grain. But no other culture invented a reaper. Most cultures met this need by forcing into backbreaking labor those who were too weak to say no—landless laborers, servants, slaves, women, and children. McCormick struggled to find a better way. The driving force in his life becomes apparent when you notice that he gave substantial portions of his income to promote the Bible through several projects including newspapers* and the Presbyterian Theological Seminary in Chicago, which was renamed the McCormick Seminary.

Cyrus was born to a Puritan couple, Robert and Mary Ann McCormick, in 1809, in a log cabin in Rockbridge County, Virginia. His Scotch-Irish ancestors came to America in 1735 with little more than a Bible and the teachings of the Protestant reformers John Calvin and John Knox.

These reformers had embraced the Hebrew ideal of the dignity of labor. In addition, reformers, such as Luther and Calvin, introduced to the European mind the radical biblical idea that the calling or vocation of a peasant or a mason was as high as that of a priest or a monk. Every believer was a saint and ought to fulfill his or her vocation for the glory of God. In the words of sociologist Max Weber:

But at least one thing [in the Protestant mind-set] was unquestionably new: the valuation of the fulfillment of duty in worldly affairs

---

* The modern press is a product of the Puritan revolution in England, and a substitute for the biblical institution of the prophet. A century ago, most newspapers in America were Christian.

as the highest form which the moral activity of the individual could assume. This it was which inevitably gave every-day worldly activity a religious significance, and which first created the conception of a calling in this sense. . . . The only way of living acceptably to God was not to surpass the worldly morality in monastic asceticism, but solely through the fulfillment of the obligations imposed upon the individual by his position in the world. That was his calling"[2]

Cyrus McCormick didn't like harvesting with a sickle or scythe. Had he lived before the Reformation, he might have escaped the drudgery of toil by going to a university or becoming a priest. This was normal in Orthodox and Catholic cultures. Even St. Thomas Aquinas—perhaps the greatest theologian of the last millennium—justified the tradition by advocating that while the biblical obligation to work rested upon the human race as a whole, it was not binding on every individual, especially not on religious individuals who were called to pray and meditate.*

The McCormick family rejected that medieval idea to follow the teachings of Richard Baxter (1615–91), the English Puritan theologian, scholar, and writer, who believed that God's command to work was unconditional. No one could claim exemption from work on the grounds that he had enough wealth on which to live. Baxter wrote, "You are no more excused from service of work . . . than the poorest man. God has strictly commanded [labor] to all."[3]

It is important to note that this work ethic, which made England and America different from Italy or Russia, was biblical—not Puritan per se. Quakers, like McCormick's rival, Obed Hussey,** shared the same worldview. This biblical work ethic, later called the "Protestant work ethic," was driven into Cyrus from childhood. Both his friends and critics acknowledged that he was a workaholic*** with an indomi-

---

* During the Middle Ages religious individuals were paid to sit the whole day and pray for the souls of their deceased relatives. In Hindu and Buddhist cultures, peasants provided for ascetics who did nothing besides meditate.

** Hussey patented his reaper in 1834 but lost the marketing race to McCormick.

*** The term "workaholic" is used only in a negative sense today. However, even our leisure-driven age accepts that no one excels in a given field and becomes a distinguished scientist, athlete,

table perseverance and a bulldog's tenacity. McCormick's passion for focused work made him very wealthy, but his work ethic was a product of his religious culture, not his desire for wealth.

The West's rapid economic progress began when it adopted the materialistic spirituality of the Hebrew Bible (the Old Testament). For it is in Genesis that God declares the material universe to be good. Many ancient worldviews, such as India's, had looked upon the material realm as intrinsically evil—something to be delivered from. Christian philosophers who studied the Bible noted that sin resulted in a breakdown of the relationship between God, man, and nature. The most influential exponent of this insight was Francis Bacon, who had a profound impact on the American mind.[4]

McCormick was nurtured on the biblical idea that through godly and creative work human beings can roll back the curse of sweat and toil and reestablish their dominion over nature. To repeat, my ancestors did not lack intelligence, but our genius was expressed in a philosophy that taught us to worship nature instead of establishing dominion over it. Economic development involves not worshipping but harnessing natural resources and energy for human consumption, albeit with foresight and a sense of stewardship.

Francis Bacon's exposition of the Bible instilled a non-fatalistic philosophy in England and America. It implied that the future could be better than the past. As explained in previous chapters, this Hebrew concept was born in Israel's collective experience of God. When God intervened in human history to liberate them from their slavery in Egypt, the Hebrews learned that God could change their destiny for the better. And since men and women were created in God's image, they, too, could forge a better future for themselves through creative efforts.

This belief became an integral feature of modern Western culture and proved to be a powerful economic asset that would set the West apart from the rest of the world. While other cultures sought magical powers through ritual and sacrifice, the West began cultivating technological and scientific powers. McCormick's grandparents, like

---

inventor, or businessman without working harder than her or his peers.

most European Puritans who fled from religious persecution to the liberty of America, interpreted their experience as being similar to that of the Israelites being set free from the bondage of slavery.

An important aspect of Moses' mission was to teach God's law to the Israelites. A cornerstone of this teaching was that while wickedness makes some individuals rich, it impoverishes entire nations. According to the Bible, a nation is exalted by righteousness.[5] Cyrus's forefathers believed that the blessings of righteousness were not exclusive to the Jews. God chose Abraham to bless all the nations of the earth. All true believers, they reasoned, were God's chosen people. Therefore, it is wrong for God's beloved to accept poverty as their fate. Even if one's poverty were a result of sin, either one's own or one's ancestors, it was possible to repent and receive God's forgiveness and the power to live a righteous life. It is not surprising, then, that within a century after Thomas McCormick's arrival in Philadelphia, his grandson's family owned an estate of twelve hundred acres.

Cyrus's family owned slaves, as did so many others of their time. They were products of their era and could have purchased more human labor to bring in their harvests. One difference the Bible made was that it demanded the McCormicks work just as hard as any of their slaves. We know that by the age of fifteen, Cyrus had despaired of seeing people slave in the fields. That's when he resolved to build upon his father's failed attempts to find a better method for harvesting grain.

SPIRITUALITY OR GREED?

The 2010 movie *Wall Street: Money Never Sleeps* powerfully shows how secularism confuses ambition and greed. Ambition is good, but it becomes greed when separated from moral absolutes. Greed is a destructive part of human nature. It brought to India not only Europeans, but also the Aryan and Muslim invaders. Greed explains the loot of Alexander the Great and Nadir Shah, but not the creativity of industrial capitalism. Pioneers of modern economic enterprise, such as Cyrus McCormick, did want to make money, but they were inspired by something nobler.

Adam Smith had observed—as do some of today's ecological economists—that the universe has been so structured by its Creator that in seeking their self-interest, creatures help to maintain a grand economic balance. We may strive to make money in our self-interest, but if we do so within the boundaries of moral limits, then the Creator's invisible hand turns our labor into a matter of public good.

In traditional cultures, including mine, people who had wealth hid it, gambled it away, or displayed it by building castles, cathedrals, or mausoleums. In contrast, McCormick's biblical upbringing encouraged him to save and reinvest his wealth in expanding his business for the glory of God and the blessing of human beings. Saving money sounds simple, but it was revolutionary. In most cultures, in most periods of history, making and saving money was a dangerous affair. It attracted both robbers and rulers, and the two were not very different. Tax collectors did not get a salary. They had to rob peasants to sustain their militia to collect taxes. Absence of a rule of law eliminated the option of banking, forcing my ancestors to hide their meager savings in the fields, walls, or floors.

The Bible created a very different culture; it inspired and enabled the habit of saving and reinvesting. This helped McCormick's factory become one of the earliest mega-industrial enterprises in America. By the time of the 1851 World's Fair, Chicago newspapers were echoing the common perception that the McCormick factory was the largest of its kind in the world, saying things like, "McCormick conquers nature to the benign end of civilization and brings bread to the mouths of the poor."[6]

Wealth accumulation via hard, creative work; saving; and reinvestment was a modern habit and a key feature of capitalism. In McCormick's hands, it made other agricultural innovations possible, empowering farmers to turn America into the breadbasket of the world. Contrary to Marxist theory, McCormick did so not by exploiting others but by liberating slaves and laborers from mindless toil and by enhancing human productivity through machines. A farmer using McCormick's reaper saved one hundred dollars for every dollar he spent on his machine.

McCormick began producing his reaper at home—as was the case with most medieval industry. But when the demand for his product grew, he subcontracted other blacksmiths to make his reaper under license to him. He soon found that some of the blacksmiths were producing substandard reapers and thus damaging his reputation. When their contracts expired, he decided to produce all of his reapers under one roof where he could effectively supervise the work and ensure quality control. The factory system made it possible for workers to specialize and excel in one or more aspects of the job.*

Buying raw materials in bulk from a single supplier and having them delivered to one location also helped McCormick to cut costs. He built his factory on the banks of the Chicago River so that boats could bring in the raw materials and then deliver the finished product. The volume of production at the factory justified the installation of a 30-horsepower steam engine that became the wonder of Chicago. Later, McCormick played a very important role in bringing the railway line to Chicago—a line that served everyone's interest.

Spirituality and Economics

How could a devoutly religious man amass a fortune of ten million dollars—a huge sum in those days? Didn't Jesus say you cannot serve both God and money?[7] How could McCormick be both devoted to Christ and dedicated to making money?

The contradiction is resolved when we realize that almost two-thirds of Jesus' parables in the Gospels are about money. They are not about rituals, meditation, mystical experiences, asceticism, or what many call "spiritual" disciplines. Christ's parable of the talents, for example, is a helpful key in understanding McCormick's apparently contradictory passions to serve Christ and make money. More than a

---

* That is not to ignore the fact that many "modern" factories became dehumanizing prisons that gave no room for creativity or personal pride in craftsmanship. From a biblical perspective, sin affects and corrupts all human endeavors. Most governments in most periods of history have been oppressive, yet anarchy is no solution to that problem. Likewise, the factory system survives because it is redeemable.

hundred years before Adam Smith, John Lilburne had used this parable to teach free market economy.

According to Jesus' parable, the kingdom of heaven "will be like a man going on a journey, who called his servants and entrusted to them his property. To one he gave five talents, to another two, to another one, to each according to his ability. Then he went away. He who had received the five talents went at once and traded with them, and he made five talents more. So also he who had the two talents also made two talents more. But he who had received the one talent went and dug in the ground and hid his master's money." When the master returned, his response to both of those who had invested and made a profit was, "Well done, good and faithful servant. You have been faithful over a little; I will set you over much. Enter into the joy of your master." But the man who hid his one talent out of fear was called "wicked."[8]

Such teachings of the Bible helped McCormick's religious tradition equate spirituality with stewardship. In fact, the word *economy* comes from the Greek word *oikonome*—which means "to manage a household with care and thrift." The English New Testament translates *oikonomos*—meaning "one who manages a household"—as *steward*, an Anglo-Saxon word that originally meant the "ward" or "keeper of a sty or cattle." For McCormick, turning five thousand dollars into ten thousand dollars was being a good steward, which, on Jesus' own authority, was synonymous with being spiritual.

Economics has become such a complex subject that our age confers Nobel Prizes on economists and routinely gives six-figure salaries to financial analysts. Therefore it could sound incredible that our complex system of capitalism was created by the Bible's simple parables. Nevertheless, McCormick was a simple man with a simple faith, and simple men and women like him made America great.

The point can be illustrated by another example: Fra Luca Bartolomeo de Pacioli (1446–1517), a fifteenth-century Franciscan monk in Venice, first described capitalism's double-entry bookkeeping system.* Without this kind of accounting, a business cannot

---

* Fra Luca Bartolomeo de Pacioli, *Summa de Arithmetica, Geometria, Proportioni et Proportionalita* (Venice 1494).

chart its profits or losses. It cannot find ways to minimize expenses and maximize income. It cannot plan for growth, nor can it know with certainty when it is best to fold up a particular venture.

Pacioli wrote on the science and theology of mathematics.[9] He explicitly recommended that people should begin all their economic transactions in the name of God. The double-entry bookkeeping system is vital not just for private entrepreneurs, but is crucial to the wealth of a nation. American and European economies appear to be headed for major disasters because they have chosen to incur huge losses and debts.

Pacioli was a contemporary of Christopher Columbus (1451–1506). Almost a century before Columbus, Chinese admiral Zheng launched a naval expedition of 317 ships with twenty-eight thousand men. The largest of these ships was 400 feet long and 160 feet wide. In contrast, the *Santa Maria*, the ship on which Columbus sailed in 1492, was only 85 feet long. The *Nina* and the *Pinta* were even smaller. The Chinese vessels had water tanks to ensure a supply of fresh water for a month or more. That expedition tells us that in some aspects of shipbuilding and sea travel, China was centuries ahead of the West. Her ships ruled the Asian seas, at least for a few years. Despite such awesome sea power, the Chinese failed to profit from it.

Couldn't they have colonized Europe, or at least Asia and Africa? They could have. But they could not even sustain their shipbuilding. An important factor behind their failure was that the Chinese did not keep account of their expenses and their income. The impressive Chinese vessels carried valuable cargo such as silk, porcelain, strange animals, jewels, and exotic foods and plants to enrich the Chinese pharmacopeia. But these treasures were not meant to serve the Chinese people. Instead, as Professor Landes pointed out, they were used to enhance Chinese prestige in the context of gift giving.[10]

The desire to impress barbarians could not feed the tens of thousands of shipbuilders, sailors, and soldiers involved in the expeditions. Nor did it help their families and relatives back home. This cultural trait—elevating prestige before profits—helped put the Chinese so far down a financial hole that they had to abandon shipbuilding and oceangoing altogether. At that time the farthest they traveled was Africa. The first Chinese ship to arrive in Europe was in 1851, for the first World's Fair, where McCormick displayed his reaper.

The power of Christ's parable becomes apparent when we realize that the mentality of preferring prestige over profits is a problem that has continued to plague nations into our own times. The unprofitable mega projects of the communist countries drove their nations to bankruptcy. They worked for the glory of the state, not for the glory of God. For them the state was the ultimate authority, and those who worked for the state were not required to give an account of how they used national resources, either materials or personnel. That mentality produced poverty, which in turn produced the revolt led by the Solidarity movement in the 1980s. The revolt began among the workers in the shipyard of Gdansk, Poland, and it triggered the collapse of communism—one of the most brilliant economic ideologies of the modern world.

One reason behind communism's failure was its refusal to accept the notion of private property rights, especially intellectual property rights. The communist countries vested all property in the state—which had the right to steal from its citizens. But states do not invent. People invent, provided their intellectual property is safe from private or public infringement.

Russia, a superpower, was reduced to bankruptcy because the state deliberately rejected one of the Ten Commandments—"You shall not steal." In the name of collectivization, it took away citizens' property. They had to work not for themselves or their children, but for their (secular) god—the state. America, on the other hand, succeeded because it had an inventive culture where people like McCormick could succeed. The Bible generated such a moral climate in America that inventors and investors could defend their rights without recruiting militia or bribing officials. That is very difficult in most nonbiblical cultures even today.

Even if it is true that five centuries ago imperial China slid back economically because it did not operate on biblical principles of stewardship, what about the success of nonbiblical nations, such as modern Japan, China, and India?

JAPAN, CHINA, AND INDIA

Japan and contemporary China and India illustrate my thesis equally well. Let us focus on Japan, since it was the first Asian country to overtake Europe. Europeans reached Japan in the middle of the sixteenth century, just after the Reformation had begun to transform Europe. The Europeans impressed the Japanese, especially with their guns and technology. They were anxious to learn the foreigners' secrets. As David Landes pointed out, learning from others had been one of the strengths of Japanese culture.[11] Much of their language, writing, silk work, ceramics, printing, painting, furnishings, and religion came from China, some of it via Korea.

Learning from others did not make the Japanese feel inferior, because they always improved upon what they learned. The Japanese soon improved on the European guns and in the process mastered related skills. Japanese sages quickly learned that in Europe eyeglasses had doubled the scholarly output of European monks and increased the productivity of skilled workers. They also learned to make watches because watchmaking had been the greatest achievement of mechanical engineering in Europe. Imitating and improving the making of guns, eyeglasses, and watches laid the foundation of mechanical skills in Japan.

But the Japanese adopted more than European science and technology. Many Japanese also adopted Christianity, the "European" religion. By the beginning of the seventeenth century, between three hundred thousand and seven hundred thousand Japanese, including many from the ruling class, had converted to Christianity. Some converted out of conviction; others sought better terms for trade. Some used their conversion as a means to ferret out technological secrets. Portuguese and Spanish sailors, merchants, and soldiers, however, did not make good missionaries. Their arrogance turned the Japanese rulers against Christianity. As a result, Shogun Ieyasu banned Christianity from Japan in 1612.

In 1616 all foreign merchant vessels—except those from China—were barred from ports other than Nagasaki and Hirado. Japan was totally off-limits to the Spanish and Portuguese in 1624 and 1639 respectively. In 1637, the Japanese people were not allowed to leave their country. During 1637 to 1638, nearly thirty-seven thousand Christians were massacred at Shimabara alone. Interestingly, following the tragedy, guns were all but banned in Japan. Gunsmiths were put out of business, and all weapons were rounded up and melted. The resulting metal was fashioned into an enormous statue of the Buddha.

The British terminated all trade with Japan. Only the Dutch continued to trade with the Land of the Rising Sun. But even they were not allowed to enter the mainland. They were restricted to just two streets on the artificial island of Deshima in Nagasaki Bay. Holland became Japan's only connection to the West. By the 1720s some Japanese individuals realized that the policy of virtual isolation was unwise. Europe was advancing rapidly, and Japan needed to learn all it could from it.

Those in power were persuaded to allow secular books from Holland to enter the country. Japanese scholars called *Rangakusha* were assigned to study those books. Some powerful and influential Japanese objected to the change in policy, so the *Rangakusha* had to tread lightly. One *Rangakusha* in particular, Otsuki Gentaku, the author of *Ladder to Dutch Studies*, defended his profession. Dutch learning is not perfect, he argued, but if we choose good points and follow them, what harm could come from that? It took almost another century for Japan to realize that while it was stagnating, Europe was growing rapidly. Finally, in 1867, the new Japanese emperor Meiji reopened the major Japanese ports for global trade.

The *Rangakusha*, the technicians, and the forward-looking bureaucrats became the new revolutionaries. Foreign experts and technicians were hired as consultants. Japanese delegates were sent to Europe and America to learn all they could about everything. In October 1871, Prince Iwakura Tomomi headed a delegation that included innovators like Okubo Toshimichi. This distinguished Japanese delegation visited factories, forges, shipyards, armories, railways, and canals on two continents. It did not return until two years later, in September 1873. They were laden with the spoils of learning and on fire with enthusiasm for reform. Japan became the first non-Western nation to begin the process of imitating and improving upon Western science and technology, economic philosophy and infrastructure.

Contact between the West and Japan has run the gamut of commerce, conversion, tragedy, competition, and peace. The strength of the Japanese culture is its willingness to learn from the success of the Protestant nations. Even the Catholic and Orthodox Christian nations were slow to learn the principles of economic development from nations transformed by the Bible. The Japanese penchant for learning, modifying, and nurturing is a cultural norm that was applicable to more and more complexity and quality.

After World War II, Japan invited American Dr. W. Edwards Deming, the leading expert in the quality revolution, to teach them how to improve on quality.[12] Today, Japanese products, competitiveness, and quality are second to none. Japan brought its inherent cultural strengths to bear on its economy. The Japanese economy began to flounder in the twenty-first century because it has not yet found the spiritual resources to deal with corruption in high places. In addition, nonobservance of the Sabbath resulted in the neglect of the family. Office and factory workers worked for six days, and on the Sabbath they attended company related parties.

Frustrated and insecure wives decided that they did not want to have children if they had to bring them up by themselves. Fewer children meant an aging population. That has now become the most serious concern for the future of the Japanese economy. Japan recognizes the problem and has invested more on robotics than almost any other nation. Robots can increasingly do a lot of things. The problem is that they are a poor substitute for children because they don't pay into the social security system. Be that as it may, for decades Japan did better than India or China because those nations envied and hated the West. Some Asian nations demanded aid, but India was too proud to learn from the West as Japan did. Our fortunes began to change only after we realized that humility is a virtue.

We cannot understand Japan without understanding Holland

and its impact on Japan. Before the Reformation, Roman Catholic Churches were open seven days a week in Holland. The devout went to the church whenever they wanted to meet with God. They would light their candles, kneel, and pray. After the Reformation, the Church leaders decided to lock their churches on Sunday nights. Not because they became less religious, but because they became more religious.

Reformers learned from the Bible that the church was not the only place to meet with God. If God had called you to be a woodcutter, then on Monday morning you ought to meet with God in the forest. If he had called you to be a shoemaker, then on Monday morning he expected you to meet with him on the workbench. If he had called you to be a homemaker, you needed to serve God while taking care of your window plants. This made Dutch homes beautiful and eventually impacted Japanese homes.

When a shoemaker begins to make his shoes for God, he does not use substandard material or workmanship. He does not cut corners; his work is of the highest standards. This biblical doctrine of *calling*, rediscovered during the Reformation, was at the root of Holland's excellence. Japanese workmen had to compete against it and learn to outdo it. Some sociologists argue that the modern world is a product of the biblical doctrine of "vocation" or calling.[13]

Why has the Japanese economy begun to stagnate now? Why are the prime ministers of Japan forced to resign one after another under charges of corruption? Many observers feel that Japan has gone as far as a nation can by imitating biblical economic principles. To move to the next level, it has to find spiritual resources to become an open, transparent, trustworthy, moral society. Otherwise the wealthy in Japan will save more of their money in Swiss banks, rather than invest within Japan. Likewise, if the Bible was the force that kept corruption down in Europe and America, then its rejection now is bound to increase corruption, destroying the moral climate required for the success of men like McCormick.

Integrity is not a natural, universal human trait. An economic system built on trust is bound to collapse without the spiritual resources that served as its foundations.

Spirituality That Saved Industrial Capitalism

Cyrus McCormick was not merely an inventor; he was also an innovative marketing strategist. His goal was to make the best and most affordable reaper available to as many people as possible. Following the teachings of the Bible as expounded by Luther, Calvin, and other reformers, McCormick believed that the business of selling his reaper was God's will for his life. So he strove to become the best salesman possible. *The Dictionary of American Biography* records that McCormick was among the first to introduce the use of field trials, guarantees, testimonials in advertising, cash, and deferred payment.[14]

McCormick invited farmers to take the reaper in May, before the harvest, without paying for it. Over the summer, his salesmen would train the farmers how to use the machine. During the harvest, McCormick's salesmen were readily available with spare parts. The farmers didn't have to pay for the reaper until December—when they were sure that the reaper was cost-effective. Deadlines for payment were routinely extended if a farmer was unable to pay on time. Little wonder Mr. McCormick became extremely popular with his customers. No inventor in the Middle Ages had advertised his product or promoted his services the way McCormick did.

The issue of honesty in advertising and marketing is becoming important in the West. There are hundreds of pieces of legislation that require honesty, but the human heart seems to be far more ingenious than the legislators. In McCormick's religious culture, integrity in marketing came from within and was reinforced by the society. Science and technology do not drive evil out of our hearts. In fact, technology can increase our capacity for evil. Identity theft and the abuse of Internet banking are very good current examples of sin in the human heart. America went on to produce many successful innovators-cum-businessmen because its culture was shaped by the gospel that deals with the inner problem of sin.

Bill Gates is currently the richest man in the world. His success is not simply because he is a great inventor-businessman. China and

India have equally gifted individuals. If India failed to produce a Bill Gates, then it is because our markets have been filled with pirated copies of his software. He couldn't have succeeded without a relatively moral culture built by the gospel. In our domestic economies, black-marketers tend to make more money than honest businessmen. America takes for granted what the Bible has done for its economy. The consequences of changing Wall Street's motto from "In God We Trust" to "In Greed We Trust" are apparent even to Hollywood scriptwriters.*

THE BIBLE, WOMEN, AND ECONOMY

Cyrus's mother, Mary Ann McCormick, exercised strong and efficient management of their farm. She created and maintained order while her husband, Robert, provided inventiveness and leadership. Working as a team, Mary Ann and Robert were able to more than double the wealth they had inherited from their parents. Cyrus and his wife, Nancy, were also an effective team. Nancy proved an efficient aid to her husband's career. Cyrus was able to manage a constantly growing business, travel the globe to promote his reaper, fight endless legal battles to protect his patent rights, and take on religious, political, and publishing responsibilities because of his wife's support. She had a "practical mind, keen perception, and rare charm." They were partners.

After Cyrus's death, Nancy took charge of the firm. In her elder years she supported the Presbyterian economist-turned-agriculturist Sam Higginbottom in establishing the Allahabad Agricultural Institute, now recognized by the Indian government as a university. The institute passed on the blessing of agricultural development to some of the poorest people in the world. (My stepmother served as a doctor in the public health clinic at this institute.)

The Puritans who migrated to America are often criticized for their

---

* "In Greed We Trust" appears on a dollar bill at the end of the movie *Wall Street: Money Never Sleeps*.

biblically derived strict sexual ethic and rigid family values, including their opposition to divorce. Yet their belief system created America's moral and family infrastructure on which to build its national wealth. Educational opportunities and the status of women substantially determine the poverty or wealth of the nation. An increasing number of Americans are rejecting the Bible and depriving themselves of the spiritual resources necessary to sustain monogamy. The glamorization of the single-parent family is condemning an increasing number of American women and children to poverty.

A powerful factor in McCormick's success was the stable base of political and personal liberties in America. The next chapter will explore the source of Western freedom—the secular myth and the historical truth.

Chapter Eighteen

LIBERTY

WHY DID FUNDAMENTALISM PRODUCE FREEDOM?

Hollywood director Steven Spielberg teamed up with George Lucas to make the hit movie, *Raiders of the Lost Ark*. The movie is set during World War II, and the Nazis are looking for the Ark of Moses, a chest that made ancient Israel invincible. The Pentagon panics and hires an archaeologist to locate the Ark first. He does find it, launching the Indiana Jones franchise and misleading a generation into the occult. What was in the ark? Why did Moses, David, and Solomon place it in the very heart of their nation—in the Holiest of Holies? Here we explore the real secret of the West's liberty and power—and it did come from that Ark.

In 1998, some friends took me to see the Huguenot monument in the village of Franschhoek in South Africa. This powerful marble statue—of a woman standing under a triune arch, atop a globe of the world—explains modern political freedom more meaningfully than does the forty-five-thousand-pound Statue of Liberty in New York. A cross, suspended from a scepter, is at the top of the three tall white marble connecting arches. The woman wears no crown, for she is neither a queen nor a goddess. She represents ordinary people. She wears a broken chain in her right hand and holds a Bible in her left hand.

Franschhoek Valley is famed for producing some of the finest wines in all of Africa. Many French Calvinists (Huguenots/

reformers) settled there after fleeing the massacre of thousands of fellow Protestants.[1] A general edict in 1536 had ordered their extermination and three thousand Waldenses (a sect affiliated with the Lutheran "heresy") were killed in Provence in 1545.[2] In 1562, the Vassy slaughter of twelve hundred launched the Wars of Religion, and uncounted thousands were butchered in the St. Bartholomew Massacre in 1572. The Dutch resettled Huguenot refugees in South Africa to provide food and wine to replenish their ships sailing to Asia via Cape Town.

Why is this sixteenth-century European woman holding the Bible instead of Plato's *Republic* or Aristotle's *Politics*? Christendom had been studying European classics for centuries before the Huguenots began their struggle for freedom. During the fifteenth- and sixteenth-century Renaissance, Europe's Christian universities taught more Aristotle than they did the Bible. In the 1540s, a woman could have been burned at the stake as a heretic for even holding a French Bible in her hands. Her children could have been murdered before her eyes or kidnapped and raised in Catholic monasteries.

The woman does not hold a Greek political treatise because, contrary to what my secular professors taught me, it was the Bible, not Greek political ideals, that fired the modern quest for freedom. This monument honors the cross at the pinnacle because the Bible empowered these French Protestants to accept suffering, exile, and even martyrdom in their quest for liberty. This chapter will explore how the Bible forged the cultural ingredients that founded modern liberties.

Small city-states in Greece had tried democracy five centuries before Christ. These city-states beat the much greater Persian army (490–479 BC). Herodotus, an early Greek historian, credited democracy as the source of that Greek strength. This cameo opinion of a Greek victory was turned into the twentieth-century secular myth that pre-Christian Greece was the source of Western democracy. John Herman Randall of New York's Columbia College and Mortimer Adler and

Robert Maynard Hutchins of the University of Chicago forged the myth. Will Durant (1885–1981) popularized the myth in his multi-volume *The Story of Civilization*. It was exposed as myth by historians like David Gress (b. 1953), in books such as *From Plato to NATO*.[3]

In reality Greek democracies never worked for more than a few decades. They always degenerated into mob rule. Plato experienced Greek democracy as the social chaos that murdered his mentor Socrates. Therefore he condemned pure democracy as the worst of all political systems. He advocated rule by a "Philosopher King" as the best form of government. His protégé, Aristotle, trained Alexander the Great to become Plato's Philosopher King. Alexander became one of history's most ambitious but ruthless conquerors. Alexander's tyranny is the true legacy of Greek political thought. The Renaissance version of Plato's Philosopher King is Polybian Republicanism promoted by Niccolo Machiavelli (1469–1527) in his treatise *The Prince*. That cynical grabbing and maintaining of power through political manipulations, coercion, and oppression became the Fascist handbook for Benito Mussolini and Adolf Hitler and continues to inspire politicians in many "democracies."

Alexander's conquests of the known world spread the Greek language, literature, art, and culture. The Hellenization was so effective that Jews translated the Torah into Greek, and Jewish followers of Jesus wrote the New Testament in Greek rather than in Hebrew. Greek art and ideas spread to India and farther east. Yet nowhere did Hellenization inspire democratic freedom. The Greeks knew their democracies had failed. Europe's Reformation and democratization began with the sixteenth-century rediscovery of the Bible and a biblical understanding of governance. It led to America's founders explicitly rejecting Greek democracy for a constitutional republic. The constitutional republic required that peoples' as well as rulers' power be constrained by the rule of law.

The Bible is not a book of abstract philosophical ideas. Moses led the Hebrews from slavery in Egypt by a miraculous deliverance during the Exodus. That is the context for Moses writing the early books of the Bible—to secure that hard-won liberty and ensure that Hebrew despots did not replace Egyptian despots. The Exodus experience had powerful philosophical implications that set the Hebrews apart from all other ancient peoples. It revealed that God was free. He was not limited by either the political or military might of Egypt, however oppressive or brutal. Nor was God limited by historical factors, oppressive armies, or insurmountable natural obstacles such as the Red Sea. God was not part of the cosmic machine. He was free and wanted his children to be free like him. Oppression and slavery were evils to be routed. They were evil because they were contrary to all that God had intended for the human beings made in his own image.

The rest of biblical history, from Moses to the Messiah, is a story of repeated loss and recovery of freedom. Jesus declared that he had been sent to "proclaim liberty to the captives."[4] Horace Greeley (1811–72), founder and editor of the *New York Tribune*, is said to have observed: "It is impossible to enslave mentally or socially a Bible-reading people." Not every culture has produced patriots like Patrick Henry, who declared, "Give me liberty or give me death!" In fact, only cultures founded on the Bible have viewed freedom as a virtue worth dying for. Biblical cultures highly value freedom as the essence of God and of his image—humanity.

The process of losing and recovering freedom recorded from Genesis through Chronicles, gave birth to political ideas that were revived during the sixteenth-century European Reformation. They are the most important pillars of modern democracy. In Genesis, Abraham was told that he would become a great nation because he would teach God's ways to his descendants. The giving of the Ten Commandments is recorded in the Bible's second book—Exodus. Moses put that Law into the Ark of the Covenant and placed it at the very heart of the nation to make the point that durable freedom is possible only under the rule of God, the rule of law, and the rule of elders (representatives). This fundamentally contrasts with Greek democracies, which made citizens (the majority or mob) the ultimate rulers of the state.

The 2000 presidential election powerfully highlighted this foundational difference between the modern American republic and ancient Greek democracies. Al Gore won the popular vote, but George W. Bush became president because he won the majority of Electoral College votes as required by the Constitution. In many non-Western countries, Al Gore's followers would have slaughtered their rivals to grab political power in the name of "democracy" (majority/mob rule). But in his concession speech, Mr. Gore said: "Over the library of one of our great law schools is enscribed the motto, 'Not under man, but under God and law.'"*

Mr. Gore conceded the presidency to Mr. Bush on the ground that the rule of law superseded the majority. Paul Johnson, Britain's widely read contemporary historian, argues that this concept of the rule of law was "the most important political development of the second millennium."[5] He must know that the idea of the rule of law had been present in the pre-Christian world; for example, in Persia and Rome. But neither the Persians nor the Romans had immutable transcendent law on which to base their national laws. So practically, the "rule of law" generally meant the rule of the ruler. The modern principle of law as sacred, above human rulers, above the majority, came not from Rome but from the Bible.

The Exodus and the Ten Commandments were not Moses' ideas. They were God's acts and words, seen, heard, and affirmed by the whole community. The Jews believed that God himself wrote the Ten Commandments on two tablets of stone on Mount Sinai. God's words had greater authority than human constitutions. As Israel's liberator, God asserted his right as ultimate ruler: "I am the LORD your God who brought you out of the land of Egypt, out of the house of slavery."[6] Mr. Al Gore alluded to the fact that the modern Western idea of the rule of law flowed from the idea that God is our ultimate ruler. Huguenots understood that the absolute sovereignty of God overrides the sovereignty of sinful men, and this liberates the common people. Thus the liberated woman of the Huguenot monument stands beneath a triple arch representing her triune God.

---

* The statement comes from Henry de Bracton, who helped codify British Common Law and is engraved at Harvard Law School.

The covenant of the Ten Commandments founded the modern principle of constitutionalism, or rule of law, by a perpetual written and binding law. Britain's submission to the rule of law was institutionalized with the Magna Carta (1215), founded on common law, tracing to the code of Alfred the Great. The Mosaic code was the foundation for such legal codes in the West. One-third of Alfred's "Dooms" (AD 893) quoted biblical law while collating the laws of three Christian kingdoms.[7] Ultimately, the Word of God was the basis for law and government. A good illustration is Paul Robert's painting *Justice Lifts the Nations*, which hangs in the Supreme Court of Switzerland. In this painting, the litigants stand before the judges. How will the judges decide? Lady Justice points her sword to an open book on which is written, "The Law of God."

Does the American notion of "one nation under God" or "in God we trust" imply theocracy or democracy? The biblical tradition rediscovered during the Reformation viewed theocracy and democracy as necessary complements: human rule flowed from God's rule. The Bible depicts God as the ultimate ruler. The first two chapters of Genesis, however, record that God created us—male and female—to rule his earth. Human beings have the right to rule on this planet because God gave us that right. The Lord Jesus claimed he had come to bring God's kingdom to this earth. His mission was to give the kingdom not to aristocrats, but to the poor, meek, and the righteous.[8]

The Huguenots' understanding of the Bible's political philosophy turned an ancient and medieval idea on its head. Plato had no respect for the "voice of the people." In AD 798, the English scholar Alcuin expressed the same wisdom to Emperor Charlemagne: "*And those people should not be listened to who keep saying the voice of the people is the voice of God, since the riotousness of the crowd is always very close to madness.*"* Once the Reformation taught those riotous mobs to become the people of God's Word, it became possible for Christian nations, such as Scotland, to view the "voice of the people" as the

---

* *Nec audiendi qui solent dicere, Vox populi, vox Dei, quum tumultuositas vulgi semper insaniae proxima sit.*

"voice of God." Nations were not bound to obey wicked commands of popes and kings claiming to be the "voice of God." Since God had given his Word, the people could read and know God's will. When popes, church councils, and theologians disagreed, the people had a responsibility to study God's Word and determine what was God's voice. On the authority of God's Word, the voice of the people could reject the voice of kings or popes when it violated God's principles.

Islam also had the notion of the ultimate authority of God and his word. Why, then, did Islam fail to produce liberty? A key factor is that Islam denied God the power and love to come to this earth to establish his kingdom. If God does not come to establish his rule, then we have no option but to be ruled exclusively by sinful men. This chapter's emphasis on the Bible's role in creating liberty does not undermine the Bible's emphasis on Christ's incarnation as the source of liberty. Jesus claimed that "if the Son sets you free, you will be free indeed."[9] Islam has never been able to foster a reformation that could undermine human totalitarianism, because it rejects the very notion of God coming to establish his kingdom. It also fails to empower the people by its refusal to translate the Qur'an into the languages of the people.

THE RULE OF ELDERS

Moses' brother, Aaron, was his right-hand man. His family was accorded permanent priesthood. Moses' tribe, the Levites, supported him more fervently than the other eleven tribes did. The Levites were appointed to care for the tabernacle and teach the people God's laws. The other eleven tribes resented this and questioned Moses' and Aaron's leadership.

In most ancient cultures, rulers would have crushed any opposition. Tribal leadership, when it was not hereditary, usually rested either on terror or on deception by the priesthood. But Moses was unusual. He had never wanted to go to Egypt and become their deliverer. He went only because God sent him. He even complained to God, "Why should I have to bear the responsibility of leading these rebellious people?" God told Moses to bring seventy elders of the Israelites to the tabernacle, to the sacred tent where people went to meet with God.[10]

That formalized the rule by elders. Two of the elders refused to come to make the point that they were under no obligation to obey Moses. Contrast these elders with the wise men and counselors of most of medieval Europe—who held office at the pleasure of the king and could be removed by him at any time. Initially, assemblies and parliaments met when kings called them for consultation. In contrast, the Hebrew elders did not owe their position to Moses. They were respected community leaders long before Moses went back to Egypt. He had to gain their confidence before going to Pharaoh.[11]

In Numbers 11, the Bible records that God anointed these seventy elders, who represented the people, to help Moses lead the nation. Joshua, Moses' young assistant, wanted to exclude from leadership the two rebels who had defied Moses. Moses insisted that all the elders, including the two who defied him, were to be accepted as leaders because they represented the people, and God had endorsed their leadership. This biblical governmental principle of the rule of elders became foundational to modern constitutional republics as the rule by elected representatives and not by hereditary aristocrats as in Rome.

The early church adopted this Old Testament approach to the leadership of elders. It was very different from the direct and vulnerable democracy in Greece. It was also radically different from the supreme authority assumed by medieval kings, popes, emperors, and lords.

DIVISION OF POWERS

Biblical history contributed another critical principle of just governance: the division of powers and checks and balances. By appointing Saul as king, the Israelites established political authority independent of religious authority, by regulations codified by Moses.[12] Samuel remained the prophet who kept a check on any abuse of political power. We can better appreciate the importance of this biblical principle of government by considering what happened in Rome. Until the time of Augustus (63 BC–AD 14), Rome was a republic with no king. A senate of aristocrats governed the republic, ensuring that none of them became dominant. But power struggles and civil wars eroded the republican system. Then Augustus eradicated those who had killed his uncle, Julius Caesar. By doing so, he became a dictator, subtly manipulating public opinion.

Rome knew no separation between church and state. Jesus' dictum that what belongs to God should not be given to Caeser came as a fundamental constraint to Roman totalitarianism. Jesus' words reminded his listeners that government had limited, not absolute, power. Caesar could not demand worship that belonged to God. Rome rejected Christ's challenge to its claim to totalitarian power. It retaliated by persecuting Christians.

Nero (AD 15–AD 68) began to light his garden paths with Christians bound to stakes and set afire. Christians died by the thousands under Rome's tyranny, which continued through ten emperors until Diocletian's vicious persecution 250 years later. But the Church resisted its pagan enemies. The Church also resisted Christian kings who usurped their status as heads of state and claimed the right to rule over the Church. While Constantine I tolerated Christianity in AD 311, Theodosius I (379–395) made Christianity the only legal religion in Rome. This raised the bishop of Rome to an unusually powerful position. Rome now had two independent centers of power—religious and secular (pope and emperor). As the prophet Samuel confronted King Saul, Nathan confronted King David, and Elijah confronted King Ahab, some popes and bishops continued to confront kings to preserve unalienable rights and restore the rule of law.

For example, when fans rioted and killed an officer and his aides for arresting a famed charioteer, Emperor Theodosius had his troops massacre more than seven thousand innocent spectators at the coliseum. The archbishop of Milan forced Theodosius to undergo penance for eight months. The bishop was following the prophet Nathan, who confronted King David concerning his adultery with Bathsheba and the murder of her husband. Theodosius had to dress as a pauper and beg forgiveness from the multitudes in front of the cathedral in Milan. This humiliation confirmed the impact of biblical governance on the emerging modern principle of checks and balances.

Pope Gregory VII (ca. 1015–85) affirmed these limits on the government's power. The Holy Roman emperor Henry IV (1050–1106) insisted that, as God's divinely appointed ruler, he had the right to appoint bishops. Pope Gregory responded by excommunicating him. That "mighty" ruler was forced to humble himself in the snowy Canossa pass of the Italian Alps. After three days, Emperor Henry IV was finally forgiven by Pope Gregory VII and readmitted to the Church. Gregory drew on arguments by theologian Manegold of Lautenbach that a king's office was by consent for definite government purpose, based on a contract (*pactum*) with the people. If the king breaks this *pactum*, however, then the people are set free from that subjugation.[13]

The importance of the role of the Church or prophet in constraining secular abuses of power is epitomized by Archbishop Stephen Langton mediating between the English king John I and his barons. To redress King John's pillaging of the Church and its people, Archbishop Langton put the barons under oath to restore the rule of law. Drawing on Manegold and the Charter of Liberties (1000) of King Henry I, Langton drafted the Magna Carta in 1215, preserving "The Church shall be free." This charter codified limitations on the powers of the king. He could not impose arbitrary taxes but was required to have the consent of the common council of the kingdom—which became Parliament and thence, Congress in the USA.

Nor could the king arrest or punish any "freeman" merely on rumors or suspicion. This codification of English civil liberties secured that "[n]o free man shall be taken or imprisoned or disseised* or outlawed or exiled or in any way ruined, nor will we go or send against him, except by the lawful judgement [*sic*] of his peers or by the law of the land."[14] In other words, neither life, liberty, nor property could be taken from anyone without judgment by the person's peers and then

---

* To disseise someone meant to strip that person of a lawfully held estate.

only by due process of the law of the land. Langton established this principle of supremacy of law over the authority of rulers by requiring immediate redress of any breach, even by the king, and authorizing armed opposition by the barons if he refused. On June 15, 1215, the barons then bound King John by oaths before God and the assembled bishops to uphold the Magna Carta in perpetuity.

The regularization of England's judicial system began with the Magna Carta. Within three decades, one of England's most famous and godly judges, Henry de Bracton, began to systematize English common law. By the mid-thirteenth century, he had explicitly derived from the Bible the principle of rule of justice rather than force. By 1258, England's House of Commons was formed. The "Model Parliament" of Edward I in 1295 consisted of bishops and abbots, peers,* two knights from each shire, and two representatives from each town.

Just government was the ideal. Secular and sacred authorities often exceeded their positions, however, assuming absolute power in their own sphere. Kings tolerated no political dissent, and the church tolerated no religious dissent. Then all hell broke loose when church and state joined hands to do evil. One of the most dramatic expressions of religio-political corruption took place at the height of the sixteenth-century Renaissance in Paris, the city of romance, great art, and culture. Twenty-two-year-old King Charles IX and his mother, Catherine de Medici** bankrupted their country through government excesses.

In a country of one state religion, Catholicism, Huguenots prayed at their personal peril. Any show of Protestant affiliation in public was punishable by the severest penalties. In Paris, public hangings of Huguenots were frequent. Women and children were not spared. As tensions became unbearable in August 1572, Catherine brought in mercenary troops from Switzerland.

At three in the morning, August 24, Saint Bartholomew's Day, the gates of Paris were locked and the church bells began to ring. Officers of the king's militia were ordered to kill every last Huguenot. The slaughter began. Within a few hours Catherine tried to call it off, but

---

* Members of the nobility.
** Machiavelli dedicated his book, *The Prince*, to Catherine's father.

it was too late. The massacre was spreading, not just in Paris but all across France. The country exploded with religious ire. No household was immune from violent reprisals and religious hatred. Historians are unsure as to the extent of the carnage. Estimates range from five thousand to thirty thousand.

How could any church join hands with a demented monarchy to sanction such slaughter? The pope allowed the people to die because they defied his authority. The Huguenots held the Bible as their authority because they believed God's Word superseded the authority of both the king and the pope. In an age when kings, judges, and bishops indulged unabashedly in corruption, Bible believers demanded that political, civic, and religious authorities conform to God's standard of righteousness.

Could the basic freedoms we've been tracking have come about in any case, regardless of the Bible, through the sheer power and inevitability of progress, the redemption of wounds, the memory of avoidable catastrophes, and the general growth of knowledge? This is difficult to imagine. People with strong convictions lead reform movements. Skeptics are, by definition, unsure in their beliefs. A lack of conviction does not inspire people to die for their beliefs and values. Fundamental reforms require the faith of ardent believers, so certain of their convictions that they would take up their crosses and go to the stake for them. Fanaticism can, of course, lead to bigotry— unless one is following a God who sacrifices himself to serve others and commands you to love your neighbor as yourself. Conviction that God is on your side makes you a powerful person.

The Trilogy of Freedom

The Huguenots' traumatic experience on Saint Bartholomew's Day gave birth to three books that triggered a veritable revolution from the medieval form of government to the modern form of constitutional government. François Hotman, Theodore Beza, and possibly Philippe du Plessis-Mornay wrote the three treatises. The transition unleashed by these writings ensured that the rule of law and the rights of the people took precedence over the tyranny of monarchs and popes. The primacy of the law and the authority of the people were expressed in concrete institutions such as parliaments and courts that were no longer subject to the whims of kings. These three books, collectively referred to as the "Trilogy of Freedom," demonstrate the role the Bible played in giving birth to modern liberties.

François Hotman (1524–90), a professor of law, was one of the most distinguished jurists of his day. He narrowly escaped death on St. Bartholomew's Day. His book, *Francogallia*, became one of the earliest sources for the rejection of political absolutism. Hotman argued that a king is nothing more than a magistrate for life. The people create kingships. Kings are responsible to the people for their conduct while in office and constantly subject to removal by the people for violation of the duties of their office. Hotman's important argument was that "royal majesty," the supreme administration of the government, was not a quality inherent in a king's person. It was an attribute that belonged to the "Three Estates"—the king, the high counselors, and the people represented by their elders—assembled as a whole, in which the king was but the presiding officer.

The General Assembly of the Estates, in Hotman's scheme, was not merely a consultative body whose consent was required by the king on exceptional occasions. Hotman considered the assembly to be the very center of the government—as in the British parliament or the United States Congress. Hotman propounded the principle of the rule of law. The way to establish the rule of law, Hotman said, was to rely on the Bible alone, instead of Roman and biblical laws, especially now that the Bible had become available and had presented a clearer understanding of God's moral requirements.

Theologian Theodore Beza's book *The Right of Magistrates* was published in 1573, one year after Hotman's book and in consultation with him. It was one of the original sources of the idea of inviolable human rights that expressed itself two hundred years later in the American Bill of Rights. Prior to Beza, the general intellectual consensus in Europe—argued by eminent thinkers such as St. Thomas Aquinas—was that kings could only be removed by the people above them; that is, either by the emperor or by the pope. Beza, in contrast, provided a biblical basis for investing that political authority in the lower officials—the magistrates. Beza argued that the magistrates or civic leaders were servants not of the king but of the kingdom. Their primary duty was not to obey the king but to defend the kingdom. The American idea that a president can be impeached and removed by the Congress came from Beza's book.

Beza built on Hotman's dictum that "a people can exist without a king . . . whereas a king without a people cannot even be imagined."[15] In God's view, people come first. God gave kings and magistrates their offices on some definite conditions, such as, to serve the people. When a king issues an unjust order, for example, to arrest or kill an innocent citizen, then the magistrates have the right and duty to disobey the king in order to obey God and defend his people. The king is like a vassal to his kingdom and forfeits his office if he violates the faith. Furthermore, following the Councils of Basel and Constance, Beza argued that the Church council had a right to depose a pope, since Christ, not the pope, was the real head of the Church. Hence, the notion of the infallibility of popes was challenged by this breakthrough in Protestant ethical thinking.

While secular Western scholarship ignores Beza's foundational role in shaping Western political thought, his principle of an independent judiciary has become the heritage of every person in the West. As an Asian, I began to appreciate its seminal virtue when I experienced the opposite. Petty politicians were able to ask corrupt magistrates to throw me in jail on trumped-up charges. Our prime minister, Mrs. Indira Gandhi, during her brief stint with authoritarianism from 1975 to 1977, talked of India's need to have a "committed judiciary"—one that would enforce the orders of rulers, not the rule of law. Thankfully, her experiment did not bcome the established practice in India, but that is the way most of the world lives.

Many nations have accepted the United Nations' notion of "human rights" without Theodore Beza's theology of the *Rights of Magistrates.* Nevertheless, "unalienable human rights" make no sense without the biblical principle of the unique worth granted to all individuals by their Creator. Also, human rights become powerless ideals without magistrates exercising their right to enforce them over the abuse of authority by rulers.

Vindiciae Contra Tyrannos (Defense of Liberty Against Tyrants) became the most popular of the Trilogy of Freedom because of its straightforward and action-oriented style. There is some dispute about the authorship of the book because it was published pseudonymously. Many scholars think that Philippe du Plessis-Mornay wrote it, perhaps with the help of his older friend, Hubert Languet.

Following Beza, Mornay drew important lessons from the coronation of King Joash in the Old Testament. During the coronation, a twofold covenant was made under the guidance of the godly high priest, Jehoiada. One covenant was between God and the king—the king would faithfully serve God—while the other was between the king and the people. Mornay demonstrated from this that people had an obligation to obey their kings, who in turn were obliged to obey God. When kings disobeyed God's law in the Bible and became unjust and oppressive, the people had a responsibility to restrain, and if necessary, to depose them. The American idea that the ruler should not be a king but a president came from this book. A president is simply the first among equals. He or she presides in an assembly of equals. Collectively, they have more power than he has.

THE HUGUENOTS' POLITICAL INFLUENCE

The St. Bartholomew's Day massacre in 1572 turned Scotland decisively against the old oppressive religio-political system that had existed for centuries. Like Beza, John Knox, Scotland's most popular reformer, had studied under Calvin in Geneva. Many of the French reformers were Knox's personal friends. Knox and the Scottish reformers had already won the religious reforms by 1560. The political battles, which were, in fact, a civil war between the Protestants and Catholics, continued until 1572. The Holy Roman Empire had a vested interest in keeping the old religious structure intact. The Roman Church's hierarchical organization was a replica, not of the New Testament church but of the Roman Empire. It gave absolute power to kings and popes over the people. But the massacre in France so repulsed the Scots that in 1573 they gave a decisive military victory to the reformers.

Queen Mary's forces were defeated, and the first fully blossomed modern democracy—already established in the Scottish church—was established in the state. In a radical overturning of the notion of the divine rights of kings or popes, it affirmed the supremacy of the "voice of the people" rooted in the Word of God. People could hear, understand, and articulate God's voice because they now had God's Word in their hands, in their own language. The Bible thus transformed medieval theocracy into modern democracy in a manner that served the people, served justice, and was eminently practical.

The Huguenots' "Trilogy of Freedom" also had an immediate impact in Holland. William I of Orange had been fighting for Dutch independence from Spain. The French trilogy provided theological justification for his struggle. William became a personal friend of Mornay and succeeded in establishing Utrecht as a free nucleus for later Dutch liberation. Eventually Mornay's work influenced the entire world through the Dutch jurist, humanist, and statesman Hugo Grotius (1583–1645) and the Swiss philosopher, diplomat, and legal expert Emmerich de Vattel (1714–67).[16] Their legal writings laid the foundation for modern international law.

In 1688 England's king James II jailed seven bishops, including Archbishop William Sancroft, on charges of rebellion by seditious libel for their refusal to read his Second Declaration of Indulgence. The jury acquitted them, nullifying this unjust edict.[17] Six months later this led to the "Glorious Revolution" where James II was replaced by William of Orange and Mary (James's heir). Parliament then codified the (English) Bill of Rights (1689), explicitly preserving the Magna Carta's right to petition the king for redress of grievances, as restored by the seven bishops.[18]

After the Bible, *Vindiciae Contra Tyrannos* had the greatest impact in fueling the American Revolution.[19] It moved the pulpits that moved the pews to resist tyranny. Secular scholarship ignores the trilogy primarily because Reformed and Huguenot writers derived and justified every argument from the Bible. Yet the fact remains that the biblical ideas proclaimed by Reformed and Huguenot writers spread rapidly to Switzerland, Holland, Scotland, England, and America. From these countries, the torch of liberty was taken to the rest of the world.

THE BIBLE AND DEMOCRACY IN INDIA

In earlier books, such as *India: The Grand Experiment*, I discussed my surprising discovery that India's freedom, too, was a fruit of the gospel. Before leaving for India as a missionary, William Carey, the Bible translator par excellence, defended his call for mission in 1792 with these words:

> After all, the uncivilized state of the heathen, instead of affording an objection against preaching the Gospel to them, ought to furnish an argument for it. Can we as men, or as Christians hear that a great part of our fellow creatures, whose souls are as immortal as ours . . . are without the Gospel, without government, without laws, without arts, and sciences, and not exert ourselves to introduce amongst them the sentiments of men, and of Christians? Would not the spread of the Gospel be the most effectual means of their civilization? Would not that make them useful members of society?[20]

The evangelical movement turned Carey's vision into the British mission in India. As noted in an earlier chapter, Lord Macaulay summed up that mission in his speech to British Parliament in 1833:

> It may be that the public mind of India may expand under our system till it has outgrown that system; that by good government we may educate our subjects into a capacity for better government; that having become instructed in European knowledge, they may, in some future age demand European institutions (of liberty).[21]

Critics, such as Arun Shourie, condemn Macaulay for bringing biblical ideas and institutions to subvert oppressive Indian culture and free the Indian mind. Without the Bible's political ideas, however, Muslim emperors, Hindu militia, or European merchants would still be ruling India.

MODERN POLITICAL THOUGHT

One of the most important exponents of a biblical political theory came a few decades after Huguenot refugees fled the French inferno of the 1570s. A Scottish pastor and theologian named Samuel Rutherford (1600?–1661) summarized the teachings of Hotman, Beza, and Mornay in his book *Lex, Rex—The Law and the Prince*. The very title of Rutherford's book set it in opposition to Machiavelli's *The Prince*. Rutherford's title can be translated as *The Law [Is] King* because it defined modern democracy as the rule of law, rather than as the rule of monarchs or majorities.

John Milton and James Harington were other biblical Puritan political theorists who, following the Huguenots, rejected the divine right of kings. Milton introduced the modern ideas of tolerance and freedom of expression. These ideas bore practical fruit in his own day and more fully after 1688—the very year in which the Huguenots came to South Africa from Holland. That was also the year in which William III of Orange sailed from Holland to England to lead the "Glorious Revolution." He put those Reformed ideals into practice by institutionalizing the rights of Parliament.

John Locke (1632–1704), who returned from Holland to England with William III that year, became one of the most important philosophers and political theorists in the decades that followed. Locke was the son of a Puritan pastor and studied in Westminster Abbey when Rutherford was there writing *Lex, Rex*. Locke articulated the biblical political vision of his predecessors systematically in 1690, when he wrote the following:

> I will not dispute now whether princes are exempt from the laws of their country, but of this I am sure, they owe subjection to the laws of God and Nature. Nobody, no power can exempt them from the

obligations of that eternal law. Those are so great and so strong in the case of promises, that Omnipotency itself can be tied by them. [In the Bible] Grants, promises, and oaths, are bonds that hold the Almighty, whatever some flatterers say to princes of the world, who, all together, with all their people joined to them, are, in comparison of the great God, but as a drop of the bucket, or a dust on the balance—inconsiderable, nothing![22]

Locke's political philosophy won only because his readers knew that he was biblical and wise.

Quantitatively, the Bible was most frequently quoted by America's Founding Fathers, followed by Montesquieu, Blackstone, and Locke.[23] This brief chapter cannot examine the Bible's influence on every political theorist or on the development of important pillars of liberty, such as freedom of conscience, freedom of speech, the press as the prophet, checks and balances, and autonomy of institutions such as family and university in their own spheres. Political philosophy gleaned from the Bible was indeed transmitted to America effectively via John Locke's writings. Secular historians pervert history, however, when they fail to confess that Locke was followed because he was channeling a biblical philosophy of governance. No Indian thinker found similar political ideas in any of our scriptures and epics.

French Protestant ideas reformed the political life of neighboring countries, but France paid heavily for suppressing the Reformation. The corruption of church and state turned its keenest thinkers against religion. For example, Rousseau reduced Mornay's twofold God-king and king-people covenant to one "social contract" between the king and people. He shared the Huguenots' love of liberty but defined freedom as the people's right to depose kings and nobles when they became corrupt and oppressive. He excluded God. His teachings helped spawn the French Revolution, but without the mobs submitting to God's Word, the revolution ended in disaster.

The Bastille perhaps symbolizes the worst of that revolution, which backfired in the name of Napoleon Bonaparte, a dictator. The high-minded rhetoric of the French Enlightenment proved powerless to control the evil in the human heart. Without the Bible, democracy became what Plato had condemned as the worst of all political systems. Napoleon was a grotesque throwback to the authoritarian Roman Empire at a time when the rest of Europe—indeed, much of the world—was looking toward a new paradigm. America, not France, became the beacon of liberty, precisely because it allowed the Bible to shape its cultural ethos.[24]

British statesman Edmund Burke was one contemporary who carefully studied the French failure. In "A Letter to a Member of the National Assembly" (1791) Burke wrote:

> What is liberty without virtue? It is the greatest of all possible evils . . . it is madness without restraint. Men are qualified for civil liberty in exact proportion to their disposition to put moral chains upon their own appetite . . . Society cannot exist, unless a controlling power upon will and appetite be placed somewhere; and less of it there is within, the more there must be without.[25]

Robert C. Winthrop, Speaker of the U.S. House of Representatives (1847–1849) and leader of the Bible Society, articulated this indispensable principle of liberty:

> All societies of men must be governed in some way or other. The less they may have of stringent State Government, the more they must have of individual self-government. The less they rely on public law or physical force, the more they must rely on private moral restraint. Men, in a word, must necessarily be controlled, either by a power within them, or by a power without them; either by the word of God, or by the strong arm of man; either by the Bible or by the bayonet.[26]

SLAVERY IN SOUTH AFRICA

When the Huguenots first came to South Africa, their spiritual leader, Pierre Simond, proposed teaching agriculture and literacy to the local people called the Hottentots. He wanted to impart the blessings of civilization to a people who did not know even the elementary principles of agriculture. Unfortunately, succeeding generations of Huguenots adopted the Dutch colonial practice of using slave labor in their homes and farms. Slavery was abolished in South Africa in 1833, after the British evangelicals led by William Wilberforce returned to the Bible. In the twentieth century, secular humanists introduced apartheid in South Africa. Sadly, many white Christians justified this form of social engineering. Thankfully, other Christians who remained faithful to the Bible helped defeat that evil.

Did the slavery and apartheid practiced by many white Christians turn the native blacks against the Bible? I proposed that question to Wynoma Michaels, then a PhD student at the University of Stellanbosch and the first black woman to become the student president of that university. I was not surprised when she replied that studying and teaching the Bible was her first love. She reported what I had suspected—more blacks study the Bible than do the whites.

Why? Because, she said, although the Bible was abused, nothing else gave her people a greater sense of their own worth and meaning than the Good Book. This was one book the slave-owner and the slave shared in common. As the master sat down to read it aloud to his slaves, they both knew they stood under its authority as equals. The blacks in South Africa had nothing else through which they could know that they were precious to God. Wynoma said that a great number of her people took the trouble to become literate for one reason alone—they wanted to read the Bible. They did not learn to read in order to find jobs. She referred to a newspaper story published that very week about a sixty-five-year-old woman who had joined an adult literacy class because she wanted to read the Bible.[27]

Today the Bible is the chief factor in opening of the African mind, just as it was the key to opening the Western mind.

Part VII

GLOBALIZING MODERNITY

Evangelical Protestantism brings about a cultural revolution in its new territories . . . It brings about radical changes in the relations between men and women, in the upbringing and education of children, in the attitudes toward traditional hierarchies. Most importantly, it inculcates precisely that "Protestant ethic" that Max Weber analyzed as an important ingredient in the genesis of modern capitalism—a disciplined, frugal, and rationally oriented approach to work. Thus despite its indigenization . . . [biblical faith] is the carrier of a pluralistic and modernizing culture whose original location is in the North Atlantic societies.

—PETER BERGER

Chapter Nineteen

MISSION

CAN STONE AGE TRIBES
HELP GLOBALIZATION?

My friend Ro does not fit conventional categories. He is neither right nor left. He would neither bomb a tribe of terrorists nor respect any culture in its entirety. Ro, short for Dr. Rochunga Pudaite (b. 1927), believes in transforming negative aspects of every culture. He believes that all cultures reflect human goodness as well as baseness. He comes from a tribe of headhunters—the Hmars of northeast India. And he has played a critical role in the transformation of his people.

Ro's Mongolian ancestors migrated from central China to the jungles between Myanmar (Burma) and India. The British found them ferocious warriors. In 1870, the Hmars took five hundred British heads during a single raid on a remote tea plantation. General Frederick Roberts, the British commander, went after them in two columns.* He killed a few, but most of them disappeared into the dense forest. The British had learned *not* to follow. Five hundred heads, the general felt, was more than enough loss for one day.

The British eventually taught the Hmars not to mess with their Indian Raj (Empire). Yet they never forgot that the Hmars were

---

* The general was later knighted and became known as Lord Roberts of Kandahar, in Afghanistan.

dreadful—a tribe of savages who decorated their huts with their ene-mies' heads. No British officer went into their jungles without a large armed guard.

While there is plenty to be said against imperialism—one culture dominating another—not enough is said against selfish indiffer-ence, against choosing not to help people who are victims of their own cultures. Ro's parents' generation, for example, lived in poverty and squalor. Alcoholism destroyed the "fortunate" who survived early death from poor hygiene, sanitation, and nutrition. Illiteracy, quarrels, and violence were the norm. Women and children were the primary victims of those evils.

The Hmars worshipped rivers, mountains, rocks, stars, the sun, and the moon. But Mother Nature showed no compassion on them. Evil spirits—real or imaginary—constantly harassed the Hmars. Demons were feared and worshipped because they brought disease. Medicine was unknown. Revered priests and witch doctors killed endless numbers of chickens, goats, and pigs as sacrifices to appease the angry spirits.

Ro believes that only exceptionally callous people would say that his tribe should have been left alone in its (imagined) "pristine way of life." The majority would agree that their way of life was sick and needed healing. The disagreement would be on how to heal it.

Some Americans, who opposed the 2002 operation to democratize Afghanistan by militarily overthrowing the Taliban regime, proposed that a culture that was housing Al Qaeda should be bombarded only with satellite television that would transmit the Western values of tol-erance and freedom.

How would a tribe in the remote mountains of Afghanistan, Africa, or India begin to understand those televised ideas? They don't know English. What if a savage tribe watched action films and became better at head-hunting? Or worse, what if the Hmars watched Hannibal Lector films and added cannibalism to their head-hunting? If they've no cash, no jobs, and no banks, then who will give them televisions? Why would anyone do business with people who produce nothing, except those who intend to sell them as slaves or prostitutes, or perhaps to procure their lungs, livers, kidneys, or hearts for organ transplant in affluent countries?

Surely, someone might argue that Stone Age tribes can become productive, profitable partners in the global economy, provided someone educates them.

There are some to whom the very idea of "educating" tribes stinks of a condescending missionary attitude—"civilizing" the savages. But the critics might be persuaded by the argument that education need not change anything. It could be used to empower tribes at the margins of the modern world; that is, to give them options. They would be free to keep their way of life or choose an alternative lifestyle. The dispute would be over who would do the educating.

"The state, of course!" would be the contention of some.

"But wouldn't that condition them," others would no doubt question, "to accept the Western form of welfare state as the ideal?" Moreover, how well would state-run schools function in remote jungles where illiterate parents and chiefs cannot possibly supervise them?

The Hmars' Isolation

In the case of the Hmars, a more basic problem was that they had no "state." They were an autonomous tribe even in the middle of the nineteenth century. The early *Gazettes* of the government of independent India did not even record their existence. They paid no taxes because the Mogul empire (1526–1757) did not extend to their area, and the (multinational) British East India Company that ruled much of India from 1757 to 1857[1] wasn't interested in tribes that didn't trade. To maximize profits, the company had to cut costs, not add schools.

William Wilberforce and Charles Grant, two evangelical members of Parliament, fought political battles for twenty years (1793–1813) to persuade the British parliament to require the company to spend one hundred thousand Indian rupees[2] per year from its profits to educate Indians. That amount, however, was not enough to run even one school in each large urban area of British India. There was no way the company could assume the responsibility of educating the Hmars.

Even if money had been available to start schools, what teachers would go to such barbarians? Educating a people is a lifelong commitment. In order to educate a tribe, one must live with them, learn their dialect, and then turn their dialect into a literary language. To become a means of transferring complex ideas, their language would need literature, grammar, and a dictionary. Educating barbarians requires missionary heroism. It begins with men like the missionary Watkins R. Roberts, who risked his life for the Hmars—people who, at best, could never repay him for his services. At worst, his head would decorate one of their huts.

As it happened, the Hmars wanted change, so they did not kill Roberts. Instead, they honored him. It was the British who threw him out of India for defying their order against going to the Hmars.

The Hmars had lived on the periphery of the Hindu, Buddhist, and Muslim civilizations. Today some Hindus claim the Hmars as a part of Hinduism. But Hindu priests never attempted to educate them. They considered it bad karma and ritual-pollution for priests to serve outcastes.* The Brahmins held their sacred language, Sanskrit, and their sacred scriptures, the Vedas, in such high regard that they taught them neither to Brahmin women nor to any lower-caste Hindus. The question of teaching them to outcastes never arose. Hindus did not convert others to their faith because they have no magic that can make a non-Brahmin into a Brahmin. Hinduism is a "racial" religion. Children are born into a particular Hindu caste (race) according to the karma of their previous lives. Non-Hindus are excluded from the Hindu caste system as "untouchable" races.

The Muslims did take their language, literature, and religion to others. But they believed the Qur'an could only be written in the "heavenly" language—Arabic. It could never be translated into other languages without distortion. So to learn the Qur'an, one first had to learn Arabic. Therefore, Islam never developed the languages of the peoples it conquered. In contrast, as mentioned in earlier chapters, it was Bible translators who developed the national languages of modern

---

* Tribals in India are non-Hindus; therefore they are classified as "outcastes."

Muslim nations, such as Urdu in Pakistan and Bengali in Bangladesh. Language and literature, as we have seen, are keys to a people's development. The Bible translators knew that a people couldn't progress without first having their language developed and enriched so that it could communicate complex ideas.

Some Indian nationalists, of course, would not blame the Hmars for beheading the British. They might even call them heroic—one of the few peoples in India valiant enough to maintain their independence. They might consider their head-hunting stories sensational and argue that they weren't horrendous, all things considered. Almost all peoples of the world, from the Assyrians to the Romanians, have at one time or another indulged in macabre enemy dismemberment. Today's "civilized" world does that to its own almost-born babies. The Germanic Goths drank from the cups made of their enemy's skulls. Vlad the Impaler could have taught the Hmars a thing or two.

Even if it were true that all cultures rest on violence, the question remains: Is a tribe really better off if it retains its isolation, beliefs, and values that keep it poor and vulnerable to preventable and curable diseases, at the mercy of uneducated witch-doctors and warrior-chiefs? Were the Hmars wrong in desiring fundamental change?

THE HEADHUNTERS FIND A BOOK

In 1909 a mail runner brought a book to the chief of the village of Senvon in the state of Manipur. It was *The Gospel of John* written in the Lushai language, using the Roman alphabet. The Hmar chief could not read. Nor was he used to receiving junk mail. No one had ever considered his tribe important enough to put him on their mailing lists! The chief deduced that someone thought this book was important for his people. A traveler who passed through the village read the words but did not understand their meaning. Finally, on the back page he found the address of the sender, Mr. Watkins R. Roberts, a businessman from Wales.

Chief Kamkhawlun sent messengers to bring Mr. Roberts to his village to explain the book's message. To visit Senvon, Mr. Roberts needed permission from Colonel Locke, the superintendent of the Lushai Hills district. The colonel was stern: "The Hmar people are the most savage headhunters in the world. They will lop off your head and make a great celebration over your dead body. When we go there we take at least fifty soldiers to guard us. I cannot spare even one for you."

Undaunted, Mr. Roberts found a few young men to guide him to Senvon in late January 1910. (It is possible that the Indian Maharaja of Manipur had granted him the permission.) After seven days of trudging some hundred miles over rugged mountain trails, they reached Senvon. Mr. Roberts met with the chief and the villagers. At first no one was interested in his stories. But the lights turned on for the Hmars when he explained the gospel using their traditions for settling tribal wars.

Imagine, he said, that two tribes have warred against each other for several years. Then one of the tribes decides that it wants peace. It sends its offer by beating a huge war drum on the mountaintop nearest the enemy camp. The other tribe responds by beating its drum before sundown. The tribe who first beat the drum brings an animal, often a mithun, or a cow, to the boundary between the two tribes. The two chiefs and their men arrive at the carefully drawn boundary. They sacrifice the mithun and let its blood flow across the boundary line.

The two chiefs then put their hands on the sacrificial animal, and the spokesmen from both tribes discuss the terms of peace. As soon as they reach an agreement, the two chiefs embrace each other over the slain animal. Then the spokesmen pronounce peace. The people embrace. Peace is restored. They were set free from their destructive animosities and insecurities. That, Mr. Roberts said, is how God made peace with us, his enemies. God made Jesus Christ the sacrificial lamb: "For God so loved the world, that he gave his only Son, that whoever believes in him should not perish but have eternal life."[3]

Mr. Roberts explained to the chief that God made human beings special—in his own likeness—good, happy, and free. Through sin, Satan deceived human beings and enslaved us to all kinds of evils that harass us—spiritual, social, and natural evils. By rebelling against God, human beings lost their relationship with God and much of his character. Becoming like Satan, we started committing sins against God and our neighbors—oppressing or murdering people, violating women, hurting our loved ones and families, robbing others, being greedy, envious, quarrelsome, and immoral.

God sent prophets and priests to show us the way to harmonious living, contentment, personal happiness, and eternal life. But men and women could not change their ways in their own strength. They needed a Savior, so God took the initiative. He beat the peace drums. He came to us in human form and revealed his love, his way of salvation, and eternal happiness. God made peace with us—his enemies. He can enable your tribe to make peace with other people, including neighboring tribes that have fought against you for generations.

Roberts left Senvon with a promise to return and open a school and a medical clinic to serve them. But at Aizwal, he found that Colonel Locke had expelled him from the Lushai Hills for disobeying orders and for "demeaning" the high British culture by sleeping in tribal homes and eating tribal food. Roberts was never again allowed to return to the Hmar areas and villages of Manipur and Mizoram. The tribe, however, kept talking about the Gospel. The Savior, dying as a sacrificial lamb, sounded very different from every other religious story they had ever heard. It didn't sound like a moralizing myth. Mr. Watkins said that it was not a story but news—good news. If so, it had to be either false or true. Ro's father, Chawnga Pudaite, then a teenager, heard the good news that God had sacrificed his own son on the cross to make peace with us—his enemies. Chawnga became one of the earliest Christians and along with his friends learned to read the Lushai language to memorize *The Gospel of John*. They shared the gospel with their people, but they had no Bible in the Hmar language.

Chawnga's son Rochunga decided to become a follower of Jesus Christ when he was only ten years old. His parents asked him to study at the nearest upper primary school—only a ninety-six-mile walk from home! To reach his school, the ten-year-old Ro had to walk through dense forests infested with tigers, bears, pythons, and wild elephants. Why would parents take such a risk? Incomprehensible as it may sound, their command to their son was: "You must translate the Bible for us." As all parents, they, too, would have liked their son to get a good job and to provide for them financially in their old age. But they knew that their jungle had no jobs to offer. "Undeveloped" communities create few jobs.

Chawnga came to recognize the Bible as the primary difference between the culture of the Hmars and the culture of Mr. Roberts. He concluded that the greatest thing he could do for his people was to ask his son, Ro, to translate the Bible into their language. After completing middle school, Rochunga traveled three hundred miles to Jorhat to prepare himself to fulfill his father's request.

From Jorhat, Ro went to Saint Paul's College in Calcutta, then to Allahabad University, where I followed him two decades later. Our university did not teach Greek and Hebrew—the original languages of the Bible. To study them Ro traveled to Glasgow, Scotland. There, he began translating the Bible into the Hmar language. From Scotland, he went to Wheaton, Illinois, USA, to complete his theological training and Bible translation. Finally, in 1958, Rochunga returned to India with a complete Hmar New Testament, translated from the original languages. It was edited and improved with others' help, then published in 1960. The Hmar New Testament became an instant best seller. The first five thousand copies sold out within six months. But Chawnga's dream was just beginning to be fulfilled.

After three months at home, Ro decided to travel the hills of Manipur, Mizoram, and Assam to retrace his boyhood adventures. He found that there was only one government school among the Hmar villages of the Manipur hills. The people wanted to read the Bible that he had translated for them, but to do so they needed schools. He began nine village schools and a high school. Within ten years, the organization he founded had opened eighty-five schools, a college, and a hospital—all without any help from the government. Today 85 percent of the Hmars know the joy of reading and writing. India's average literacy rate is less than 60 percent. Emancipation from illiteracy and superstitions was just the beginning. The Hmars were now set on a course to develop their God-given potential and use it to serve God and their homeland.

In their schools, the Hmars taught the Bible to build character and to instill a spirit of self-reliance. Traditionally, their culture understood heroism as a pursuit of physical prowess. To be a good Hmar was to be a great warrior. Ro realized that transforming his tribe required giving them a vision of new and nobler values. He believed in the wisdom of his father's dream and was personally committed to it. What could fire the hearts of young Hmars with a passion for pursuing excellence in service instead of warfare?

Ro had studied in a secular university. He knew that secular literature—Western or Indian—had nothing as liberating as the Bible, unless it was based upon the Bible itself. His people needed to cultivate their minds as much as their muscles. But what use is a good mind unless it is also moral? Haim G. Ginott (1922–73), clinical psychologist, educator, and best-selling author said:

> I am a survivor of a concentration camp. My eyes saw what no person should witness. Gas chambers built by learned engineers. Children poisoned by educated physicians. Infants killed by trained nurses. Women and babies shot and burned by high school and college graduates.
>
> So I am suspicious of education. My request is: help your students become more human. Your efforts must never produce learned monsters, skilled psychopaths, or educated Eichmanns. Reading, writing, and arithmetic are important only if they serve to make our children more human.[4]

Ro, the Bible translator turned educator, made sure that his schools were not intimidated by secular ideologues. They taught the Bible as the basis of holistic human growth—physical, mental, social, and spiritual.

Those schools' graduates became India's ambassadors, chief secretaries of state, a director general of police, high-ranking officers of the Indian Administrative Services (IAS), doctors, lawyers, engineers, professors, and pastors. Some well-known Hmars are H. T. Sangliana, former director general of police, member of Parliament, and now vice chairman of the Minorities Commission; L. T. Pudaite, ambassador to five or more countries, including Hungary, S. Korea, and Myanmar; and L. Keivom, high commissioner to New Zealand.[5] Mr. Sangliana's character has made him a national legend. In the midst of my country's all-pervasive and oppressive corruption, Bollywood found his integrity so fascinating that his story has already inspired three full-length feature films.

The following incident illustrates how seriously the Hmars took the Bible. Their college needed a library; the lieutenant governor saw their need and helped them obtain one hundred thousand rupees from the University Grants Commission. When the inspector of colleges saw that they had obtained government funding, he demanded that they stop teaching the Bible in their college. Instead of surrendering their liberty, the Hmars chose to close down their college. Ro explained this decision to me: "The young people must have intellectual freedom to pursue truth. But how can we cultivate in them a love for intellectual freedom if we surrender our freedom to teach the Bible?"

In the 1970s, while many universities were singing the praises of communism, Ro saw through its bankruptcy. What the Bible did for the West and for his people was better than the terror and poverty Marx's *Das Capital* was inflicting on the people of USSR. The communist government had banned the Bible. But Ro wanted to bless India's Russian friends, so he took advantage of an Indo-USSR friendship treaty and mailed hundreds of thousands of Russian Bibles from India to every address in Russia's telephone directories. Through the years, Ro's organization, Bibles for the World, has continued mailing Bibles to more than a hundred countries.

Head-hunting is now history. The Hmars are well on their way to health and cultural vitality. Each year, two dozen Hmar schoolchildren spend eleven months in the United States, giving musical concerts and performing tribal dances. Born in 1927, Ro has not taken his well-earned retirement. He continues as the founder and chairman of Bibles for the World. His heart aches for the soul of our nation, lying under the curse of the twin evils of caste and untouchability. When Ro was a child, his tribe did not know how to live civilly with others. As an adult, he finds it painful that his countrymen do not know how to live in brotherly love with fellow Hindus.

To transform a social order built on caste and untouchability, Ro coined the slogan, *"Transforming a Nation through Education."* His family and organization give a great deal of time and effort to first transforming their teachers by encouraging them to study the Word of God. Ro encourages them to teach every subject with biblical principles. In my state of U.P., more than a thousand miles west of Ro's home state, in a large village inhabited mostly by lower castes, Ro started a model school in an attempt to provide education to India's untouchables. Their school has already received recognition from the state government.

This is significant because the popular assumption that all religions teach the same principles is simply untrue. The Hindu social order is based on the teaching, "Exclude some of your neighbors as untouchables." Ro wants to rebuild India on Jesus' dictum, "Love your neighbor as yourself." Caste, he believes, is the most significant cause of India's weaknesses—political, social, and economic. It was because of the caste system that small bands of foreigners were able to come and colonize the large and prosperous, but deeply divided, Hindu society.

Ro played an important role as a peacemaker between the government of India and the militant Mizo rebels who began an armed rebellion against the government in 1965. In 1975, our prime minister, Mrs. Indira Gandhi, asked Ro to serve as her unnamed special emissary to negotiate peace with the underground Mizos. As I write this, he is contributing to change in the Indian subcontinent. Former president Clinton described it as "the most dangerous place on earth" because of the hostilities between nuclear neighbors India and Pakistan. Ro is striking at the root of the problem—the spirituality of hate[6] that prevents our people from loving one another.

Rochunga Pudaite's family continues to promote the Bible worldwide. He has been championing the cause of a new university in

India—one that will be founded on the biblical worldview. He wants our future generations to have a wholesome intellectual foundation on which to build a new India, and he knows that all the great universities that built modern Western civilization—Oxford, Paris, Cambridge, Princeton, Harvard, and so forth—were established to teach the Bible. Ro, a Bible translator and distributor, has been laying the foundations for a university.

Ro agrees with Bible translators before him that the pen is mightier than the sword. That is the distilled wisdom of the second millennium after Christ. The millennium had its fair share of heroes and villains. They fought their wars and left their mark on history. The world, however, recognized that ultimately it is ideas, not might, that rule the world. Ideas create cultures. Ideas build industries, services, and jobs, ultimately materializing into civilizations. Ro believes the ideas that built the best nations came from the Bible and only arrogance can motivate tribes like his to reject what is true and good.

The Bible generates hope for all peoples. Ro thinks that it is no virtue to romanticize the miseries of a primitive tribe that lives at the mercy of natural elements, germs, demons, and unscrupulous, authoritarian priests. The Bible set his imagination free to dream what his tribe ought to be—educated; free to interact with neighbors and enemies; able to overcome hunger, hate, and disease; and ready to contribute to the world. Some advocates of "multiculturalism" condemn people to live in the Stone Age.

Ro believes imagination that sets us free is a component of our distinctly human gift—creativity. That is why he made the film *Beyond the Next Mountain*,[7] based on his life. Ro became a linguist because he believes that language links our minds together to make us the only culture-creating creatures on this planet. It enables us to store and transmit ideas and to improve upon existing ideas. He is proud to have been part of the historic tradition that made the Bible the book of the last millennium.

This fascinating story of the Bible lifting Stone Age tribes out of oppression, chronic poverty, and subsistence living into freedom and abundance can be multiplied tens of thousands of times across every continent and country. Educated, upper caste Hindus, such as Arun Shourie, despise these heroic efforts to transform cultures—without realizing that most of them would not have been much better without the Bible creating modern India. I have told the story of India's modernization in three books. Admittedly my books are journalistic. Thankfully, they have begun to inspire young people to research the social history of India's modernization at the doctoral level.

In the years to come, the real history of modern India will be rescued from the distortions of leftists, liberals, and politically motivated Hindutva historians. Similar historical research has begun in many nations to demonstrate that globalization is a result neither of military colonization nor of coca-colonization. It is partial fulfillment of God's promise to Abraham that he would bless all the nations of the earth by his children who obey his Word.

Chapter Twenty

THE FUTURE

MUST THE SUN SET ON THE WEST?

Mark Zuckerberg, the creator of Facebook, is history's youngest billionaire. David Fincher "celebrated" Zuckerberg's life in the movie *The Social Network*, judged by America's national board of film review as the best film of 2010. The film's most pathetic character is Harvard University, represented by its committees and president. Zuckerberg, a law unto himself, shows total contempt for Harvard, its values, and its rules. Yet, the university cannot hold him accountable for anything. It retains absolutely no philosophical basis for invoking conscience or character. The film sends the message that now the university exists only to teach skills. Character has been excluded by the secular worldview. The best it can do is to teach you how to avoid the long arm of the law.

This loss of a sense of truth and goodness hit me when a doctoral scholar at Harvard protested William Carey's campaign against "widow-burning" in India. Imposing her values on another age, she demanded, "Why couldn't this white Christian male respect other people's beliefs and cultures?" Her moral outrage exposed clichés of multiculturalism and relativism that poorly camouflage the intellectual and moral bankruptcy of the West's elite. *Relativism* is now its only virtue. This transformed "tolerance" undermines the compass of truth—the Bible—which Harvard originally had and which could have helped Zuckerberg succeed as an innovator, while also loving his neighbors, respecting his partners, and honoring those in authority.

As brilliant but amoral graduates from secular universities such as Harvard gain control of America's economic and political life, the world has every reason to cease trusting America. The trust that made the dollar the reserve currency of the world came from the original Harvard created by the Bible.

Sunsets are spectacular. People revel in them. Sunsets also tell us that it is time to light our lamps. Many cultures that followed the West into brilliant modernity are now dusting off their rusty lamps. Russia and China have decided to trade in their own currencies, not in dollars. Even Saudi Arabia my soon sell oil for euros and yen. Loss of trust has consequences beyond economics. In 1987, a significant section of Hindu leadership backed a mass movement to legalize *Sati*—widow-burning. The British banned *Sati* as inhumane in 1829, but why should India follow British prejudices? Appealing to the "clash of civilizations," non-Western cultures are returning to traditional worldviews, including Jihad.

Relativism is the only value a truthless culture can dictate. The only thing its "tolerance" finds hard to tolerate is the West's traditional value system.[1] Goodness and truth are being replaced by debauchery and depravity. The culture celebrates porn stars. Drug peddlers are powerful and respected political lobbyists. At least until 9/11, both the West's intellectual elite and Islamic countries were urging our nations to save themselves from the West's "corrupting influence." Must the West continue on its path to the "Endarkenment" that follows sunsets?

At the dawn of the third millennium, the West resembles the legendary fish in a large tank. A researcher blocked off a section of the tank with a transparent wall and put fish food in the sealed-off section. The fish tried to get to its food but could not. After repeated failed attempts the fish learned that its nourishment was beyond reach, so it stopped trying. At that point the researcher removed the wall, but the fish did not try to get to the food. The researcher added fresh food, but the fish had given up trying. It died of starvation.

That fish died because it believed the food was inaccessible. What if the researcher could tell the fish that the wall had been removed? What if the fish was a spiritual being with free will? What if it could choose to believe a word that contradicted its earlier experience? In that case the fish might have survived. Communication and belief matter. Revelation generates hope and effort. At times, believing what you are told means the difference between life and death. The issue is not whether there is hope for the West but whether the West has the humility to return to revelation, whether it can recover the faith that generates hope.

Hope and confidence that the human spirit can overcome obstacles were defining features of modern Western civilization. But now the secular West is unsure if the human spirit even exists except as a word. At the same time, one result of denying the soul is that Western philosophers no longer know what a "word" is. Many are following India's philosophy of Silence as the ultimate reality. Having rejected the divine *logos* (the Word) as its foundation, now the West is unsure if language has anything to do with truth. Even though the West's history confirms the Bible's teaching that human beings are endowed with unique dignity, its universities now claim that history can be nothing but a point of view.

Secular universities have blocked the West from truth. Consequently, it assumes that man is merely biology, that there is no One out there who cares enough to reveal saving truth. Is man nothing more than a fish, without purpose, dignity, or responsibility? Is free will a fiction? Are we determined by our chemistry and environment? Psychologist John B. Watson (1878–1958) summarized this secular worldview in a classic lecture in 1913. He said, "The behaviorist recognizes no dividing line between man and brute."[2] American psychologist B. F. Skinner understood that this philosophy required the secular West to go "beyond freedom and dignity."[3] Billions are descending from freedom and dignity into fatalistic despair. A divorce may be necessary but at the end of the day it is resignation. Abortion is sold as "choice" but in most cases, it is fatalism—a belief that the child or the mother cannot have a good life without taking the baby's life. Individuals resigning themselves to the death of their marriage or baby are like the fish that lost faith, and therefore hope. Even the mainstream Western church is being corrupted.[4]

SECULAR FATALISM

Ruth and I celebrated the dawn of the new millennium in Cambridge, England, where we were researching for this book. In early 2000, while copying some material at the library, Ruth met Thomas Dixon, a young doctoral student who became fascinated by our project. Dixon had published a paper[5] explaining how the flawed secular notion of physiological emotions had replaced clinical use of the more helpful biblical paradigm of the soul having passions and affections.

We had not heard of Jonathan Edwards's book *The Religious Affections* (1746). Edwards, America's first philosopher, based his teaching on St. Augustine's trinitarian view of man derived from the New Testament. Edwards's paradigm, Dixon said, was far more useful for clinical psychology than Charles Darwin's 1872 book *The Expressions of the Emotions in Man and Animals*. Most twentieth-century scientists, philosophers, and psychologists—including Freud and Watson—had adopted Darwin's paradigm.

The young man told Ruth he was not a Christian but that his research had convinced him that Christians had lost the wealth of their biblical heritage, and the world was poorer for it. As Ruth tried to comprehend the enormity of this thought, Dixon asked what a clinical psychiatrist should do for a patient filled with rage, jealousy, and hatred. What if the patient's situation is so complex and so hopeless that he is contemplating divorce, murder, or suicide? The psychiatrist can only address the patient's "emotions." He cannot take on the role of a priest who can listen to the patient's confession and forgive in order to heal.

The patient could go to a therapist, who would describe his anger and hatred as secular emotions. These are treated as chemical and physiological changes in his brain and the muscles. The therapist could refer him to a doctor for a prescription that would change his chemistry and relax the muscles. But does a drug exist that has the ability to produce the "emotions" of forgiveness or love for his enemy, meaning and purpose for his life, and a hope for the future? Can chemistry create inner peace that comes from repentance and promotes positive relationships or faith in a future dispensation of justice?

Ruth knew that many suicidal men like Kurt Cobain continue in their despair, anger, or mania in spite of taking psychiatric medication. Medication may help superficially, but it cannot cure the deepest maladies of our humanity. Since Ruth knew that Dixon's ideas would interest me, she invited him over.

Dixon explained to me that in the final analysis the patient's anger may not be a result of his chemistry. It may be caused by a belief—true or false—that he has been insulted, cheated, treated unjustly, or is in great danger. His hatred and fear may be based on a belief that he might lose something precious—his job, honor, life, position, possession, spouse, or child. His beliefs may be true, but such emotions make matters worse. Jonathan Edwards called these negative emotions the "passions of the soul."[6] Often these are involuntary or at least reactionary.

Likewise, desirable emotions of repentance or forgiveness may only come from a belief that God commands us to repent or forgive others because he has forgiven our sins. Love for an enemy may come from prayer for supernatural help. Hope and joy may follow a theological assurance that God is in control. The decision to return good for evil might come from a desire to obey God's Word, or from a reliance on God's future justice. These positive emotions are crucial for one's healing. Edwards called them the "soul's affections." The Bible describes them as the "fruit of the Spirit."

Dixon added that it did not matter to him whether or not a human being has a spirit. What seemed obvious is that to lump passions (works of the flesh) and affections (the fruit of the Spirit) into a single category of amoral animal emotions is unhelpful and intellectually untenable. These positive and negative emotions are more than chemistry. They are based on beliefs, knowledge, cognition, choice, or prayer. They are more than biological phenomenon. Philosophers who reject the mystery of the soul have to explain away our experience of free will as something other than what it appears—free will. Yet, an act of the will, such as repentance, faith, or forgiveness, may be the best means of transforming one's inner emotions and external situations.

He admitted that no one knows what free will is and how we came to possess it. He insisted, however, that we cannot deny we have free will—the ability to choose to forgive or retaliate. One can call this aspect of our being mental rather than spiritual, but that is semantic slight-of-hand. To claim that free will is sheer chemistry is to assert an unprovable philosophical dogma. Chemistry offers us no explanation for our experience of ourselves. Chemistry does affect the mind. The mind affects the body. Nevertheless, the mind is clearly more than chemistry as we know it.

What he seemed sure of was that changing our beliefs can transform negative, harmful, or destructive emotions into life-affirming ones. We also know that not every belief is equally conducive to a happy and hopeful life. Every day, therapists confront beliefs that make life a tortuous hell. What a person chooses to believe strongly influences whether he lives in peace or in torment.

Why do we believe that human emotions are merely evolved versions of animal emotions? Dixon explained that American philosopher William James popularized this idea in his 1884 essay entitled "What Is an Emotion?" James opined that "an emotion was nothing but [the] combination of various sensations resulting from bodily disturbances."[7] This became the default assumption in the West as the culture drifted from the Bible's spiritual worldview to the presupposition that material nature is all that exists—philosophical materialism.[8]

Thanks to Dixon's discourse, I became aware that many research scientists had become suspicious of the simplistic, reductionist view of the human mind and emotions promoted by Darwin and James. Dr. Jeffrey M. Schwartz, professor of psychiatry at UCLA, explained why "mind" cannot be reduced to "brain."[9] Neuroscientist Beauregard similarly reviewed evidence for the Soul.[10] Suppose someone's brain is badly wired and he suffers from anxiety disorder, obsessive thoughts, and compulsive behavior. Can his mind (soul or psyche) teach his brain to act responsibly? Schwartz's discipline, neuroplasticity, harnesses our mind's capacity to rewire our brain.

The principles are not difficult to understand: If you have diabetes or high cholesterol, then you don't eat what your body craves. You choose to eat the food that is right for you. The nonphysical parts of us, our soul (mind, will, and emotion) and spirit (intuition, communion, conscience) help us separate good from bad, right from wrong. Our minds rule—at least ought to rule—over our bodies and cravings. Humans differ from animals in that we subject (or ought to subject) our bodily passions to choices that are wise and moral. This phenomenon of "ought to" makes us moral or spiritual creatures, different from other species.[11]

Let us assume that humans have no soul or mind and that the brain is but a biochemical machine. Then it could react to its environment but it could not initiate anything new out of its own "free will." Our law does not hold a mentally sick person responsible for "criminal" actions. Our entire legal system is based on the assumption, however, that a person who makes free choices is responsible for them. If no one were really free, then our emotions would be culturally conditioned chemical responses. Their evolutionary purpose would be to aid our chances to survive and procreate. In other words, it would be natural for an endangered organism to retaliate. When threatened, that organism would fight back in fear. If an individual is weaker than his enemy, he might retaliate with words—curses and abuses—or he might plan to take revenge at a more favorable moment. This is what the Bible calls the life of a "natural"[12] man.

In contrast, consider the story of Gladys Stains, an Australian missionary to India. Her husband, Graham, had devoted his life to serving lepers in India's eastern state of Orissa. Gladys was an ordinary housewife, but she stunned our nation by spontaneously, unpretentiously, humbly, and genuinely forgiving militant Hindus for their atrocities. They had burned alive her husband, Graham, and two little sons, Philip (eleven) and Timothy (seven) on January 23, 1999.[13] On January 26, 2005, the government of India honored Gladys with one of our highest civilian honors—*Padma Bhushan*.

Why should an individual be given a national honor simply for forgiving murderers? To appreciate that forgiveness, remember that India's and Pakistan's births as free nations came with the terrible pain of Hindu-Muslim-Sikh sectarian riots. About ten million were made homeless. One-half to one million people were killed, including Mahatma Gandhi. Fifty years of secular democracy and education could not free us from this destructive chain of violence and revenge. Hindu-Muslim clashes have burned trainloads of innocent passengers, leading to riots that last for weeks. Frequent riots have reduced Indian Muslims to relative poverty and powerlessness. Any successful Muslim businessman is a marked target for the next round of riots. Even sympathetic bankers hesitate to lend to him.

Gladys's simple act of forgiveness became a national phenomenon because it broke this common chain of cause and effect. In city after city, Hindu, Muslim, Sikh, Buddhist, Jain, and secular leaders gathered to publicly honor Gladys as a saint to emulate. The government of India was simply the last in line to acknowledge that Gladys Stains is an ordinary woman with an extraordinary spirit—possessed of a spirituality that could heal our nation.

THE SAVIOR

How are we to understand a biochemical organism who forgives and blesses those who ridicule, mock, strip, insult, and beat him? How can he love those who spit on him, put a crown of thorns on his head, and then murder him by nailing him to a wooden cross?

Jonathan Edwards understood spiritual revival by reading the apostle Peter's first letter in the New Testament. Peter praises believers for glorying in their humiliation. Why should biochemical organisms struggling for physical survival rejoice when they are discriminated against and unjustly treated?[14] How could they bless those who persecute them?[15] How could they respond to injustices "with joy inexpressible and filled with glory"?[16]

Is it possible for anyone to be honest when his personal needs and social environment encourage or advocate moral compromise and corruption? Jonathan Edwards triggered America's first Great Awakening and England's Methodist revival because the Bible taught him that "religious affections" were [super]natural fruit of a spiritual revival. These fruits appear when people are "born again" into a spiritual life by God's living Word.

Are these pious platitudes? The Great Awakening was not a religious dogma. It exemplified the historical secret of America's greatness. It is the reason why England escaped bloody revolution. The sun shone on the West when its cultural leaders understood that the Holy Spirit had actually enabled Peter's original readers—the believers—to live the way that Christ lived.

Clearly, a spiritual revival that fills people with personal joy and purpose, that gives them staying power in the midst of severe trials, and that enables them to love those who ill-treat them, would save much more than the Western family. It would solve the social problems that drove Kurt Cobain and many others to suicide. It would reinvigorate economies sapped by loss of morale, mutual distrust, frivolous litigation, stifling regulations, private theft, and corporate corruption. Jonathan Edwards triggered the Great Awakening by expounding 1 Peter 1:8–9:

> Though you have not seen him [Christ], you love him. Though you do not now see him, you believe in him and rejoice with joy that is inexpressible and filled with glory, obtaining the outcome of your faith, the salvation of your souls.

The believer's joy was produced not by chemistry but by a "faith more precious than gold" and a "living hope" produced by the "resurrection of Jesus Christ." The "living and abiding Word of God"[17] gave them a "new birth," making possible a life of uncompromising holiness.

AMERICA'S GREAT AWAKENING

The Great Awakening was not a cure-all. Nor were Jonathan Edwards, George Whitefield, and John Wesley perfect. It is right to submit them to critical scrutiny as we would any public figure or social movement. It is secular bigotry, however, to speak of them only with negative overtones. The fact is that the American Awakening in the 1730s and its British counterpart became the watershed movements in shaping America and Great Britain. By teaching people to revere God's Word and its principles, it ensured the success of America's independence and Britain's democracy. In contrast, the secular Enlightenment in France led to a revolution that catastrophically degenerated into totalitarianism. Every country in South and Central America and the Caribbean that followed the French Revolution fell into dictatorship. Secular revolutions merely replace one sinful authority with another.

In contrast, at the heart of the Great Awakening was a revival of personal piety. Its social consequences were far reaching. It united 80 percent of all Americans in a common world-and-life view, which ensured that America remained one nation even though Americans were divided among many denominations. Thanks to later contributions by men such as Roger Williams, the Awakening made it possible for America to accept the nonestablished denominations of European dissenters. A cultural precedent was set that has made religious tolerance a defining characteristic of American life.

In an earlier chapter we noted that the spiritual Great Awakening led to "grassroots intellectualism." Its emphasis on studying the Bible inspired people to enhance the quantity and quality of American educational opportunities. Edwards became president of Princeton University. George Whitefield, the second most important leader of the Great Awakening, founded the school that became the University of Pennsylvania. Its inaugural faculty members were Presbyterian ministers whose interest in education was rooted in their concern for souls. It reflected the peculiarly Protestant notion that education should be available for all because the Bible teaches that God wants everyone to know the truth.[18]

The Great Awakening's sense of responsibility for human souls extended to Native Americans and slaves. George Whitefield was the first European to preach to black people. As a result of his efforts, American slaves began to cherish literacy. They wanted to read the

Bible and were encouraged to do so. While the First Great Awakening did not address slavery, it did become the force that democratized America and led to the American Revolution. That inspired many more quests for political liberty, eventually ending colonialism. Some evangelicals began denouncing slavery as sinful. The British revival led to ending the slave trade. In the United States, the abolition of slavery followed the Second Awakening, which began under antislavery preachers such as Charles Finney, Lyman Beecher, his sons, and his daughter Harriet, who wrote *Uncle Tom's Cabin*.[19]

The Great Awakening took Jesus' promise of "rest for your souls"[20] to the masses. That promise released many from anxiety at the core of their being. On the authority of God's Word, the revivalists assured believers that God had accepted them as his own children.[21] This helped ordinary people find meaning in their lives. A housewife could read the Bible and relate her everyday life, her joys, and her sorrows to the Bible's cosmic framework of the kingdom of God. God's Word motivated her to love God by worshipping with other Christians, loving her neighbors, and serving her community. This generated the peculiar volunteerism that defined American compassion, until the socialist mind-set began dismantling it in favor of entitlement attitudes. Yet, it was the power of American volunteerism, fired by the Bible's vision of the kingdom of God, which enabled a ragtag army to win history's most successful revolution.

Historian Gregory Nobles is one of many who documented how the Great Awakening forced communities to take a more active role in local political and religious affairs, creating the community vibrancy that fostered the spirit driving the American War of Independence.[22] After studying sermons of that era, historian William McLoughlin concluded that "the roots of the Revolution as a political movement were so deeply imbedded in the soil of the First Great Awakening forty years earlier that it can be truly said that the Revolution was the natural outgrowth of that profound and widespread religious movement."[23]

A few leading lights of the American Revolution were indeed Deists, but it is foolish to conclude that Deism or secularism birthed American democracy. McLoughlin clarifies:

[T]he impetus for [the American] revolt came from non-scientific sources, and one of the most important of these was pietistic religion. Jonathan Edwards understood better than most deists the well-springs of human action . . . The knowledge historians have about the deistic views of Jefferson, Adams, Franklin, and Washington was not known to the people of their day, for these men wisely confined their heterodoxy to their private correspondence.[24]

The American Revolution was fueled by the covenant theology that began with the Huguenots and came to America with Puritans and Presbyterians. Daniel Elazar is one of many who have documented that "the covenants of the Bible are the founding covenants of Western civilization."[25] George Washington honored this cornerstone of American liberty on April 30, 1789, in the Federal Hall in New York before his people and his God. Raising his right hand and placing his left on the Bible, he took his oath as the first president of the United States, adding "so help me God."[26] Since then, virtually every United States president has taken his oath of office with right hand upraised and left hand on the Bible. Some who did not do so were also following their understanding of Jesus, who asked his disciples not to swear. For some it was but a tradition. But not so for General Washington, who led America from 1755 to her liberty and served as her first president. With biblical Christianity in mind, Washington said: "Religion and morality are the essential pillars of civil society."[27]

Washington was not alone in believing the Bible was the key to American character. President John Quincy Adams said, "So great is my veneration of the Bible, that the earlier my children begin to read it the more confident will be my hope that they will prove useful citizens of their country and respectable members of society. I have for many years made it a practice to read through the Bible once every year."[28] President Abraham Lincoln stated that "the Bible is the best gift God has ever given to men. All the good from the Savior of the world is communicated to us through this Book."[29] In a public message to the American Bible Society in August 1956, President Dwight

D. Eisenhower summed up the Bible's place in America: "The Bible is endorsed by the ages. Our civilization is built upon its words."

SINNERS IN THE HANDS OF A LOVING FATHER

The chief criticisms of Edwards are rooted in dislike of his sermon "Sinners in the Hands of an Angry God," preached on July 8, 1741. In this, the revival's best-known sermon, Edwards compared the human condition to that of a spider dangling by his web over a hot fire. He pointed out that an individual could lose his hold on life at any moment and his soul be plunged into the fires of eternal damnation. People who reject Edwards's teaching on the soul or of God's hatred for sin dislike this sermon. They dislike the thought that God holds human beings accountable to an absolute standard of right conduct.

The principles of responsibility and accountability are but the flip side of dignity and freedom. For a person to be free to choose, she or he must accept responsibility and be judged for the choices she or he makes. Some hold that a serial rapist and murderer should not be punished, for example, because his behavior was conditioned by the way his father treated him. This reduces a human person to the level of a fish that can make no free choices, doing only what it has learned. The atheistic USSR, China, and Kampuchea demonstrate that when you exclude the spiritual dimension and abolish the fear of God, as Watson and Skinner did, you replace them with fearsome totalitarianism. Sermons such as Edwards's helped create the West's freedom[31] because Edwards's hearers knew that, like Jesus, Edwards was inviting sinners to the eternal bosom of a loving and forgiving Father.

DIGNITY AND IMMORTALITY

Since before St. Augustine, the issue of man's unique dignity has been inseparably tied to the question: Do we have a nonmaterial soul and do we exist beyond physical death?

The belief in the immortality of the soul was a huge factor behind the West's respect for the inalienable rights of every individual.

Individual liberty meant respecting individual conscience and not sending dissenters into concentration camps. This respect came out of the belief that there will be a final judgment; therefore, individuals ought to have the liberty to live by their conscience. Is this concept of the soul's immortality religious mumbo jumbo? Believing in a future judgment by the Supreme Judge, the Magna Carta was secured by oaths before God. So, too, America's founders required every legislator and officer to swear to uphold the Constitution. Before the law, every witness must first swear to tell the truth. It was customary for them to do so with a hand on the Bible. Why is the Word so important?

What is life? Biology tells us that at its root, life is information—DNA.[32] What is word? Information! What is faith? Believing information! Jesus said that God's Word is the seed that blossoms into eternal life when combined with our faith.[33]

IS RESURRECTION PLAUSIBLE?

During my undergraduate years, the toughest challenge to my faith came from Chatterjee, mentioned earlier, who rejected even the possibility that Jesus had been resurrected. He argued, "I do not know who moved the stone that had sealed Jesus' tomb, why his tomb was empty, or what happened to his corpse. What I know is that Jesus did not rise from the dead, because resurrection is impossible. Once you are dead, you are dead. Death is the end of our existence. There is no soul that continues beyond death." I thought over my friend's challenge seriously. Jesus may or may not have risen from the dead, but could he logically assert that resurrection is *impossible*? What is ultimate reality: death or life?

It is possible to believe that death is the original and the ultimate reality. In the beginning, there was no life, no God, no angels, no spirits, no cells, and no amoebae. Life emerged in a cosmic accident and has been evolving ever since. One day, perhaps a few billion years from now, another accident will cause life to completely disappear from the cosmos. That makes death the ultimate reality.

But, if that is true, then I have already conceded that all life came out of death! How, then, is resurrection impossible? On the other hand, if the ultimate reality is life—a "living" God who lives outside the space-time continuum, who seeded life into our cosmos—then resurrection must be possible and should be expected.

WORD AND THE SOURCE OF LIFE

Our age trivializes words and personhood because many assume that impersonal, physical energy is the ultimate reality. Therefore intelligence, information, and communication cannot possibly be a part of ultimate reality. The fact is, our words do describe and encapsulate invisible laws that govern unknown galaxies. Words help us plan successful trips to outer space. Our unique gift of language enables us to create culture. Words are creative. Word (information) is life because the Bible says that God created the universe with his words. Jesus made an astounding claim about the relationship of his words to life when he said,

> Truly, truly, I say to you, whoever hears my word and believes him who sent me has eternal life. He does not come into judgment, but has passed from death to life.
> Truly, truly, I say to you, an hour is coming . . . when the dead will hear the voice of the Son of God, and those who hear will live. For as the Father has life in himself, so he has granted the Son also to have life in himself. And he has given him authority to execute judgment . . . an hour is coming when all who are in the tombs will hear his voice and come out, those who have done good to the resurrection of life, and those who have done evil to the resurrection of judgment.[34]

Such a claim is either lunacy or Truth. Christ's critics condemned him for claiming to be divine.[35] His disciples, on the other hand, saw his words bring a man back to life who had been dead for four days.[36] The disciples heard Jesus predict his death and resurrection. They saw Jesus die. Then they saw him resurrected. This took away their fear of death.

At the imminent risk of martyrdom, they proclaimed Jesus to be the creator and savior of the world, the one who gives us eternal life with God. The apostle John described God's power to give us eternal life in these words:

> See what kind of love the Father has given to us, that we should be called children of God; and so we are. The reason why the world does not know us is that it did not know him. Beloved, we are God's children now, and what we will be has not yet appeared; but we know that when he appears we shall be like him, because we shall see him as he is. And everyone who thus hopes in him purifies himself as he is pure.[37]

THE PARABLE OF TWO EGGS

I used a parable with some international scholars in California. I held an egg in each hand, and I asked if they could tell any difference between the two. The students responded that the eggs looked identical to them. They could well be from the same farm, even from the same hen.

"Neither of these is boiled or rotten," I assured them. "But if you incubate them, one of them will hatch, the other will not. Can you tell me which of these will change into a chicken?"

No one had a clue.

"The difference," I explained, "is that the egg in my right hand is fertilized, the other is not. Both are living organisms, but the egg in my right hand has received 'life.' Right now, that life is transforming it from the inside. Soon it will cease being an egg. Its identity as an egg will die, but it will be reborn as something more glorious. It will become like its parents. What does it mean when we say that an egg has been fertilized, that it has received new life through a sperm?"

One of the students instantly got the point: "It has received certain information encoded in some chemicals."

Exactly! That information established what this egg will become. That information determined its gender, color, and size, in fact, its every cell and organ, as well as most traits. At its core, life is information. Biological information is encoded in DNA. Our minds', our souls' information is encapsulated in words. Those who receive God's Word receive God's own eternal life. The Bible says that

> if you confess with your mouth that Jesus is Lord and believe in your heart that God raised him from the dead, you will be saved. For with the heart one believes and is justified, and with the mouth one confesses and is saved.[38]

Once we receive and believe God's Word, it begins transforming our souls into God's likeness. As illustrated by this egg's transformation, ultimately our biological lives receive God's imperishable seed that rebirths us into God's eternal likeness. The apostle Peter said, "You have been born again, not of perishable seed but of imperishable, through the living and abiding word of God."[39] The Scriptures were given to educate us to receive life by receiving God's living Word into our lives. The Bible says,

> [Jesus] came to his own, and his own people did not receive him. But to all who did receive him, who believed in his name, he gave the right to become children of God, who were born, not of blood nor of the will of the flesh nor of the will of man, but of God.[40]

THE WORD AND INDIVIDUAL TRANSFORMATION

The Word of God is the power that transforms our character. The apostle Paul wrote to Timothy:

> [F]rom childhood you have been acquainted with the sacred writings, which are able to make you wise for salvation through faith in Christ Jesus. All Scripture is breathed out by God and profitable for teaching, for reproof, for correction, and for training in righteousness, that the man of God may be competent, equipped for every good work.[41]

Harvard was named after Rev. John Harvard. Its 1692 motto is: *Veritas, christo et ecclesiae* (Truth, for Christ and the Church). Harvard's 1646 Rules and Precepts read:

> 2. Let every Student be plainly instructed, and earnestly pressed to consider well, the maine end of his life and studies is, to know God and Jesus Christ which is eternal life (John 17:3) and therefore to lay Christ in the bottome, as the only foundation of all sound knowledge and Learning. And seeing the Lord only giveth wisedome, Let every one seriously set himself by prayer in secret to seeke it of him (Proverbs 2:3).

> 3. Every one shall so exercise himselfe in reading the Scriptures twice a day, that he shall be ready to give such an account of his proficiency therein, both in Theoreticall observations of Language and Logick, and in practical spiritual truths, as his Tutor shall require, according to his ability; seeing the entrance of the word giveth light, it giveth understanding to the simple (Psalms 119:130).

Universities like Harvard were institutions that produced leaders who built the greatest nation in history. Yet now they turn out graduates brilliant in abilities but not always great in character. How can a young man keep himself pure?[42] Jesus overcame temptation by holding to the Scriptures that he studied, internalized, and obeyed.[43] The Word of God was his compass for determining right and good. It shaped his character. It gave him the strength to refuse shortcuts to meet his needs. It enabled him to refuse to sell his soul to the devil.[44]

For Jesus, as for the psalmist, God's Word was the lamp for his feet and the light for his path.[45] The Bible is not merely a handbook of private piety. It is the very foundation of Western civilization.

A VISION OF NATIONAL RESURRECTION

The Bible prepared colonial Americans for liberty because it taught the truth of God's redemptive intervention in history. God liberated a bunch of Hebrew slaves and transformed them into a mighty nation. The Old Testament describes the struggle of twelve tribes to become one nation. Glorious reigns of David and Solomon were followed by political tyranny that inflamed latent tribalism and split the nation.

The Israelites' rejection of God led to their apparent rejection by God. He punished their intellectual, moral, religious, and political corruption by destroying both nations—Israel and Judah. On August 14, 586 BC, God destroyed his own temple and Jerusalem, sending his chosen people into exile in Babylon. Many Jews thought that their sun had finally set. They saw no hope for their nation's resurrection. The prophet Jeremiah lamented:

> How lonely sits the city that was full of people! How like a widow has she become, she who was great among the nations! She who was a princess among the provinces has become a slave.[46]

The tribes that lost their faith in their Scriptures also lost their hope and disappeared from the canvas of history. Those that kept their faith alive became the model for the present state of Israel. After destroying Jerusalem, Nebuchadnezzar took the prophet Ezekiel to Babylon as a captive. Ezekiel's people were like the fish in our opening parable.* They believed that their nation was dead and they were like dry bones with no future. Ezekiel, however, sought God and internalized the divine scroll.[47] In a dramatic vision, God then asked Ezekiel:

> "Son of man, can these bones live?" . . . Then he said to me, "Son of man, these bones are the whole house of Israel. Behold, they say, 'Our bones are dried up, and our hope is lost; we are clean cut off.' Therefore prophesy, and say to them, Thus says the Lord GOD: Behold, I will open your graves and raise you from your graves, O my people. And I will bring you into the land of Israel. And you shall know that I am the LORD, when I open your graves, and raise you from your graves, O my people. And I will put my Spirit within

---

* page 371–72

you, and you shall live, and I will place you in your own land. Then you shall know that I am the LORD; I have spoken, and I will do it, declares the LORD."[48]

The fulfillment of Ezekiel's prophecy and Israel's great awakening began when the Persian emperor Cyrus conquered Babylon and came face to face with Daniel's knowledge of God, nationalism, and obedience of faith, discussed in the Appendix. Against the king's own feelings Daniel was thrown into the lion's den. His miraculous deliverance resulted in the king issuing his revolutionary proclamation in 538 BC:

Thus says Cyrus king of Persia, "The LORD, the God of heaven, has given me all the kingdoms of the earth, and he has charged me to build him a house at Jerusalem, which is in Judah. Whoever is among you of all his people, may the LORD his God be with him. Let him go up."[49]

This began the fulfillment of Isaish's prophecy:

Your sun will never set again, and your moon will wane no more; the Lord will be your everlasting light, and your days of sorrow will end. Then will all your people be righteous and they will possess the land forever. (Isaish 60:20–21 NIV)

THE BIBLE

Is It a Fax from Heaven?

In his novel *The Da Vinci Code*, Dan Brown wrote that since "the Bible did not arrive by fax from heaven," it cannot be the Word of God.[1]

Can the president of the United States of America use a speechwriter to craft his State of the Union address? Can he have dozens of associates amend, rewrite, revise, and edit that speech? If, in an emergency, the president asked someone else to deliver his speech to the Congress, would it still be the president's word?

The Da Vinci Code assumes that the Creator cannot do what a president can do. Worse, it assumes that since the Creator cannot communicate, the human mind cannot know the truth. It creates a myth to revive Gnostic/Tantric teaching that we can experience enlightenment by silencing our minds through mystical sex. Dan Brown implements Joseph Campbell's recommendation that having lost its hope of finding truth, the West ought to invent stories to imagine the meaning of existence. Brown's hero also examines symbols hidden by fictional mystics such as Leonardo da Vinci, a Renaissance Rationalist, who is turned into a Gnostic Master.

If it is true that we cannot know what is true, then what happens with America's 1776 Declaration of Independence? The Founders said, "We hold these truths to be self-evident that all men are created equal and are endowed by their Creator with certain undeniable rights, that among these are life, liberty and the pursuit of happiness." Are these truths self-evident to the human mind?

A postmodernist would be absolutely right in insisting that the Declaration of Independence was wrong. These "truths" are not "self-evident." Human equality is not self-evident anywhere in the world—not even in America. Women and blacks were not treated as equal in America. Equality was never self-evident to Hindu sages. For them, inequality was self-evident. Their question was, why are human beings born unequal? Hinduism taught that the Creator made people different. The higher castes were made from his head, shoulders, and belly, and the lower castes were made from his feet. The law of karma accentuated these basic differences. The Buddha did not believe in the Creator, but he accepted the doctrine of karma as the metaphysical cause for the inequality of human beings.

Nor were unalienable rights self-evident to Rome. During Jesus' trial, Pilate, Rome's governor and chief justice over Israel, declared: "I find no basis for a charge against this man."[2] Pilate then said to Jesus, "You will not speak to me? Do you not know that I have authority to release you and authority to crucify you?"[3]

Wait a minute! Do you have the power to crucify someone whom you declare to be innocent? Isn't it self-evident to you that he has an unalienable right to life?

Or take the case of the apostle Paul. A number of Roman commanders, judges, governors, and kings tried him. Everyone agreed that he was innocent. Did anyone set him free? No, they kept him imprisoned for years to please his accusers and try to extract bribes from him.[4] It was not self-evident to any of them that Paul had an unalienable right to liberty.

Equality and human rights are not self-evident truths. In his original draft, Thomas Jefferson penned, "We hold these truths to be *sacred and unalienable*." That was the truth. That's why the Declaration grounded the "unalienable" rights in the Creator rather than in the state. The most honest declaration would have been, "We hold these truths to be divinely revealed." Revelation is the reason why America believed what some Deists ascribed to "common sense." To be precise, these truths appeared common sense to the American Founders because their sense was shaped by the common impact of the Bible—even if a few of them doubted that the Bible was divinely revealed.

Does all of this matter?

Yes, it is a matter of life and death. Jesus and Paul were highly respected public servants. Yet even their lives were not safe in a culture that had lost the very notion of truth. Jesus told Pilate that he had come to reveal truth.[5] What an opportunity! Pilate could have said to his accusers: "I have never met anyone who knew truth. Now that you have brought him to me, I will keep him at least for a while to learn all about truth." But Pilate had no patience for "nonsense." How could this carpenter know truth when the greatest Greek philosophers and Latin poets were clueless? By Pilate's time, Europe had lost hope of knowing truth and even interest in seeking it. Like the postmodern West today, Pilate believed that no one knows truth—not in any rational sense that could be explained in words. The Gnostics who talked about "experiencing" mystical truth used the same type of mythical verbage as Dan Brown. And this is far from a theoretical discussion.

What happens to a culture that is clueless about what is true, good, and just? Pilate answered that question when he declared: "I have the power to crucify you or set you free." When we believe truth is unknowable, we rob it of any authority. What is left is brute power wielding arbitrary force. Whether a person or an ethnic minority is guilty or innocent becomes irrelevant. His or her right to life depends exclusively on the whims of whoever has power. Any nation that refuses to live under truth condemns itself to live under sinful man.

Dan Brown is quite right that the Bible was not faxed from heaven. It is very different from other books like the Qur'an that claim to be inspired. It usually does not use the phrase "the Word of God" as other ancient and contemporary "revelations" do. For example, unlike the Prophet Muhammad, none of the writers of the four Gospels claim to have received their information in a prophetic trance by revelation from God or from an angel. Nor do the Gospel writers claim that a spirit entity used them as channels for "automatic writing."

Private revelations cannot generally be confirmed as divinely inspired. They may be supernaturally inspired, but how would we know if they are from God or from the devil, angels, or demons?[6] Most books of the Bible are not revelations received in a subjective, trancelike experience.[7] The Gospels, for example, claim to be objective public truth. They bear courageous witness to the public events of Jesus' teaching, miracles, prophecies, crucifixion, resurrection, and ascension—witnessed by five hundred people. The Gospel writers—"the evangelists"—challenged the interpretations of Jewish scholarship and a brutal Roman state. They opened themselves to cross-examination. Matthew, Mark, and John gave eyewitness accounts as evidence for their truth. Luke described how he systematically researched the facts, carefully checking them out with eyewitnesses. This is a very human, scholarly way of writing indeed!

Can men record the Word of God?

The apostle Paul wrote to the Thessalonians: "When you received the word of God, which you heard from us, you accepted it not as the word of men but as *what it really is, the word of God*."[8] Documented fulfillment of earlier prophecies provides strong evidence of writers communicating "the word of God." J. Barton Payne, for example, details 1,817 Bible predictions involving 8,352 predictive verses (27 percent of the Bible).[9] Systematic fulfillment of short- and midterm prophecies have given strong encouragement that the canon reflects the word of God as spoken by prophets.

Can the words of men be the Word of God?

Ill-informed critics assume that Christians believe the Bible because the Roman Catholic Church councils declared it was God's Word. The reality is that the Church believes the Bible because Jesus lived and died "in accordance to the scriptures."[10]

The Gospels make it clear that Jesus did not have a martyr complex: he did not want to die.[11] He could have escaped arrest in the garden of Gethsemane. In fact, at the moment of his arrest Peter gave Jesus an excellent opportunity to escape into the dark, but Jesus rebuked him.[12] Jesus could also have saved his life during his trial, for his judges found him innocent. Instead of trying to save his life, Jesus laid it down. And he did it for one reason alone: so that the Scriptures may be fulfilled.[13] Why did Jesus take the Jewish Scriptures so seriously that he chose to die to fulfill them?

Scientists have just begun to discover awe-inspiring communication that happens in communities of the single cell creatures we call amoeba.[14] We are far from figuring out why life is so inseparably related to information and its transmission. From the very beginning, the Hebrew Scriptures (the Old Testament) reveal a God who speaks: "And God said, 'Let there be light,' and there was light."[15] Thus the Jewish worldview sees language as foundational to reality. We human beings speak because we are made in the image of a Spirit who said, "Let us make man in our image."[16] Man became a "living soul" when God breathed his spirit ("breath") into a body of clay.[17] Thus, human language has both spiritual and physical aspects.

The Bible teaches that God is love. Love includes communication. Both Old and New Testaments teach that God speaks to us because he loves us. He gave us the gift of language so we may know and love him and one another as his children. Love, Jesus taught, was the whole point of divine revelation, that is, communication.[18] In the Judeo-Christian understanding, love and language are aspects not of chemistry but of our *psyche* or soul. Our chemistry is designed to facilitate love, knowledge, communication, and worship.

Jesus, Daniel, and the Jewish Scriptures

Jesus treated the Hebrew Scriptures in the same way as did the Hebrew prophet, Daniel, an administrator in Babylon.

Daniel was a young contemporary of the prophet Jeremiah in whose day, many prophets claimed to receive revelations from God. The prophets who predicted peace and prosperity for Jerusalem enjoyed religious and political patronage. Yet their prophecies turned out to be false. Jeremiah, on the other hand, called his nation to repentance. Otherwise, he said, God would bring doom and destruction through the Babylonians. Jeremiah was condemned for treason and almost killed, but subsequent events proved him right. Daniel, therefore, took Jeremiah's prophecies seriously.

Decades after Jeremiah was gone, Daniel kept reading Jeremiah's scrolls, even though Jeremiah's work was not yet in the Jewish canon. The more Daniel read, the more convinced he became that since Jeremiah's predictions had come true, he was a prophet from God.[19] Finally Daniel became so convinced that Jeremiah's words were God's words that he was willing to be thrown into a den of lions.[20] Here is what happened:

Jeremiah prophesied that Jerusalem would be rebuilt seventy years after its destruction.[21] That was about the time when the Medo-Persian coalition defeated Babylon. Jeremiah's prophecy, in conjunction with dreams of Nebuchadnezzar and Daniel himself, helped Daniel understand the significance of that momentous event. He believed "the word of the LORD to Jeremiah the prophet"[22] and began to pray for the rebuilding of Jerusalem.[23] Then the king was duped into issuing a devastating edict: No one was to pray to any god except to the king for thirty days. The penalty for violation was the lions' den!

Daniel, by then administrator-in-chief for the empire, knew that his rivals had engineered that edict specifically to destroy him. He had to choose. Would he stop praying for the dead city of Jerusalem to save his life, or would he trust Jeremiah's words at the risk of his life?

The deeper question was, who was sovereign—God or the king? Daniel had no other basis for disobeying the king and risking his life except his confidence that Jeremiah's words were God's words. God was sovereign over history. God had used Babylon to destroy wicked Jerusalem to fulfill the words spoken by numerous prophets, beginning with Moses. Now God was going to use the Persian emperor to rebuild his temple, notwithstanding the schemes of Daniel's rivals.[24] Daniel believed Jeremiah's prophecy. Therefore he kept his practice of opening his windows to Jerusalem and praying three times a day.

Daniel was arrested, tried, and thrown into the lions' den. After a sleepless night, the king was astonished to discover that something— or rather, someone—had kept the lions from harming Daniel. His miraculous escape so moved the king that he issued an edict encouraging Jews to return to build a temple for the living God in Jerusalem and pray for the king![25]

As Daniel did, Jesus treated the words of the Hebrew Scriptures as God's Word. He lived by the Scriptures,[26] died, and was buried according to the Scriptures, and on the third day he rose again "according to the Scriptures"[27] and his own prophecies.[28] Jesus' apostles, including Peter and Paul, followed Jesus in teaching that the Hebrew Scriptures were written by men but inspired by God.[29]

Did Jesus lay down his life to fulfill the Scriptures because he was but a first-century Jew conditioned by his culture's mistaken view of the Scriptures? Or was the Old Testament his own Word? In that case, Jesus would be teaching the lesson that John Locke drew from it, that is, to use our gift of language responsibly, to say what we mean and mean what we say, and to keep our word, as God does, whatever the cost.[30]

Even a superficial reading of the Gospels is sufficient to show a skeptic that Jesus' culture rejected him because he overturned their understanding of the Scriptures.[31] He was anything but a product of his culture. He spoke not as an exegete, but as someone with a unique authority to expound God's original intention behind the words of Scripture.[32] The Jews persecuted Jesus because he claimed to have greater authority than Moses,[33] who had received the *"very words of God."*[34]

IS THE NEW TESTAMENT THE WORD OF GOD?

The epistle to the Hebrews exhorts the Jewish followers of the Messiah to "remember your leaders, who spoke *the word of God* to you."[35] How could the apostles' words be regarded as "the words of God"?

The apostles already believed that God's word created the universe.[36] They had seen Jesus' words still the storms, heal the sick, and raise the dead. Jesus assured them: "The words that I say to you I do not speak on my own authority, but the Father who dwells in me does his works."[37] He promised that if they would abide in his word, they would know the truth, the truth would set them free,[38] and that their prayers would be answered if they remained in his word.[39]

Having seen Jesus' words raise several people from death, what were the apostles to do with his claim that the day was coming when the dead would hear his voice, and those who hear would rise again and live eternally?[40]

To make matters worse, the apostles thought the Messiah would conquer Rome, but Jesus predicted he would be crucified and three days later be raised again. The apostles witnessed Jesus' words come true. Their firsthand experiences of Christ's death and resurrection compelled them to conclude that Jesus' words were God's words. Jesus was the eternal, creative Word of God (*logos*) become flesh.[41] Jesus himself used the testimony of the Scriptures—more than his incredible miracles—as the proof of his divinity.[42]

In his prayer to his Father, Jesus said, "For I have given them [the disciples] the words that you gave me."[43] He breathed his Spirit upon the apostles,[44] assuring them that the Holy Spirit would remind them what he had taught them[45] and would guide them into all truth.[46] Jesus did not send them merely to teach and preach what they had heard and seen. He also gave them authority to heal the sick and cast out demons with their words.[47] The apostles became the servants or "ministers of the word."[48] They devoted themselves to "the ministry [service] of the word."[49] God's Spirit confirmed the apostles' words by supernatural signs and wonders.[50] What would you have thought if you saw Peter's words heal a man born lame?[51] Even unbelievers treated the words of the apostles as the words of God.[52]

The apostles' contemporaries interpreted the growth of the church as the growth of the word of God: "And the word of God continued to increase, and the number of disciples multiplied."[53] Following Jesus' example, the apostles sealed their words with their blood. They did not struggle for personal survival, because Christ's word assured them of their eternal survival.

Contrary to Bible critics, such as Dan Brown and Arun Shourie, the church did not invent the Word of God: the church was "built on the foundation of the apostles and the prophets," that is, on the New and the Old Testaments.[54]

Ill-informed skeptics assume that the Bible—especially the New

Testament—was deemed to be the Word of God in AD 325 by the Church Council of Nicaea, which collated the canon of Scripture. The following verses show that Jesus believed that his message was God's word. His apostles believed that what they were preaching was God's word. Long before any church council met Christ's original companions and followers in Jerusalem accepted the apostles' words as the Word of God, just as the Thessalonian believers accepted Paul's words as the Word of God.

How could the apostle John say to his readers that they already knew the truth and did not need anyone (not even a church council) to determine for them the word of God?[55] The first- and second-century church already knew which books had genuine apostolic authority behind them. They did not require canonization of the apostles' writings by a church council to begin laying down their lives for the Word of God. They had been affirming their faith in these writings, by choosing martyrdom, for more than two hundred years before Constantine.[56]

The Old Testament canon existed before Jesus' time. Canonization of the New Testament became necessary only because spurious books began to appear claiming to have been written by the original apostles. Canonization did not turn Paul's epistles into God's word. The purpose of canonization was to refute the spurious works as inauthentic, such as the alleged "Gospel of Thomas" and the "Gospel of Barnabas."

It is important to note that only one book in the New Testament, the Revelation (to John), claims to have been received supernaturally in visions, and this book met with the toughest scrutiny before being included in the canon. A book with a similar title, *The Revelation of Peter*, was rejected. Why? Because Christianity is about public truth, not about private, subjective, unverifiable, secret, inner, "religious" experience. Private intuition may indeed be from God, but it has to be publicly authenticated before the public can follow it. The Revelation of John was included in the canon precisely because it is not a "fax from heaven." John "saw," "looked," and "heard" certain things and then wrote down his eyewitness account—exactly as he did in the gospel of John.[57] The church canonized books with known apostolic authority to undercut the deception of power-hungry "religious" prophets, apostles, and mystics.

The authorship of Revelation has been disputed, but it is clear that if someone other than John the apostle forged the book in John's name, then the forger would have made an effort to establish his credentials as an apostle. The author of the book of Revelation simply states that his name was John, and he expects the intended readers to recognize his apostolic authority.

The point is this: the church does not believe the Scriptures because the Council of Nicaea canonized some books. Roman Catholics acknowledge that Church councils have sometimes been wrong. The Council of Nicaea did not create the Bible. The process of canonization of the New Testament began with a heretic, Marcion (AD 90–160), who identified a widely accepted canon in order to challenge it. In response to such attempts, the church affirmed the New Testament canon in order to repudiate heresies.

Inclusion in the canon was not dependent on unverifiable "divine inspiration" but on verifiable matters. The first was apostolic authority, including implied apostolic authority as in the case of the books of Mark, Luke, Acts, and the epistle to Hebrews. Equally important was theological harmony with the Old Testament canon that Jesus confirmed as the Word of God. The Gnostic forgeries did claim apostolic authorship, but they did not and could not claim harmony with the Old Testament. For example, John's Revelation is a very deliberate unpacking of the book of Daniel. In Revelation 5, for example, the Lamb of God receives the title deed of the earth that had been promised to the Messiah in Psalm 2 and Psalm 110. The chapters that follow become the key to explaining how Jesus was the Messiah prophesied by the Old Testament.

CAN THE NATURAL ALSO BE SUPERNATURAL?

The church fathers knew that fallible men had authored the books of the New Testament. The Council of Nicaea wrestled with a worldview issue raised by Gnosticism: Could the natural (material/physical) be simultaneously spiritual, nonmaterial, supernatural, and good?

The Gnostics presupposed that the natural realm was evil. Therefore, they concluded that human words cannot be God's word; the Christ Spirit could not become incarnate; Christ could not have died on the cross; it was the evil, material body of a man—Jesus—that was crucified; the Christ Spirit was laughing at the folly of his enemies as they were crucifying Jesus, thinking that they were killing the Christ.

The Council of Nicaea rejected this Gnostic worldview in favor of the Old Testament teaching that the material world—the tangible, physical expression of God's words—was good. Man (male and female) really was made in God's image; the human body was good. God could become man, and our physical bodies can be, and ought to become, the temple of the Holy God.[58]

Just as Satan could enter Judas to do evil,[59] God's Spirit can and does use human beings to speak his words[60] and do his will. The work and words of men and women can be human, satanic, or divine. Just as Jesus could be fully man and fully God, so man's words could be God's words. If a president can take a speechwriter's words and make them his own, why couldn't Paul communicate God's words? He can, just as an ambassador can speak the king's words.[61] It is absurd to claim that Jesus was the greatest prophet, as Dan Brown implies, and to simultaneously claim that the Scripture Jesus believed in, to the extent of laying down his life, was merely a human hoax.

The church fathers did not understand the mystery of human language any more than we do. Nor did they conclude that the New Testament was God's Word based on abstract philosophical arguments. They relied on eyewitnesses who saw the words of Jesus and his apostles make the lame to walk and the blind to see, drive out demons, and raise the dead back to life. The Holy Spirit confirmed Jesus' and the apostles' words with signs and wonders, just as God's supernatural acts had confirmed Moses' words.[62] Future generations may understand language better than we do. Contemporary medicine has just begun to study the healing power of human words. However, at present, even our science fiction is clueless about how words could possibly bring a dead person back to life or, as Einstein marveled, how our minds and words could comprehend the physical universe.*

Rome's collapse meant that Europe lost its soul—the source of its civilizational authority—and descended into the "Dark Ages." The Bible was the power that revived Europe. Europeans became so enthralled with God's Word that they rejected their sacred myths to hear God's Word, study it, internalize it, speak it, and promote it to build the modern world. At the dawn of the twenty-first century, the West is again losing its soul. Will it relapse into a new dark age or humble itself before the Word of the Almighty God?

The following verses demonstrate that the New Testament viewed Jesus and his apostles' teaching—speaking and writing—as "the Word of God" centuries before church councils.

On one occasion, while the crowd was pressing in on him to hear the word of God, he was standing by the lake of Gennesaret. (Luke 5:1)

For he whom God has sent utters the words of God, for he gives the Spirit without measure. (John 3:34)

The words that I say to you I do not speak on my own authority, but the Father who dwells in me. (John 14:10)

For I have given them [the apostles] the words that you [Father] gave me. (John 17:8)

They were all filled with the Holy Spirit and continued to speak the word of God with boldness. (Acts 4:31)

---

* See chapter 4.

It is not right that we should give up preaching the word of God to serve tables. (Acts 6:2)

And the word of God continued to increase. (Acts 6:7)

Now when the apostles at Jerusalem heard that Samaria had received the word of God, they sent to them Peter and John. (Acts 8:14)

The Gentiles also had received the word of God. (Acts 11:1)

But the word of God increased and multiplied. (Acts 12:24)

They proclaimed the word of God in the synagogues of the Jews. (Acts 13:5)

Sergius Paulus, a man of intelligence, who summoned Barnabas and Saul and sought to hear the word of God. (Acts 13:7)

And Paul and Barnabas spoke out boldly, saying, "It was necessary that the word of God be spoken first to you." Since you thrust it aside and judge yourselves unworthy of eternal life, behold, we are turning to the Gentiles. (Acts 13:46)

And he stayed a year and six months, teaching the word of God among them. (Acts 18:11)

For we are not, like so many, peddlers of God's word, but as men of sincerity, as commissioned by God, in the sight of God we speak in Christ. (2 Corinthians 2:17)

WE REFUSE TO PRACTICE CUNNING OR TO TAMPER WITH GOD'S WORD. (2 CORINTHIANS 4:2)

I BECAME A MINISTER . . . TO MAKE THE WORD OF GOD FULLY KNOWN. (COLOSSIANS 1:25)

LONG AGO, AT MANY TIMES AND IN MANY WAYS, GOD SPOKE TO OUR FATHERS BY THE PROPHETS, BUT IN THESE LAST DAYS HE HAS SPOKEN TO US BY HIS SON. (HEBREWS 1:1–2)

THE REVELATION OF JESUS CHRIST, WHICH GOD GAVE HIM TO SHOW TO HIS SERVANTS THE THINGS THAT MUST SOON TAKE PLACE. HE MADE IT KNOWN BY SENDING HIS ANGEL TO HIS SERVANT JOHN, WHO BORE WITNESS TO THE WORD OF GOD. (REVELATION 1:1–2)

AND THE ANGEL SAID TO ME, "WRITE . . . THESE ARE THE TRUE WORDS OF GOD. (REVELATION 19:9)

AND HE SAID TO ME, "THESE WORDS ARE TRUSTWORTHY AND TRUE. AND THE LORD, THE GOD OF THE SPIRITS OF THE PROPHETS, HAS SENT HIS ANGEL TO SHOW HIS SERVANTS WHAT MUST SOON TAKE PLACE. (REVELATION 22:6)

NOTES

FOREWORD

1. Alan Bloom, *The Closing of the American Mind: How Higher Education Has Failed Democracy and Impoverished the Souls of Today's Students* (NY: Simon & Schuster, 1987), 58.
2. Richard Rorty and Gianni Vattimo, *The Future of Religion* (NY: Columbia University Press, 2005), 72.
3. C. S. Lewis, *Surprised By Joy* (NY: Harcourt, Brace, and World, 1955), 207–208.

PROLOGUE

1. *Missionaries in India: Continuities, Changes, Dilemmas* (New Delhi: ASA Publications, 1994) and *Harvesting Our Souls: Missionaries, Their Designs, Their Claims* (New Delhi: ASA Publications, 2000).
2. Both the books are available from www.RevelationMovement.com.

PART I

Epigraph: H. Grady Davis, "History of the World," http://all-history.org/religions17.html (accessed December 5, 2010).

CHAPTER ONE

Epigraph: George Orwell's "Notes on the Way" was first published in *Time and Tide*, March 30–April 6, 1940. It is reprinted in *Collected Essays, Journalism and Letters of George Orwell* (Harcourt, Brace & World, 1968). See http://orwell.ru/library/articles/notes/e/e_notew.htm.

1. "Endless, Nameless" on *Nevermind* (Los Angeles: Geffen Records, 1991). This song is a hidden track at the end of some copies of the CD.
2. The *Rolling Stone* editors, *Cobain* (Boston: Little, Brown and Company, 1994), 128. See "Suicidal Tendencies" by Diana Grains, 128–32.
3. Ibid.
4. Charles R. Cross, *Heavier Than Heaven* (NY: Hyperion, 2001), 15.
5. Freud's second topography undermines the modern, Cartesian understanding of selfhood that most in the West understand by "self." Freud's self is decentered.
6. Band AC/DC.
7. For a simple summary see Connie Zweig's essay, "The Death of the Self in a Postmodern World" in *The Truth About The Truth: Deconfusing and Re-Constructing the Postmodern World*, ed. Walter Truett Anderson (NY: Penguin Putnam, 1995), 145–150.
8. *Rolling Stone*, November 3, 2005, 54.
9. Kurt Cobain, *Journals* (NY: Riverhead Books, 2003), 108–09.
10. Steven Blush, *American Hardcore: A Tribal History* (Los Angeles; NY: Feral House, 2001), 9.

11. A lyric by Agent Orange, "Living in Darkness," *Agent Orange* (Warner/Elektra/Atlantic, 1981).

12. On February 25, 2009, the Bureau of Democracy, Human Rights and Labour submitted the 2008 Human Rights Report for Turkmenistan: "The government demonstrated little or no support for non-Turkmen music, but classical music was taught and performed throughout the country. The previously banned government-supported symphony orchestra was reestablished at the National Cultural Center and began monthly concerts of Turkmen and world classical music. The president decreed that the circus reopen, and the first opera performance took place in June. Traditional local music, which had not been performed for years, was played in concerts and social events." http://www.state.gov/g/drl/rls/hrrpt/2008/sca/119142.htm (accessed January 16, 2011).

13. Ephesians 5:18–20 NIV.

14. For a biblical description of music in heaven, please see Revelation 5:7–9, 14:1–3, 15:1–4.

15. "Tibetan Buddhist Monk Nominated for Grammy award," 3 February 2006, International Campaign for Tibet, http://www.savetibet.org/media-center/ict-news-reports/tibetan-buddhist-monk-nominated-grammy-award (accessed December 4, 2010).

16. Job 38:4–7.

17. J. R. R. Tolkien, *The Silmarillion* (Boston and NY: Houghton Mifflin Company, 2001), 15–16. Tolkien's fictional passage is an expression of the Bible's teaching in Job 38, John 1, and the book of Revelation.

18. Martin Luther's Foreword to Georg Rhau's *Symphoniae Lucundae*, a collection of chorale motets published in 1538, reprinted in *From Liturgy and Hymns*, ed. Ulrich S. Leupold; trans. Paul Zeller Strodach; vol. 53 of *Luther's Works*, American Edition, ed. Jaroslav Pelikan and Helmut T. Lehmann (Philadelphia: Fortress, 1965).

19. Martin Luther, *The Table Talk of Martin Luther*, trans. and ed. William Hazlitt (London: H. G. Bohn, 1857), 340.

20. For example, see 1 Samuel 19:18–24 or 1 Chronicles 25:1–6. "David and the chiefs of the service also set apart for the service the sons of Asaph, and of Heman, and of Jeduthun, who prophesied with lyres, with harps, and with cymbals. The list of those who did the work and of their duties was: Of the sons of Asaph . . . who prophesied under the direction of the king. Of Jeduthun, the sons of Jeduthun . . . who prophesied with the lyre in thanksgiving and praise to the LORD. Of Heman, the sons of Heman . . . the king's seer, according to the promise of God to exalt him . . . They were all under the direction of their father in the music in the house of the LORD with cymbals, harps, and lyres for the service of the house of God."

21. Acts 2:30.

22. 1 Corinthians 14:1.

23. Wilfrid Mellers, *Bach and the Dance of God* (Oxford: Oxford Univ. Press, 1981), 82.

24. Christoph Wolff, *Johann Sebastian Bach: The Learned Musician* (NY: Norton, 2000), 8.

25. Ulrich Meyer, *Biblical Quotations and Allusions in Cantata Libretti of Johann Sebastian Bach* (London: Scarecrow Press, 1997), 177–216. Bible references that Bach quoted or alluded to in his compositions and writings.

26. Romans 8:28.

27. Jacques Barzun, *From Dawn to Decadence: 1500 to the Present, 500 years of*

Western Cultural Life (NY: HarperCollins, 2000). His concept of "decadence" is explained in his introduction.

28. Stanley Fish, who retired as the Dean of the College of Liberal Arts and Sciences at the Univ. of Illinois at Chicago argued in an article, "Why We Built the Ivory Tower," *NY Times*, May 21, 2004, that the Univ. should not even try to teach morality or good citizenship. He wrote, "Performing academic work responsibly and at the highest level is a job big enough for any scholar and for any institution. And, as I look around, it does not seem to me that we academics do that job so well that we can now take it upon ourselves to do everyone else's job too. We should look to the practices in our own shop, narrowly conceived, before we set out to alter the entire world by forming moral character, or fashioning democratic citizens, or combating globalization, or embracing globalization, or anything else."

29. Ibid. Quoted by Orwell.

PART II

CHAPTER TWO

1. Sri Jayaprakash Narayan is sometimes referred to as a "second Gandhi."
2. Biogas digesters convert waste materials into methane gas for energy. Our biogas digester, installed on the Kadari farm, was the first in the area. The Gandhi Ashram in Chhatarpur partnered with us to bring in experts to teach local masons how to make one, and peasants how to maintain them.
3. Exodus 3.
4. Genesis 15:1 NKJV.
5. 2 Corinthians 1:3.
6. My study of popular Indian gurus was published by Vikas Publishing House (Delhi). It had been serialized by India's foremost weekly, *Sunday*.
7. Romans 13:1–2; 1 Peter 2:13–17. Soon I discovered the Bible provided theological grounds for civil disobedience.
8. Association for Comprehensive Rural Assistance (ACRA) was registered as a nonprofit organization in 1977 with Dr. D. W. Mategaonker as the chairman of a nine-member governing body. I served as the CEO and operated it out of our home. Others who joined us became an extension of our family—hence a "community." An inner core, in theory, made day-to-day decisions. In practice, however, the whole community met every morning for prayers and participated in making decisions that affected everyone.
9. Matthew 7:7.
10. James 4:2.
11. Acts 4:19. The first chapter of my book *Truth and Social Reform* discusses a biblical theology of civil disobedience as it was forged in this confrontation.
12. The Lord Jesus was on a confrontation course with the socio-religio-political establishment of his time. This was to culminate in his crucifixion. Therefore, he asked all who wished to follow him to take up their cross and be prepared for martyrdom. See, for example, Luke 9:23–26.

CHAPTER FOUR

1. John 8:12.
2. Helen Keller, *The Story of My Life* (NY: Grosset and Dunlap, 1905), 23–24.

3. Albert Einstein, "Physics and Reality," *Journal of the Franklin Institute*, vol. 221, issue 3, March 1936, 349–382.
4. Genesis 2:9.
5. Isaiah 66:2 NIV.
6. Genesis 12:3, 18:18, 22:18, 26:4, etc.
7. Revelation 22:2.
8. Three of my books study the last point: (1) *William Carey and the Regeneration of India*, (2) *Missionary Conspiracy: Letters to a Postmodern Hindu*, and (3) *India: The Grand Experiment.*

Part III

Epigraph: *The Broken Covenant: American Civil Religion in Time of Trial* (NY: Crossroad Books, 1975), 12–13.

Chapter Five

1. Proverbs 31: 8–9 NIV.
2. Bhagavad Gita II.22.
3. Bhagavad Gita II.12–13.
4. Genesis 39–41.
5. Scholars dispute the exact title of *Oration on the Dignity of Man* by Giovanni Pico Della Mirandola (1463–94).
6. Henry Thode, *Franz von Assisi und die Anfange der Kunst der Renaissance in Italien* (Berlin: G. Grote, 1885).
7. Paul Sabatier, *Vie de S. François d'Assise* (Paris: Fischbacher, 1894).
8. Wallace K. Ferguson, "The Reinterpretation of the Renaissance," *Facets of the Renaissance: the Arensberg Lectures* (Los Angeles: HarperCollins, 1959).
9. Charles Trinkaus, *In Our Image and Likeness* (London: Constable, 1970). Another important scholar to develop this line of thinking was Charles Norris Cochrane, whose study *Christianity and Classical Culture* (Oxford: Oxford Univ. Press, 1940) demonstrated that the Western confidence in the human ability to change history originated in the work of the Church Fathers such as St. Augustine. Most important, these men taught the biblical grounds for critiquing the classical faith in *Fortune and Fate* as divine entities.
10. Genesis 1:26.
11. Trinkaus, *In Our Image and Likeness*, vol. 1, 3.
12. Genesis 1:1.
13. Trinkaus, *In Our Image and Likeness*, 510.
14. Quoted by Trinkaus, *In Our Image and Likeness*, 510.
15. Hebrews 1:7, 14 NIV.
16. Trinkaus, *In Our Image and Likeness*, 37.
17. Ibid.
18. Francesco Petrarca, *On Religious Leisure (De Otio Religioso)* (ca. AD 1357), ed. and trans. by Susan S. Schearer (NY: Italica Press, 2002), 60–61.
19. Mark Kramer et al. *The Black Book of Communism: Crimes, Terror, Repression* (Cambridge: Harvard Univ. Press, 1999).
20. Exodus 3.
21. Richard Hell, *Hot and Cold* (NY: powerHouse, 2001).
22. Wesley J. Smith, *A Rat Is a Pig Is a Dog Is a Boy: The Human Cost of the Animal Rights Movement* (NY: Encounter Books, 2010).

23. Gene Edward Veith and Marvin Olasky, *Postmodern Times: a Christian Guide to Contemporary Thought and Culture* (Wheaton, IL: Crossway Books, 1994), 76.

24. "Zoo in Copenhagen Exhibits New Primates (Fully Clothed)," *NY Times*, August 29, 1996.

CHAPTER SIX

1. E. Haldeman-Julius, *The Meaning of Atheism*, Little Blue Book #1597 (Girard, KS: Haldeman-Julius Company).

2. George Holmes, ed., *The Oxford History of Medieval Europe* (Oxford: Oxford Univ. Press, 1992), 1.

3. Edward Grant, *God and Reason in the Middle Ages* (Cambridge: Cambridge Univ. Press, 2001), 1.

4. L. C. Goodrich, "Revolving Book Case in China," *Harvard Journal of Asiatic Studies*, VII (1942), 154.

5. Lynn White Jr., *Medieval Religion and Technology* (Berkeley: Univ. of California Press, 1978), 47.

6. See, for example, Maharishi Mahesh Yogi, *Science of Being and Art of Living: Transcendental Meditation* (NY: New American Library, 1963 [copyright], 1968 [first printing]), 294ff.

7. A. L. Basham, *The Wonder That Was India*, 3rd ed. (New Delhi: Rupa, 2000), 269–270.

8. Raoul Mortley, *From Word to Silence* (Bonn: Peter Hanstein Verlag GmbH, 1986).

9. Ibid., 33–34.

10. Ibid., 160.

11. Ibid., 43.

12. John 14:6.

13. John 18:37.

14. John 1:1, 14.

15. Mortley, *From Word to Silence*, 50.

16. Ibid., 50–51.

17. Quoted by Cochrane in *Christianity and Classical Culture* (Oxford: Oxford Univ. Press, 1940), 401.

18. Ibid., 37.

19. Edward Grant, *God and Reason*, 29.

20. Ibid., 39.

21. Ibid., 41.

22. For example, John 17:3; Colossians 2:3.

23. John of Damascus, *The Fount of Knowledge, from Writings*, trans. Frederic H. Chase, Jr., in *The Fathers of the Church* series, vol. 37 (NY: Fathers of the Church, 1958), 7.

24. David S. Landes, *The Wealth and Poverty of the Nations* (NY: Norton, 1998), 139.

25. Revisionist historian Eamon Duffy illustrates this in his controversial study, *The Stripping of the Altars: Traditional Religion in England 1400–1580* (New Haven: Yale Univ. Press, 1992). As a Catholic, Duffy holds Henry's move responsible for promoting factionalism and division. "[Henry VIII] had hoped that the English Bible would be read 'with meekness . . . and not to maintain erroneous opinions.' Instead, the people disputed 'arrogantly' in the churches, alehouses, and taverns, and slandered each other 'as well by word as writing,' one part of them calling the other papist, the other part calling the other heretic,'" 422.

26. See, for example, Jared M. Diamond's *Guns, Germs and Steel: The Fates of Human Societies* (NY: Norton, 1997).

27. Cedric B. Cowing, *The Great Awakening and the American Revolution: Colonial Thought in the 18th Century* (Chicago: Rand McNally, 1971), 72.
28. Isaiah 11:2.
29. Proverbs 1:7.
30. Landes, *Wealth and Poverty of the Nations*, 317.
31. Ibid.
32. Ibid.
33. Acharya Rajneesh, *Beyond and Beyond* (Bombay: Jeevan Jagruti Kendra, 1970), 15.

CHAPTER SEVEN

1. "The Historical Roots of Our Ecological Crisis," *Science*, vol. 155, 1967, 1203–07.
2. Lynn White Jr., *Medieval Religion and Technology: Collected Essays* (Berkeley: Univ. of California Press, 1978), 22.
3. David S. Landes, *Revolution in Time* (Cambridge, MA: Harvard Univ. Press, 2000), 39–44.
4. Ibid., 20.
5. His thesis is presented more popularly in the chapter "The Christian Expectation of the End Time and the Idea of Technical Progress," in his book *Evolution and Christian Hope: Man's Concept of the Future from the Early Fathers to Teilhard de Chardin* (NY: Garden City, 1966).
6. Genesis 2:15.
7. For a more expanded summary of Benz's view, see Lynn White Jr., *Medieval Religion and Technology*, 236–37.
8. 2 Thessalonians 3:10.
9. Cardinal Gasquet, trans., *The Rule of St. Benedict* (London: Medieval Library, 1925), chapter 48.
10. Genesis 1:3—2:2.
11. Genesis 3:17–19.
12. White, *Medieval Religion and Technology*, 22.
13. Ibid., 131.
14. Barzun, *From Dawn to Decadence*, 600–601.
15. White, *Medieval Religion and Technology*, 22.
16. For further discussion see *Angels in the Architecture* by Douglas Jones (Moscow, ID: Canon Press, 1998). The authors argue that the Dark Ages weren't "dark" but were actually a beginning of a culture molded by the Bible. Critics may find some romanticizing of the Dark Ages, but the authors do bring up fascinating points generally ignored by scholars.
17. Lynn White Jr., "Technology and Invention in the Middle Ages," *Speculum: A Journal of Medieval Studies* (April, 1940), 141–159.
18. Ibid., 291.
19. Ibid., 245.
20. Hollywood actress Shirley MacLaine effectively introduced the Indian concept of time to Western readers. See her concept of eternal "Nowness" in her book *Going Within* (NY: Bantam Books, 1989).
21. Genesis 2:7.
22. Acts 18.3.
23. 2 Thessalonians 3:10.
24. Quoted by Philip Mason, *The Men Who Ruled India* (Calcutta: Rupa, 1992), 12.
25. Stanley Wolpert, *A New History of India*, 5th ed. (NY: Oxford Univ. Press, 1997), 155–56.

26. Rodney Stark, *For the Glory of God: How Monotheism Led to Reformations, Science, Witch-hunts, and the End of Slavery* (Princeton: Princeton Univ. Press, 2003), 359, 360, 244.

PART IV

CHAPTER EIGHT

1. Jonathan Swift, "Cadenus and Vanessa," in *Jonathan Swift: The Complete Poems* Pat Rogers, ed. (New Haven: Yale Univ. Press, 1983), 149, lns. 740–41.
2. See Jacques Ellul, *Subversion of Christianity*, trans. Geoffrey W. Bromiley (Grand Rapids: Eerdmans, 1986), chapter 5.
3. For a firsthand account of the atrocities of the conquistadors, see Bartolomé de Las Casas, *The Devastation of the Indies: A Brief Account*, trans. Herma Briffault (Baltimore: Johns Hopkins Univ. Press, 1992). While there were significant movements in Spain resisting the abuse of the West Indians, the momentum of the conquistadors proved difficult to stop.
4. *Lord Curzon in India: Being a Selection from His Speeches as Viceroy and Governor-General of India, 1898–1905* (London: MacMillan, 1906), 393.
5. See my books *India: The Grand Experiment; Missionary Conspiracy: Letters to a Postmodern Hindu;* and *William Carey and the Regeneration of India.*
6. The new expanded edition is called *Truth and Transformation: A Manifesto for Ailing Nations* (Seattle, WA: YWAM, 2009).
7. Luke 9:23–24.
8. I inherited a .22 rifle from my mother-in-law. The police refused to give me a license, so I could not keep it for more than a few months. For a while, I also had an air-pistol, which was good for chasing monkeys. Our most dreaded weapon, however, was Ruth's hair-dryer—believed to be a laser gun!
9. William Blake, "Auguries of Innocence," line 97.
10. Sidney Painter, *French Chivalry: Chivalric Ideas and Practices in Medieval France* (Baltimore: Johns Hopkins Press, 1940), 150. Most of the information on pages 129–31 on the medieval hero comes from this book.
11. Roland Bainton, *Here I Stand* (England: Lion Publishing, 1978), 174.
12. Ibid., 181–82.
13. Matthew 20:27–28.
14. 1 Corinthians 1–3.
15. Hebrews 2:14–15.
16. John 15:13.

CHAPTER NINE

1. John 18:37.
2. John 14:6.
3. Matthew 22:21.
4. Matthew 26:52.
5. St. Cyprian, *Letters: 1–81* (AD 249–58) in *The Fathers of the Church*, vol. 5, trans. Sister Rose Bernard Donna (Washington, DC: Catholic Univ. of America Press, 1964), 43.
6. For examples of such abuse of the alleged power to grant indulgence, see Henry C. Sheldon's *History of the Christian Church*, vol. 2, 320–21.
7. 1 Peter 2:9.

8. *The Catholic Encyclopedia*, eds. Charles G. Herbermann, Edward A. Pace, Thomas J. Shahan, Condé B. Pallen, John J. Wynne, "Donation of Constantine," (NY: The Encyclopedia Press, 1913), 119, says, "This document is without a doubt a forgery, fabricated somewhere between the years 750–850." Although John Wycliffe and other critics of Rome had called the legitimacy of this document into question before Valla's critique, it was the work of Valla that proved indisputably the document was indeed illegitimate.

9. David Daniell, *William Tyndale: A Biography* (New Haven: Yale Univ. Press, 1994), 181–185.

10. Quoted by Henry C. Sheldon, *History of the Christian Church*, vol. 2, (Peabody, MA: Hendrickson Publishers, 1988), 411.

11. Nietzsche was much closer to the truth when he wrote, "Christianity, sprung from the Jewish roots and comprehensible only as a growth on this soil, represents the countermovement to any morality of breeding, or race, or privilege: it is anti-Aryan religion par excellence." From "The Twilight of the Idols," in *The Portable Nietzsche*, trans. Walter Kaufmann (NY: Viking Press, 1954), 504–505.

12. Alister McGrath, *In the Beginning: The Story of King James Bible* (London: Hodder & Stoughton, 2001), 19.

13. Ibid., 20.

14. Douglas C. Wood, *The Evangelical Doctor* (Herts, UK: Evangelical Press, 1984), 82.

15. Christopher de Hamel, *The Book: A History of the Bible* (London: Phaidon Press, 2001), 168–169.

16. Hebrews 11:25.

17. Luke 7:22.

18. Desiderius Erasmus, "The Paraclesis" in *Christian Humanism and the Reformation: Selected Writings of Erasmus*, ed. and trans. John C. Olin (NY and Evanston: Harper and Row, 1965), 97.

19. "There were more than 50 editions between 1522 and 1529 alone, not including further editions of separate portions of the New Testament. The peak was in 1524, when there were 47 different editions of parts of Luther's translation." (de Hamel, *The Book*, 232).

20. John F. D'Amico, *Renaissance Humanism in Papal Rome: Humanists and Churchmen on the Eve of the Reformation* (Baltimore: Johns Hopkins Univ. Press, 1983), 5–6. The Bible did not require clerical vows of chastity. It did require spiritual leaders to act with integrity. But the pope, not the Bible, governed the Church.

21. Joseph McCabe, *Crises in the History of the Papacy: A Study of Twenty Famous Popes Whose Careers and Whose Influence Were Important in the Development of the Church and in the History of the World* (NY: G. P. Putnam's Sons, 1916), 263.

22. Daniell, *William Tyndale*, 77.

23. F. Douglas Price, "Gloucester Diocese under Bishop Hooper, 1551–3," *Transactions of the Bristol and Gloucestershire Archaeological Society*, 55 (1938): 101.

24. John Foxe, *The Acts and Monuments of John Foxe*, vol. 5 (London: R.B. Seeley and W. Burnside, 1837–41), 117.

25. William Barclay, *New Testament Words* (Norwich, UK: SCM Press, 1964), 68–69.

26. Alister McGrath, *In the Beginning: The Story of the King James Bible* (London: Hodder & Stoughton, 2001), 127–129.

27. R. C. Sproul, ed., *The Reformation Study Bible* (Nashville: Thomas Nelson, 1995), iv.

28. McGrath, *In the Beginning*, 140.

29. Ibid., 143, 144.

30. http://bible.crosswalk.com/Commentaries/GenevaStudyBible/gen.cgi?book=da&chapter=006.
31. http://bible.crosswalk.com/Commentaries/GenevaStudyBible/gen.cgi?book=da&chapter=011.
32. McGrath, *In the Beginning*, 143.
33. Genesis 12:3; 18:18, Hosea 4:6 & 14; Romans 1:18–32; Matthew 28:18–20, etc.
34. John 8:31–32.

PART V

Epigraph: Fred Kaplan, *Lincoln: The Biography of a Writer* (NY: HarperCollins, 2008), 3–4.

CHAPTER TEN

1. *Christianity and Conservatism*, the Rt Hon Michael Alison MP and David L. Edwards, eds. (London: Hodder and Stoughton, 1990), 337–338.
2. Claudius Buchanan, *Christian Researches in Asia: With Notices of the Translation of Scriptures into the Oriental Languages*, 9th ed. (London: G. Sidney, 1812), 213–14.
3. The Kashi Society for Promotion of Nagari Script.
4. Shabd Sagar (Varanasi: Nagri Pracharini sabha, 1924).
5. Hugh Tinker, *South Asia: A Short History* (London: Macmillan, 1989), 100–101.
6. Acts 17:26–27.
7. Genesis 12:1–4; 15:4–7; 18:18–19.
8. Psalm 102:13–14.
9. Psalm 137:1, 5–6.
10. 1 Chronicles 23:25.
11. Jeremiah 29:7.
12. Matthew 10:6.
13. Matthew 28:18–20, Acts 1:8, etc.
14. Genesis 18:18.
15. Translated by Nivad C. Chaudhuri in *The Autobiography of an Unknown Indian*. http://books.google.com/books.
16. Michael Madhusudan Dutt, *The Anglo-Saxon and the Hindu* (Madras, 1854).

CHAPTER ELEVEN

1. Ruth apRoberts, *The Biblical Web* (Ann Arbor, MI: Univ. of Michigan Press, 1994), 10.
2. Genesis 20:1–17.
3. Erich Auerbach, *Mimesis: The Representation of Reality in Western Literature*, trans. Willard R. Trask (Princeton: Princeton Univ. Press, 2003), 14.
4. Genesis 18.
5. Genesis 12:1.
6. Genesis 17:1 NKJV.
7. Meenakshi Mukherjee, *Realism and Reality: The Novel and Society in India* (Delhi: OUP, 1996), 7.
8. Auerbach, *Mimesis*, 15.
9. T. S. Eliot, *Selected Essays* (London: Faber and Faber, 1999), 390.
10. Bede the Venerable, *Bede's Ecclesiastical History of the English Nation*, trans. J. Stevens, rev. J. A. Giles (NY: E.P. Dutton, 1st ed. 1910, reprinted 1958), 205–208.

11. Matthew 10:29.
12. William Shakespeare, *The Tragedy of Hamlet, Prince of Denmark* (Scene 2).
13. Shakespeare, *King Lear* (Act 4, Scene 1).
14. *Invitation to the Classics*, ed. by Louise Cowan and Os Guinness (Grand Rapids, MI: Baker Books, 1998), 19–20.
15. 1 Peter 2:11.
16. Hebrews 11:10.
17. Dante Alighieri, *The Divine Comedy* (1320) Canto XXXIII.
18. Matthew 6:10.
19. John Bunyan, *The Pilgrim's Progress*, ed. W. R. Owens (Oxford: Oxford Univ. Press, 2009) xii, 10.
20. John Bunyan, *Works*, vol. III, p. 235 (edition by George Offor). This great hymn has many versions, some of which bring out Pilgrim's heroism better than the original itself.
21. Barzun, *From Dawn to Decadence*, 264.
22. Ibid., 270.
23. Romans 2:11 KJV and Romans 10:12 NIV.
24. Henry Van Dyke, *The Poetry of Tennyson*, 10th ed. (NY: Charles Scribner's Sons, 1905), 391–437.
25. Cleland Boyd McAfee, *The Greatest English Classic: A Study of the King James Version of the Bible and Its Influence on Life and Literature* (Harper, 1912), 286.
26. Stephen King, *On Writing: A Memoir of the Craft* (NY: Scribner, 2000), 197.

CHAPTER TWELVE

1. Michael Edwardes, *British India 1772–1947* (New Delhi: Rupa & Co., 1994), 110.
2. For detailed documentation of this point see my book, *India: The Grand Experiment*.
3. Edwardes, *British India*, 115–117.
4. For the text of his letter, see my book, *Missionary Conspiracy* (Mussoorie: Good Books), 154–159.
5. *Selections from the Educational Records* (New Delhi: National Archives of India), 81–90.
6. Samuel Wilberforce, *The Life of William Wilberforce* (London: John Murray, 1872), 340.
7. Matthew 28:28.
8. The Danish king granted Serampore a Royal Charter in 1827. Sadly, in 1883, Serampore began to confer only theological degrees. Instead of teaching "secular" subjects from the perspective of a Christian worldview, it abandoned them to the ideology of secularism.
9. In North India, for example, Tulsidas had produced a Khari Boli (old "Hindi") version of the Ramayan. But the Brahmins refused to accept it as scriptures.
10. The letter written from Calcutta, dated 11 Dec 1823. *Selections from the Educational Records* (New Delhi: National Archives of India), 81–90.
11. Charles Trevelyan, *On the Education of the People of India* (London: Longman, Orme, Brown, 1838), 192–93.
12. Mr. Macaulay, on 1833 July 26, Hansad Parliamentary Debates, Third Series, vol. xx (London, 1833).
13. Thomas Babbington Macaulay, "Minute of the 2nd of February, 1835" in *Speeches by Lord Macaulay with His Minute on Indian Education* (London: Oxford Univ. Press, Humphrey Milford, 1935), 359.

14. Matthew 5:5.
15. Charles H. Haskins, *The Rise of Universities* (NY: Henry Holt, 1923), 3.
16. R. W. Southern, *The Making of the Middle Ages* (1953) (London: Pimilco, 1993), 164.
17. Ibid., 165.
18. Ibid., 207.
19. Ibid.
20. Ibid., 208.
21. H. G. Wells, *The Outline of History* (NY: Garden City Books, 1961), 587–88.
22. *Luther's Works*, vol. 44, *The Christian in Society*, ed. James Atkinson (Philadelphia: Fortress Press, 1966), 202.
23. Ibid., 200.
24. Ibid.
25. Ibid., 201.
26. Ibid., 202.
27. Ibid.
28. Ibid., 203.
29. Ibid.
30. Ibid., 204. Lombard's sentences were comments or commentaries on the Bible.
31. Ibid., 205.
32. John Dewey, "The American Intellectual Frontier," *New Republic*, 10 May 1922, vol. 30 (NY: Republic Publishing, 1922), 303.
33. Hermann Weimer, *Concise History of Education* (NY: Wisdom Library, 1962), 78.
34. In his book *The Soul of the American University: From Protestant Establishment to Established Nonbelief* (NY: Oxford Univ. Press, 1994), 33, George Marsden writes, "One of the remarkable facts of American history is that only six years after their settlement in the Massachusetts wilderness the Puritans established what soon became a reputable college. Higher education was for them a high priority in civilizational building."
35. Ibid.

Chapter Thirteen

1. Genesis 1:27–29.
2. Thomas Sprat, *History of the Royal Society*, 62 (quoted by Peter Harrison, *The Bible*, 231).
3. Genesis 1:25, 31. "And God saw that it was good. . . . God saw all that he had made and it was very good."
4. Proverbs 27:17 NIV.
5. Fritjof Capra, *Tao of Physics* (Flamingo S. 1975), 317. The ideas of Aldous Huxley and Lynn White Jr. had begun to circulate in India in the 1960s. Later, Capra, physicist-turned-mystic/environmentalist became very popular in India. Capra is one of many who condemn Christianity for creating science and the ecological mess. Also popular was Marilyn Ferguson's book *Aquarian Conspiracy* (Los Angeles: J. P. Tarcher, 1980), which blamed Christianity for science, technology, social oppression, and ecological crisis.
6. See Oakley's essay, "Christian Theology and the Newtonian Science: The Rise of the Concept of the Laws of Nature," in *Church History*, vol. 30 (The American Society of Church History, 1961), 433–457.
7. Proverbs 8:29 NIV. Such verses, explains historian Francis Oakley, shaped the original idea of "natural laws." See his essay, "Christian Theology and the Newtonian Science," *Church History*, vol. 30, 1961.

8. U.S. Constitution, Declaration of Independence, 1776.

9. Genesis 1:26, 17. "Let us make mankind in our image, in our likeness, so that they may rule over . . ."

10. Alfred North Whitehead, *Science and the Modern World: Lowell Lectures, 1925* (NY: Macmillan, 1967), 12.

11. Joseph Needham, *Science and Civilisation in China*, vol. 2 (Cambridge: Cambridge Univ. Press, 1956), 581.

12. *More Letters of Charles Darwin*, ed. by Francis Darwin and A. C. Seward, vol. 1 (NY: Appleton & Co., 1903), 195.

13. Genesis 1:28 KJV.

14. Peter Harrison, *The Bible, Protestantism, and the Rise of Natural Science* (Cambridge Univ. Press, 1998), 207.

15. Hindu scriptures have many creation stories. Kurma—the great tortoise—is the second incarnation of the god Vishnu. He came to support the earth when gods and demons were churning the ocean of milk to find the nectar of life. See Bramhi Samhita of the Kurma Purana, ~ AD 500–800. India's first Anglican Bishop, Reginald Heber (1783–1826), learned this was taught at the Sanskrit College in (present-day) Varanasi. Heber's report, "A Journey Through India" (1828), helped force the East India Company to introduce modern education in India. Mangalwadi, *Missionary Conspiracy: Letters to a Postmodern Hindu* (1996).

16. Scholars have shown that university politics led by the Liga was the primary cause of Galileo's persecution. See Roy E. Peacock, *A Brief History of Eternity: A Considered Response to Stephen Hawkings' A Brief History of Time* (Wheaton, IL: Crossway Books, 1991).

17. Allocution of the Holy Father John Paul II, October 31, 1992, the Holy See.

18. Richard Lewontin, "Billions and Billions of Demons" (*review of The Demon-Haunted World: Science as a Candle in the Dark* by Carl Sagan, 1997), *The NY Review*, 9 January 1997, 31.

19. Rodney Stark, *For the Glory of God: How Monotheism Led to Reformations, Science, Witch-Hunts and the End of Slavery* (Princeton: Princeton Univ. Press, 2003), 178–192; 394.

20. Michael J. Behe, *The Search for the Limits of Darwinism* (NY: Free Press, 2008). ISBN: 0743296222.

21. J. Sanford, J. Baumgardner, W. Brewer, P. Gibson, and W. Remine, "Mendel's Accountant: A biologically realistic forward-time population genetics program," SCPE. 8(2), July 2007, pp. 147–165. http://mendelsaccount.sourceforge. net/ (accessed January 15, 2011).

22. William A. Dembski and Jonathan Wells, *The Design of Life* (Dallas: The Foundation for Thought and Ethics, 2007).

23. Harrison, *The Bible*, 18.

24. Ibid., 4.

25. For a good introduction see *Biblical Origins of Modern Secular Culture: An Essay in the Interpretation of Western History* by Willis B. Glover (Macon, GA: Mercer Univ. Press, 1984).

26. See Stark, *For the Glory of God*, 160–163 and 198–199.

27. Elaine Howard Ecklund, *Science vs. Religion: What Scientists Really Think* (Oxford Univ. Press, 2010).

28. Stark, *For the Glory of God*, 159.

29. Ibid., 171. Newton wrote long commentaries on the Bible's books of Daniel and Revelation

30. See Oakley, "Christian Theology," 438–39. Metaphysical necessitarianism meant that things behaved in a certain way because of their inherent "form" or inner logic. Natural laws were thus "immanent" in nature, not imposed on nature by God. Because they were immanent in things, they were binding on God.
31. M. B. Foster, "Christian Theology and Modern Science of Nature," *Mind: A Quarterly Review*, vol. 44, 1935, 31.
32. M. B. Foster, "The Christian Doctrine of Creation and the Rise of Modern Natural Science," *Mind: A Quarterly Review*, January 1934, 448.
33. Glover, *Biblical Origins*, 10–11.
34. See James MacLachlan, *Galileo Galilei, First Physicist* (NY: Oxford Univ. Press, 1997).
35. Francis Bacon, *The Advancement of Learning* (London: Henrie Tomes, 1605). The 1893 edition by David Price (Cassell & Company) is online at www.fullbooks.com.
36. Galileo Galilei, "Letter to the Grand Duchess Christina of Tuscany, 1615."
37. U.S. Constitution, The Declaration of Independence, 1776.
38. Glover, *Biblical Origins*, 83–85.
39. Ibid., 84.
40. Proverbs 25:2.
41. Glover, *Biblical Origins*, 84–85.
42. 1 John 4:1–3.
43. See 1 Timothy 4:1–5.
44. Psalm 19:1; Revelation 4:11.
45. Genesis 3:17–18; 2 Chronicles 7:14; Hosea 4:1–6.
46. Harrison, *The Bible*, 58.
47. Genesis 4:10–12; 6:3–7.
48. Matthew 1:21.
49. Galatians 3:13.
50. 1 Corinthians 15:3.
51. 1 John 1:8–9.
52. 2 Chronicles 7:14.
53. Romans 8:19–23.
54. Francis Bacon, *Novum Organum with Other Parts of the Great Instauration*, trans. and eds. Peter Urbach and John Gibson (Chicago: Open Court, 1994), 292–293.
55. Harrison, *The Bible*, 194.
56. Sir Thomas Browne, *Religio Medici*, in *Browne's Religio Medici and Digby's Observations*, ed. Henry Frowde (London: Clarendon Press, 1909), 32.
57. Tertullian, *Adversus Marcionem*, ed and trans. by Ernest Evans (Oxford: Clarendon Press, 1972), 47.
58. Harrison, *The Bible*, 63.
59. John 8:32.
60. 1 Peter 2:9.
61. 1 Corinthians 10:31.
62. Revelation 4:11.
63. Psalm 19:1.

Part VI

Epigraph: "Constitutional Practice of Community of Memory? Some Remarks on the Collective Identity of Europe,"*Reflections on Multiple Modernities: European, Chinese, and Other Interpretations*, eds. Dominic Sachsenmaier and Shmuel Eisenstadt (Boston: Brill, 2002), 211.

CHAPTER FOURTEEN

1. http://www.finfacts.com/corruption.htm.
   Eigen Press Release 27 Aug 2002, Bribe Payers Index 2002 Transparency International, p 34.
2. Hebrews 4:13 NIV.
3. Malachi 3:8–9.
4. Ephesians 4:28.
5. Lord Macaulay's essay, *Clive*, is published as appendix 3 in the Indian edition of my book, *Missionary Conspiracy: Letters to a Postmodern Hindu* (Mussoorie: Nivedit Good Books, 1996).
6. Ian Bradley, *The Call To Seriousness: The Evangelical Impact on the Victorians* (NY: Macmillan Publishing, 1976).
7. Mangalwadi, *Missionary Conspiracy* (Mussoorie: Nivedit, 1996) and *India: The Grand Experiment* (UK: Pippa Rann Books, 1997).
8. 1 Corinthians 1:18–25.
9. 1 Corinthians 15:3–4.
10. Revelation 20:11–15.
11. Revelation 3:20.
12. The full text of the lecture is published in my book *Missionary Conspiracy*. In this lecture he summarized the classic 1939 study by J. W. Bready, *England Before and After Wesley*.
13. *Journal of John Wesley*, Christian Classics, Ethereal Library, www.ccel/wesley/Journal.

CHAPTER FIFTEEN

1. Alexis de Tocqueville, *Democracy in America*, trans. George Lawrence, ed. J. P. Mayer (HarperPerennial, 1988), 603.
2. Ibid., 590.
3. Ibid., 261.
4. Ibid., 291.
5. Matthew 19:4–6.
6. Ibid., 603. Emphasis added.
7. Genesis 1:26–27.
8. Genesis 3:16.
9. Tocqueville, *Democracy in America*, 731.
10. For the full story see, *Why I Am not a Muslim* by Ibn Warraq (NY: Prometheus Books, 1995), 99–101.
11. "You have heard that it was said, 'You shall not commit adultery.' But I say to you that everyone who looks at a woman with lustful intent has already committed adultery with her in his heart. "It was also said, 'Whoever divorces his wife, let him give her a certificate of divorce.' But I say to you that everyone who divorces his wife, except on the ground of sexual immorality, makes her commit adultery, and whoever marries a divorced woman commits adultery" (Matthew 5:27–32).
12. For more detailed discussion, see my chapter "Tantric Sex—A Celebration of Life?" in my book *When The New Age Gets Old: Looking for a Greater Spirituality* (Downer's Grove, IL: IVP, 1992).
13. Ibid. See the chapter "Doing Ecology Is Being Human."
14. Nicol McNicol and Vishal Mangalwadi, *What Liberates a Woman: The Story of Pandita Ramabai—A Builder of Modern India* (Landour, Mussoorie, UA, India:

Nivedit Good Books, 1996). Also *The Legacy of William Carey: A Model for Transforming a Culture*.

15. Tocqueville, *Democracy in America*, 287.

16. For the full story see Ibn Warraq, Ibid., 100–101. In Sura 66.15 God says, "O Prophet! Why have you forbidden yourself that which God has made lawful unto you [i.e. Mary], out of desire to please your wives, for God is forgiving and merciful? Verily God has sanctioned the revocation of your oaths [to stay away from Mary] . . . If he divorces you [wives], God will give him in your stead wives more submissive unto God, believers, pious, repentant, devout, fasting; both Women married previously, and virgins." The Sura was to Mary's advantage, but she saw through it and never converted to Islam. Therefore, she could never become a wife.

17. Matthew 19: 9–11.

18. Stark, *Rise of Christianity* (Princeton: Princeton Univ. Press, 1996).

19. "You shall not murder" (Exodus 20:13).

20. "For the man who does not love his wife but divorces her, says the LORD, the God of Israel, covers his garment with violence, says the LORD of hosts. So guard yourselves in your spirit, and do not be faithless" (Malachi 2:16).

21. Leviticus 18:6–18.

22. "You shall not commit adultery" (Exodus 20:14).

23. "Therefore an overseer must be above reproach, the husband of one wife" (1 Timothy 3:2).

24. Stark, *Rise of Christianity*, 104–105.

25. "Religion that is pure and undefiled before God, the Father, is this: to visit orphans and widows in their affliction, and to keep oneself unstained from the world" (James 1:27).

26. Stark, *Rise of Christianity*, 106.

27. Ibid. See also Keith Hopkins, "The Age of Roman Girls at Marriage," *Population Studies* 18 (1965), 309–27.

28. C. Schmidt, *The Social Results of Early Christianity*, trans. Mrs. Thorpe (London: William Isbister, 1889), 47.

29. Quoted by ancient historian Aulus Gellius in *The Attic Nights of Aulus Gellius*, vol. 1, trans. John C. Rolfe (NY: G.P. Putnam's Sons, 1927), 31.

30. Beryl Rawson, "The Roman Family" in *The Family in Ancient Rome: New Perspectives*, ed. Beryl Rawson (Ithaca: Cornell Univ. Press, 1986), 11.

31. Minucius Felix, *The "Octavius" of Minucius Felix*, trans. J. H. Freese (NY: Macmillan), 83.

32. Heiko A. Oberman, *Luther: Man Between God and the Devil* (NY: Image Books, 1992), 277.

33. Swami Sivananda, *Bliss Divine* (Sivanandanagar, Divine Life Society, 1974), 539–540.

34. Roland Bainton, *Here I Stand: Martin Luther* (UK: Lion, 1978), 298.

35. Ibid.

36. Genesis 1:31.

37. Genesis 2:18.

38. Genesis 2:24.

39. The apostles Peter and Paul called every believer a priest, and their bodies, temples of the Holy Spirit. See, for example, 1 Peter 2:9 and 1 Corinthians 6:19.

40. Bainton, *Here I Stand*, 352.

41. As a Catholic, he calls it "Protestantism."

42. Tocqueville, *Democracy in America*, 585–88.
43. Genesis 18:17–19.
44. Luke 1:17.
45. Ibid., 595.
46. Ibid., 42.
47. Ibid., 393–94.
48. Genesis 2:18 NIV.
49. Ephesians 5:23.
50. Martin Luther, *Treatise on Good Works* in *Luther's Works: The Christian in Society*, ed. James Atkinson, gen. ed. Helmut T. Lehmann, trans. by W.A. Lambert, vol. 44 (Philadelphia: Fortress Press, 1966), 98–99.
51. See chapters on ecology and vegetarianism in *When The New Age Gets Old* (Mangalwadi) for more detailed discussion on the biblical teaching on original sin, curse, eco-feminism, goddess worship, etc.
52. Ibid.

CHAPTER SIXTEEN

1. Friedrich Nietzsche, "The Twilight of the Idols" in *The Portable Nietzsche*, trans. by Walter Kaufmann (NY: Viking Press, 1954), 505.
2. Galatians 5:22–23.
3. Acts 1:8; John 15, etc.
4. 2 Corinthians 1:3.
5. *Culture Matters*, eds. Lawrence E. Harrison and Samuel P. Huntington (NY: Basic Books, 2000), 2.
6. This comment is not meant to suggest that all "alternative" medicine or divine healing is hocus-pocus. For a discussion of holistic healing, please see the chapter "My Course in Miracles" in my book *When The New Age Gets Old* (InterVarsity Press, 1992).
7. Lawrence E. Stager, *Ashkelon Discovered: From Canaanites and Philistines to Romans and Moslems* (Washington D.C.: Biblical Archaeology Society, 1991), 51.
8. For a discussion of the radical nature of Jesus' compassion see my chapter, "His Compassion: Jesus, The Trouble Maker" in *Truth and Transformation*.
9. Luke 4:18.
10. Matthew 9:36.
11. Matthew 10:16; John 10:11.
12. Matthew 12:10–12; Mark 3:2–5; Luke 13:10–16.
13. Matthew 19:13.
14. Matthew 8:3, 9:10–13; Luke 17:11–19; John 4.
15. St. Justin Martyr, *The First and Second Apologies*, in *Ancient Christian Writers*, vol. 56. trans., ed. by Leslie William Barnard (NY: Paulist Press, 1997), 31–32.
16. See Paul Johnson, *A History of Christianity* (NY: Atheneum, 1976), 75.
17. Swami Vivekananda (1863–1902), the founder of Ramakrishna Mission, was the first Hindu guru to imitate Christian service to try to prevent conversions to Christ.
18. St. Augustine, *On Nature and Grace* (AD 415), quoted in Charles Noris Cochrane, *Christianity and Classical Culture* (Oxford: Oxford Univ. Press, 1940), 489.
19. Thomas Sydenham, *The Works of Thomas Sydenham, MD*, Preface to 1st ed, 1666, trans. R. G. Latham, Sydenham Society, 1848, 25.
20. Dorothy Clarke Wilson, *DR. IDA: The Story of Dr. Ida Scudder of Vellore* (London: Hodder & Stoughton, 1961).

21. K. Spink, *Mother Teresa: A Complete Authorized Biography*, (NY: HarperOne, 1998).
22. For a discussion, see my earlier books, for example, *Missionary Conspiracy: Letters to a Postmodern Hindu* and *India: The Grand Experiment*.
23. Malcolm Muggeridge, *Jesus Rediscovered* (NY: Pyramid, 1969), 157.

CHAPTER SEVENTEEN

1. Reuben G. Thwaites, *Cyrus Hall McCormick and the Reaper*, vols. 1–2, (State Historical Society of Wisconsin, 2009).
2. Max Weber, *The Protestant Ethic and the Spirit of Capitalism*, trans. Talcott Parsons (NY: Charles Scribner's Sons, 1958), 80.
3. Richard Baxter, *Baxter's Practical Works*, vol. 1 (Letterman Assoc., 2007), 115.
4. See for example, George Marsden, *Fundamentalism and American Culture* (Oxford: Oxford Univ. Press, 2006).
5. Proverbs 14:34.
6. William T. Hutchinson, *Cyrus Hall McCormick: Seed Time, 1809–1856* (NY: Century, 1930), 271.
7. Matthew 6:24.
8. Matthew 25:14–30.
9. His book was called *Summa de Arithmetica, Geometria, Proportioni et Proportionalita* (Venice, 1494).
10. David Landes, *The Wealth and Poverty of Nations* (NY: W. W. Norton, 1998), 94.
11. Ibid., 350–59.
12. Rafael Aguayo, *Dr. Deming: The American Who Taught the Japanese About Quality* (NY: Fireside, 1991).
13. See, for instance, Max Weber, *The Protestant Ethic and the Spirit of Capitalism* (cited above) or Talcott Parsons, "Christianity and Modern Industrial Society" in *The Talcott Parsons Reader*, ed. Bryan S. Turner (Malden, MA: Blackwell, 1999), 23–50.
14. *The Dictionary of American Biography* (NY: Charles Scribner's Sons, 1946).

CHAPTER EIGHTEEN

1. O. I. A. Roche, *The Days of the Upright: A History of the Huguenots* (NY: Clarkson N. Potter, 1965), 340.
2. "Cambridge History of the Reformation," http://www.third-millennium-library.com/readinghall/MODERN-HISTORY/REFORMATION/9/5-Massacre-of-the-Waldenses.html (accessed November 27, 2010).
3. David Gress, *From Plato to NATO* (NY: Free Press, 1998). See Chapter 1, "The Grand Narrative and its Fate."
4. Luke 4:18.
5. Paul Johnson, "Laying Down the Law," in *The Wall Street Journal*, 10 March 1999, A22.
6. Exodus 20:2.
7. F. N. Lee, *Alfred the Great and Our Common Law* (Queensland Presbyterian Theological Seminary, 2000).
8. Luke 1:52–53; Matthew 5:3, 5, 10; Luke 12:32.
9. John 8:36.
10. Numbers 14.
11. Exodus 3:13–20; 4:29.
12. Deuteronomy 17:14–20.

13. Manegold of Lautenbach, *Liber ad Gebehardum*, AD 1085.
14. J. C. Holt's translation in *Magna Carta* (Cambridge, UK: Cambridge Univ. Press, 1965), 327.
15. François Hotman, *Francogallia in Constitutionalism and Resistance in the Sixteenth Century: Three Treatises by Hotman, Beza, & Mornay*, ed., trans, and abr. by Julian H. Franklin (NY: Penguin, 1969), 79.
16. Hugo Grotius, *The Law of War and Peace*, 1625; Emmerich de Vattel, *The Law of Nations or the Principles of Natural Law*, 1758.
17. Seven Bishops' Trial, 12 Howell's State Trials 183 (1688).
18. English Bill of Rights, 1 Will. & Mar., Sess. 2, C. 2.
19. Mark Hall, *Vindiciae Contra Tyrannos: The Influence of the Reformed Tradition on the American Founding*, annual mtg. American Political Science Assoc. Washington, D.C. Sept. 2010.
20. William Carey, *An Inquiry into the Obligations of Christians* (London: Baptist Missionary Society, 1991), 95–96.
21. Records of the House of Commons, July 26, 1833. For the text of his speech, see the chapter, "The Evangelical Manifesto For India's Freedom" in *India: The Grand Experiment*, 87–108.
22. John Locke, *Two Treatises on Civil Government*, 2nd ed. (London: George Routledge & Sons, 1887), 293.
23. Donald S. Lutz, "The relative influence of European writers on late eighteenth-century American political thought," *The American Political Science Review*, 1984, 189. In analyzing 3,154 documents from 1760 to 1805, Hyneman and Lutz found that 34 percent cited the Bible, 8.4 percent cited Montesquieu, 7.9 percent Blackstone, and 2.9 percent Locke.
24. Gary T. Amos details "How the Bible and Christianity Influenced the Writing of the Declaration of Independence" in *Defending the Declaration* (Providence Foundation, 1994).
25. Edmund Burke, *A Letter from Mr. Burke to a Member of the National Assembly: In Answer to Some Objections to His Book on French Affairs* (NY: Hugh Gaine, 1791), 31.
26. Robert C. Winthrop, "The Bible: An Address Delivered at the Annual Meeting of the Massachusetts Bible Society in Boston, May 28, 1849" in *Addresses and Speeches on Various Occasions*, vol. 1 (Boston: Little, Brown, and Co., 1852), 172.
27. Conversation with author in 1999.

PART VII

Epigraph: Peter Berger in *Globalization and the Challenges of a New Century: A Reader*, eds. O'Meara, Mehlinger, and Krain (Bloomington, IN: Indiana Univ. Press, 2000), 425.

CHAPTER NINETEEN

1. From 1857 to 1947 most of India was governed directly by the British Crown.
2. In 1813, Indian Rupees 2.13 = US$1 or Rs 8 = 1 £. In 2010, Indian Rupees 48 = US $1.
3. John 3:16.
4. Haim G. Ginott, *Teacher and Child: A Book for Parents and Teachers* (NY: Avon Books, 1975).

5. The story of the Hmar people is taken from Rochunga Pudaite, *The Book That Set My People Free* (Wheaton, IL: Tyndale House, 1982); Joe Musser and James and Mari Hefley, *Fire on the Hills: The Rochunga Pudaite Story* (Wheaton, IL: Tyndale House, 1998).
6. See the author's booklet *Spirituality of Hate: A Futuristic Perspective on Indo-Pakistan Conflict*. Available from www.VishalMangalwadi.com.
7. *Beyond the Next Mountain*, 1987, James F. Collier, director; Rolf Forsberg, producer (Vision Video, DVD 2004). Available from Netflix.

CHAPTER TWENTY

1. William J. Federer, *Backfired: A Nation Born for Religious Tolerance No Longer Tolerates Religion* (St. Louis: Amerisearch, 2007).
2. The lecture "Psychology as the Behaviorist Views It" was delivered at Columbia University.
3. B. F. Skinner, *Beyond Freedom and Dignity* (Indianapolis: Hackett Publishing, 2002). Originally published in 1971.
4. Nancy Pearcey, *Total Truth: Liberating Christianity from Its Cultural Captivity* (Wheaton, IL: Crossway Books, 2004).
5. In the following "conversation" I have taken the liberty to simplify Dixon's academic arguments. Therefore, I am putting some words in his mouth. Those who want to read his brilliant essay, "Theology, Anti-Theology and Atheology: From Christian Passions to Secular Emotions," can find it in *Modern Theology*: vol. 15, no. 3 (Oxford: Blackwell Publishers, July 1999).
6. An earlier meaning of *passion* was to be committed to a cause or person enough to suffer for that thing/person. Mel Gibson used that meaning in his film *The Passion of the Christ*. Paul calls negative and positive passions the "acts (works) of the flesh" and "fruit of the Spirit." "The acts of the flesh are obvious: sexual immorality, impurity and debauchery; idolatry and witchcraft; hatred, discord, jealousy, fits of rage, selfish ambition, dissensions, factions and envy; drunkenness, orgies, and the like . . . But the fruit of the Spirit is love, joy, peace, forbearance, kindness, goodness, faithfulness, gentleness and self-control" (Galatians 5:19, 21a, 22–23a NIV).
7. Dixon, "Theology," 308.
8. Nancy Pearcey, *Saving Leonardo: A Call to Resist the Secular Assault on Mind, Morals, and Meaning* (Nashville: B&H, 2010).
9. Jeffrey M. Schwartz and Sharon Begley, *The Mind and the Brain: Neuroplasticity and the Power of Mental Force* (NY: Regan Books, 2002).
10. Mario Beauregard and Denyse O'Leary, *The Spiritual Brain: A Neuroscientist's Case for the Existence of the Soul* (NY: HarperOne, 2007).
11. In 2005, Schwartz, theoretical physicist Henry P. Stapp, and psychologist Mario Beauregard challenged the materialist interpretation that mind is but brain. See "Quantum Physics in Neuroscience and Psychology: A Neurophysical Model of Mind/Brain Interaction," *Philosophical Transactions of the Royal Society* (UK).
12. Romans 6:19; 9:8; Corinthians 15:46; Jude 1:19.
13. Vijay Martis et al. *Burnt Alive: The Stains and the God They Loved* (GLS, Mumbai 1999, 2008).
14. Matthew 5:11–12.
15. Matthew 5:44.
16. 1 Peter 1:8.

17. See 1 Peter 1:14–23.
18. Jesus: "Then you will know the truth, and the truth will set you free" (John 8:32 NIV).
19. Timothy L. Smith, *Revivalism and Social Reform* (Eugene, OR: Wipf & Stock, 2004).
20. "Take my yoke upon you and learn from me, for I am gentle and lowly in heart, and you will find rest for your souls" (Matthew 11:29 NKJV).
21. John 1:11–12.
22. See Gregory H. Nobles, *Divisions Throughout the Whole: Politics and Society in Hampshire County, Massachusetts, 1740–1775* (Cambridge: Cambridge Univ. Press, 1983).
23. William G. McLoughlin, "'Enthusiasm for Liberty': The Great Awakening as the Key to the Revolution," *Preachers and Politicians: Two Essays on the Origins of the American Revolution* (Worcester: American Antiquarian Society, 1977), 48.
24. Ibid., 49–50.
25. A good study is by Daniel J. Elazar, *Covenant and Commonwealth: From Christian Separation Through the Protestant Reformation, the Covenant Tradition in Politics*, vol. 2 (New Brunswick: Transaction Pub., 1996), 2.
26. "Abram said to the king of Sodom, 'I have lifted my hand to the LORD, God Most High, Possessor of heaven and earth'" (Genesis 14:22).
27. David Barton, *Original Intent* (Aledo, TX: WallBuilders, 2008), 182.
28. Quoted in www.Americanchronicle.com from John Quincy Adams, *Letters of John Quincy Adams to His Son on the Bible and Its Teachings* (Auburn: James M. Aden, 1850).
29. *Washington Daily Morning Chronicle*, September 8, 1864, cited in *The Collected Works of Abraham Lincoln*, vol. 7, 543.
30. *America's God and Country: Encyclopedia of Quotations*, William J. Federer, ed., (St. Louis: Amerisearch, Inc., 2000), 227.
31. For the pulpit's role in creating modern England, see Herbert Schlossberg's *The Silent Revolution and the Making of Victorian England* (Columbus, OH: Ohio State Univ. Press, 2000).
32. Werner Gitt, *In the Beginning Was Information, A Scientist Explains the Incredible Design in Nature* (Green Forest, AR: Master Books, 2006).
33. Luke 8:4–15.
34. John 5:24–29.
35. "The Jews answered him [Pilate], 'We have a law, and according to that law he ought to die because he has made himself the Son of God'" (John 19:7).
36. John 11.
37. 1 John 3:1–3.
38. Romans 10:9–10.
39. 1 Peter 1:23.
40. John 5:24–26.
41. 2 Timothy 3:15–17.
42. Psalm 119:9.
43. Dietrich Bonhoeffer, *Meditating on the Word* (Cambridge, MA: Cowley,1986) A. W. Tozer, *The Pursuit of God* (Camp Hill, PA: WingSpread, 1992).
44. Matthew 4:1–10.
45. Psalm 119:105.
46. Lamentations 1:1–3.
47. Ezekiel 2:9—3:3.

48. Ezekiel 37:1–3, 11–14. See also Isaiah 45.
49. 2 Chronicles 36:23. See also Ezra 1.
50. Deuteronomy 30:19.

APPENDIX

1. Dan Brown, *The Da Vinci Code* (NY: Doubleday, 2003), 231.
2. Luke 23:4 NIV.
3. John 19:10.
4. Acts 24:26–27.
5. John 18:37.
6. In Acts 10:9–19, Peter received a revelation in a trancelike vision. Subsequent events in chapters 9 and 10 confirmed that the vision was from God.
7. Daniel, who did receive private visions, did not try to get his contemporaries to believe his prophecies. "I, Daniel, was deeply troubled by my thoughts, and my face turned pale, but I kept the matter to myself" (Daniel 7:28). "Here is the end of the matter. As for me, Daniel, my thoughts greatly alarmed me, and my color changed, but I kept the matter in my heart." Later generations, including Jesus Christ, believed him because his prophecies turned out to be so true that many modern scholars thought his book must have been written centuries after Daniel's time.
8. 1 Thessalonians 2:13, emphasis added.
9. Barton Payne, *Encyclopedia of Biblical Prophecy* (NY: Harper & Row, 1973).
10. 1 Corinthians 15:2–3; Luke 24:44–48.
11. Luke 22:41–42.
12. Luke 22:49–51.
13. Matthew 26:54; Mark 14:49.
14. http://www.cosmicfingerprints.com/blog/intelligent-bacteria/John Tyler Bonner, *The Social Amoeba: The Biology of Slime Molds* (Princeton: Princeton Univ. Press, 2008).
15. Genesis 1:3.
16. Genesis 1:26.
17. Genesis 2:7.
18. Matthew 22:37.
19. Deuteronomy 18:21, 22.
20. Deuteronomy 4:7, 29; 9:26; Jeremiah 29:7, 12–13; 31:4–14, 23–28; 50:4. Lamentations 2:18, 19.
21. Jeremiah 25:11–12.
22. Jeremiah 1:1–3; Jeremiah 25:3; 2 Chronicles 36:21; Ezra 1:1; Daniel 9:2.
23. Daniel 9:2.
24. 2 Chronicles 36:21–23; Isaiah 44:24–28; Isaiah 45:1, 13.
25. See passages such as Daniel chapters 9 and 6, Ezra 1:1: "In the first year of Cyrus king of Persia, that *the word of the* LORD *by the mouth of Jeremiah might be fulfilled*, the LORD stirred up the spirit of Cyrus king of Persia, so that he made a proclamation throughout all his kingdom and also put it in writing (emphasis added)."
26. Matthew 4:1–10.
27. 1 Corinthians 15:2–3.
28. Mark 8:31–33; 9:30–32; 10:32–34.
29. 2 Peter 1:19–21; 2 Timothy 3:15–16.

30. Matthew 5:37.
31. Matthew 22:29.
32. Matthew 7:28–30.
33. Matthew 19:1–11.
34. Romans 3:2; Hebrew 3:1–6.
35. Hebrews 13:7 NIV (emphasis added).
36. Genesis 1; John 1:1–3.
37. John 14:10.
38. John 8:32.
39. John 15:7.
40. John 5:24–25.
41. John 1:1, 14.
42. John 5:39.
43. John 17:8.
44. John 20:22.
45. John 14:26.
46. John 16:13.
47. Matthew 10:1–8.
48. Luke 1:2.
49. Acts 6:4.
50. Acts 2:42–44; 5:12; 14:3.
51. Acts 3:1–10.
52. Acts 13:7.
53. Acts 6:7.
54. Ephesians 2:20.
55. 1 John 2:19–21.
56. Revelation 20:4.
57. In Revelation 1:11 John is told: *"Write what you see in a book and send it to the seven churches."* Although John was "in the spirit" when he saw his visions, it is very clear from the book that John's rational functions were never arrested. His book is not "automatic" spirit writing. This is eyewitness testimony. Revelation 1:2 states that John *"bore witness to the word of God and to the testimony of Jesus Christ, even to all that he saw."* In John's writings, *marturew*—"bear witness" means "eyewitness." See John 1:32: And John (the Baptist) bore witness: *"I saw the Spirit descend from heaven like a dove, and it remained on him."*
58. 1 Corinthians 6:19.
59. John 13:27.
60. Isaiah 59:21; 1 Corinthians 2:13.
61. 2 Corinthians 5:20.
62. Exodus 7:2–4; Deuteronomy 6:22; Acts 2:22, 43; 14:3.

WITH GRATITUDE

This book is merely a milestone in a journey that Ruth and I began a long time ago. Professor Prabhu Guptara encouraged us at the very beginning and has remained available as a source of wisdom, guidance, and practical support. Long conversations with Udo and Debbie Middelmann helped shape my perspective. Ranald Macaulay, Larry and Melinda Landis, Christine Colby, Darrow Miller, Bob Moffitt, Bob Osburn, Art Lindsley, Jim and Betsy Burkett, Brad Bailey, the late Dr. Ralph Winter, Rich and Sue Gregg, David and Amber McDonald, Graham and Ann Fraser, Tim Mahoney, Rob Hoskins, Steve Ferguson, James Catford, Mark Elliott, Babu Verghese, Jeff Fountain, and Ivan and Silvia Kostka have been other key encouragers along the way.

Besides Ruth, who was my main researcher in 1999 and 2000, the following have assisted with research, writing, and editing: David Hagen, Tracey Finck, Jonathan Rice, Doug Gallo, Scott and Mary Keyes, and Jesse Bjoraker. Nate Andrews made a significant contribution to the chapter on literature. Ranjeet Guptara researched the history of medicine and compassion. Our daughter Nivedit helped research Indian nationalism and M. M. Dutt. Ro and Mawii Pudaite contributed to the chapter that tells Ro's story. Donald Drew gave his research on John Wesley. Art Lindsley, Chris Watkins, Ian Cooper, David Hagen, Scott and Mary Keyes, Peyton Beard, Ranjeet Guptara, and many others read the manuscript to make helpful suggestions and minimize errors.

During these years of wandering, the following have offered us "long-term" shelters: Hugh and Ruth Bradby, Basil and Shirley Scott,

Pat Babbington Smith, Alice Landis, Thom and Linda Wolf, Moses and Mercy David, Ron and Colleen Johannsen, Bob and Nancy Brydges, Mike and Beth Keglar-Gray, Ray and Anita Sandberg, Alan Meenan, Susan Rigby, Paul and Sue Sailhamer, Tim and Becky Lewis, and now our daughter Anandit and her husband, Albert.

The number of people who have helped us with prayers and finances in this journey is too large to recount. None of them are likely to read this page, looking for their names. Yet, I must mention a few: Doug and Beth Heimberger, Jay and Ruth Story, Galen Watje, Alice Landis, Gene Willlis, David and Pamela Makela, Howard and Roberta Ahmanson, the late Dr. Ken Taylor, Promod and Dorcas Haque, Senthil and Malathy Nathan, Bob and Mahinder Guibord, Bonagh and Mark Dalton, Bob and Cathie Baldwin, Terry and Karen Thigpen, Gwen Henson, Jim and Marlys Manthei, Tim and Pam Manthei, Del and Geri Weirich, Terry and Pamela Bosgra, Dean Cozzens, Marlys Sanford, Satish and Gladys Amancharla, Larry and Mary Ehrlich, Alex and Robin George, Chander and Geri Mehta, Warren and Nancy Martin, Solomon and Margaret, Marilyn Bohne, Daniel and Sunita Pardhe, Jyoti Guptara, Kent Larue, Clell and Marcella Rogers, Dennis and MaryAnn Barnett, Andrew and Kris Engles, Scott and Carol Bertilson, (late) Stan and Marilyn Reuter, Davis and Renee Citron, Luis and Doris Bush, Jeff and Dawn Siemon, (late) Pierre and Sandra Tullier, Richard and Susan Kendal-Bell, Ron Williams, David and Catherine Hicks, Ranjeet Guptara, Dwight and Christine Erickson, Archie and Barbara Linert, Sushil Singh, Thomas and Mary Kraft, Tom and Marty Hoag, Craig and Sonia Andersen, Tim and Kim Dulas, Erik Barr, Michael and Jayati Chelian, B. J. Dabhade, Joseph and Subhashini Ladella, Nelson and Naomi Hard, Jane McNally, Ann Hillstrom, Rishi and Eunice Goel, Phil and Lois Svalya, Daniel Thomas, Hugh and Nancy Maclellan, and Vinay Mangalwadi.

In this journey, Mark Harris has been a huge source of practical counsel and administrative help. Others who offered notable administrative assistant are Brad Olson, Samraj Gandhi, Anjali Guptara, Marla Muckala, and Elizabeth Skrivanek. Legal assistance was provided by Galen Watje and Scott Moen. Larry Frenzel made it unnecessary to work through a literary agent. Mahoney Media, Ted and Yvonne McDonald, Steve Law, Andre Dantzler, Carolyn Rafferty, Lee Behar, and Allan Carrington are making it possible to package my research for the digital media such as www.RevelationMovement .com.

Joel Miller, Vice President, Thomas Nelson, had the vision to publish this book, and it was an extremely pleasant experience to work with Janene MacIvor as the editor.

In the final months of birthing this book, Surya, our eighteen-month-old fifth grandchild, remained the ever-present source of humanizing joy. She made sure that I didn't disappear into an ivory tower.

ABOUT THE AUTHOR

Vishal Mangalwadi (b. 1949) studied philosophy in Indian universities, Hindu Ashrams, and L'Abri Fellowship in Switzerland.

In 1976, along with his wife Ruth, he founded the Association for Comprehensive Rural Assistance to serve the poor and low-caste peasants in central India. Vishal's first book, a study of contemporary Hinduism, *The World of Gurus* (1977) was written in the company of his illiterate friends, far from the ivory tower. It became an instant hit and has remained a textbook in many universities.

From initiating and managing service projects, Vishal moved into organizing peasants and untouchables into political parties, ultimately serving in the national headquarters of two political parties in New Delhi, India. For his writings, backed by his service to the poor, the *Bhartiya Dalit Sahitya Academy* honored him with the "Distinguished National Service Award," the William Carey International University, Pasadena, California, honored him with an LL.D, and the county government of Los Angeles honored him with a scroll of commendation.

Vishal and Ruth have two daughters and five grandchildren.

An inspirational speaker, Vishal has lectured in thirty-three countries. Many of his videos are available at www.RevelationMovement.com.

INDEX